STRATEGIC FINANCIAL PLANNING ⌣

This book on personal financial planning and wealth management employs the lifecycle model of financial economics. The central idea of "consumption smoothing" is used to connect chapters and topics such as saving and investment, debt management, risk management, and retirement planning. The first part of the book is nontechnical and aimed at a wide audience with no special technical background. The second part of the book provides a rigorous presentation of the lifecycle model from first principles using the calculus of variations. The accompanying website is found at http://www.yorku.ca/milevsky/?page_id=185.

Narat Charupat is an associate professor at the DeGroote School of Business, McMaster University, Ontario, Canada. His research has been published in journals such as the *Journal of Economic Theory, Journal of Banking and Finance, Journal of Risk and Insurance,* and the *Journal of Financial and Quantitative Analysis.* Professor Charupat's areas of professional interest include annuity and insurance products, financial innovation, arbitrage, and behavioral finance. He has taught courses in financial derivatives and personal and international finance.

Huaxiong Huang is a professor of applied mathematics at York University, Toronto, Canada, where he has taught since 1999. He has published more than 60 articles in peer-reviewed journals including the *Journal of Banking and Finance, Insurance: Mathematics and Economics, Journal of Risk and Insurance,* and the *Financial Analysts Journal.* He is an associate editor of the *Journal of Engineering Mathematics* and *Advances in Applied Mathematics and Mechanics* and managing editor of the *Mathematics-in-Industry Case Studies.* A Fellow of the Fields Institute, he has held visiting positions in China, Japan, the United Kingdom, and the United States.

Moshe A. Milevsky is a finance professor at York University, Toronto, Canada; executive director of The IFID Centre in Toronto; and president and CEO of the QWeMA Group. He has written eight books, more than 60 peer-reviewed journal articles, and more than 200 articles in the popular press on insurance, investments, pensions, retirement, and annuities, including *The Calculus of Retirement Income: Financial Models for Pension Annuities* and *Life Insurance* (Cambridge University Press, 2006). A Fellow of the Fields Institute, Professor Milevsky has received two National Magazine (Canada) awards and the Graham and Dodd scroll award and has been honored by the Retirement Income Insurance Association for lifetime achievement in applied research. In 2009, *Investment Advisor* magazine named him one of the 25 most influential people in the financial advisory business.

Strategic Financial Planning
over the Lifecycle

A Conceptual Approach to Personal Risk Management

NARAT CHARUPAT
McMaster University, Canada

HUAXIONG HUANG
York University, Canada

MOSHE A. MILEVSKY
York University and the IFID Centre, Canada

CAMBRIDGE
UNIVERSITY PRESS

CAMBRIDGE
UNIVERSITY PRESS

32 Avenue of the Americas, New York NY 10013-2473, USA

Cambridge University Press is part of the University of Cambridge.

It furthers the University's mission by disseminating knowledge in the pursuit of
education, learning, and research at the highest international levels of excellence.

www.cambridge.org
Information on this title: www.cambridge.org/9780521148030

First published 2012
Reprinted 2013

A catalog record for this publication is available from the British Library.

Library of Congress Cataloging in Publication data
Charupat, Narat.
Strategic financial planning over the lifecycle : a conceptual approach to personal risk
management / Narat Charupat, Huaxiong Huang, Moshe A. Milevsky
    p. cm.
Includes bibliographical references (p.   ) and index.
ISBN 978-0-521-76456-8 (hardback)
1. Finance, Personal.   2. Risk management.   3.Wealth–Management.   I. Huang,
Huaxiong.   II. Milevsky, Moshe Arye, 1967–   III. Title.
HG179.C5354   2012
332.024–dc23   2011050681

ISBN 978-0-521-76456-8 Hardback
ISBN 978-0-521-14803-0 Paperback

Additional resources for this publication at http://www.yorku.ca/milevsky/?page id=185

To our wives...

. . . As far as I am aware, no one has challenged the view that if people were capable of it, they ought to plan their consumption, saving, and retirement according to the principles enunciated by Modigliani and Brumberg in the 1950s . . .

Angus S. Deaton, Princeton University, 2005

Contents

Acknowledgments

The authors would like to thank Zvi Bodie, Simon Dabrowski, Faisal Habib, Mark Kamstra, Larry Kotlikoff, David Promislow, Thomas Salisbury, Ling-wu Shao, and Pauline Shum for helpful comments, conversations, and discussions as this book was being written.

In addition, the authors would like to acknowledge our editor Scott Parris at Cambridge University Press for encouraging us to reach a wider audience; Tanya Bass for editorial and typesetting assistance; Mirela Cara for help with the lecture slides; Warren Huska for setting up the book's website; Shana Meyer at Aptara, Inc., for supplying editorial and composition services; the CFA Institute for allowing us to use material in Chapter 12; and Alexa Brand, the office manager at the IFID Centre, for ensuring that we were never bogged down by minutia.

Finally, we would like to recognize thousands of our students who have motivated us to "explain things better" during the last twenty years of our teaching careers. We look forward to meeting thousands more over the next twenty.

ONE

Introduction and Motivation

This book grew out of the deep frustration two of the three authors have experienced for many years, trying to teach a practical yet rigorous course on personal – in contrast to corporate or investment – finance, to undergraduate and graduate students at Canadian business schools. Although there are many college-level textbooks that discuss the *tactical* aspects of personal finance – nuggets such as: credit card debt is bad; reduce fees on mutual funds; regular saving is important; have a budget; and so on – we have not come across a textbook that integrated all these disparate concepts into a conceptual or *strategic* framework for financial decision making, *based on sound economic principles.*

For the most part, personal finance is being taught as a collection of stand-alone facts about "smart" money management. Most existing textbooks are written assuming a (very) basic background in mathematics on the part of the student, which limits the financial and economic level at which such a course can be delivered and the material discussed. Moreover, in today's Google and YouTube world, curious students could obtain more relevant, accurate, and up-to-date information about most (if not all) of the products that are part of the personal financial toolkit. In our opinion, a textbook that allocates most of its pages to the *tactical* aspects of financial planning, such as explaining how to read a credit card statement or how to get a copy of your credit report from your local credit bureau, or how to open up a brokerage account, is not advanced enough for a third or fourth year course in a business school. Many personal finance textbooks – whose first editions were written before Internet browsers existed – are a relic from a bygone era in which good information could not be located on the Web within seconds.

On a related note – to make things more difficult for us as instructors – the recent "discoveries" by behavioral economists that individuals do not

1

adhere to the most basic axioms of rational choice, and the overwhelming evidence that most consumers make systematic and persistent mistakes with their money, create an even greater need for *a conceptual framework* that goes beyond amusing anecdotes regarding dollar bills left lying on the street.

Likewise, from the perspective of students in the engineering and sciences, it is often difficult for those who are interested in personal finance problems to find a background textbook that provides an overview of the relevant institutional features of personal finance and insurance together with the mathematical treatments used to solve these problems. Often, mathematics students have to sit through various courses offered in business schools, occasionally extracting useful information from a mountain of tangential material.

So, like any authors embarking on an ambitious writing project, we believe there is a niche to be filled. In particular, our goal in writing this book – and the way we approach the topic in class – is to *teach personal finance from the perspective of the lifecycle model* (LCM), originally formulated mathematically by Ramsey (1928), economically by Fisher (1930), then refined by Modigliani and Brumberg (1954) as well as Friedman (1957), and finally adjusted for lifetime uncertainty by Yaari (1965). Our intention is to extract as many practical insights as possible in an accessible and analytically tractable manner. If there is one question that links every single dilemma in personal finance, it is: **What course of action will help me maximize my standard of living – in the smoothest way possible – over the rest of my life?**

To avoid distraction, mathematical techniques are only presented when they are absolutely needed. Our emphasis is on the practical aspects of these techniques rather than mathematical rigor. The first twelve chapters of this book – which are geared toward undergraduates in business and finance – present the lifecycle model of investment and consumption under very simple assumptions about wages, retirement dates, and investment returns. The final two chapters (13 and 14) are (much) more mathematical and present advanced material related to the LCM, leading up to the Merton (1990) work on asset allocation in continuous time. The two final chapters are more suitable for an advanced undergraduate audience in economics and applied mathematics, or perhaps a first year graduate course, assuming they have the mathematical maturity and interest. As far as the numerical examples and case studies are concerned, we focus our examples on the Canadian environment (and in particular the tax material in Chapter 6) mainly because this is where we are located and where we currently teach. The other chapters or sections that contain a substantial amount of Canadian content are so designated. That said, most of the conceptual material – which forms the majority of this book – is universal enough to apply anywhere.

In writing this book we aimed to "prove" that personal finance can be taught to university students in an intellectually satisfying manner, within a rational and strategic framework. We hope you agree.

TWO

Mathematical Preliminaries – Working with
Interest Rates

Learning Objectives

In this chapter, we will review the concepts of interest rates and time value of money (TVM). There are several types of present-value and future-value formulas, each of which is used in specific circumstances. Our goal is to make sure that you understand when (i.e., in what context) these formulas should be used. A good understanding of this chapter is needed to proceed to future chapters, where we will need to calculate the amounts of your consumption and savings at various points in time.

Although we believe that most of you have covered these materials in your previous finance courses, we recommend that you take another look at them and familiarize yourself with the notations we will use in the rest of this book.

2.1 Interest Rates

As you may recall, an interest rate is the rate of return that a borrower promises to pay for the use of money that he or she borrows from the lender. Normally, it is expressed in terms of per-annum percentage rates (e.g., 4% p.a.). To express it properly, however, we also need to state the compounding frequency of the rate, which is the number of compounding periods in one year. In other words, it is the number of times in a year that interest is calculated and added to the principal of the loan.

For example, annual compounding means that interest is added to the principal once a year. Suppose you invest \$1 for one year at the interest rate of 4% p.a., annual compounding. At the end of the year, you will receive:

$$(1 + 0.04)^1 = 1.04.$$

Suppose instead that the interest rate is 4% p.a., semi-annual compounding. In this case, interest will be added to the principal every six months (i.e., a compounding period is six months). In other words, you earn 2% every six months, with the interest being reinvested. So, after one year you will get:

$$\left(1 + \frac{0.04}{2}\right)^2 = 1.0404,$$

which is slightly more than the annual-compounding case. On the other hand, if the rate is 4% p.a., monthly compounding (i.e., a compounding period is one month), you now earn $0.04/12 = 0.3333\%$ per month, with the interest being reinvested. As a result, you will end up with:

$$\left(1 + \frac{0.04}{12}\right)^{12} = 1.040742,$$

which is even higher.

As you can see, the higher the frequency of compounding, the more money you will receive at the end of your investment horizon. Note from these calculations that what we do in each of the three cases is: (i) we figure out the rate per compounding period based on the stated compounding frequency, and (ii) add that per-period rate to 1 and then raise the whole thing to the power of the number of compounding periods. Formally, if you invest $\$A$ for n years at an interest rate of $i\%$ p.a., compounded m times per year, at the end of n years, you will receive:

$$A \cdot \left(1 + \frac{i}{m}\right)^{mn}. \tag{2.1}$$

2.1.1 Effective Annual Rate (EAR) and Annual Percentage Rate (APR)

Next, we want to introduce a term that reflects the returns that you get under various compounding frequencies. That term is **effective annual rate (EAR)**. An EAR is simply the interest rate that you actually earn after taking compounding into account. For example, when the stated interest rate is 4% p.a., annual compounding, the EAR is also 4% because this is the rate that you actually earn after one year. On the other hand, when the stated interest rate is 4% p.a., semi-annual compounding, the EAR is 4.04%. Finally, when the stated interest rate is 4% p.a., monthly compounding, the EAR is 4.0742%. Given a per-annum interest rate, the higher the frequency of compounding, the higher the EAR will be.

Formally, suppose the stated interest rate is i% p.a., compounded m times per year. Its EAR is:

$$\left(1 + \frac{i}{m}\right)^m - 1. \tag{2.2}$$

Obviously, if you know the EAR and the compounding frequency, you can use equation (2.2) to work backward to find the stated interest rate, i.

In practice, some lenders express their interest rates in terms of **annual percentage rates (APRs)**. This is common among, for example, car dealers and credit card issuers. An APR is a simple interest rate per year, and is expressed without an associated compounding frequency. A good way to think of an APR is as follows. Suppose the lender wants to charge you some interest rate per payment period (which can be of any length – a month, a quarter, a year, etc.). The APR is calculated by multiplying that rate per payment period by the number of payment periods in one year. For example, suppose you are quoted an interest rate of 4% APR, and the lender requires you to make a payment every month (i.e., payment period is one month). This means that the lender is charging you a rate of 0.3333% per payment period (i.e., a month). This is because if you multiply the rate per period by the number of periods in a year, you will get 0.3333% × 12 = 4%.

There are two things to note about APRs. First, because an APR quote does not come with an associated compounding frequency, it is up to the borrower to know the number of payment periods per year. Secondly, an APR does not take into account the compounding effect. Consider the previous example where you were quoted an interest rate of 4% APR, payable monthly, which means the rate per payment period is 0.3333%. The effective annual rate (EAR) in this case is:[1]

$$(1.003333)^{12} - 1 = 0.040742 \text{ or } 4.0742\%.$$

In other words, when the payments are required more often than once a year, the effective interest rate that you pay will be higher than the quoted APR. Now you can see that the quoted APR of 4% is not the rate that you effectively end up paying over a year. That effective rate is the EAR, which in this case is 4.0742%. This is why an APR quote is ambiguous. You need to know the payment frequency in order to figure out the effective annual rate.

---

[1] Note that the EAR in this case is the same as the EAR when the rate is quoted as 4% p.a., monthly compounding. This is because the rate per period in both cases is the same, which is 0.3333% per month.

Of course, given a quoted APR, different frequencies of payments will lead to different EARs.

In the previous example, the difference between the APR (4%) and the EAR (4.0742%) may not appear to be significant. However, with a higher quoted APR, the difference can be substantial. For example, many credit cards charge interest at an APR of 25% (or higher) with daily compounding. At first glance, 25% would translate to $250 on a credit card balance of $1,000, which is already a bit of money. However, that amount has not yet taken into account the compounding effect. What you actually end up paying is the EAR, which in this case is:

$$\left(1 + \frac{0.25}{365}\right)^{365} - 1 = 0.283916 \text{ or } 28.3916\%,$$

which is almost 3.40% more than the stated APR.

Before we move on, we want to emphasize three things from this section. First, it is important to understand the different ways under which interest rates can be expressed (e.g., 4% p.a., semi-annual compounding vs. 4% APR). Secondly, you should be able to distinguish between rates per year and rates per period (where a period can be of any length). Finally, you should be able to work with different compounding frequencies.

2.2 Time Value of Money – Definitions

Because money can earn a rate of return, the value of $1 to be received today is not the same as the value of $1 to be received some time in the future (say, one year from now). Therefore, in order to compare properly cash flows that occur at different points in time, we need to apply the concept of time value of money (TVM) so that those cash flows are valued as of one common time point. To this end, we define **present value** as the current worth of an amount of money or a sequence of cash flows. Also, we define **future value** as the value as of a specified date in the future of an amount of money or a sequence of cash flows.

Present value and future value are linked by rates of return. Note that we use the term **rates of return**, which is a more general term than **interest rates**. This is because people can invest their money in many different ways. If they lend it out, they will earn a rate of return equal to the prevailing interest rate. On the other hand, if they invest it some other way (say, buying a stock), they will earn a rate of return that reflects the nature of that investment. Therefore, the use of a more general term is appropriate.

In addition, note that from now on, we also refer to a rate of return as a **valuation rate**.

2.3 Present Value and Future Value of a Single Cash Flow

The present value of $1 to be received N periods from now (note that a period can be of any length) where the valuation rate is v% per period is:

$$\mathbf{PV}(v, N) := \frac{1}{(1+v)^N} = (1+v)^{-N}. \tag{2.3}$$

For example, suppose the valuation rate is $v = 2$% per period. The present value of $1 to be received five periods from now is:

$$\mathbf{PV}(0.02, 5) = \frac{1}{(1.02)^5} = 0.9057.$$

Next, let us suppose that you now have $1. What is the future value of it five periods from now? It must be equal to $1 compounded over five periods at the valuation rate; that is,

$$\mathbf{FV}(0.02, 5) = 1 \cdot (1.02)^5 = 1.1041.$$

Formally, the future value of $1 after N periods from now at the valuation rate of v% per period is:

$$\mathbf{FV}(v, N) := (1+v)^N. \tag{2.4}$$

Note that we have kept the length of a period unspecified and that the valuation rate v is expressed as a rate per period. When you want to calculate present values or future values, it is up to you to find the correct rate per period to use. For example, suppose the length of a period is one month and we are dealing with an interest rate quote of 6% APR. It is now up to you to recognize that because the length of a period is one month, the rate per period (based on your knowledge of what an APR is from the previous section) is 6%/12 = 0.5% per period.

Just to make sure that you are comfortable with finding the rate per period, let us consider another example.

Practice Question *Suppose you are quoted an interest rate of 6% p.a., semi-annual compounding. What is the equivalent rate per month?*

This is not as straightforward as in the earlier APR case. In the APR case, you know that the rate per period is simply the APR divided by the number of periods in a year. Here, the equivalent rate per month must be such that it compounds to the same effective annual rate (EAR) as the EAR of the quoted rate, which is:

$$\left(1 + \frac{0.06}{2}\right)^2 - 1 = 0.0609 \text{ or } 6.09\%.$$

As a result, the equivalent rate per month must be such that:

$$(1 + v)^{12} - 1 = 0.0609.$$

Solving for v, we get $v = 0.004939$ or 0.4939% per month.

Next, we will look at the present value and the future value of a sequence of cash flows. A typical example is an annuity. An annuity represents a sequence of payments that are made over many consecutive periods. Those payments can be of an equal amount or can vary. Each payment can occur at either the beginning or the end of a period. If the payment is made at the beginning of a period, that annuity is typically referred to as an **annuity due**. On the other hand, if the payment is made at the end of a period, that annuity is typically referred to as an **ordinary annuity**.

We divide our discussion into different cases depending on (i) whether the annuity is an ordinary annuity or an annuity due, and (ii) whether its payments remain the same or vary.

2.4 Present Value of an Annuity with Constant Payments

We start with an annuity whose payments remain the same through time.

2.4.1 Ordinary Annuity

Let us consider an ordinary annuity that pays $1 at the end of a period for N periods (i.e., there are N payments). How do we find the present value of this ordinary annuity? The logic must be the same as in the case of the present value of a single amount. Here, what you can do is find the present value of each of the N payments and then add them up. That is, the present value is equal to:

$$\mathbf{PVA}(v, N) := \frac{1}{1+v} + \frac{1}{(1+v)^2} + \frac{1}{(1+v)^3} + \cdots + \frac{1}{(1+v)^N}, \quad (2.5)$$

which, after some manipulation, reduces to:

$$\mathbf{PVA}(v, N) = \left[\frac{1 - (1+v)^{-N}}{v}\right]. \quad (2.6)$$

The square bracket on the right-hand side of equation (2.6) is what we call a **present-value-of-annuity factor** or PVA factor, denoted by $\textbf{PVA}(v,\ N)$. It gives you the present value of an annuity per \$1 of payoff per period for N periods. So, if the annuity's payment is some other amount (say, \$$X$) per period, you can simply multiply \$$X$ by the PVA factor to get the present value of that annuity.

Practice Question   *Suppose that you are earning a salary of \$5,000 per month, payable at the end of the month. What is the present value of your future salary, assuming that you will work for another thirty years and that the valuation rate is 6% APR?*

Here, the payment period is monthly and so the valuation rate per period is $0.06/12 = 0.005$ or 0.5% per month. The number of periods is 360 months. The PVA factor is:

$$\textbf{PVA}\,(0.005,\ 360) = \left[\frac{1 - (1.005)^{-360}}{0.005} \right] = 166.7916.$$

As a result, the present value of your lifetime salary is \$5,000 $\cdot$ 166.7916 = \$833,958.

Note how the present value depends on the assumption that 6% APR is the appropriate rate to use to value your future salary. Of course, if we used a higher rate (e.g., 8%), the present value will be lower, and vice versa. We discuss in the next chapter how the appropriate rate can be determined.

Practice Question   *You have just won a lottery worth \$1,000,000. You are going to put the winnings in a bank account earning 6% p.a., annual compounding. You plan to withdraw \$70,000 from this account at the end of every year. How many years will the money last?*

This is a simple present-value-of-annuity problem. The present value of the yearly withdrawals must equal the amount of the winnings, \$1,000,000. In this case, the payment period is one year. Let N be the number of years that you can make the withdrawals. Then,

$$70,000 \cdot \textbf{PVA}\,(0.06,\ N) = 1,000,000.$$

Using the formula for PVA, we have

$$70,000 \cdot \left[\frac{1 - (1.06)^{-N}}{0.06} \right] = 1,000,000,$$

which, after some manipulation, reduces to:

$$(1.06)^N = 7.$$

To solve for N, we take a natural log of both sides.

$$\ln (1.06)^N = \ln 7,$$

which leads to

$$N \ln(1.06) = \ln 7$$

or

$$0.05827 N = 1.9459.$$

Solving for N, we have $N = 33.40$ years. This means that you will be able to take out \$70,000 per year for thirty-three years. At the end of the thirty-fourth year (i.e., just before you make the final withdrawal), the account will have less than \$70,000 left for you to withdraw.

2.4.2 Annuity Due

In the previous examples, the payments are made at the end of the periods (i.e., ordinary annuity). What if the payments are made at the start (i.e., annuity due)? In this case, the PVA factor becomes:

$$\overline{\text{PVA}}(v, N) := 1 + \frac{1}{1+v} + \frac{1}{(1+v)^2} + \frac{1}{(1+v)^3} + \cdots + \frac{1}{(1+v)^{N-1}}, \tag{2.7}$$

which reduces to:

$$\overline{\text{PVA}}(v, N) = \left[\frac{1 - (1+v)^{-N}}{v} \right] \cdot (1+v). \tag{2.8}$$

There is obviously a connection between the PVA factor for an annuity due and the PVA factor for an ordinary annuity. If you compare equation (2.8) to equation (2.6), you can see that equation (2.8) is simply equation (2.6) multiplied by $(1 + v)$; that is,

$$\overline{\text{PVA}}(v, N) = \text{PVA}(v, N) \cdot (1 + v).$$

This should not be surprising if you look at the long-form expressions of both PVA factors in equations (2.5) and (2.7). Because the cash flows of an annuity due occur at the beginning of the periods, each of them is discounted

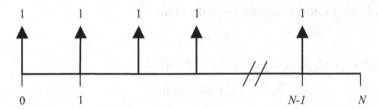

Figure 2.1. Cash flow pattern of an annuity due.

over a shorter time (by one period, to be exact) than their counterpart for an ordinary annuity.

Figure 2.1 displays the cash flow pattern for an annuity due, in which payments grow.

Practice Question *Suppose that you are earning a salary of $5,000 per month, payable at the start of the month. What is the present value of your lifetime salary assuming that you will work for another thirty years and that the valuation rate is 6% p.a., monthly compounding?*

The PVA factor in this case is:

$$\overline{\mathrm{PVA}}\,(0.005,360) = \left[\frac{1 - (1.005)^{-360}}{0.005} \right] \cdot (1.005) = 167.6256.$$

As a result, the present value of your lifetime salary is $5,000 \cdot 167.6256 = $838,128.

Recall from the previous subsection that if your salary is paid at the end of each month (i.e., ordinary annuity), the present value of your lifetime salary is $833,958, which is lower than the present value in this case. This is, as mentioned earlier, due to the timing of the cash flows. The later the payments occur, the longer the time period over which you discount them, and thus the lower their present values.

2.5 Future Value of an Annuity with Constant Payments

2.5.1 Ordinary Annuity

Next, let us consider the future value of an ordinary annuity that pays $1 per period at the end of each period for N periods. Assume, as before, that the valuation rate is v% per period. The future value is equal to:

$$\mathbf{FVA}(v, N) := 1 \cdot (1 + v)^{N-1} + 1 \cdot (1 + v)^{N-2} + 1 \cdot (1 + v)^{N-3} + \cdots + 1.$$
$$(2.9)$$

To be clear, the first term in Eq. (2.9) is the future value of $1 received at the *end* of the first period. As a result, this amount can be invested for $N - 1$ periods. The second term is the future value of $1 received at the end of the second period and invested for $N - 2$ periods, and so on. Finally, the last term is the $1 received at the end of the last period, and so there is no time to invest it.

After some manipulation, Eq. (2.9) reduces to:

$$\text{FVA}(v, N) = \left[\frac{(1 + v)^N - 1}{v} \right]. \tag{2.10}$$

The square bracket on the right-hand side of equation (2.10) is what we call a **future-value-of-annuity factor** or FVA factor, denoted by **FVA**(v, N). It gives you the future value of an annuity per $1 of payoff per period for N periods. So, if the annuity's payment is some other amount (say, X) per period, you can simply multiply X by the FVA factor to get the future value of that annuity.[2]

Practice Question *Suppose you set aside $1,000 to invest every month for the next thirty years (i.e., until you retire). The investment will be made at the end of each month. Assuming that the investment rate is 6% p.a., monthly compounding, how much money will you have at the start of your retirement?*

The FVA factor is:

$$\text{FVA}\,(0.005,360) = \left[\frac{(1.005)^{360} - 1}{0.005} \right] = 1{,}004.5150.$$

As a result, by the time you retire, you will have $1,000 \cdot 1,004.5150 = $1,004,515. This is the future value of all your savings over the next thirty years.

2.5.2 Annuity Due

In the previous example, the investment is made at the end of the months (i.e., ordinary annuity). What if you decide to invest at the start of each

---

[2] You should convince yourself that the FVA factor for an ordinary annuity in equation (2.10) is related to the PVA factor for an ordinary annuity in equation (2.6) as follows:

$$\text{FVA}(v, N) = \text{PVA}(v, N) \cdot \text{FV}(v, N).$$

month (i.e., annuity due)? In this case, the FVA factor becomes:

$$\overline{\text{FVA}}(v, N) := 1 \cdot (1 + v)^N + 1 \cdot (1 + v)^{N-1} \tag{2.11}$$
$$+ 1 \cdot (1 + v)^{N-2} + \cdots + 1 \cdot (1 + v),$$

which reduces to:

$$\overline{\text{FVA}}(v, N) = \left[\frac{(1 + v)^N - 1}{v} \right] \cdot (1 + v) \tag{2.12}$$

or, equivalently,

$$\overline{\text{FVA}}(v, N) = \left[\frac{(1 + v)^{N+1} - 1}{v} \right] - 1. \tag{2.13}$$

You should be able to verify that in this case, the future value of your savings will be \$1,009,538, which is higher than the future value in the ordinary-annuity case (i.e., \$1,004,515). This should be intuitive because when you start saving earlier (in this example, by one month), your savings have more time to earn income, and so the final result should be higher.

2.6 Present Value of an Annuity Whose Payments Change at a Constant Rate

Next, let us consider a slightly more complicated form of annuity. Suppose that the payments are no longer the same period after period. Rather, they change at a constant rate of $g\%$ per period, where g can be positive or negative. We refer to this type of annuity as a **constant-growth annuity**. Note that because g can be negative, the annuity payments may indeed decline over time.

2.6.1 Constant-Growth Ordinary Annuity

Consider first the case where each annuity payment occurs at the end of a period. Suppose there is a constant-growth ordinary annuity that lasts N periods and whose payments start at \$1 per period and change at the rate of $g\%$ per period. This means that the first payment is \$1 and is paid at the end of the first period. The second payment is $\$1 \cdot (1 + g)$ and is paid at the end of the second period, and so on. As before, the present value of this sequence of payments is simply the sum of the present values of each payment; that is,

$$\text{PVA}(\overline{g}, v, N) := \frac{1}{1+v} + \frac{1 \cdot (1+g)}{(1+v)^2} + \frac{1 \cdot (1+g)^2}{(1+v)^3} + \cdots + \frac{1 \cdot (1+g)^{N-1}}{(1+v)^N},$$

(2.14)

which, after some manipulation, reduces to:

$$\text{PVA}(\overline{g}, v, N) = \left[\frac{1 - \left[(1+g)^N \cdot (1+v)^{-N} \right]}{v - g} \right].$$

(2.15)

When $v = g$, the PVA factor reduces to:

$$\text{PVA}(\overline{g}, v, N) = \frac{N}{(1+v)}.$$

(2.16)

$\text{PVA}(\overline{g}, v, N)$ is the present-value-of-annuity factor. Note that we use the notation $\overline{g}$ instead of g in the PVA bracket. This does not mean that they have different values. Rather, the purpose is simply to distinguish this PVA factor from a slightly different version of it that will be discussed next.

In the description of the earlier annuity, it is clear that the first payment (which is to occur at the end of the first period) is equal to $1, and equation (2.15) was derived accordingly. In some personal-finance applications, you will require a slightly different version of a constant-growth ordinary annuity. In this different version, the first payment is not $1, but $ (1 + g). In other words, although this annuity is based on the same base amount of $1, the first payment (which, recall, is made at the end of the first period) already takes into account the growth in the first period. Consequently, the present value of this sequence of payments is:

$$\text{PVA}(g, v, N) := \frac{1 \cdot (1+g)}{1+v} + \frac{1 \cdot (1+g)^2}{(1+v)^2} + \frac{1 \cdot (1+g)^3}{(1+v)^3}$$

$$+ \cdots + \frac{1 \cdot (1+g)^N}{(1+v)^N},$$

(2.17)

which, after some manipulation, reduces to:

$$\text{PVA}(g, v, N) = \left[\frac{1 - \left[(1+g)^N \cdot (1+v)^{-N} \right]}{v - g} \right] \cdot (1+g).$$

(2.18)

When $v = g$, the PVA factor reduces to:

$$\textbf{PVA}(g, v, N) = N. \tag{2.19}$$

$\textbf{PVA}(g, v, N)$ is the present-value-of-annuity factor in this case. Note that in contrast to the PVA factor in equation (2.15), here we use the notation g, not $\overline{g}$.

For future reference, we refer to the first version of this annuity (i.e., whose first payment is \$1) as a **delayed constant-growth ordinary annuity (DGOA)**, and the second version (whose first payment is $\$(1 + g)$) as a **regular constant-growth ordinary annuity (RGOA)**.

To make sure that you understand the difference between these two annuities, consider the following examples.

Practice Question *Your current salary is \$5,000 per month. Suppose that it grows at the rate of 3% APR (i.e., 0.25% per month). What is the present value of your lifetime salary, assuming that you will work for another thirty years and that the valuation rate is 6% p.a., monthly compounding?*

This example shows that an ambiguity can exist. It is not completely clear from the context whether \$5,000 is the amount that you were most recently paid (i.e., from the most recent month), or the amount that you are going to be paid at the end of next month. If the latter, then this is a DGOA, and so the calculation is:

$$5{,}000 \cdot \textbf{PVA}(\overline{g}, v, N) = 5{,}000 \cdot \textbf{PVA}(0.0025, 0.005, 360)$$

$$= 5{,}000 \cdot \left[\frac{1 - \left(1.0025^{360} \cdot 1.005^{-360}\right)}{0.005 - 0.0025} \right]$$

$$= 5{,}000 \cdot 236.8245$$

$$= 1{,}184{,}122.$$

On the other hand, if \$5,000 is the amount from the previous month, your next paycheck will be $\$5{,}000 \cdot 1.0025 = \$5{,}012.50$. Accordingly, this is a RGOA, and the present value of your future lifetime salary will be:

$$5{,}000 \cdot \textbf{PVA}(g, v, N) = 5{,}000 \cdot \left[\frac{1 - \left(1.0025^{360} \cdot 1.005^{-360}\right)}{0.005 - 0.0025} \right] \cdot 1.0025$$

$$= 5{,}012.50 \cdot 236.8245$$

$$= 1{,}187{,}083.$$

As you can see, it is very important to make sure what the first payment is.

To make sure you understand how to work with the PVA factor in this case, let us look at another example.

Practice Question *Refer to the previous lottery example. Recall that your lottery winning: is $1,000,000, and is now in the bank earning 6% p.a., annual compounding. Suppose you do not want to withdraw the same amount every year. Rather, you want each subsequent amount to be 3% higher than the one before in order to account for the fact that prices of goods and services rise over time. If you want to do this for exactly thirty-three years, what is the amount that you can withdraw in the first year? Remember that the withdrawals are done at the end of each year.*

In this case, you want the present value of this constant-growth sequence of withdrawals to equal the lottery winnings, $1,000,000. Let the first-year amount, which is to be withdrawn at the end of the year, be $\$A$. So, we are dealing with a DGOA whose first payment is $\$A$. Using the PVA factor in equation (2.15), we have:

$$A \cdot \left[\frac{1 - \left(1.03^{33} \cdot 1.06^{-33}\right)}{0.06 - 0.03} \right] = 1,000,000.$$

Solving for $\$A$, we get $\$A = \$48,998$. At the end of the second year, you make your second withdrawal in the amount of $50,468, which is 3% more than the first withdrawal. This will go on until the end of year thirty-three, at which point your bank account will be exhausted.

Table 2.1 displays the amounts withdrawn, their present values as of the start of the first year (i.e., now), and the balances of your bank account. You can see that the withdrawn amounts grow by 3% every year. The sum of the present values of the thirty-three withdrawals is equal to $1,000,000, which is what you currently have in the account. This verifies that the calculations are correct. Another way to verify it is to look at the balance of the account after thirty-three years, which is down to zero.

Note also that the balance at the end of each year is equal to the beginning balance plus the return on it (at 6% per year) minus the amount withdrawn. For example, the ending balance for year 1 is calculated by:

$$1,000,000 \cdot (1.06) - 48,998.38 = 1,011,001.62.$$

Table 2.1. *Amounts withdrawn and their present values*

Year	Beginning A/C balance	Amount withdrawn	Ending A/C balance	Present value of withdrawn amount
1	$1,000,000.00	$48,998.38	$1,011,001.62	$46,224.89
2	$1,011,001.62	$50,468.33	$1,021,193.38	$44,916.64
3	$1,021,193.38	$51,982.38	$1,030,482.60	$43,645.41
.	.	.	.	.
10	$1,061,146.96	$63,931.77	$1,060,884.00	$35,699.17
.	.	.	.	.
20	$947,915.52	$85,918.96	$918,871.50	$26,789.94
.	.	.	.	.
30	$417,576.57	$115,467.89	$327,163.27	$20,104.13
31	$327,163.27	$118,931.93	$227,861.13	$19,535.15
32	$227,861.13	$122,499.89	$119,032.91	$18,982.26
33	$119,032.91	$126,174.89	$0.00	$18,445.03
				$1,000,000.00

Source: Author Calculations.

2.6.2 Constant-Growth Annuity Due

When the annuity payment occurs at the start of the period, the PVA factor for a constant-growth annuity is:

$$\overline{PVA}(g, v, N) := 1 + \frac{1\cdot(1+g)}{1+v} + \frac{1\cdot(1+g)^2}{(1+v)^2} \qquad (2.20)$$
$$+ \frac{1\cdot(1+g)^3}{(1+v)^3} + \cdots + \frac{1\cdot(1+g)^{N-1}}{(1+v)^{N-1}},$$

which, after some manipulation, reduces to:

$$\overline{PVA}(g, v, N) = \left[\frac{1 - \left[(1+g)^N\cdot(1+v)^{-N}\right]}{v - g}\right]\cdot(1+v). \qquad (2.21)$$

When $v = g$, the PVA factor reduces to:

$$\overline{PVA}(g, v, N) = N. \qquad (2.22)$$

Practice Question *Refer to the previous lottery example. Suppose each of the thirty-three withdrawals occur at the start of each year. What is the amount that you can withdraw in the first year?*

Let the first-year amount be $\$A$. Note that this withdrawal will be made at the start of the first year (i.e., now). Using the PVA factor in equation (2.21), we have:

$$A \cdot \left[\frac{1 - \left(1.03^{33} \cdot 1.06^{-33}\right)}{0.06 - 0.03} \right] \cdot (1.06) = 1,000,000.$$

Solving for $\$A$, we get $\$A = \$46,224.89$. This is the amount that you withdraw now. At the start of the second year, you make your second withdrawal in an amount of $\$47,611.63$, which is 3% higher than the first amount. This will go on until the beginning of the thirty-third year, where you make your final withdrawal and your bank account will be exhausted. As an exercise, you should try to create a table similar to Table 2.1 to track the amounts of the withdrawals and the account balances through time.

2.7 Future Value of an Annuity Whose Payments Change at a Constant Rate

Now, we look at the future value of a constant-growth annuity. As before, we separate our discussion between ordinary annuity and annuity due.

2.7.1 Constant-Growth Ordinary Annuity

Consider the future value of a DGOA that lasts N periods and whose payments start at $1 in the first period and change at the rate of $g\%$ per period. The FVA factor is:

$$\begin{aligned} \text{FVA}(\overline{g}, v, N) : = {} & 1 \cdot (1 + v)^{N-1} + 1 \cdot (1 + g) \cdot (1 + v)^{N-2} \qquad (2.23) \\ & + 1 \cdot (1 + g)^2 \cdot (1 + v)^{N-3} + \cdots + 1 \cdot (1 + g)^{N-1}. \end{aligned}$$

The first term in this expression is the future value of $1 received at the *end* of the first period. As a result, this amount can be invested for $N - 1$ periods. The second term is the future value of $\$ (1 + g)$ received at the end of the second period and invested for $N - 2$ periods, and so on. Finally, the last term is the $\$ (1 + g)^{N-1}$ received at the end of the last period, and so there is no time to invest it.

After some manipulation, this expression reduces to:

$$\text{FVA}(\bar{g}, v, N) = \left[\frac{(1 + v)^N - (1 + g)^N}{v - g} \right]. \qquad (2.24)$$

When $v = g$, the FVA factor becomes:

$$\text{FVA}(\bar{g}, v, N) = N \cdot (1 + v)^{N-1}. \qquad (2.25)$$

Next, what about the future value of a RGOA (i.e., one whose first payment is $\$(1 + g)$)? The FVA factor is:[3]

$$\text{FVA}(g, v, N) := \left[\frac{(1 + v)^N - (1 + g)^N}{v - g} \right] \cdot (1 + g). \qquad (2.26)$$

When $v = g$, the FVA factor becomes:

$$\text{FVA}(g, v, N) = N \cdot (1 + v)^N. \qquad (2.27)$$

Practice Question   *Suppose you want to set aside 10% of your monthly salary to invest for the next thirty years (i.e., until you retire). The investment will be made at the end of each month. Your current monthly salary (which will be paid at the end of this month) is \$5,000. Suppose that your salary grows at the rate of 3% APR (i.e., 0.25% per month). Assuming that the investment rate is 6% p.a., monthly compounding, how much money will you have at the start of your retirement?*

Because you want to save a fixed percentage of your monthly salary (which itself is growing at a constant rate), the amounts of your savings will also grow at that constant rate. Therefore, we are dealing with the future value of a DGOA whose first payment is 10% of \$5,000 or \$500. Each subsequent payment will be 0.25% more than the one before. Using equation (2.26), the amount of money that you will have after thirty years is:

$$500 \cdot \left[\frac{(1.005)^{360} - (1.0025)^{360}}{0.005 - 0.0025} \right] = 713{,}147.$$

2.7.2 Constant-Growth Annuity Due

Consider a constant-growth annuity due that lasts N periods and whose payments start at \$1 in the first period and change at the rate of $g\%$ per

---

[3] We are omitting the long-form expression of this FVA factor. You should try to write one out.

period. The FVA factor is:

$$\overline{\text{FVA}}(g, v, N) := 1 \cdot (1+v)^N + 1 \cdot (1+g) \cdot (1+v)^{N-1} \qquad (2.28)$$
$$+ 1 \cdot (1+g)^2 \cdot (1+v)^{N-2} + \cdots + 1 \cdot (1+g)^{N-1}(1+v).$$

The first term in this expression is the future value of \$1 received at the *start* of the first period. As a result, this amount can be invested for N periods. The second term is the future value of \$$(1+g)$ received at the start of the second period and invested for $N-1$ periods, and so on. Finally, the last term is the \$$(1+g)^{N-1}$ received at the start of the last period, and so it can be invested for only one period. After some manipulation, this expression reduces to:

$$\overline{\text{FVA}}(g, v, N) = \left[\frac{(1+v)^N - (1+g)^N}{v - g}\right] \cdot (1+v). \qquad (2.29)$$

When $v = g$, the FVA factor becomes:

$$\overline{\text{FVA}}(g, v, N) = N \cdot (1+v)^N. \qquad (2.30)$$

2.8 A Preliminary Discussion of the Effects of Inflation

An *inflation rate* is the rate of change in the general level of prices of goods and services over a period of time. If the price levels keep increasing, the purchasing power of our money will decline over time. In other words, one dollar will buy fewer and fewer units of goods and services over time. For example, suppose the inflation rate is expected to be 2% per year over the next several years. Suppose also that a product now costs \$1 per unit. So, one dollar now can buy one unit of this product. Let us look at the prices of this product at the end of each of the next five years.

As you can see from Table 2.2, in the presence of inflation, the purchasing power of one dollar declines over time. At the end of the first year, one dollar can buy 0.9804 units of the product, whereas by the end of the fifth year, one dollar can only get you 0.9057 units. We will refer to the one dollar that we have at the end of each year as a **nominal** dollar. On the other hand, we will refer to its purchasing power as the **real** value of a dollar. Note that the real value of a dollar is measured in terms of the number of units of goods and services that a dollar can buy at a given point in time. As a result, the real value of a dollar is simply the nominal value (i.e., one) adjusted by the inflation rate over time. This allows us to generalize by saying that the real value of any nominal amount of money at any point in time is that nominal amount adjusted by inflation over time.

Table 2.2. *The decay effects of inflation*

End of year	Product's price	No. of units $1 can buy
1	1.0200	0.9804
2	1.0404	0.9612
3	1.0612	0.9423
4	1.0824	0.9238
5	1.1041	0.9057

Source: Author Calculations.

It is important to recognize that the real value of a dollar is measured relative to a reference time point. In Table 2.2, that reference time point is now. This is because we assume that $1 can buy one unit of the product now. As a result, the real value of $1 today is 1 (remember that the real value is measured in terms of the number of units of goods and services). The real value of a dollar at the end of each of the next five years is defined relative to this current value. Of course, if you pick another time (say, two years ago) to be your reference time point, the real values of a dollar will be measured relative to that point. So, the numbers that you get will be different from those in Table 2.2. However, the message of those numbers will remain the same, which is that the purchasing power of a dollar declines at the rate of 2% per year.

To make sure that you understand the difference between nominal and real values of a dollar, consider the following example.

Practice Question *Suppose you invest $1,000 now in a five-year term deposit whose interest rate is 3.50% p.a., annual compounding. Suppose also that the inflation rate is 2% per year. What will be the nominal and real values of your investment after five years?*

After five years, the nominal value will be:

$$1,000 \times 1.035^5 = 1,187.69.$$

Due to inflation, the real value of this payoff is:

$$\frac{1,187.69}{1.02^5} = 1,075.72.$$

As you can see from the example, although the nominal rate of return on the term deposit is 3.50%, this is not the return that you receive if measured in terms of purchasing power. This is because inflation has eroded the purchasing power of the dollar. Consequently, the real rate of return is lower and can be calculated as:

$$\left(\frac{1{,}075.72}{1{,}000}\right)^{\frac{1}{5}} - 1 = 0.014706 \text{ or } 1.4706\% \text{ p.a.}$$

It is important to distinguish between a nominal rate of return and a real rate of return, which is the nominal rate adjusted for inflation. The two rates are related to inflation as follows:

$$(1 + \text{nominal rate}) = (1 + \text{real rate}) \cdot (1 + \text{inflation rate}). \qquad (2.31)$$

You can use this formula to verify the real rate of return in the previous example.

Later in the book, we discuss this topic in more detail. For now, please make sure that you understand the differences between real and nominal terms, and how they are related.

2.9 Appendix: Geometric Progressions and Annuity Relations

In this chapter we provided a number of closed-form expressions for the present (discounted) value of a sequence of cash flows. Although there are many ways to derive such expressions, in this technical appendix we demonstrate how the sum of a **geometric progression** can be used to discount annuity cash flows. We also take the opportunity to summarize the main formulas in a tabular format.

Let us start with a formal definition and notation for a geometric progression:

$$\mathbf{Y}_n := \xi + \xi^2 + \xi^3 + \cdots + \xi^n = \sum_{j=1}^{n} \xi^j, \qquad (2.32)$$

which is the sum of exactly n terms, where ξ can be thought of as any number. Now, if you multiply the sum-term $\mathbf{Y}_n$ by ξ and then subtract it from $\mathbf{Y}_n$ itself, you will be left with equation (2.33):

$$\mathbf{Y}_n - \xi\mathbf{Y}_n = \sum_{j=1}^{n} \xi^j - \sum_{j=1}^{n} \xi^{j+1} = \xi - \xi^{n+1}. \qquad (2.33)$$

Notice how the terms from (and including) ξ^2 to ξ^n drop out when you subtract $\xi\mathbf{Y}_n$ from $\mathbf{Y}_n$. This trick enables us to obtain a closed-form expression for any arbitrary sum. Rearranging and isolating $\mathbf{Y}_n$ in equation (2.33) and then dividing by $\xi \neq 0$ itself leaves us with a clean expression for $\mathbf{Y}_n$, namely:

$$\mathbf{Y}_n = \frac{\xi - \xi^{n+1}}{1 - \xi} = \frac{1 - \xi^n}{1/\xi - 1}, \tag{2.34}$$

which can be used over and over again to derive multiple formulas for annuities.

For example, an ordinary annuity (OA) can be valued by plugging $\xi = (1 + v)^{-1}$ into equation (2.34) and therefore:

$$\mathbf{PVA}(v, N) = \frac{1 - (1 + v)^{-N}}{v}, \tag{2.35}$$

which was one of the first annuity formulas we displayed. Likewise, the regular constant-growth ordinary annuity (RGOA) can be valued using the same technique, but by plugging $\xi = (1 + g)/(1 + v)$ into equation (2.34), leading to:

$$\mathbf{PVA}(g, v, N) = \frac{1 - (1 + g)^N \cdot (1 + v)^{-N}}{(1 + v)/(1 + g) - 1} = \frac{1 - (1 + g)^N \cdot (1 + v)^{-N}}{(v - g)/(1 + g)}. \tag{2.36}$$

The delayed constant-growth ordinary annuity (DGOA) can also be valued by dividing the RGOA expression $\mathbf{PVA}(g, v, N)$ by $(1 + g)$ to delay the growth by one period and then using the (same) expression for the geometric progression. Specifically:

$$\mathbf{PVA}(\overline{g}, v, N) = \frac{\mathbf{PVA}(g, v, N)}{1 + g} = \frac{1 - (1 + g)^N \cdot (1 + v)^{-N}}{v - g}. \tag{2.37}$$

In fact, in many (other) finance and actuarial textbooks, $\mathbf{PVA}(\overline{g}, v, N)$ is the standard definition of a growing annuity.

The *due* versions for any annuity cash flow can also be expressed by manipulating equations (2.32) to (2.34). For example, the regular constant-growth annuity due (RGAD) satisfies:

$$\overline{\mathbf{PVA}}(g, v, N) = 1 + \sum_{j=1}^{N-1} \xi^j = 1 + \mathbf{PVA}(g, v, N - 1) \tag{2.38}$$

where, once again, $\xi = (1 + g)/(1 + v)$. The summation term (Σ) only involved $N - 1$ terms, because the first term was the initial (due) cash flow

Table 2.3. *Five main PV annuity expressions with example:*
$$g = 2\%, v = 5\%, N = 30$$

	First 2 terms	Last term	PV formula	Example
$\mathbf{PVA}(v, N)$	$\frac{1}{1+v} + \frac{1}{(1+v)^2} +$	$\cdots + \frac{1}{(1+v)^N}$	$\frac{1-(1+v)^{-N}}{v}$	$OA = 15.3725$
$\overline{\mathbf{PVA}}(v, N)$	$1 + \frac{1}{1+v} +$	$\cdots + \frac{1}{(1+v)^{N-1}}$	$\frac{(1+v)-(1+v)^{-(N-1)}}{v}$	$AD = 16.1411$
$\mathbf{PVA}(g, v, N)$	$\frac{1+g}{1+v} + \frac{(1+g)^2}{(1+v)^2} +$	$\cdots + \frac{(1+g)^N}{(1+v)^N}$	$\frac{1-(1+g)^N \cdot (1+v)^{-N}}{(v-g)/(1+g)}$	$RGOA = 19.7503$
$\mathbf{PVA}(\overline{g}, v, N)$	$\frac{1}{1+v} + \frac{1+g}{(1+v)^2} +$	$\cdots + \frac{(1+g)^{N-1}}{(1+v)^N}$	$\frac{1-(1+g)^N \cdot (1+v)^{-N}}{v-g}$	$DGOA = 19.3631$
$\overline{\mathbf{PVA}}(g, v, N)$	$1 + \frac{1+g}{1+v} +$	$\cdots + \frac{(1+g)^{N-1}}{(1+v)^{N-1}}$	$\frac{(1+v)-(1+g)^N \cdot (1+v)^{-(N-1)}}{v-g}$	$RGAD = 20.3312$

of $1. Either way, by substituting into equation (2.36), this leads to:

$$\overline{\mathbf{PVA}}(g, v, N) = 1 + \frac{1 - (1+g)^{(N-1)} \cdot (1+v)^{-(N-1)}}{(v-g)/(1+g)}. \tag{2.39}$$

Rearranging terms, we can also write the RGAD as:

$$\overline{\mathbf{PVA}}(g, v, N) = \frac{(1+v) - (1+g)^N \cdot (1+v)^{-(N-1)}}{v-g}$$

$$= (1+v) \cdot \mathbf{PVA}(\overline{g}, v, N) \tag{2.40}$$

with the final equality stemming from equation (2.37). Note that when $g = 0$ we are left with an expression for the annuity due (AD) in equation (2.40).

To make certain this is all clear, we have included a matrix that summarizes the five main annuity expressions we discussed, which is used repeatedly throughout the book. See Table 2.3.

Notice how the present value of the AD is greater than the value of the OA because the first of the N cash flows occurs earlier in time and is not discounted. Likewise, notice how the PV of the DGOA is smaller than the PV of the RGOA because the numerator's cash flows are slightly smaller in each one of the N terms. Finally, the PV of the RGAD is greater than both the DGOA and the RGOA because the first cash flow occurs earlier and the periodic cash flows are greater.

To summarize, we will be using five different expressions for present values, each depending on the context of the problem. We will make sure to point out the reason we are using a particular equation when it is not clear from the context itself.

In all cases, however, the future value (FV) can be easily computed by multiplying the appropriate PV by $(1+v)^N$, independently of the five types of annuity involved. So, for example, the FV of a RGAD when $g = 2\%$ and $v = 5\%$ and $N = 30$, would be denoted by and equal to: $\overline{\textbf{FVA}}(0.02, 0.05, 30) =$

$$\left(\frac{(1+0.05) - (1+0.02)^{30} \cdot (1+0.05)^{-(30-1)}}{0.05 - 0.02}\right)(1+0.05)^{30} = 87.87033$$

and the FV of a DGOA would be: $\textbf{FVA}(\overline{0.02}, 0.05, 30) =$

$$\left(\frac{1 - (1+0.02)^{30} \cdot (1+0.05)^{-30}}{0.05 - 0.02}\right)(1+0.05)^{30} = 83.68603,$$

which is smaller in value.

In general, if the present value of a particular sequence of cash flows **A** is smaller than the present value of a sequence **B**, then the future value of **A** will be smaller than the future value of **B**, assuming you are using the exact same point in time to compare these values. Think about this for a moment and make sure you understand why. It also reduces the need for yet more formulas.

2.10 Questions and Assignments

1. Calculate the effective annual rates (EAR) of the following interest rate quotes:

Rate (% p.a.)	Compounding Frequency
6%	weekly
6%	monthly
6%	quarterly
6%	semi-annually

2. Please compute the following quantities:

$$\textbf{PVA}(0, 0.05, 20) = \text{_____}$$

$$\frac{1}{12}\textbf{PVA}(0, 0.05/12, 20 \times 12) = \text{_____}$$

$$\frac{1}{52}\textbf{PVA}(0, 0.05/52, 20 \times 52) = \text{_____}$$

3. You have just won a lottery, which gives you a choice of two prizes. You can take a lump sum payment of $100,000 now. Alternatively, you can choose to receive $10,000 per year for twelve years, where the first payment occurs now. Suppose that the interest rate is 3% p.a., quarterly compounding. Which would you choose?

4. Assume that you have $100,000 in a bank account that is earning interest of $v = 4\%$ p.a., monthly compounding. You plan to deposit (add) $1,000 at the end of each month, for the next fifteen years. Then, starting in the first month of year 16, you plan to withdraw $c per month (at the end of each month). How long will it take until the account is depleted?

5. Based on the previous question, suppose you want to make monthly withdrawals for twenty-five years. How much can you withdraw per month?

6. Currently, you have a savings of $100,000 earning a rate of return of 4% p.a., monthly compounding. You want to retire in thirty years with a nest egg of $1,000,000. How much do you have to save at the end of each month for the next thirty years in order to reach that goal?

7. You are currently twenty-five years old. You plan to retire at age sixty, and expect to live until you are eighty-five. You estimate that during retirement, your annual expense will be $60,000 and growing at the rate of 3% p.a., annual compounding. The interest rate is expected to be 6% p.a., annual compounding. Assume that all expenses occur at the end of year. How much money will you need to have at the start of your retirement?

8. Based on the previous question, suppose that you currently make $40,000 a year. You expect your income to grow at the rate of 4% p.a., annual compounding. You plan to set aside a fixed percentage of your income every year in order to meet your retirement needs. Assume that the savings occur at the end of the year and the rate of return is 6% p.a., annual compounding. What is that percentage?

9. You will retire in thirty years. You believe that you will need to spend $50,000 (in today's dollars) every year during retirement. Suppose that the interest rate and the inflation rate are expected to be 6% p.a. and 2% p.a., respectively (both rates are annual-compounding rates). If you expect to live for twenty-five years after retirement, how much money do you need to have at the start of retirement? Assume for simplicity that all expenses occur at the end of year.

10. Please figure out and then compute the quantity: $\lim_{m\to\infty} \frac{1}{m}\mathbf{PVA}$ $(0,0.05/m, 20m)$.

THREE

Personal Balance Sheet and Human Capital

Learning Objectives

In this chapter, we talk about personal balance sheets, which are snapshots of our financial position at a point in time. We then discuss the concept of human capital that, as we will argue, should be included in everyone's personal balance sheet.

3.1 Personal Balance Sheets

A starting point in the personal financial-planning process is to assess our current financial situations. This is typically done by preparing a personal balance sheet. It is a good exercise for you to create your own balance sheet. Please take out a blank sheet of paper and draw a straight line down the center, splitting the sheet into two equal parts. Write "Assets" on the top left-hand side, and write "Liabilities" at the top right-hand side. On the left-hand side, list the value of your assets, including money in bank accounts, stocks, savings bonds, pension accounts, mutual funds, equity in a small business, house, car, and any other items you can think of. The list does not have to be exhaustive (e.g., you can disregard personal-use assets such as clothing). On the upper right-hand side, make sure to include what you owe on credit cards, consumer loans, student loans, mortgage loans, and any other financial obligations.

Once you have listed all your assets and all your liabilities, add them up to get summary numbers for both. On one side of the balance sheet is the value of everything you own, and on the other side is the value of everything you owe. Finally, subtract what you owe from what you own. The resulting number is your current net worth, as seen in Table 3.1.

Table 3.1. *Personal (Accounting) balance sheet*

Assets	Liabilities
Bank Accounts	Credit Card Balance
Investment (Stocks, Bonds, Mutual Funds, etc.)	Student Loans
Vehicles	Car Loans
Housing	Mortgage Loans
Present Value of Pensions	Other Debts
Equity in Small Business	
Other Assets	
	Total Liabilities
	Total Assets − Total Liabilities
Total Assets	= Net Worth

What you have done so far is create a **traditional** (or **accounting**) balance sheet of yourself. Although this traditional balance sheet tells you what you have and what you owe, it is our belief that it does not fully capture your current financial position and, more importantly, your current financial potential. To understand our argument, consider a balance sheet of a recent college graduate. Most likely, this person does not yet have a lot of assets, but has several debts such as a credit card loan and a student loan. Consequently, her net worth will be very small. It might even be negative, which means that she is technically bankrupt. However, as a recent college graduate, she has a good future ahead of her. As she starts working, she will earn income that she can use to consume and pay down her debts. That income-earning potential is not reflected in her traditional balance sheet. Therefore, this kind of balance sheet is not very useful in making her future financial decisions.

We believe that a better kind of balance sheet is one that includes a measure of one's economic future. For this reason, we now introduce the concept of *gross human capital,* which, in a nutshell, is the present value of your expected future income. It reflects your future earning potential. At the young age of twenty or twenty-five, you have forty to fifty years of salary, bonus, and wage income ahead of you. Think of this as a physical asset that you own like a gold mine or an oil well with many more decades of proven reserves. Corporations that own such wells and mines usually cannot extract more than a small fraction of the reserves in any given year, and yet the asset has substantial value and belongs on their corporate balance sheets today. The same concept should apply to cash-generating assets on the personal balance sheet.

Table 3.2. *Economic personal balance sheet*

Assets	Liabilities
Financial Assets	*Explicit Liabilities*
Bank Accounts	Credit Card Balance
Investment (Stocks, Bonds, Mutual Funds, etc.)	Student Loans
Vehicles	Car Loans
Housing	Mortgage Loans
Present Value of Pensions	Other Debts
Equity in Small Business	
Other Assets	*Implicit Liabilities*
	Total Liabilities
Gross Human Capital	Total Assets − Total Liabilities
Total Assets	= Economic Net Worth

We believe that the most valuable asset for most people during their working years is their gross human capital. This applies not only to college kids in their early twenties or graduate students in their late twenties, but also to you in your thirties, forties, and even fifties. Accordingly, you should include the (estimated) value of your gross human capital on the asset side.

Table 3.2 displays a personal balance sheet that incorporates your financial potential. We refer to this kind of balance sheet as an **economic balance sheet**. It is at the core of lifecycle wealth management and this book. There are a few things to note from the table. First, your gross human capital now shows up as part of your assets. Secondly, your liabilities now consist of explicit and implicit ones (we will explain their differences shortly). Finally, the difference between your total assets and total liabilities is now termed **economic net worth** because it now contains the value of your gross human capital.

Let us briefly examine the individual components of this economic balance sheet.

3.1.1 Financial Assets

We define financial assets as consisting of the *market* value of all your assets; that is, all the properties that you own except your gross human capital. As defined, financial assets include not only money in your bank accounts, but also the market values of other tangible items such as a car, a bicycle, and an iPod. Basically they are all the money that you would get if you sold everything you own today.[1] For future reference, we use the symbol $\mathbf{M}_x \geq 0$ to denote them, where the subscript x denotes your age. Note that you should use their market values, not the accounting book values or their historical acquisition costs. The market values are what you would receive if you were to sell them.

In addition, your financial assets include intangible assets such as the value of your life insurance policies and the commuted value of your pension plan (although you are not legally allowed to sell these assets).

3.1.2 Gross Human Capital

As defined earlier, gross human capital is the present value of all of your expected future income. Obviously, this number will depend on your occupation and your age. For example, using data from the U.S. Census Bureau (or Statistics Canada, for that matter) and the analytic methods described in the next section, the human capital of an "average" twenty-five-year-old college graduate can be anywhere between $540,000 and $1,700,000, depending on various assumptions and parameters. Ten years older, an average thirty-five-year-old college graduate has a human capital worth between $520,000 and $1,600,000. At the age of forty-five, the number ranges between $500,000 and $1,400,000. And, even at the age of sixty-five, the value of human capital of an average college graduate is between $160,000 and $480,000. This is because many people work well into their seventies (whether by choice or by force is another matter). The earning capacity is valuable even at an age you might traditionally associate with retirement.

Here is another perspective based on degrees versus careers. Based on raw data from the U.S. Bureau of Labor Statistics, at the age of twenty-five, the human capital of a physician, a lawyer, and a civil engineer – all degreed professionals – is worth, on average, approximately $2.7 million, $2.1 million, and $1.4 million, respectively. In contrast, an average plumber's human capital is worth $960,000 and an average baker's human capital (yes, the Bureau of Labor Statistics has a category for bakers) is worth $520,000. This is the discounted sum of all the wages "an average person" in that profession is projected to earn over the course of his or her life.

We will use the notation $\mathbf{GH}_x$ to denote the value of your gross human capital at age x.

---

[1] Some people use the term *financial assets* to refer only to assets that are traded in the financial markets such as stocks and bonds. Our definition is broader than that.

3.1.3 Explicit Liabilities

Explicit liabilities, denoted by $\mathbf{eL}_x$, are the market values of all (financial) debts you owe at the age of x. Common debts that people have include credit card debt, a student loan, a car loan, and a mortgage loan. These debts are recognized by both you and the lenders, hence the term "explicit." Do not worry yet about the various interest rates and maturity dates of these loans. $\mathbf{eL}_x \geq 0$ is the amount of cash you would need today if you were to pay off all of your liabilities in one lump sum.

3.1.4 Implicit Liabilities

If you put the value of your gross human capital on your personal balance sheet (which we say you should), it is important to remember that in order to be consistent, you should try to estimate the value of your future expenses and put it on your balance sheet as well. These future expenses do not yet exist, but you know that at some point you will have to pay them. Indeed, these future expenses should be thought of as liabilities that are now hidden from view, hence the term "implicit."

What are these expenses? They are the *minimum* costs of living that you will have to spend for the rest of your life. Note that we are talking about the minimum level of expenses required to sustain yourself. In other words, these expenses are nondiscretionary. They include, for example, the costs of food, clothing, shelter, and future medical treatment. No one can survive without spending at least some minimum amounts on these expenses.

These minimum costs are not easy to quantify. This is because they are likely to be lower than what you are used to with your current standard of living. However, for the purpose of constructing a proper economic balance sheet, you need to come up with some estimate. The estimate obviously depends on several factors such as your age, your health condition, and where you live.

We will henceforth use the notation $\mathbf{iL}_x$ to denote the value of your implicit liabilities at age x.

3.1.5 Economic Net Worth

Your economic net worth, denoted by $\mathbf{W}_x$, is the difference between the values of your total assets (which now include your gross human capital) and your total liabilities (which now include your implicit liabilities). That is,

$$\mathbf{W}_x = \mathbf{M}_x + \mathbf{GH}_x - \mathbf{eL}_x - \mathbf{iL}_x \qquad (3.1)$$
$$= (\mathbf{M}_x - \mathbf{eL}_x) + (\mathbf{GH}_x - \mathbf{iL}_x)$$
$$= \mathbf{F}_x + \mathbf{H}_x.$$

As can be seen from the second equality in equation (3.1), your economic net worth consists of two components. The first component is $\mathbf{M}_x - \mathbf{eL}_x$ (i.e., financial assets minus explicit liabilities). It is simply the traditional definition of net worth. It is not your economic net worth because it does not take into account your future economic resources (i.e., earning potential). We will henceforth refer to it as **financial capital**, and denote it by $\mathbf{F}_x$. The second component, $\mathbf{GH}_x - \mathbf{iL}_x$, is the difference between your gross human capital and implicit liabilities. It reflects your expected future income and expected future minimum spending. We will henceforth refer to this second component as the **net human capital**, and denote it by $\mathbf{H}_x$.

Note that the composition of your economic net worth changes through time. When you are in school, you are building up your gross human capital. If you have a student loan, your traditional net worth is probably negative, and so your economic net worth is positive mainly because of your gross human capital. Once you start working, you gradually convert your gross human capital into income that you can use to pay down your debts, invest, and buy other assets. Therefore, as you age, the relative contribution of the two components to your economic net worth change. When you retire, your gross human capital becomes zero, and so you need to have accumulated enough financial capital to pay for your future expenses.

In the next two sections, you will learn how to estimate your gross human capital and implicit liabilities. For now, though, remember that you are much more valuable than you think! Your economic net worth is most definitely greater than zero even if your financial capital is zero or negative.

3.2 Estimation of Gross Human Capital

Gross human capital is not easy to value. You cannot quite sell yourself in the open market to obtain a price for your gross human capital (partially because slavery is illegal). So, for the purposes of this book, we use the next best thing to a quoted market price – mathematical models. Recall that gross human capital is defined as the discounted value of all the wages you expect to receive over your working life. To get this discounted value, you must (1) reasonably estimate your annual wages, (2) select a retirement date at which the wages will stop, and (3) properly discount all the wages, earned at distinct points in time, at a suitable valuation rate. None of these three steps are easy or straightforward.

Let us start with an example. Suppose you are now (exactly) twenty-two years old and still in school. You plan to start working when you turn twenty-five. You expect your salary will be $60,000 per year. It will be paid monthly (at the end of each month) and so your monthly salary is $5,000. You plan to work for forty years (i.e., until you reach sixty-five). Assuming that the valuation rate is 5% p.a., monthly compounding, what is the value of your gross human capital today (at age twenty-two)?

First, let us calculate the value of your gross human capital at the time when you start working (i.e., at age twenty-five). This is a simple present-value-of-ordinary-annuity problem. There are 480 months of salary to be received. The valuation rate per month is $v = 0.05/12 = 0.004167$ or 0.4167%. The present value of this sequence of income is:

$$\mathbf{GH}_{25} = 5{,}000 \cdot \mathbf{PVA}(v, N) = 5{,}000 \cdot \mathbf{PVA}(0.4167, 480)$$

$$= 5{,}000 \cdot \left[\frac{1 - (1.004167)^{-480}}{0.004167} \right]$$

$$= 1{,}036{,}921.$$

So the value of your gross human capital at the start of your working life, $\mathbf{GH}_{25}$, is $1,036,921. The value of it today, $\mathbf{GH}_{22}$, is the present value of that amount. That is,

$$\mathbf{GH}_{22} = \mathbf{GH}_{25} \cdot \mathbf{PV}(v, N)$$

$$= \mathbf{GH}_{25} \cdot \mathbf{PV}(0.004167, 36)$$

$$= \frac{1{,}036{,}921}{1.004167^{36}}$$

$$= 892{,}765.$$

The value of your gross human capital today is $892,765. As you can see from the calculations, this amount depends on the assumptions that you make regarding your salary, the number of working years, and the valuation rate. Different values of these parameters will result in different estimations. Consider the next example.

Practice Question *Suppose that all other assumptions remain the same except that the valuation rate is 7% p.a., monthly compounding. What is the current value of your gross human capital,* **GH$_{22}$**?

We repeat the previous calculations, but this time with $v = 0.07/12 = 0.005833$ or 0.5833%.

$$\textbf{GH}_{25} = 5{,}000 \cdot \textbf{PVA}(0.5833,480)$$

$$= 5{,}000 \cdot \left[\frac{1 - (1.005833)^{-480}}{0.005833} \right]$$

$$= 804{,}594.$$

So, in this case, the value of your gross human capital at the start of your working years (i.e., three years from now) is $804,594. As a result, its current value is:

$$\textbf{GH}_{22} = \textbf{GH}_{25} \cdot \textbf{PV}(0.005833,36)$$

$$= \frac{804{,}594}{1.005833^{36}}$$

$$= 652{,}589.$$

The fact that the value of your gross human capital is now lower should not come as a surprise to you. Because the valuation rate is used to discount your future salary, if the rate is higher, then the resulting present value is lower.

Next, let us look at the effect of changing the assumption on salary. Suppose that your salary is growing at a rate of $g_w = 3\%$ per year.

Practice Question *Suppose that the valuation rate is $v = 5\%$ p.a., monthly compounding, while your salary is $5,000 per month and increasing at the rate of $g_w = 3\%$ per year (or 0.25% per month). That is, the first salary payment is $5,000, payable at the end of your first working month. What is* **GH$_{22}$**?

In this case, we are dealing with a delayed constant-growth ordinary annuity (see equation (2.15) in Chapter 2). The value of your gross human capital at age twenty-five, **GH$_{25}$**, is:

$$5{,}000 \cdot \textbf{PVA}(\overline{g}_w, v, N) = 5{,}000 \cdot \textbf{PVA}(0.0025,0.004167,480)$$

$$= 5{,}000 \cdot \left[\frac{1 - \left(1.0025^{480} \cdot 1.004167^{-480}\right)}{0.004167 - 0.0025} \right]$$

$$= 1{,}648{,}426.$$

Table 3.3. *Value of gross human capital per one dollar of starting monthly income for 480 months, as function of valuation rate and growth rate*

v \ g_w	2% p.a.	4% p.a.	6% p.a.
1% p.a.	589.30	924.74	1,523.09
3% p.a.	394.95	588.11	922.11
5% p.a.	279.10	394.41	586.93
7% p.a.	207.28	278.86	393.88

Calculations

It then follows that:

$$\mathbf{GH_{22}} = \mathbf{GH_{25}} \cdot \mathbf{PV}(0.004167, 36)$$
$$= \frac{1,648,426}{1.004167^{36}}$$
$$= 1,419,256.$$

So, the current value of your gross human capital in this case is $\mathbf{GH_{22}} =$ \$1,419,256. If you compare this value to that under the case where there is no salary growth (i.e., $\mathbf{H_{22}} = 892{,}765$), you can see that a salary growth of 3% per year increases your gross human capital by more than half a million dollars. Remember this next time your employer wants to impose a salary freeze!

To highlight the importance of the assumptions on the values of v and g_w, we calculated the value of gross human capital at age twenty-five per one dollar of starting monthly income under various values of v and g_w (assuming that the person will work for forty years).

As can be seen from Table 3.3, the value of gross human capital is highly sensitive to the assumptions on the valuation rate and the salary growth rate. Consequently, it is important that you be as accurate as possible when you make these assumptions.

3.2.1 What Is Proper Discount Rate for Gross Human Capital?

This is one of the fundamental issues you are asked to ponder in the next few chapters. For now let us leave it at this: *You should select a discount rate (denominator) for gross human capital valuation that reflects the safety and stability of the expected wages (numerator).* If you are reasonably confident that these wages will materialize (for example if you have a very safe job), then use a discount rate that is low and close to the risk-free interest rate in the economy (which will be denoted by r), such as the investment rate on government bonds. Never use a valuation rate that is lower than the rate of return on the safest possible asset available. The risk-free interest rate determines the upper bound for the value of gross human capital.

On the other hand, if you are unsure about the safety of these projected wages, or are concerned about the stability of your job, then discount the wages at a (much) higher rate (i.e., $v > r$). In the language of financial economics, you add a wage risk premium to the risk-free interest rate. Generally, the wage risk premium would be: $v - r \geq 0$.

If you still find this rather vague and disturbing, remember that the point of deriving a gross human capital value is to make better financial decisions over your lifecycle, as opposed to determining a market price at which to IPO yourself. As you will see in future chapters, in many situations of practical interest, a suitable value for (your personal valuation rate) v can be extracted from traded market instruments.

3.3 Estimation of Implicit Liabilities

As mentioned earlier, implicit liabilities are the value of the *minimum* costs of living that you will have to spend for the rest of your life. To estimate this value, you will have to be realistic about the subsistent level of expenses that people in the same geographical location and health condition will need. This level does not reflect the standard of living that you aspire to have. Rather, it is the lowest standard that you can tolerate.

Consider the following example.

Practice Question *You are now twenty-two years old. You live with your parents (rent free) and have few expenses, all of which are generously covered by your parents. You plan to move out when you start working at twenty-five years old. You have estimated that the minimum level of expenses is $24,000 per year (or $2,000 per month, payable at the end of each month). These expenses will increase at the rate of $g_b = 2\%$ per year to reflect inflation. You also expect to live until eighty-five years old. Assuming that the valuation rate is, as before, 5% p.a., monthly compounding, what is the value of your implicit liabilities today (i.e., iL_{22})?*

In this case, you will have no expenses for the next three years. Afterwards, the nondiscretionary consumption will occur for the following sixty years (until you reach eighty-five). As before, we first calculate the value of your implicit liabilities at age twenty-five, iL_{25}. We then discount it back over three years to the current age.

$$iL_{25} = 2,000 \cdot \mathbf{PVA}(\overline{g}_b, v, N)$$

$$= 2,000 \cdot \mathbf{PVA}(0.001667, 0.004167, 720)$$

$$= 2,000 \cdot \left[\frac{1 - \left(1.001667^{720} \cdot 1.004167^{-720}\right)}{0.004167 - 0.001667} \right]$$

$$= 667,067.$$

And so:

$$iL_{22} = iL_{25} \cdot \mathbf{PV}(0.004167, 36)$$

$$= \frac{667,067}{1.004167^{36}}$$

$$= 574,329.$$

Thus, your economic balance sheet should show \$574,329 as implicit liabilities.

Next, recall from the previous section that if we assume that you work for forty years and your starting salary is \$5,000 per month and increasing at the rate of 3% per year, the value of your gross human capital today is $GH_{22} = \$1,419,256$. Therefore, your net human capital today is: $H_x = GH_x - iL_x = \$1,419,256 - \$574,329 = \$844,927$.

To get a complete picture of your economic net worth, suppose your current assets consist of cash and a few personal belongings totaling \$5,000, while your *explicit* liabilities are a student loan in the amount of \$20,000. Your economic balance sheet will look like this:

Table 3.4. *Economic personal balance sheet (at age 22)*

Assets		Liabilities	
Financial Assets		*Explicit Liabilities*	
Cash and Personal Belongings	\$5,000	Student Loan	\$20,000
		Implicit Liabilities	\$574,329
		Total Liabilities \$594,329	
Gross Human Capital	\$1,419,256		
Total Assets	\$1,424,256	Economic Net Worth	\$829,927

Source: Author Calculations.

Your current (age twenty-two) financial capital is −$15,000. Negative financial capital is not unusual for young people who are still in school or have only recently graduated. Your economic net worth, however, is positive and more than $800,000. Again, this is because it takes into account the potential income that you can make in the future. During this stage of life, net human capital typically makes up almost the entire amount of people's economic net worth. As you age, you extract dividends from your gross human capital. You convert them into financial capital by properly saving as opposed to spending.

You can see that the amount of your implicit liabilities determines how much of your wealth you can discretionarily spend. The higher your implicit liabilities, the less you have remaining to spend freely. We will talk about your discretionary decisions in detail in the next chapter.

As you age, the value of your implicit liabilities will typically decline. This is because you have fewer years to live. However, for some people, their implicit liabilities may increase. For example, someone who develops a chronic medical condition needs to spend more during the later years of his or her life. This is why it is important for everyone to regularly evaluate their financial position so that they can adjust their consumption/savings accordingly.

Note that so far we have not mentioned income taxes. When you receive income in the future, a portion of those payments will go to the government in the form of income taxes. Again, you have no choice in this matter. As long as you want to remain within the law, paying income taxes is not discretionary. Therefore, the value of your human capital must reflect the taxes.

There are two approaches to handling income taxes when preparing an economic balance sheet. First, you can take them into account directly when you calculate your human capital; that is, you use after-tax salary in the calculation. In this way, the resulting gross human capital is after-tax gross human capital. Secondly, if you prefer to use before-tax salary in the calculation of your gross human capital, you have to calculate separately the present value of future income taxes that you will have to pay, and then treat this present value as another form of implicit liabilities. Either way, the after-tax value of your gross human capital will be the same.

We will talk more about income taxes in future chapters. For now, keep in mind that you need to account for all your future nondiscretionary expenses and include them as implicit liabilities in your economic balance sheet.

3.4 An Example of Human Capital Decisions: Investing in Education

Given the escalating tuition fees for education these days, prospective students often wonder if the substantial short-term cost of school is worth the long-term benefits in wages. In this section, you will see how the concept of human capital thinking, and equation (3.1) in particular, can be applied to help shed light on the decision of whether to pursue higher education.

Practice Question *Suppose that you are thirty years old and working in the financial services industry. Your current salary is $60,000 per year, assumed to be payable in one lump sum at the end of the year. Your career has been progressing and your salary growing steadily by $g_w = 5\%$ APR. Although you started working a number of years ago with a substantial amount of student loan debt and other debts, you have recently managed to pay them all off and have now accumulated $40,000 in assets. You are now contemplating whether to go back to graduate school for a master's degree in finance. The potential "cost" of this investment in your education is threefold. First, the program itself charges $100,000, which must be paid up front. Second, it is a full-time program that takes eighteen months to complete so you cannot work or earn any wages while in school. Finally, once you graduate, there is no assurance that you will find a better job, and it might take as long as six months to find a suitable job. Therefore, going back to school will mean a two-year hiatus from the labor force, and you will have to take on a student loan. In any case, you plan to work until you are sixty-five years old. Assuming that the valuation rate is $v = 4\%$ p.a., annual compounding, is it worthwhile to invest in education?*

The answer, of course, depends on whether the degree increases the value of your economic net worth. Let us start by looking at your current economic net worth:

$$\mathbf{W}_{30}(\mathrm{A}) = \mathbf{M}_{30} - \mathbf{eL}_{30} + \mathbf{GH}_{30}(\mathrm{A}) - \mathbf{iL}_{30}$$

where the letter "A" in the parenthesis denotes the status quo. Your current financial capital is equal to $\mathbf{F}_{30} = \mathbf{M}_{30} - \mathbf{eL}_{30} = \$40,000 - \$0 = \$40,000$. Your current gross human capital is:

$$\mathbf{GH}_{30}(\mathrm{A}) = 60,000 \cdot \mathbf{PVA}(\overline{g}_w, v, N)$$

$$= 60,000 \cdot \mathbf{PVA}(0.05, 0.04, 35)$$

$$= 60,000 \cdot \left[\frac{1 - \left(1.05^{35} \cdot 1.04^{-35}\right)}{0.04 - 0.05} \right]$$

$$= 2,387,062.$$

Therefore, your current economic net worth is:

$$\mathbf{W}_{30}(A) = 40,000 + 2,387,062 - \mathbf{i}\mathbf{L}_{30} = 2,427,062 - \mathbf{i}\mathbf{L}_{30} \qquad (3.2)$$

where we leave the current value of your implicit liabilities in notation terms. You will see that there is no real need to estimate it for our current purpose, because the term will drop off the calculations later.

Now, let us calculate your economic net worth in case you decide to get the degree, in which case you quit your job, borrow the tuition fees, and disappear from the job market for two years. Under this choice, your economic net worth is:

$$\mathbf{W}_{30}(B) = \$40,000 - \$100,000 + \mathbf{GH}_{30}(B) - \mathbf{i}\mathbf{L}_{30}$$

where the letter "B" in the parenthesis denotes the degree alternative. Your financial capital is now $-\$60,000$ because you have to pay the tuition fees by using your savings (i.e., \$40,000) and borrowing the rest. Your gross human capital, $\mathbf{GH}_{30}(B)$, is the present value of the value of your gross human capital at age thirty-two, which is when you will re-start working. Assume that the salary growth rate remains the same at 5% per year, while the valuation rate is 4% p.a., annual compounding. Because you do not know for sure what your starting salary will be when you go back to work in two years' time, let us denote that starting wage by w_{32}. Then,

$$
\begin{aligned}
\mathbf{GH}_{32}(B) &= w_{32} \cdot \mathbf{PVA}(\overline{g}_w, v, N) \\
&= w_{32} \cdot \mathbf{PVA}(0.05, 0.04, 33) \\
&= w_{32} \cdot \left[\frac{1 - \left(1.05^{33} \cdot 1.04^{-33}\right)}{0.04 - 0.05} \right] \\
&= 37.1345 \cdot w_{32}.
\end{aligned}
$$

It then follows that:

$$
\begin{aligned}
\mathbf{GH}_{30} &= \mathbf{GH}_{32} \cdot \mathbf{PV}(0.04, 2) \\
&= \frac{37.1345 \cdot w_{32}}{1.04^2} \\
&= 34.3329 \cdot w_{32}.
\end{aligned}
$$

Finally, your economic net worth at age thirty under the degree choice is:

$$\mathbf{W}_{30}(B) = -60,000 + 34.3329 \cdot w_{32} - \mathbf{IL}_{30}. \qquad (3.3)$$

Comparing the economic net worth under the two alternatives in equations (3.2) and (3.3), you can see that getting a master's degree will be worthwhile if:

$$-60,000 + 34.3329 \cdot w_{32} > 2,427,062.$$

Solving for w_{32}, we have $w_{32} > \$72,440$.

So, if you believe that you can get a starting salary of more than \$72,440 in your next job, you should go ahead and quit your current job, borrow the \$60,000, and raid the piggy bank to pay the \$100,000 tuition fees. Note that if you choose the status quo (i.e., stay in the current job), your salary at age thirty-two will be \$66,150. So, a mere 10% raise above what you would otherwise be earning at the age of thirty-two is enough to offset two years of lost wages and the \$100,000 tuition fees.

Based on this comparison, you can run the same analysis for a whole collection of different assumptions and parameters to extract the break-even wage.

3.4.1 Some Caveats

Before you rush off to apply the previous idea to your particular circumstances to decide whether to drop out of school immediately and go work at Starbucks instead, please think about the many assumptions that are fused into the architecture. First, the formula is based on the premise that your current job is just as safe as the job you will get with the master's degree. The discount rate v under Plan A is the same as the discount rate under Plan B. Yet some might argue that an advanced degree might lead to greater job stability and security, which warrants a lower discount rate (i.e., lower wage risk premium) under Plan B than under Plan A.

Another factor to consider is that your projected wage growth rate g_w might actually be higher under Plan B (going back to school) than under Plan A (maintaining the status quo). An advanced degree might open up greater career opportunities. Therefore, although your initial wage (once you graduate) might not be as high as the calculated break-even rate, it might actually increase at a greater rate over time. This too might serve to tilt the scales in favor of investing in human capital. Finally, there is the psychological value and other intangibles that are impossible to quantify.

3.5 Questions and Assignments

1. You are currently twenty years old, and will spend two more years in school. Once you graduate, you will start working with a

starting salary of $w_{22} = \$50,000$ per year. Your salary will grow at the (nominal) rate of 5% per year until you retire at age sixty-five. What is the current value of your human capital H_{20}, assuming that the (nominal) valuation rate is $v = 6\%$ p.a., annual compounding, and that the salary is paid at the end of each year?

2. What if the salary growth rate is $g_w = 5\%$ per year during the first ten years and then becomes $g_w = 3\%$ per year until you retire at age sixty-five?

3. Instead of using numbers, use notations (i.e., w_{22}, g_w, and v) to derive an expression for the value of human capital at age thirty (i.e., H_{30}), assuming that you will take a five-year sabbatical between the age of forty to forty-five (during which you do not get paid), and then continue working until age sixty-five. Assume that your wage at age forty-five, denoted by w_{45}, is exactly equal to the wage you would have earned if you did not leave the labor force for five years.

4. You are twenty-five years old and earn $w_{25} = \$50,000$ per year (payable at the end of the year). Your wage is growing at the rate of 3% per year. You would like to stop working at age sixty-five. What is your human capital worth today, assuming a valuation rate of $v = 5\%$ p.a., annual compounding? In addition, you are thinking of going back to graduate school to get an advanced degree. The program will take two years, and you expect to earn $w_{27} = \$70,000$ per year when you graduate. Assuming the same wage growth rate, what is the most you are willing to pay (today) for schooling?

5. Reverse the previous problem. Assume that you have to pay $100,000 (now) for graduate schooling. What is the minimum salary that you must earn at age $x = 27$ to justify the expense?

6. You are thirty-five years old with a steady job and no debt. Your financial capital is worth $F_{35} = \$150,000$ and is invested entirely in the stock market in mutual funds. Your current salary is $w_{35} = \$50,000$ per year (payable at the end of the year), and is expected to grow by $g_w = 5\%$ per year until you retire at age sixty-two. You expect to live until you are eighty years old. Assume that the minimum level of expenses that you need is $18,000 per year, and that this amount is growing at the rate of 2% per year. What is the value of your current economic net worth, W_{35}, assuming a valuation rate of $v = 6\%$ p.a., annual compounding? Now imagine that (overnight) the stock market crashes and your financial capital falls by 40%. However, at the same time interest rates have dropped by 200 basis points so

the "new" valuation rate is $v = 4\%$ p.a., annual compounding. What is the revised value of your economic net worth W_{35}? Has it declined/increased? Explain.

7. In the previous question, by how much would interest (valuation) rates have to decline, so that the drop in the stock market is entirely offset by the increase in human capital value?

8. You are now twenty-three years old and have just finished university. You have two job offers. The first offer (Job A) is with a municipal government (i.e., low risk). Your salary will start at $40,000 per year and will grow at the rate of 4% p.a. If you take this job, you will retire at age sixty-five. The second offer (Job B) is with a private company and involves a higher risk. Your salary will start at $55,000 per year and will grow at the rate of 7% p.a. If you take this job, you want to retire when you reach age sixty. Suppose that you believe that the valuation rates appropriate for the two jobs are 2% p.a., and 5.5% p.a. respectively (both are annual-compounding rates). Suppose also that your salary is paid at the end of the year. Strictly on financial terms, which job will you choose?

9. Jane is a sixty-year-old bank manager. She is now making $80,000 per year. Her bank is not doing very well, and she recently was asked by the head office whether she would consider an employment termination package. If she leaves her job now, she will be paid a lump-sum compensation of $300,000. Because of her age, she will not be able to find another job. On the other hand, if she chooses to remain with the bank, she will have to accept a pay cut of 25%, starting immediately. The growth rate of her salary is expected to be only 1% p.a. until she reaches her retirement age of sixty-five. Suppose that the valuation rate is 3% p.a., annual compounding. Should she accept the termination package?

10. Natalie is eighteen years old, and is about to finish her last year of high school. She is a very good student, and now has a choice of two prestigious university programs. The first choice is an engineering program at a Canadian university, which takes four years to complete and costs $80,000 in total (in present value term). When she graduates (i.e., at age twenty-two), she expects her starting salary to be $70,000 per year (payable at the end of the year). The salary will grow at the rate of $g_w = 5\%$ p.a. The second choice is a medical program at an American university, which takes seven years to complete and costs

$200,000 in total (in present value term). When she graduates, her starting salary is expected to be $100,000 per year (payable at the end of the year). It is expected to grow at the rate of $g_w = 4\%$ p.a. Regardless of the choice, she plans to work until she reaches sixty-five years old. Assume that the valuation rate is 4.50% p.a. Which program of study should she choose?

FOUR

Consumption Smoothing and Optimal Savings

Learning Objectives

In this chapter, we look at consumption/investment decisions. During your working years, you have to decide how much of your salary you want to spend immediately and how much to save for the future. We use an economic concept called **consumption smoothing**, which suggests that people want to optimize their standard of living over their lifetime. They do so by balancing the spending and savings during different stages of their lives. We will see that under this concept, people's standard of living will not wildly fluctuate. Rather, it either remains the same or changes in a smooth fashion over their lifetime.

You will learn to derive your optimal consumption and savings at various ages. You will also see how your financial and economic net worth change over time.

4.1 Consumption Smoothing

Imagine the following situation. You are twenty-five years old, and your long-lost and rather eccentric uncle, whom you rarely met and barely know, has just passed away. When the lawyers vet his will, they discover that he left you $25 million as an inheritance. Unbeknownst to your family, he was quite wealthy and he took a liking to you personally. Unfortunately (and there always is a but), the money has been placed in an iron-clad trust that you cannot access for the next twenty-five years. Even the best lawyers in town cannot break or dissolve the trust documents. Your uncle was concerned about your financial maturity, and he decided it would be best to wait until you are (much) older before giving you the title to this unprecedented sum of cash. Therefore, the money is inaccessible for the next quarter century.

The question to you is: How do you manage your financial life in the meantime? You have little, if any, financial capital right now and have been living hand to mouth so far. Will you live like a pauper until the age of fifty waiting for the trust fund to be unlocked? Or will you spend your way recklessly into debt (perhaps using credit cards) and count on your windfall to bail you out in twenty-five years?

When this question is posed to students in class, one of the first issues that comes up is whether you can now borrow against this guaranteed source of money at a reasonable cost. Well, imagine you can. In addition, to make life easier, imagine for now that the borrowing rate is zero. So now the question becomes how much of this $25 million would you borrow against today? In other words, how would you spread your consumption expenditures over your lifecycle?

The answer to such a question is obviously a matter of personal preferences and your financial "relationship" with money. There is no right or wrong answer. The responses from individual students can be (and often are) all over the map. Some want to borrow against only a small fraction of the funds today, whereas others want to borrow against the entire amount and spend it all. Some argue it would be best to wait and live within current means for now, and then retire once the money is unlocked at age fifty. Others claim it would be silly to live an impoverished life for twenty-five years, and only enjoy wealth in the later part of life.

Anyway, this (rather pleasant) dilemma also ties in with what happens once you actually get access to the $25 million. Do you spend it all then? Assume you will live to the age of seventy-five, which then leads to twenty-five years of life before money and twenty-five years of life after money. *What is the plan?*

When multiple generations of students were asked to ponder this in small groups, and were then instructed to come up with a plan, they usually arrived at a rather intuitive consensus plan for this dilemma. Their solution? Spend the $25 million evenly over the next fifty years. The consensus plan is for you to borrow exactly $500,000 at the age of twenty-five and spend (i.e., consume) every penny of it within the year. So, you now owe $500,000 to the bank. Then, when you turn twenty-six, you borrow another $500,000 and spend it all before your twenty-seventh birthday. You then continue this process every single year – borrowing $500,000 on your birthday and spending it all by the next one – for the next twenty-five years until you reach the age of fifty. Remember, that is the age when you receive the $25 million payoff. Note that after twenty-five years of this highly indebted lifestyle, you owe exactly $12.5 million to the bank, and you pay it back immediately on the day you get the $25 million. After paying off your debts, you are left with (only) $12.5 million that must last you for the remaining twenty-five years of your life. And, because you probably (and it makes perfect sense to) want to maintain the same standard of living as before, you continue to spend the same $500,000 each year from the age of fifty to seventy-five, although there is no need to borrow anymore. This is the consensus view from a large number of students who have been asked this question.

Some of you may not fully agree with this plan. You may prefer to borrow a bit more earlier on in life – call it financial impatience – and thus enjoy $550,000 or $600,000 per year when you are still young and energetic. There is nothing wrong with this. However, remember, this impatience will force you to live on less than $500,000 per year when you are older. After all, there is only $25 million to spend. On the flip side, perhaps your grandparents, who lived through the Great Depression of the 1930s, might counsel that you live on only $400,000 for now. Have some patience, they say, and then live it up later. However, this is just a matter of tweaking or tilting the consumption plan backward and forward like a seesaw.

Although this example is rather far-fetched, the outcome is consistent with the economic concept of **consumption smoothing**. Loosely speaking, this concept states that "maximal happiness" is associated with the highest possible *total* standard of living over your lifetime. As such, you should regularly update the value of your *discretionary* lifetime resources and spread the consumption of those resources evenly or close to evenly over the rest of your life. This implies that you should borrow when necessary – typically early in life – and save when necessary, irrespective of when exactly you earn the high versus low wages. You should not be a slave to this year's salary. In other words, this year's cash flow and the size of your current financial capital should have a minimal impact on this year's consumption or savings. What matters more is the stream of income that you will receive throughout your life.

This concept prevents people from oversaving and living like a pauper early in life so as to enjoy a disproportionately high standard of living during retirement. It also precludes overspending and having an artificially high standard of living when young only to suffer a steep drop later.

Now back to the previous example, dividing $25 million into fifty years to arrive at $500,000 per year is trivially simple because you did not have to worry about the time value of money (i.e., paying interest on the debt) or uneven cash flows over different periods of time. Doing the same kind of smoothing for a more realistic setup such as one with irregular cash flows of wages and salary that are earned over different time periods and spread over a working period (e.g., age twenty-five to sixty-five) that differs from a retirement period (e.g., age sixty-five to ninety-five), requires some additional computational power. We next present a model for it. However, for a more formal structure, you may want to refer to Chapter 13 of this book.

4.2 Assumptions for Consumption Smoothing

As mentioned earlier, the goal of consumption smoothing is to spread your discretionary lifetime resources (i.e., your economic net worth) over your life so as to obtain the highest possible total standard of living. Recall from the previous chapter that your economic net worth, $\mathbf{W}_x$, is the difference between the values of your total assets (i.e., financial capital plus gross human capital) and your total liabilities (explicit and implicit debts); that is,

$$\mathbf{W}_x = (\mathbf{M}_x - \mathbf{eL}_x) + (\mathbf{GH}_x - \mathbf{iL}_x) \tag{4.1}$$
$$= \mathbf{F}_x + \mathbf{H}_x,$$

where, as before, $\mathbf{M}_x$ is the value of your financial assets, $\mathbf{F}_x$ is your financial capital, $\mathbf{GH}_x$ and $\mathbf{H}_x$ are your gross and net human capital, respectively, and $\mathbf{eL}_x$ and $\mathbf{iL}_x$ are explicit and implicit liabilities, respectively.

Recall that implicit liabilities are the present value of the minimum expenditures that you have to make in order to survive the rest of your life. These expenses are nondiscretionary, so you have no control over them. As $\mathbf{W}_x$ is already free of implicit liabilities, it is indeed your discretionary lifetime resources. It then follows that the decisions that you are about to make in this chapter will be on the optimal amounts of your discretionary consumption for the rest of your life. To emphasize, the optimal consumption that you are going to derive here represents what you will consume *in addition to* your minimum, subsistent (i.e., nondiscretionary) level of consumption. Later in this chapter, we put both the subsistent and discretionary parts of your consumption together. For now, let us concentrate on the discretionary part.

To obtain optimal consumption and savings rules, we will make the following four assumptions:

1. Your economic net worth is completely and totally available to you to spend or invest today. You can borrow against it (all), and so you do not face what economists call a "liquidity" constraint. Note that this assumption implies that everyone lives to earn their entire wage

profile. There is no death and no disability that will reduce the value of gross human capital or economic net worth.

2. The valuation rate, v, used to quantify your gross human capital, GH_x, and implicit liabilities, iL_x, is the same as the interest rate that you pay on all your explicit debts, eL_x, and also the same as the rate at which your assets, M_x, grow over time. In theory and also in practice, these three rates – valuation, interest, and investment – could be completely different. You might have a very safe, secure job whose wage flows should be discounted at the risk-free rate. You might be paying onerous interest rates on your credit cards and mortgages while your investments earn lower returns. For now, assume all three numbers are the same (i.e., v per year) and are universally accepted and agreed upon.

3. You like the consumption-smoothing concept. In other words, you plan to spread the benefits of your economic net worth smoothly over your entire life. The only feature in which humans differ from one another is in their *patience*. You prefer to increase the amount of your discretionary consumption at the constant rate of g_c each year.

4. The time of death is known with certainty, and you plan to die with zero leftovers. In the language of economics, you have no bequest motives. You do not intend to pass on any of your wealth as inheritance to anyone. All you want is an optimal consumption plan that will leave zero net worth at the end of your life.

Based on these four assumptions, we can derive your optimal consumption and savings rules. We note, however, that in Chapter 13, we present another approach to solving this problem. That approach involves maximizing a concave utility of consumption (when interest rates are assumed to be constant). The two approaches yield identical results, and in this chapter we take the easier route that does not involve too much advanced mathematics.

In this chapter we do all the analyses in real (rather than nominal) terms. That is, we will work with real values of the cash flows. Recall from the discussion in Chapter 2 that this means that all the cash flows that we are going to work on will be expressed in today's dollar (i.e., after adjusting for inflation). For example, if we say that your salary is constant at $50,000 per year for the rest of your working years, we are referring to its real value. Suppose the inflation rate is 2% per year. Then, this is the same as saying that your *nominal* salary is growing at 2% p.a. to keep pace with inflation.

Working in real terms also means that all the rates (e.g., v, g_c, and g_w) are expressed as real rates. For example, if we say that your salary is growing at the rate of $g_w = 1\%$ p.a., it means that your *nominal* salary is increasing at a higher rate than required to keep pace with inflation. Recall from Chapter 2 that:

$$(1 + \text{nominal rate}) = (1 + \text{real rate}) \cdot (1 + \text{inflation rate}).$$

Then, the salary growth rate of $g_w = 1\%$ p.a. means that your *nominal* salary is growing at the rate of:

$$(1.01 \cdot 1.02) - 1 = 0.0302 \text{ or } 3.02\% \text{ p.a.}$$

One of the benefits of working in real terms is that it provides us with better intuition for the value of cash flows that will occur at various future points in time. This is because those cash flows are all expressed in today's dollars. This advantage is particularly important for this chapter because we are about to talk about the optimal amounts of consumption at various ages.

4.3 Solving for Smoothness

Before we discuss the process of consumption smoothing, let us take a look at Figure 4.1. This figure displays four of the possible different patterns of lifetime consumption that the consumption-smoothing framework can generate – constant, moderately increasing, steeply increasing, and declining. You will soon see that the pattern that you have depends on the value of your patience parameter, g_c. Regardless of the patterns, however, note that all four of them do not have any break or jump. This is precisely the idea of consumption smoothing. Whatever pattern of consumption you choose, the change from year to year will never be abrupt.

Assume that you have just turned x years old. You are now earning w_x per year, to be paid at the end of the year (i.e., just before you turn $x + 1$ years old). The salary is growing at the rate of g_w per year. You plan to work until you reach R years old, at which point you will retire. You will then live until age D.

Your current financial assets are $\mathbf{M}_x$, while your explicit liabilities are $\mathbf{eL}_x$. You have determined that the subsistent level of expenses for this year is b_x per year, payable at the end of the year. These expenses are growing at the rate of g_b per year. The valuation rate is v per year, annual compounding.

Based on this information, you can calculate your current gross human capital to be:

$$\mathbf{GH}_x = w_x \cdot \mathbf{PVA}(\overline{g}_w, v, R - x)$$

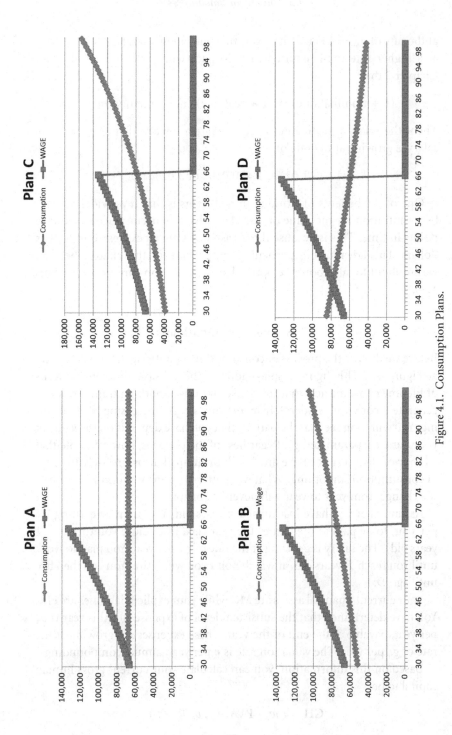

Figure 4.1. Consumption Plans.

and your implicit liabilities to be:

$$\mathbf{iL}_x = b_x \cdot \mathbf{PVA}(\overline{g}_b, v, D - x),$$

where both PVA factors are as defined in Chapter 2. Note that we use the PVA factors for delayed constant-growth ordinary annuities because we assume that the salary and the subsistent expenses are paid at the end of the year.

Consequently, your current economic net worth is:

$$
\begin{aligned}
\mathbf{W}_x &= (\mathbf{M}_x - \mathbf{eL}_x) + (\mathbf{GH}_x - \mathbf{iL}_x) \qquad\qquad (4.2) \\
&= \mathbf{M}_x + \left[w_x \cdot \mathbf{PVA}(\overline{g}_w, v, R - x) \right] \\
&\quad - \mathbf{eL}_x - \left[b_x \cdot \mathbf{PVA}(\overline{g}_b, v, D - x) \right].
\end{aligned}
$$

This is the amount of your discretionary lifetime resources.

Next, we want to figure out your optimal consumption and savings plan. To do so, we will need to make one more assumption about your preference. We assume that you want your *discretionary* consumption to change at the rate of g_c per year (remember that you have no control over your non-discretionary consumption). For example, suppose c_n is the amount of your discretionary consumption at age n. You want your discretionary consumption in the following year to be $c_{n+1} = c_n(1 + g_c)$. Note that g_c can be positive, zero, or even negative. This parameter g_c indeed measures your financial patience. The higher the value of g_c, the more patient you are (i.e., you are willing to wait to consume more later). When $g_c < 0$, you exhibit negative patience (i.e., impatience). As a result, we will refer to g_c as the **patience parameter**.

It is important to note that while the patience parameter g_c determines how the amounts of your discretionary consumption change from year to year, it does not *necessarily* determine how your standard of living will change. This is because your standard of living is determined by your total consumption (subsistent plus discretionary). For example, suppose that your $g_c = 0$ (which means your discretionary consumption will be constant through time), but that your subsistent consumption is increasing over time. Then, your total consumption and thus standard of living will increase over the years. This is true because the two amounts of consumption are expressed in real terms. Therefore, if the sum of them is increasing over time, then it must mean that the total *nominal* consumption is increasing by more than the rise in the price levels. That is, as you age, you will be able to buy more and more units of what you need or want, resulting in an increase in standard of living over time.

Now your task is to come up with the optimal sequence of yearly discretionary consumption amounts from now (i.e., age x) to your death (i.e., age D) such that two conditions are satisfied. First, you have exhausted your economic net worth by age D (remember that you have no bequest motive). In other words, your discretionary lifetime resources in equation (4.2) are your budget constraint. You cannot consume over your lifetime more than this amount. Nor do you want to consume less because you do not intend to leave anything for your children. Secondly, the amounts of your yearly discretionary consumption change by the rate of g_c per year. Solving for the optimal consumption sequence is not really difficult to do. You know from our discussion of present values in Chapter 2 that the constant-growth sequence of consumption that meets these two requirements is one that has the same present value as your current economic net worth. Let c_x be the amount of your discretionary consumption for this year (again, payable at the end of the year). This is the first amount in the sequence (and so the amount for the second year is $c_x(1 + g_c)$, and so on). The present value of this sequence is:

$$c_x \cdot \mathbf{PVA}(\overline{g}_c, v, D - x).$$

Equating this present value to your current economic net worth, $\mathbf{W}_x$, and solving for the optimal c_x^*, we have:

$$c_x^* = \frac{\mathbf{W}_x}{\mathbf{PVA}(\overline{g}_c, v, D - x)}. \tag{4.3}$$

This is the optimal amount of discretionary consumption for the current year (age x). It is a function of four variables – your current economic net worth ($\mathbf{W}_x$, which is the budget constraint); the valuation rate (v); the growth rate that you want for your discretionary consumption (g_c); and the remaining length of your life ($D - x$). Note, however, that your current economic net worth ($\mathbf{W}_x$) depends on the value of your gross human capital ($\mathbf{GH}_x$), which, in turn, is a function of your current wage (w_x), the time to retirement ($R - x$), and the valuation rate (v). The current economic net worth also depends on the value of your implicit liabilities, which, in turn, is determined by the subsistent level of expenses (b_x), the remaining length of your life ($D - x$), and the valuation rate (v). As a result, your optimal discretionary consumption depends on these factors as well.

When $v = g_c$, the optimal c_x^* becomes:

$$c_x^* = \frac{\mathbf{W}_x \cdot (1 + v)}{D - x}. \tag{4.4}$$

It is important to recognize that the optimal discretionary consumption derived in equations (4.3) and (4.4) is under the assumption that all payments occur at the end of the year. Obviously, if we assume that payments occur at the beginning of the year, the expressions for c_x^* will change. However, the logic of the derivation remains the same. We solve for c_x^* by equating the present value of the discretionary consumption sequence to the current economic net worth. In other words, the logic is that the present value at any point in time of future discretionary consumption must be the same as the economic net worth (which is the budget constraint) at that point.

Once we have figured out this optimal amount, we can calculate your optimal savings amount for the current year. That amount must be what you have left of your salary after paying for both nondiscretionary and discretionary consumption. The optimal savings amount for the current year, s_x^*, is:

$$s_x^* = w_x - b_x - c_x^*.$$

There are two things to note about the optimal savings amount. First, they are by-products of your optimal consumption decisions. Once you decide to consume a certain amount in any given year, the optimal savings amount in that year is also determined. Secondly, during your working years, the optimal savings amount can be negative in some years if your consumption is greater than your salary. Negative savings mean you borrow to consume in those years. Of course, your savings cannot remain negative forever. At some point, you will have to repay the loans, which requires that you consume less than your salary.

Finally, we can look at the evolution of your *financial* capital. Recall that your current financial capital is defined as:

$$\mathbf{F}_x = \mathbf{M}_x - \mathbf{eL}_x.$$

Then, at the end of the current year (which is the same as the start of next year), your wage is paid and your consumption takes place. Your financial capital at the start of next year must be:

$$\mathbf{F}_{x+1}^* = \mathbf{F}_x \cdot (1 + v) + s_x^* \tag{4.5}$$
$$= \mathbf{F}_x \cdot (1 + v) + w_x - b_x - c_x^*.$$

Your financial capital at the start of next year is equal to the future value of your current financial capital (i.e., after it has been invested for one year) plus your savings in the current year. The value of your financial capital in any other year can be calculated in the same way.

Next, let us look at a numerical example. To simplify the calculations, we will again do the analysis on real terms.

Practice Question *You have just turned twenty-five years old today. You are about to start working. Your starting annual salary (payable at the end of this year) is $50,500, and is growing at a real rate of 1% per year. You plan to work until you are sixty-five years old, and expect to live until ninety years old. Currently, you only have $3,000 in a savings account, but you have no debt. Assume that the real valuation rate is $v = 3\%$ per year, and that you want your consumption to remain constant in real terms (i.e., real value of patience parameter is $g_c = 0$). Assume also that the subsistent level of expenses is $20,000 per year, which will remain constant in real terms throughout your life (i.e., the real growth rate is $g_b = 0$). What are the optimal amounts of discretionary consumption and savings for the current year?*

Based on this information, the current value of your gross human capital is:

$$GH_{25} = 50,500 \cdot \mathbf{PVA}(\overline{g}_w, v, R - x)$$

$$= 50,500 \cdot \left[\frac{1 - \left[(1.01)^{40} \cdot (1.03)^{-40}\right]}{0.03 - 0.01} \right] = 1,372,536$$

while the current value of your implicit liabilities is:

$$iL_{25} = 20,000 \cdot \mathbf{PVA}(\overline{g}_b, v, D - x)$$

$$= 20,000 \cdot \left[\frac{1 - (1.03)^{-65}}{0.03} \right] = 569,058.$$

As a result, your current net worth is:

$$W_x = (M_x - eL_x) + (GH_x - iL_x)$$
$$= (3,000 - 0) + (1,372,536 - 569,058)$$
$$= 806,478.$$

This is the amount of your discretionary lifetime resources.

Now we are ready to figure your optimal discretionary consumption for the current year, c_{25}^*. As discussed earlier, the optimal consumption at any age x, c_x^*, must be such that the present value of the consumption sequence (which does not grow in real terms) is equal to your current economic net worth. Equating the two and solving for c_{25}^*, we have:

$$c_{25}^* = \frac{806{,}478}{\left[\frac{1-(1.03)^{-65}}{0.03}\right]}$$

$$= 28{,}344.3329 \approx 28{,}344.$$

The optimal discretionary consumption for the current year is $28,344. It then follows that the optimal savings for the current year is:

$$s_{25}^* = w_{25} - b_{25} - c_{25}^*$$

$$= 50{,}500 - 20{,}000 - 28{,}344$$

$$= 2{,}156,$$

which translate to a savings rate of:

$$\frac{2{,}156}{50{,}500} = 0.0427 \text{ or } 4.27\%.$$

As a result, when you receive your salary at the end of the current year, you use it to pay for your total consumption (subsistent and discretionary) of $48,344. You then save the remaining amount, which is $2,156. Your financial capital at the start of next year is then:

$$\mathbf{F}_{26}^* = [\mathbf{F}_{25} \cdot (1 + v)] + s_x^*$$

$$= [3{,}000 \cdot 1.03] + 2{,}156$$

$$= 5{,}246.$$

What about the optimal consumption and savings for next year? We know that your salary for next year will be $50,500 \cdot 1.01 = \$51{,}005$. Your optimal discretionary consumption for next year remains at $c_{26}^* = 28{,}344$ because your patience parameter is $g_c = 0$. Because your subsistent consumption also remains the same at $20,000, the optimal savings for next year is:

$$s_{26}^* = 51{,}005 - 20{,}000 - 28{,}344$$

$$= 2{,}661$$

or 5.2171% of your salary next year.

Practice Question *Based on the previous example, suppose you want to know how much your financial capital is at some future point in time, say, ten years from now or at the start of your retirement.*

Obviously, what you can do is to use equation (4.5) and repeat the calculations until you reach the desired years (i.e., $\mathbf{F}_{35}^{*}$ or $\mathbf{F}_{65}^{*}$). However, it would be time-consuming because you would have to figure out the consumption and savings of every year in the period. A better method is to rely on the logic that the present value at any point of future discretionary consumption must be the same as the value of the economic net worth (which is the budget constraint) at that point. We can equate the two and back out the value of your financial capital as follows.

Based on the setup in the previous example, when you *turn* thirty-five years old (i.e., ten years from now), the present value of your future discretionary consumption is:

$$c_{35}^{*} \cdot \left[\frac{1 - (1.03)^{-55}}{0.03} \right] = 28,344.3329 \cdot \left[\frac{1 - (1.03)^{-55}}{0.03} \right] = 758,903$$

where we use the fact that your annual discretionary consumption does not change from year to year because your patience parameter is $g_c = 0$ (remember that we work in real terms here). Next, your economic net worth at age thirty-five, $\mathbf{W}_{35}$, is equal to:

$$\mathbf{W}_{35} = \mathbf{F}_{35}^{*} + \mathbf{GH}_{35} - \mathbf{iL}_{35}.$$

Because $\mathbf{W}_{35}$ is the budget constraint, it must equal the present value of your future consumption; that is,

$$\mathbf{W}_{35} = \mathbf{F}_{35}^{*} + \mathbf{GH}_{35} - \mathbf{iL}_{35} = 758,903$$

or

$$\mathbf{F}_{35}^{*} = 758,903 - \mathbf{GH}_{35} + \mathbf{iL}_{35}.$$

At age thirty-five, your gross human capital is:

$$\mathbf{GH}_{35} = w_{35} \cdot \left[\frac{1 - \left[(1.01)^{30} \cdot (1.03)^{-30} \right]}{0.03 - 0.01} \right]$$

$$= 55,783.42 \cdot \left[\frac{1 - \left[(1.01)^{30} \cdot (1.03)^{-30} \right]}{0.03 - 0.01} \right]$$

$$= 1,240,356$$

where your wage at age thirty-five is $w_{35} = \$55,783.42$, and is equal to the wage at age twenty-five (i.e., \$50,500) compounded at the growth rate of 1% per year over ten years.

Similarly, your implicit liabilities at age thirty-five is:

$$\mathbf{iL}_{35} = 20{,}000 \cdot \left[\frac{1 - (1.03)^{-55}}{0.03} \right]$$

$$= 20{,}000 \cdot \left[\frac{1 - (1.03)^{-55}}{0.03} \right]$$

$$= 535{,}489,$$

where your nondiscretionary consumption at age thirty-five is the same as at any age because its growth rate is zero. It then follows that your financial capital at age thirty-five is:

$$\mathbf{F}_{35}^* = 758{,}903 - 1{,}240{,}356 + 535{,}489 = 54{,}036.$$

Table 4.1 tracks the amounts of your salary, consumption, savings, gross human capital, financial capital, and economic net worth through time. As you can see, your gross human capital gradually declines over the years until it becomes zero when you retire (age sixty-five). As you work, you gradually convert your gross human capital into consumption and savings. The amounts of savings continue to grow throughout your working years. In the first working year (age twenty-five), you save \$2,156 or 4.27% of your salary. In the last working year (age sixty-four), you will save more than \$26,000 or approximately 35% of your salary. You need to save this much in order to prepare for your retirement years. Your financial capital keeps rising until it reaches its maximum of approximately \$840,000 at the start of your retirement. This is the amount that allows you to continue your consumption pattern until you pass away.

In contrast, your economic net worth keeps declining as you age. Recall that economic net worth at any age x is defined as:

$$\mathbf{W}_x = (\mathbf{M}_x - \mathbf{eL}_x) + (\mathbf{GH}_x - \mathbf{iL}_x)$$
$$= \mathbf{F}_x + \mathbf{H}_x.$$

As a result, the change in its value is the sum of the changes in the values of financial capital, gross human capital, and implicit liabilities. In this case, the net effect is negative for every year, which means that the annual decline in gross human capital cannot be made up for by the increase in financial capital plus the decline in implicit liabilities. Note that this result is specific to the setup of this example. We will see a different case shortly.

Now that you know how to calculate the amount of your financial capital at age thirty-five, you can use the same technique to figure out its value at any other age. We leave the calculation of $\mathbf{F}_{65}^*$ to you as an exercise.

Table 4.1. *Projected salary, consumption, savings, gross human capital, financial capital, and economic net worth at various ages ($g_c = 0$)*

Age	At the beginning of the year			Salary	Nondiscretionary consumption	Discretionary consumption	Savings	At the end of the year		
	Gross human capital	Financial capital	Economic net worth					Gross human capital	Financial capital	Economic net worth
25	$1,372,536	$3,000	$806,478	$50,500	$20,000	$28,344	$2,156	$1,363,212	$5,246	$802,328
26	$1,363,212	$5,246	$802,328	$51,005	$20,000	$28,344	$2,661	$1,353,104	$8,064	$798,054
35	$1,240,356	$54,036	$758,903	$55,783	$20,000	$28,344	$7,439	$1,221,783	$63,096	$753,326
45	$999,502	$185,839	$694,967	$61,620	$20,000	$28,344	$13,275	$967,867	$204,689	$687,471
55	$605,986	$432,799	$609,041	$68,066	$20,000	$28,344	$19,722	$556,099	$465,505	$598,968
64	$72,275	$791,969	$506,707	$74,443	$20,000	$28,344	$26,099	$0	$841,827	$493,564
65	$0	$841,827	$493,564	$0	$20,000	$28,344	−$48,344	$0	$818,737	$480,027
75	$0	$577,132	$338,373	$0	$20,000	$28,344	−$48,344	$0	$546,101	$320,180
85	$0	$221,403	$129,809	$0	$20,000	$28,344	−$48,344	$0	$179,701	$105,359
89	$0	$46,936	$27,519	$0	$20,000	$28,344	−$48,344	$0	$0	$0
90	$0	$0	$0	$0	$0	$0	$0	$0	$0	$0

Source: Author Calculations.

We want to emphasize that under the consumption-smoothing framework, the amounts of your savings are dictated by the pattern of discretionary consumption that you desire. That pattern, of course, depends on the value of your patience parameter g_c. Up to this point, we have assumed that your g_c is zero (in real terms). In other words, you want your discretionary consumption to remain constant in real terms. Next, we want to see the effect of the change in the value of the patience parameter. Suppose you no longer want your discretionary consumption to remain the same in real terms throughout your life. Rather, you want it to either increase or decrease. We will look at the case of an increase first.

Practice Question *Based on the same setup as in the previous examples, suppose that you want your discretionary consumption to increase by 1% per year (i.e., your real $g_c = 1\%$). What is the effect of this change on the consumption, savings, and financial and economic net worth?*

This is the case where you want your discretionary consumption to increase (smoothly) by 1% per year. We will repeat the previous calculations, but this time with $g_c = 1\%$. First, we note that this change does not affect the value of your gross human capital or implicit liabilities, and so your economic net worth (i.e., the budget constraint) remains the same at \$806,478. However, the pattern of your discretionary consumption will change. Let c_{25}^* be the optimal discretionary consumption at age twenty-five in this case. The present value of this new consumption sequence is:

$$c_{25}^* \cdot \left[\frac{1 - \left[(1.01)^{65} \cdot (1.03)^{-65} \right]}{0.03 - 0.01} \right] = 36.0222 \cdot c_{25}^*.$$

Equating this present value to the budget constraint and solving for c_{25}^*, we have $c_{25}^* = \$22,388.3843 \approx \$22,388$. This means that the optimal savings for the current year is:

$$\begin{aligned} s_{25}^* &= w_{25} - b_{25} - c_{25}^* \\ &= 50{,}500 - 20{,}000 - 22{,}388 \\ &= 8{,}112, \end{aligned}$$

which translate to a savings rate of:

$$\frac{8{,}112}{50{,}500} = 0.1606 \text{ or } 16.06\%.$$

Comparing these results to those in the previous example (when $g_c = 0$), we see that your optimal discretionary consumption at age twenty-five is now lower by almost $6,000. This means that the optimal savings for the current year is higher by the same amount. These results should not be surprising to you. Here, you want to increase gradually your standard of living (i.e., to be able to consume more in real terms later in your life). Because the lifetime budget constraint is still the same as before, you now have to accept lower discretionary consumption in the early years. This enables you to save more in order to finance your higher consumption in later years.

Table 4.2 tracks the amounts of your salary, consumption, savings, gross human capital, financial capital, and economic net worth through time. Your discretionary consumption increases at the rate of 1% per year. In the last year of your life (i.e., age eighty-nine), you will consume $42,324. Because you have to save more during the early years (compared to the case where $g_c = 0$), your financial capital increases at a faster rate during your working years until it reaches its maximum of $994,100 when you start your retirement (age sixty-five). Note that this maximum is greater than in the case where $g_c = 0$. Again, this is because with $g_c = 1\%$, your consumption in the retirement years is higher, and so you need a bigger nest egg to finance it.

Your economic net worth follows a different time pattern from the case where $g_c = 0$. Here, it increases in the early years. Then by the time you reach thirty-five years old, it starts to decline. The reason for this pattern is that in the early years, your high savings (plus accrued interest on past savings and the decline in implicit liabilities) more than compensates for the decline in your gross human capital. This is no longer true from age thirty-five on.

Finally, let us look at the case where the value of your patience parameter is negative (i.e., you want to consume more in the early years and less later).

Practice Question *Again, based on the same setup as in the previous examples, suppose that you want your discretionary consumption to decline by 1% per year (i.e., your $g_c = -1\%$). What is the effect of this change on the consumption, savings, and financial and economic net worth?*

As the calculations in this case are similar to the previous two cases, we will skip them and present the corresponding table. There are a few things to note from Table 4.3. First, you now consume a lot more in early years than later. Your discretionary consumption at age twenty-five is $34,919, which is higher than in the cases where $g_c = 0$ and $g_c = 1\%$. In the last

Table 4.2. *Projected salary, consumption, savings, gross human capital, financial capital, and economic net worth at various ages* ($g_c = 1\%$)

| | At the beginning of the year | | | | | | | At the end of the year | | |
Age	Gross human capital	Financial capital	Economic net worth	Salary	Nondiscretionary consumption	Discretionary consumption	Savings	Gross human capital	Financial capital	Economic net worth
25	$1,372,536	$3,000	$806,478	$50,500	$20,000	$22,388	$8,112	$1,363,212	$11,202	$808,284
26	$1,363,212	$11,202	$808,284	$51,005	$20,000	$22,612	$8,393	$1,353,104	$19,930	$809,920
.	.	.	.	.	.	.	.	.	.	.
35	$1,240,356	$111,102	$815,969	$55,783	$20,000	$24,731	$11,053	$1,221,783	$125,487	$815,717
.	.	.	.	.	.	.	.	.	.	.
45	$999,502	$291,570	$800,698	$61,620	$20,000	$27,318	$14,302	$967,867	$314,619	$797,401
.	.	.	.	.	.	.	.	.	.	.
55	$605,986	$572,976	$749,218	$68,066	$20,000	$30,176	$17,890	$556,099	$608,056	$741,518
.	.	.	.	.	.	.	.	.	.	.
64	$72,275	$944,330	$659,069	$74,443	$20,000	$33,003	$21,440	$0	$994,100	$645,837
.	.	.	.	.	.	.	.	.	.	.
65	$0	$994,100	$645,837	$0	$20,000	$33,333	-$53,333	$0	$970,590	$631,879
.	.	.	.	.	.	.	.	.	.	.
75	$0	$707,887	$469,129	$0	$20,000	$36,821	-$56,821	$0	$672,303	$446,382
.	.	.	.	.	.	.	.	.	.	.
85	$0	$281,515	$189,921	$0	$20,000	$40,673	-$60,673	$0	$229,288	$154,946
.	.	.	.	.	.	.	.	.	.	.
89	$0	$60,509	$41,092	$0	$20,000	$42,324	-$62,324	$0	$0	$0
90	$0	$0	$0	$0	$20,000	$0	$0	$0	$0	$0

Source: Author Calculations.

Table 4.3. *Projected salary, consumption, savings, gross human capital, financial capital, and economic net worth at various ages* ($g_c = -1\%$)

Age	At the beginning of the year			Salary	Nondiscretionary consumption	Discretionary consumption	Savings	At the end of the year		
	Gross human capital	Financial capital	Economic net worth					Gross human capital	Financial capital	Economic net worth
25	$1,372,536	$3,000	$806,478	$50,500	$20,000	$34,919	-$4,419	$1,363,212	-$1,329	$795,753
26	$1,363,212	-$1,329	$795,753	$51,005	$20,000	$34,570	-$3,565	$1,353,104	-$4,935	$785,055
30	$1,317,779	-$11,167	$753,100	$53,076	$20,000	$33,208	-$132	$1,304,236	-$11,634	$742,485
31	$1,304,236	-$11,634	$742,485	$53,607	$20,000	$32,876	$731	$1,289,756	-$11,253	$731,884
35	$1,240,356	-$4,735	$700,132	$55,783	$20,000	$31,581	$4,203	$1,221,783	-$675	$689,555
45	$999,502	$84,773	$593,900	$61,620	$20,000	$28,561	$13,059	$967,867	$100,375	$583,157
55	$605,986	$308,074	$484,315	$68,066	$20,000	$25,830	$22,236	$556,099	$339,552	$473,015
64	$72,275	$664,531	$379,269	$74,443	$20,000	$23,596	$30,847	$0	$715,314	$367,051
65	$0	$715,314	$367,051	$0	$20,000	$23,360	-$43,360	$0	$693,413	$354,702
75	$0	$475,355	$236,596	$0	$20,000	$21,126	-$41,126	$0	$448,489	$222,568
85	$0	$177,414	$85,820	$0	$20,000	$19,106	-$39,106	$0	$143,630	$69,288
89	$0	$37,236	$17,819	$0	$20,000	$18,354	-$38,354	$0	$0	$0
90	$0	$0	$0	$0	$20,000	$0	$0	$0	$0	$0

Source: Author Calculations.

year of your life (age eighty-nine), your discretionary consumption is only $18,354. Secondly, in the early years (up to age thirty), you actually consume (subsistent plus discretionary) more than what you make (i.e., your savings are negative). This requires that you draw from your initial financial capital (i.e., $3,000) and also borrow. As a result, your financial capital becomes negative. After age thirty, you start to have positive savings, and you use them to pay down the loan gradually. The loan is fully paid off by the time you reach age thirty-seven (not shown in the table), after which your financial capital turns positive and grows. It reaches its peak of $715,314 when you start your retirement. This amount is lower than in the previous two cases because the consumption in your retirement years is not as high as in those two cases.

Figure 4.2 plots the pattern of salary, subsistent consumption, and total consumption (subsistent plus discretionary) from age twenty-five to ninety for the case where $g_c = -1\%$. Because you are impatient, your discretionary consumption in the early years is higher than in the later years. Because your subsistent consumption remains the same throughout your life, this means that your total consumption will also decline over time, as shown in the graph.

Figure 4.3 displays the patterns of financial capital and gross and net human capital from age twenty-five to ninety under the same case. Here you can see that as you approach your retirement (i.e., age sixty-five), your gross human capital approaches zero. As a result, your net human capital will start to become negative. This occurs around age fifty-nine, which is where your gross human capital declines to the point where it is less than your implicit liabilities (please try to verify this by your own calculations). However, by that time, you will have built up sufficient financial capital to finance your consumption during the remaining period of your life.

4.3.1 Effects of Changes in Other Parameter Values

So far, we have looked at the effect of changes in the patience parameter on the optimal consumption pattern. What about the effect of wage growth rate, g_w? Obviously, you can see for yourself by repeating the previous calculations where you alter g_w but leave the value of every other parameter unchanged. In general, if g_w is higher, the value of gross human capital, H_{25}, will increase. This, in turn, increases the economic net worth W_{25}, resulting in a "looser" lifetime budget constraint. It then follows that the optimal current discretionary consumption rate, c_{25}^*, will be higher. The same effect will be observed if you increase the age of retirement R, or increase the

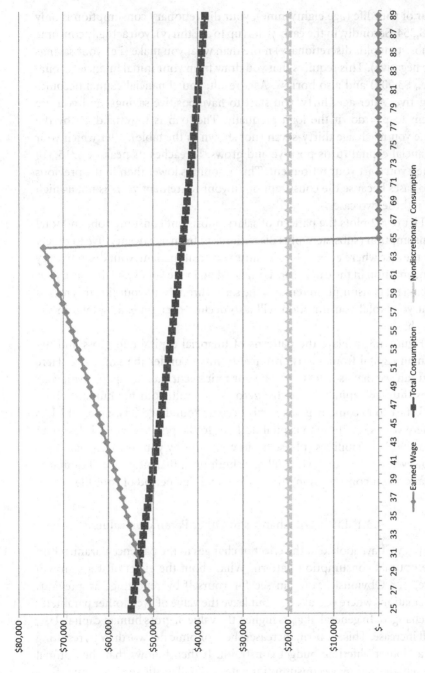

Figure 4.2. Wages vs. Nondiscretionary and Total Consumption: Wage growth of $g_w = 1\%$, personal patience of $g_c = -1\%$, and valuation $v = 3\%$.

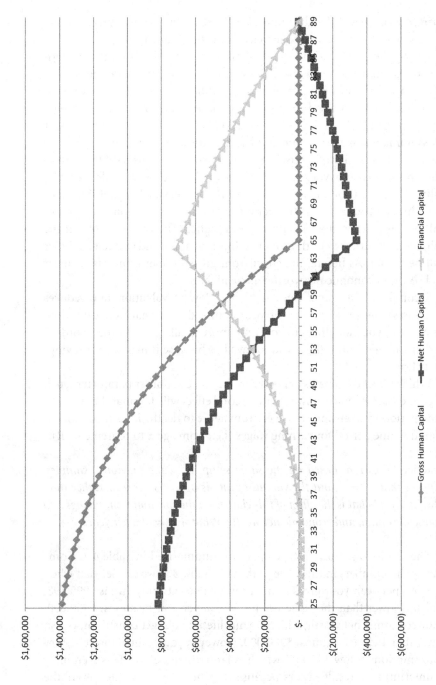

Figure 4.3. Financial Capital and Gross vs. Net Human Capital: Wage growth of $g_w = 1\%$, personal patience of $g_c = -1\%$, and valuation $v = 3\%$.

Gross Human Capital   Net Human Capital   Financial Capital

current wage w_{25}. They all (uniformly) increase the value of gross human capital, which then flows into increased consumption at all ages.

The impact of the valuation rate v on the optimal consumption pattern is generally more ambiguous. This is because v affects the determination of the optimal consumption rate in two different ways. First, because it is the discount rate used in the calculation of your gross human capital and implicit liabilities, a higher valuation rate reduces the value of your gross human capital and your implicit liabilities. The two reductions have opposite effects on your economic net worth. The lower value of gross human capital causes your economic net worth to be lower, while the lower value of implicit liabilities makes your economic net worth higher. Typically, gross human capital has a stronger effect and so your economic net worth will be lower when the valuation rate is higher. The reverse is true if the valuation rate is lower. Both your gross human capital and implicit liabilities will be higher. As before, the effect from gross human capital is stronger and so your economic net worth will be higher.

Secondly, at the same time, a higher (lower) valuation rate reduces (increases) the present value of your future discretionary consumption. As a result, you can afford to consume more at all ages. In other words, a higher valuation rate allows you to save less because it makes your savings grow faster.

Which effect dominates depends on the values of other parameters such as g_c and g_w. Generally, however, the second effect will dominate because the time period for consumption (i.e., from age x to death, D) is much longer than the time period for earning wages (i.e., from age x to retirement, R).

Practice Question *Based on the same setup as in the previous examples. suppose that $g_c = 0$, but the valuation rate is $v = 5\%$ per year rather than 3% per year. What is the effect of this change on the consumption, savings and financial capital, and economic net worth? What if $v = 2\%$ per year?*

The results when $v = 5\%$ per year are summarized in Table 4.4. Comparing the numbers in this table to those in Table 4.1, we can see that when $v = 5\%$ per year, your gross human capital at age twenty-five is $995,498, which is lower than the value when $v = 3\%$ per year by almost $400,000. Your economic net worth, which is your lifetime budget constraint, is also lower than before by almost $200,000. However, your annual discretionary consumption is now $32,111, which is larger than before. This seemingly counterintuitive result occurs because a higher valuation rate lowers the present value of your future consumption, and so you can consume more

Table 4.4. *Projected salary, consumption, savings, gross human capital, financial capital, and economic net worth at various ages (v = 5%)*

Age	At the beginning of the year			Salary	Nondiscretionary consumption	Discretionary consumption	Savings	At the end of the year		
	Gross human capital	Financial capital	Economic net worth					Gross human capital	Financial capital	Economic net worth
25	$995,498	$3,000	$615,277	$50,500	$20,000	$32,111	−$1,611	$994,773	$1,539	$613,930
26	$994,773	$1,539	$613,930	$51,005	$20,000	$32,111	−$1,106	$993,507	$510	$612,515
35	$959,667	$11,337	$598,335	$55,783	$20,000	$32,111	$3,673	$951,867	$15,577	$596,141
45	$832,054	$94,166	$570,739	$61,620	$20,000	$32,111	$9,509	$812,037	$108,383	$567,165
55	$547,692	$305,579	$525,788	$68,066	$20,000	$32,111	$15,956	$507,011	$336,814	$519,967
64	$70,898	$678,204	$461,598	$74,443	$20,000	$32,111	$22,332	$0	$734,446	$452,567
65	$0	$734,446	$452,567	$0	$20,000	$32,111	−$52,111	$0	$719,058	$443,085
75	$0	$540,892	$333,299	$0	$20,000	$32,111	−$52,111	$0	$515,826	$317,853
85	$0	$225,612	$139,023	$0	$20,000	$32,111	−$52,111	$0	$184,782	$113,863
89	$0	$49,629	$30,582	$0	$20,000	$32,111	−$52,111	$0	$0	$0
90	$0	$0	$0	$0	$20,000	$0	$0	$0	$0	$0

Source: Author Calculations.

and still stay within the budget. Note also that in early years, you consume more than your salary, which means that you have to borrow. This course of action is optimal even though the interest rate is higher than before.

The results when $v = 2\%$ per year are summarized in Table 4.5. Although your gross human capital and economic net worth at age twenty-five are both higher than when $v = 3\%$ per year, you end up with lower discretionary consumption. Even though your budget is larger, you cannot consume as much because you have to save more to compensate for the fact that the rate of return on your savings is now lower.

Finally, we note that although the examples so far assume that payments occur once a year, the same logic applies to any frequency of payments (e.g., monthly, weekly, etc.).

4.4 Consumption Smoothing vs. Other Approaches

Next, we want to compare the consumption-smoothing framework to other approaches that individuals can use to make their consumption/savings decisions. In particular, we will consider two recommendations that financial planners commonly give. They are the fixed-percentage savings rules and the so-called 70% income replacement rule.

4.4.1 The Fixed-Percentage Savings Rules

Some common advice that financial planners give to their clients is that the clients should set aside a fixed percentage of their wages for savings. For example, the best-selling book by David Chilton entitled *The Wealthy Barber* recommends that you "save 10 percent of all that you earn and invest it for long-term growth." The appeal of this advice is that it is simple, straightforward, and does not require much calculation (if at all). However, it does not take into consideration (at least directly) each person's lifetime budget and preference. Once that fixed percentage is saved, the person then consumes the remaining amount. Therefore, depending on how much savings have been accumulated during the working years, the resulting consumption can be substantially different between the working years and the retirement years. In other words, the resulting standard of living can change significantly once the person retires.

To see this, suppose you were to follow this advice. We can calculate the amounts of savings and consumption throughout your life under the following rules. First, during your working years, you will save a fixed percentage of your salary, and consume the rest. Note that in this framework,

Table 4.5. *Projected salary, consumption, savings, gross human capital, financial capital, and economic net worth at various ages* ($v = 2\%$)

	At the beginning of the year							At the end of the year		
Age	Gross human Capital	Financial Capital	Economic Net Worth	Salary	Nondiscretionary consumption	Discretionary consumption	Savings	Gross human capital	Financial capital	Economic net worth
25	$1,644,825	$3,000	$923,876	$50,500	$20,000	$25,523	$4,977	$1,627,221	$8,037	$916,830
26	$1,627,221	$8,037	$916,830	$51,005	$20,000	$25,523	$5,482	$1,608,761	$13,679	$909,643
35	$1,427,452	$82,771	$846,727	$55,783	$20,000	$25,523	$10,260	$1,400,218	$94,686	$838,138
45	$1,102,049	$240,438	$752,684	$61,620	$20,000	$25,523	$16,096	$1,062,470	$261,343	$742,214
55	$638,634	$499,384	$638,045	$68,066	$20,000	$25,523	$22,543	$583,340	$531,915	$625,283
64	$72,984	$842,991	$513,553	$74,443	$20,000	$25,523	$28,920	$0	$888,770	$498,301
65	$0	$888,770	$498,301	$0	$20,000	$25,523	−$45,523	$0	$861,023	$482,744
75	$0	$584,940	$327,954	$0	$20,000	$25,523	−$45,523	$0	$551,115	$308,990
85	$0	$214,572	$120,303	$0	$20,000	$25,523	−$45,523	$0	$173,340	$97,185
89	$0	$44,631	$25,023	$0	$20,000	$25,523	−$45,523	$0	$0	$0
90	$0	$0	$0	$0	$20,000	$0	$0	$0	$0	$0

Source: Author Calculations.

Table 4.6. *Projected salary, savings, and consumption under various fixed-percentage savings schemes*

Age	Salary	10% Savings	10% Total consumption	15% Savings	15% Total consumption	20% Savings	20% Total consumption
25	$50,500	$5,050	$45,450	$7,575	$42,925	$10,100	$40,400
26	$51,005	$5,101	$45,905	$7,651	$43,354	$10,201	$40,804
35	$55,783	$5,578	$50,205	$8,368	$47,416	$11,157	$44,627
45	$61,620	$6,162	$55,458	$9,243	$52,377	$12,324	$49,296
55	$68,066	$6,807	$61,260	$10,210	$57,856	$13,613	$54,453
64	$74,443	$7,444	$66,999	$11,166	$63,277	$14,889	$59,555
65–90		−$26,274	$26,274	−$39,130	$39,130	−$51,986	$51,986

Note: The amounts of consumption from age 65 to age 90 under each savings scheme are calculated based on the amount of financial net worth as of the start of age 65 and on the assumption that consumption during these retirement years will be constant. The amount of financial net worth as of the start of age 65 is $457,513 under the 10% savings scheme, $681,376 under the 15% savings scheme, and $905,239 under the 20% savings scheme.
Source: Author Calculations.

there is no need to distinguish between nondiscretionary and discretionary consumption any more. Secondly, your savings will earn a rate of return equal to the valuation rate v. Thirdly, once you reach your retirement age (age sixty-five), you will start to consume from the savings that you have built. We will assume that you will consume the same amount every year until you pass away. Because we are doing this calculations in real term, this means that your standard of living is the same for every retirement year.

Table 4.6 displays the amounts of savings and consumption at various ages under three different fixed percentages of savings (10%, 15%, and 20%). By comparing these numbers to those in Table 4.1, you can see that if you save 10% of your salary, you will enjoy a high standard of living during your working years. In the year before you retire, your total consumption is $67,000. However, this high standard of living comes at a cost. You will have to accept a sharp drop in consumption once you retire. During your retirement years, you will only consume about $26,000 per year – a drop of more than 60%. The 10% savings rate is not high enough for you to enjoy the same standard of living once you retire.

What if you set aside 15% of your salary for savings? The outcome looks slightly better. Your standard of living during retirement will only be about 38% lower than what you have in the year before you retire. It is not until you save 20% of your wage that your standard of living becomes more even throughout your life.

The point of this example is that a hard-and-fast rule such as the fixed-percentage savings rule does not always lead to a desirable outcome. Once the savings rate is fixed, consumption and thus standard of living are a by-product of it. The fixed percentage has no direct connection with your lifetime budget. As a result, if you choose a wrong percentage, you can get a nasty surprise when you reach your retirement. We believe that the consumption-smoothing framework is more sensible because it allows you to take into consideration your lifetime budget and then choose the standard of living that you desire. The amounts of your savings will then vary from year to year to adjust for the consumption amounts that you choose.

Another advantage of the consumption-smoothing framework is that it allows shocks to your income to be absorbed by spreading it throughout your life. For example, suppose you became ill and could only work part-time for the next year. Your income next year would be much lower than before. Under the consumption-smoothing framework, your consumption next year would not be correspondingly lower. This is because the framework takes into account your income in all future years when determining your yearly optimal consumption. A sudden drop in income for a short period of time would not have a serious effect on your consumption during that period.

4.4.2 The 70% Income Replacement Rule

Financial planners and the business media often refer to the so-called 70% **replacement rate** for retirement income. This rule states that individuals should target and aim to generate an income in retirement that is 70% of their pre-retirement income. For example, if you were earning wages and salary of $100,000 per year before you retired, you will need $70,000 per year in income after you retire. And if you were (only) earning $50,000 per year before, then you need $35,000 after, and so on. Some advocates of this rule believe that it should be closer to 80%, while others believe that 60% might be enough. The debates about suitable retirement replacement rates can get heated and passionate, and so we provide some references to this literature in the bibliography.

After reading this chapter you might ask yourself where we – the authors – fall in this debate, and more importantly how it ties into consumption smoothing. Well, as you might suspect, picking a number out of thin air, whether it is 50% or 100% or anything in between, and advocating that it should be a target for retirement does not make much sense to us. It is not very logical. As you learned and we argued in this chapter, some people have preferences for increasing ($g_c > 0$) or declining ($g_c < 0$) or constant ($g_c = 0$) discretionary consumption pattern. This is not something that can be or should be imposed from above or outside.

That said, there is a way to think about these replacement rate debates within our framework. This is by focusing on the implicit liabilities and the nondiscretionary consumption that we denoted by b_x. After all, it is quite reasonable to argue that your b_x is age-dependent and maybe lower after retirement compared to before retirement. For example, once you are retired you might be able to save on work-related travel and commuting expenses. You might also be entitled to senior discounts, extra tax credits, free medical insurance, and other retiree benefits. All of these reduce your nondiscretionary consumption expenditures b_x for ages $x > R$ compared to ages $x < R$. In fact, you might actually have more leisure time on your hands, which then enables you to drive across town to look for a better deal on vegetables or toilet paper, or perhaps to save money by making dinners. In other words, you can substitute time for money. Therefore, your subsistent consumption will drop after you retire.

If that is the case, then perhaps b_{65} (the first year you are retired) might actually be $(0.7) \cdot b_{64}$ or even $(0.6) \cdot b_{64}$ or perhaps $(0.8) \cdot b_{64}$. This, however, is an empirical question that is context- and lifestyle-specific. There is no philosophy or theory that one can draw upon to measure these things. Continuing with this line of thought, the value of implicit liabilities at retirement would then be equal to $\mathbf{iL}_{65} = (0.7) \cdot b_{64} \cdot \mathbf{PVA}(\overline{g}_b, v, D - 65)$, where g_b denotes the growth rate of your nondiscretionary consumption and $(D - 65)$ is the time you plan to spend and live in retirement. Finally, because your gross human capital $\mathbf{GH}_{65} = 0$ once you retire, then your financial capital F_{65} must be at least greater than $\mathbf{iL}_{65}$. We have always maintained that $\mathbf{iL}_{65}$ was rather subjective and never claimed that $b_{64} = b_{65}$, for example.

Here is the bottom line. After you retire we believe that you should (and will) continue to grow your discretionary consumption smoothly and by g_c per year. Consumption smoothing should be the retirement goal – not an arbitrary replacement rate. Note, however, that your total consumption might drop (discontinuously) because your b_x has suddenly declined.

This is perfectly consistent with consumption smoothing, which has always been and will always be about spreading your economic net worth over time.

For example, if you believe that a proper retirement replacement rate is only 60%, then your implicit liabilities **iL** at any age (which is the present value of all your subsistent consumption from that age on) will be lower. This means that your net human capital is higher, and thus your economic net worth is greater. All of this translates into a larger discretionary consumption rate over your entire life, and especially during your pre-retirement years. In plain English you will *save less*. On the other hand, if you believe (or hopefully, estimate) that a proper retirement replacement rate is 80%, then your implicit liability **iL** at any age is greater, and so your net human capital is lower. You will therefore spend less on discretionary items. This is rather obvious.

4.5 Practical Considerations

To implement the consumption-smoothing framework in practice, there are a few things that you may want to keep in mind. First, the previous analyses were done in real terms. As a result, all the optimal consumption and savings amounts were expressed in today's dollar. However, because we pay for goods and services (and save) in nominal dollars, you have to translate those real amounts into nominal amounts. As you already know from Chapter 2, this is done by multiplying the real amounts by the rates of inflation over the relevant periods. For example, suppose that the optimal (real) amount that you should save in two years' time is $10,000, and that the inflation rate is expected to be 2% per year. Then, the (nominal) amount that you will have to save when you reach that point is:

$$10{,}000 \cdot 1.02^2 = 10{,}404.$$

The second thing that you should keep in mind is that we have assumed in our analyses that there is no uncertainty is your wage cash flows. You can count on receiving the amounts that you expect to get. In practice, however, there is always a chance of your employment being disrupted (e.g., by illness, injury, or being laid off). This is why in practice we observe that people will attempt to build up **precautionary savings**. This is especially true during the early working years where their financial capital is still low. People do not want to have a wildly fluctuating consumption pattern, and so they want to build up their savings to use as a buffer in case something unexpected happens.

Obviously, different people will react differently toward their income risk. Nevertheless, the implication of this risk on the results that we obtained in this chapter is that people may choose not to consume as much as what the model suggests. Some may not want to borrow to consume even though that would be the optimal course of action if there was no income risk.

In a few chapters from now, we discuss available mechanisms that individuals can use to hedge their income risk and thus help to make their consumption patterns as smooth as possible. These mechanisms include medical insurance and disability insurance. With these mechanisms in place, the income uncertainty is reduced and individuals should behave more closely to what the consumption-smoothing framework suggests.

4.6 Questions and Assignments

1. You have just turned twenty-three years old, and are about to start working. Right now, you do not have any assets but have a student loan debt of $40,000. Your starting salary is $w_{23} = \$40,000$ per year. You expect your salary to grow at the rate of $g_w = 2\%$ per year until you retire at age sixty-five. Suppose that you live until you are ninety years old. Your patience parameter g_c is 1% p.a., while the valuation rate and the borrowing rate are $v = 3\%$ p.a. Suppose also that your current minimum, subsistent level of consumption is $15,000 per year, which is growing at the rate of $g_b = 2\%$ per year. What are the optimal current discretionary consumption and savings levels? What is the fraction of your salary that you save?

2. Based on question (1), what are the optimal consumption and savings levels when you reach fifty years old? What is the fraction of your salary at that time that you save? What is the value of your economic resources at that time?

3. Based on question (1), what are the optimal current discretionary consumption and savings levels if your subsistent level of consumption changes to $10,000 per year once you retire?

4. Again, based on question (1), if the valuation rate becomes 5% p.a., what are the optimal current consumption and savings levels? What is the current value of your economic resources? What is the value (in real terms) of your optimal consumption at age fifty?

5. Suppose that the patience parameter in question (1) is 2% p.a. and that the valuation rate is 5% p.a. How long will it take you to completely repay your student loan?

6. You have just turned twenty-five years old, and are about to start working with no current assets or debt. Your current salary is $w_{25} = \$50,000$ per year, payable at the end of the year. You expect your salary to grow at the rate of 2% p.a. until you retire at age sixty-five. Suppose you live until you are ninety years old. Suppose also that your patience parameter g_c is 1% p.a., while the valuation rate is 3% p.a. Your current minimum, subsistent level of consumption is $12,000 per year, which is growing at the rate of $g_b = 1\%$ per year. Create a table that shows the optimal consumption and savings rates from age twenty-five to ninety, and compare that to the consumption and savings rates according to the *fixed percentage savings rule*.

7. You have just turned twenty-seven years old, and are about to start working with no current assets or debt. Your starting salary is $w_{27} = \$70,000$ per year, payable at the start of each year. You expect your salary to grow at the rate of 3% p.a. until you retire at age sixty-seven. Suppose you live until you are ninety years old. Suppose also that your patience parameter g_c is 1% p.a. until the age of sixty-seven at which point it decreases to 0% p.a. for as long as you live. Your current minimum, subsistent level of consumption is $20,000, which is growing at the rate of $g_b = 1\%$ per year. Assume the valuation rate is 4% p.a. What is the optimal consumption and savings rates at age twenty-seven?

8. Assume that you are thirty years old, with $F_{30} = \$200,000$ in financial capital. You currently earn $w_{30} = \$50,000$ per year, which is expected to grow by $g_w = 1\%$ until you retire at the age of sixty-five. Assume you plan to live to age ninety and the valuation rate is $v = 3\%$. Your minimum, subsistent level of consumption is $12,000 per year, which will not change. Compute the optimal consumption rate (today) at age $x = 30$. What percentage of your wage should you optimally save at age thirty? (This is the savings ratio.) Assume that your personal patience factor is $g_c = 2\%$, which means that your consumption should grow at 2% per year. All cash flows occur annually at the end of each year.

9. Jack has just turned 30, and has no savings (i.e., financial capital). He expects to earn $100,000 per year until the age of 40, and then he expects to earn $200,000 until the age of 60, at which point he will retire. He plans to live until 90 years old, and would like to have a flat (constant) consumption profile for the rest of his life. Assume that all cash flows occur at the end of each year, and that

all values are in inflation-adjusted terms. More importantly, assume that the valuation rate is 0% over the entire life horizon. In other words, money earns nothing, and it costs nothing to borrow. Ignore implicit liabilities. What is Jack's optimal consumption rate, and at what age will he no longer have any debt? Next, assume that although investment rates are zero (over the entire life horizon), Jack cannot actually borrow at 0%. If he borrows money, he is charged 5% interest. How does this change your answers?

10. Please solve the previous question assuming $v = 3\%$ instead of $v = 5\%$. What is the impact of a higher valuation rate?

FIVE

Debts, Loans, and Mortgages
[Canadian Content]

Learning Objectives

In this chapter, we cover various issues concerning usage of debt. In particular, we look at how mortgage financing works. We then talk about the advantages and shortcomings of investment loans (i.e., borrowing money to invest). Finally, we discuss the benefits of debt consolidation (i.e., combining debts of various sources into one).

5.1 Mortgage Financing

Suppose you want to buy a house. After visiting several potential choices, you decide on one house that you like the most. You then negotiate with the seller on the price. Now, you have to decide how much of the payment will come from your own money (i.e., down payment) and how much from borrowing.

In many countries, there is a rule governing the minimum down payment that a buyer needs to make. Typically, the minimum is expressed as a percentage of the house's price or appraised value. For Canada, that minimum is 5% (as of early 2011). Obviously, you can make a larger down payment than the minimum if you want. Depending on the amount of your down payment, your mortgage can be classified as conventional or high-ratio. A **conventional mortgage** is one where the buyer makes a down payment of at least 20% of the purchase price and borrow the rest (or, equivalently, the loan-to-value ratio is 80% or below). On the other hand, a **high-ratio mortgage** is one where the down payment is between 5% and 20% (or the loan-to-value ratio between 95% and 80%). This classification is important because the *Canadian Bank Act* prohibits most federally regulated lending institutions from providing mortgage loans to high-ratio borrowers without mortgage insurance, which protects lenders against borrowers' default (and not to be confused with mortgage *life* insurance, which protects lenders in case the borrowers pass away prematurely). Insurance premium is to be paid up front in one lump sum, and depends on the amount of down payment that the buyer makes.

In addition to the amount of the loan (denoted by L), there are typically four issues that you have to decide on. They are:

1. Amortization period (denoted by N). This is the period over which the loan is amortized (i.e., repaid). Common lengths of amortization periods are fifteen, twenty, and twenty-five years. Because mortgage repayments are typically made in equal monthly installments, this means that mortgage loans are commonly amortized over 180, 240, or 300 months. Some borrowers may choose to repay more frequently such as every two weeks (or every week), in which case the amortization will be done based on biweekly (or weekly) periods. The more frequent the repayments, the less interest (in total) borrowers have to pay. In any case, you need to know what the amortization period is in order to calculate the amount of each payment.

2. Term of mortgage. A mortgage loan is granted for a specific term, typically between one and ten years. After the term is over, the borrower has to renew or renegotiate it. Note that the term of mortgage is different from the amortization period. The term of mortgage tells you how long the current loan is in effect, whereas the amortization period is used to calculate your payments.

3. Is the mortgage rate floating or fixed? If the mortgage rate (denoted by i) is fixed, then it is constant through the term of the mortgage. Once the term is over, the loan has to be renewed, and a new rate will apply. The new rate can be different from the old one, depending on the level of market interest rates at that time. In contrast, a floating-rate mortgage loan will have its interest rate adjusted periodically based on the movement of market interest rates. We discuss the pros and cons of these two types later.

4. Is the mortgage open or closed? An open mortgage allows you to pay off part or all of the loan at any time without penalties. Typically, open mortgages are floating-rate or very short-term fixed-rate mortgages. In contrast, a closed mortgage typically imposes restrictions on the amount of extra payments that you can make (e.g., up to 15% of the original principal per year), and might charge considerable penalties if you do so.

5.1.1 Mortgage Amortization

Based on the loan principal, mortgage rate, and amortization period, you can calculate the amount of mortgage payments that you have to make. Consider the following example.

Practice Question *Suppose you want to buy a house that costs $500,000. You will make a down payment of $100,000, and borrow the rest. You choose a five-year term, fixed-rate mortgage with a mortgage rate of 4.50% p.a., monthly compounding, and an amortization period of twenty years. The loan will be repaid with equal monthly payments. What is the amount of each monthly payment?*

Before we do the calculations, we note that in practice, mortgage rates are typically expressed with semi-annual compounding. However, as you learned in Chapter 2, you can always convert these rates into appropriate rates per payment period. We choose to express the rate under monthly compounding in this example so that you do not have to go through the conversion step.

This example is a straightforward present-value-of-an-annuity problem. The amount of each monthly payment must be such that by the end of the amortization periods, you will have completely paid off the loan. Therefore, the present value of all the payments must be equal to the principal. In this case, the down payment is 20%, and so no mortgage insurance is required. The principal is $400,000, the rate per month is $4.50\%/12 = 0.375\%$, and the amortization period is 240 months. Let A be the monthly payment. Then,

$$A \cdot \mathbf{PVA}(0.00375, 240) = 158.0654 \cdot A = 400,000.$$

Solving for A, we have $A = \$2,530.5957 \approx \$2,530.60$.

Each monthly payment is a **blended payment**. It includes both an interest payment and a principal repayment. For example, consider the payment of the first month. The outstanding principal at the beginning of the first month is, of course, $400,000. The interest charge for this month is:

$$400,000 \cdot 0.00375 = 1,500.$$

As a result, the portion of the monthly payment that goes toward interest is $1,500. The rest of it (i.e., $1,030.60) goes toward reducing the principal. It then follows that the outstanding principal at the end of the first month is:

$$400,000 - 1,030.60 = 398,969.40.$$

Table 5.1. *Mortgage repayment schedule*

Principal = $400,000; Amortization period = 240 months; Rate = 4.50% p.a., monthly compounding

Month	Beginning principal	Interest portion of payment	Principal portion of payment	% Principal repayment portion	Ending principal
1	$400,000.00	$1,500.00	$1,030.60	40.73%	$398,969.40
2	$398,969.40	$1,496.14	$1,034.46	40.88%	$397,934.94
.	.	.	.	.	.
12	$388,448.46	$1,456.68	$1,073.92	42.44%	$387,374.54
.	.	.	.	.	.
24	$375,292.32	$1,407.35	$1,123.25	44.39%	$374,169.07
.	.	.	.	.	.
60	$332,085.24	$1,245.32	$1,285.28	50.79%	$330,799.96
.	.	.	.	.	.
120	$245,784.55	$921.69	$1,608.91	63.58%	$244,175.64
.	.	.	.	.	.
180	$137,753.70	$516.58	$2,014.02	79.59%	$135,739.68
.	.	.	.	.	.
239	$5,032.87	$18.87	$2,511.72	99.25%	$2,521.14
240	$2,521.14	$9.45	$2,521.14	99.63%	$0.00

Source: Author Calculations.

This amount will then be the beginning principal for the second month, on which you can calculate interest charge and figure out how much of the second monthly payment is for principal reduction. You can continue to do this until you reach month 240, by the end of which the outstanding principal should be zero.

Table 5.1 displays selected portions of the repayment schedule. Note that the portions of interest and principal repayments change every month. As the principal is gradually repaid, the monthly interest charge becomes smaller and smaller, and the portion of the monthly payment that goes toward principal repayment is getting larger and larger. In the first month, the portion of principal repayment is approximately 41%. It rises to about 50% by the end of five years and almost 80% by the end of fifteen years. In the final month, the portion is more than 99%.

The table also tracks the amounts of outstanding principal through time. For example, after five years, you have managed to reduce the mortgage principal down to $330,799.96. Over five years, you have made a total mortgage payment of $2,530.5975 · 60 = $151,835.85. Out of this

Table 5.2. *Amortization periods of Canadian mortgages: 2007–2010*

When mortgage was issued	Amortization period (% of total)			
	<=25 years	30 years	35 years	40 years
Fall 2007	63%	11%	11%	15%
Fall 2008	50%	5%	13%	32%
Fall 2009	53%	19%	23%	6%
Fall 2010	58%	12%	30%	N/A

Source: Globe and Mail, Winter 2011.

amount, $82,635.81 is interest, while the rest (or $69,200.04) is principal repayment.

Another way to find out the outstanding principal at any point in time is to discount all the remaining payments back to that point. For example, at the end of year 5, there will be 180 monthly payments remaining. The present value of this sequence of payments is:

$$2,530.5975 \cdot \mathbf{PVA}(0.00375, 180) = 330,799.96.$$

Note from the example that because the term of the original mortgage is five years, you will have to renegotiate the loan and get a new term after sixty months. As calculated, the outstanding principal at that point will be $330,799.96. This will be the starting principal of the second term, on which the amount of your new monthly payments are calculated. If the mortgage rate for the second term is the same as in the first and the amortization period remains the same, then the new payments will also be the same as before. However, if the new mortgage rate is higher (lower), you will end up with a higher (lower) monthly payment (see problem 5 at the end of this chapter).

Next, if you assume that the mortgage rate remains the same throughout the amortization period and add up all the monthly payments over twenty years (without taking into account time value of money), you will get $2,530.5975 \cdot 240 = $607,343.40$. So, over twenty years, the total amount of interest that you pay on the loan is $207,343.40. You should be able to verify that the total amount of interest will increase if the mortgage rate is higher and/or the amortization period is longer.

Finally, let us look at the length of the amortization period that Canadians have been choosing over the years. Table 5.2 shows the selected lengths as reported by the *Globe & Mail* newspaper every fall since 2007. As you can see, at least half of the buyers picked amortization periods that are within

Table 5.3. *Mortgage insurance charged by Canadian mortgage and housing corporation (Feb. 2011)*

Loan-to-value ratio	Standard premium (% of original loan principal)
Up to and including 65%	0.50%
From 65% up to and including 75%	0.65%
From 75% up to and including 80%	1.00%
From 80% up to and including 85%	1.75%
From 85% up to and including 90%	2.00%
From 90% up to and including 95%	2.75%

Source: http://www.cmhc-schl.gc.ca/en/index.cfme.

twenty-five years. Prior to October 2008, periods of forty years were quite popular. However, the Canadian government, in order to prevent a housing problem such as the subprime crisis in the United States, tightened mortgage rules and so periods of such a length no longer exist. (The percentage of forty-year amortization periods in the fall of 2009 is likely due to applications that were submitted before the rule changed.)

As you have seen, the length of the amortization period is one factor that determines the amount of your monthly mortgage payments. Your choice of the length will depend on your monthly cash flows (i.e., your ability to repay the loan). You will see in the next subsection that banks impose conditions on the percentage of your income that goes toward servicing debts. Therefore, given the price of the house, this percentage will influence your choice of amortization period.

5.1.2 Mortgage Insurance

As mentioned earlier, if the buyer puts down less than 20% down payment, mortgage insurance will have to be purchased. Buyers with down payments over 20% might also choose to buy it. One possible reason for this is that with the insurance, the risk to the lender is lower and so the mortgage loan will likely be at a more favorable rate. It is also possible that the lender might require the buyer to be insured if the loan is considered to be high risk.

Currently, there are a few providers of mortgage insurance in Canada, with the largest being the Canada Mortgage and Housing Corporation (CMHC) with approximately two-thirds of the market share. The insurance premium that they charge is summarized in Table 5.3.

The premium depends on the amount of down payment that the buyer makes (or, equivalently, the loan-to-value ratio). The more the down payment (and thus the lower the loan-to-value ratio), the less the premium. Currently (early 2011) the standard premium ranges from 1% (for loan-to-value ratio of 80%) to 2.75% (for loan-to-value ratio of 95%) of the original loan principal.[1] The buyer can pay the premium in cash. However, most buyers cannot afford to do so, and choose to add the premium onto the mortgage loan (that is to be amortized), thus making it more expensive because they will have to pay interest on it.

Practice Question *Based on the previous example, suppose you wish to make a down payment of only $50,000. Because the down payment is only 10% of the purchase price, you will have to get mortgage insurance. You will add the insurance premium to the principal of the loan. How much is the amount of the monthly payment in this case?*

The loan-to-value ratio in this case is 90%. According to Table 5.2, the insurance premium is 2% of the principal. Therefore, the total amount that you will borrow is $450,000 · 1.02 = $459,000. Using the same calculation technique as in the previous example, you can verify that the monthly payment in this case is $2,903.86, which is $56.94 per month higher than the payment in case of no insurance. Multiplying $56.94 per month by the number of months in the amortization period (i.e., 240), we get $13,665.60. If you choose to amortize the insurance premium over twenty years, the total amount that you end up paying on it is $13,665.60 (i.e., principal of $9,000 plus interest of $4,665.60).

Note that the premium is based on the loan-to-*value* ratio. The lender may appraise the value of the house that you are buying, and the appraised value may not be the same as the price that you are paying, in which case the loan-to-value ratio will be different from what you think. Note also that lenders will also try to make sure that you do not end up with too much debt if they grant you a mortgage loan. For this reason, they generally impose conditions on your **gross-debt-service (GDS) ratio** and **total-debt-service (TDS) ratio**. The GDS ratio is typically defined as the ratio between your monthly housing cost and your gross monthly income; that is,

$$\text{GDS} = \frac{\text{Monthly Housing Costs}}{\text{Gross Monthly Income}}, \tag{5.1}$$

---

[1] Standard premium is for buyers whose sources of income can be verified and whose down payment money comes from "traditional" sources such as savings.

where monthly housing costs are typically defined as the sum of (i) monthly mortgage payment; (ii) property taxes; (iii) heating expenses; and, if applicable, (iv) all or part of condominium fees. It is important to note that for the purpose of calculating the GDS (and also TDS) ratios, the monthly mortgage payment is to be calculated based on the rate that is the greater of (a) the contract rate (i.e., the rate that the borrower will actually be paying), or (b) the interest rate that is posted by the bank (i.e., before any discount) for a five-year, fixed-rate mortgage. Therefore, the amount of monthly mortgage payment in the GDS calculation may not be the same as (and is likely to be higher than) the actual payment that the borrower will pay if the mortgage is granted.

As defined, the GDS ratio provides the lender with an estimate of the proportion of your income that is needed for housing costs. Commonly, lenders will not lend you an amount that will result in a GDS ratio exceeding 32%.

The TDS ratio is typically defined as the ratio between (i) your monthly housing costs plus debt-service costs and (ii) your gross monthly income. Monthly debt-service costs are monthly payments for all your debts including the monthly mortgage payment determined in the previously explained manner. As such, they also include payments on your student loans, car loans, and credit card loans.

$$\text{TDS} = \frac{\text{Monthly Housing Costs} + \text{Monthly Debt-Service Costs}}{\text{Gross Monthly Income}}. \quad (5.2)$$

Typically, lenders will not lend you an amount that will result in a TDS ratio exceeding 40%.

Practice Question *Suppose you want to buy a house that costs $500,000. You make a down payment of $100,000, and borrow $400,000 (and thus no mortgage insurance is required because your down payment is 20%). The posted mortgage rate for a five-year, fixed-rate term is 5.00% p.a., monthly compounding. You want the amortization period to be twenty years. Suppose also that your gross monthly income is $9,000, property taxes (per year) are 1% of the house price, heating costs are $150 per month, and you have a car loan outstanding that requires a monthly payment of $600. Will the bank grant you the mortgage loan?*

Based on the posted five-year mortgage rate, the amount of mortgage payment per month is:

$$\frac{400,000}{\text{PVA}(0.004167, 240)} = \frac{400,000}{151.5253} = 2,639.82.$$

Based on the information, the amount of property taxes per month is:

$$\frac{500{,}000 \cdot 0.01}{12} = 416.67,$$

where we note that property taxes are actually based on the assessed value of your property. The assessed value can be different from the price that you pay for it. For the purpose of this example, we assume that the two are the same.

As a result, your GDS ratio will become:

$$\frac{2{,}639.82 + 150 + 416.67}{9{,}000} = 0.3563 \text{ or } 35.63\%,$$

which exceeds the limit of 32%. In addition, your TDS ratio will become:

$$\frac{2{,}639.82 + 150 + 416.67 + 600}{9{,}000} = 0.4229 \text{ or } 42.29\%,$$

which is also greater than the limit of 40%. As a result, the bank will not lend you this much. You must make a larger down payment.

Practice Question *Based on the previous example, what is the maximum house price that you can afford in order to be within the ratio limits? Assume that the heating costs and property taxes are at the same rate as before.*

Let L be the maximum amount of mortgage loan that the bank will give you (which means the maximum house price that you can afford is L plus your down payment or $L + 100{,}000$). The monthly mortgage payment is then:

$$\frac{L}{\mathbf{PVA}(0.004167, 240)} = \frac{L}{151.5253}.$$

The monthly property taxes are:

$$\frac{0.01 \cdot (L + 100{,}000)}{12} = \frac{0.01L + 1{,}000}{12}.$$

As a result, your monthly housing costs are:

$$\frac{L}{151.5253} + \frac{0.01L + 1{,}000}{12} + 150.$$

This amount must be equal to the limit under the GDS ratio, which is $\$9{,}000 \cdot 32\% = \$2{,}880$. Equating the two and solving for L, we have $L = \$356{,}075$.

Therefore, the maximum amount that the bank will lend to you is $\$356{,}075$. You can verify that this amount will not breach the 40% limit of your TDS ratio either. It then follows that the maximum house price that you can afford is $456,075.

5.1.3 Mortgage Refinancing

Suppose you took out a mortgage loan several years ago, and that interest rates have been declining since. Obviously, you want to take advantage of the new, lower rates, but the current term of your existing mortgage is not yet over. You could wait until the end of the term and hope that the rates will still be low by then. Alternatively, it may be worth it for you to refinance your existing mortgage. To do so, you will have to borrow a new loan from another lender and use the proceeds to prepay your existing loan. As mentioned earlier, if your mortgage is of a closed type (which most long-term, fixed-rate mortgages are), the lender will typically charge a prepayment penalty. In Canada, the penalty is the greater of (i) three months worth of interest; and (ii) the **interest rate differential (IRD)**. The IRD is the difference between the interest amount payable on your mortgage (or, in case you do not fully prepay the loan, on the amount of principal that you want to prepay) for the remaining mortgage term and the interest amount that your bank could earn in the same duration by re-lending the prepaid amount at the current interest rate. The only exception to the penalty rule is when the term of your existing mortgage is more than five years *and* more than five years have elapsed. In such a case, the maximum penalty is three-month interest.

Different banks use different methods in calculating the three-month interest and the IRD. Here, we present the most typical one. Let P be the amount of mortgage principal that you want to prepay. Note that if you do not fully prepay the loan, P will be less than the current outstanding principal. Also, let v_{old} be the rate *per month* under your existing mortgage, N be the number of months *remaining* under the existing mortgage term, and v_{new} be the current interest rate per month for a new mortgage with a term closest to N. The three-month interest is calculated as follows:

$$\text{3-month interest} = P{\cdot}v_{old} \cdot 3,$$

while the IRD is equal to:

$$\text{IRD} = P \cdot (v_{old} - v_{new}) \cdot N.$$

Practice Question *Three years ago, you borrowed a mortgage loan with a principal of $300,000 and a term of five years with monthly payments. The*

*loan was to be amortized over twenty years at the mortgage rate of 6% p.a.
semi-annual compounding. If you want to prepay the whole loan now, how
much money do you need? Assume that the current interest rate for the term
of two years is 4.50% p.a., semi-annual compounding.*

First, we figure out the current outstanding principal. The mortgage rate
of 6% p.a. semi-annual compounding is equivalent to 0.4939% per month.
Based on the information, your monthly mortgage payment is:

$$\frac{300{,}000}{\mathbf{PVA}(0.004939, 240)} = \frac{300{,}000}{140.4123} = 2{,}136.5653.$$

As three years have passed, the current outstanding principal must be:

$$2{,}136.5653 \cdot \mathbf{PVA}(0.004939, 204) = 2{,}136.5653 \cdot 128.3668 = 274{,}264.05.$$

Next, we calculate the penalty. The amount of interest on the current
outstanding principal over three months is:

$$274{,}264.05 \cdot 0.004939 \cdot 3 = 4{,}063.46.$$

To calculate the IRD, we first convert the current mortgage rate (i.e.,
4.50% p.a., semi-annual compounding) into the equivalent monthly rate
of 0.3715%. Then,

$$\text{IRD} = 274{,}264.05 \cdot (0.004939 - 0.003715) \cdot 24 = 8{,}052.19.$$

The prepayment penalty is the maximum of the two, which is $8,052.19. As
a result, to prepay this loan in full now, you will need:

$$274{,}264.05 + 8{,}052.19 = 282{,}316.24.$$

It should be noted from these calculations that the three-month interest of
$4,063.46 is not exactly the same as the actual amount of interest embedded
in the mortgage payments of the next three months (that you will have to
make if you do not prepay the loan). If you create a mortgage amortization
schedule similar to one in Table 5.1, you will see that the sum of the interest
portion of your next three monthly payments is $4,051.85, as shown in
Table 5.4.

The difference occurs because the straightforward method does not
account for the fact that the principal declines month after month. Note,
however, the difference is quite small, and thus the straightforward method
can be used as a reasonable approximation.

We also note that there is currently no uniformity in how banks calculate
IRD. For example, in the previous calculations, we used v_{old} as the mortgage

Table 5.4. *Mortgage repayment schedule for months 37, 38, and 39*

Original Principal = $300,000; Amortization period = 240 months; Rate = 6% p.a., semi-annual compounding

Month	Beginning principal	Interest portion of payment	Principal portion of payment	% Principal Repayment portion	Ending principal
37	$274,264.05	$1,354.49	$782.08	36.60%	$273,481.97
38	$273,481.97	$1,350.62	$785.94	36.79%	$272,696.03
39	$272,696.03	$1,346.74	$789.82	36.97%	$271,906.21
Total		$4,051.85			

Source: Author Calculations.

rate that you are actually paying. Due to the negotiation that you had with your bank when you took out this loan, this rate is likely to be below the "posted" rate for your mortgage term at that time. The rate that you got, v_{old}, is likely after some discount. However, some banks use the posted rate (which is higher) instead of v_{old} in their IRD calculations. This results in a higher amount of IRD that they can charge.

In addition, the remaining duration under the existing mortgage term, N, may lie between the standard terms of new mortgages, in which case banks will have to either round it up or round it down in order to find the rate v_{new} to use in the calculations. Here again lies a difference in banks' practice.

Practice Question *Suppose that there is a bank that is willing to help you refinance your existing mortgage. You will get a new five-year mortgage with the same remaining amortization period (i.e., seventeen years). The mortgage rate will be 5% p.a., semi-annual compounding. Should you take this offer?*

The benefit of refinancing is the savings in interest payments. To calculate the savings, we need to compare the monthly mortgage payments if you do not refinance the loan to what they would be if you do.

Case 1: Do Not Refinance the Loan

We look first at the payments if you do not refinance the loan (i.e., do nothing). Currently, the loan has two years left under the current term. So, the monthly payments will remain the same (i.e., $2,136.57) for the next twenty-four months, after which the loan will have to be renewed at the then-prevailing mortgage rate. We will assume that the loan will be renewed for another five years, and then when that term is up, it will be renewed again for another five years, and so on. In other words, after the current term is over in twenty-four months, you renew the loan three times, each for five years. More crucially, we assume that the rates for the next three renewals is the same as the now-prevailing five-year rate (i.e., 5% p.a., semi-annual compounding). You may think that this assumption is a bit of a stretch. However, *some* rate has to be assumed, and in the absence of any power to predict the movements of interest rates, we will use the now-prevailing rate as a proxy for the subsequent rates.

Under these assumptions, we can calculate the monthly mortgage payments for the three renewals. Note that because the three renewals are assumed to be done at the same mortgage rate, we can simply lump them up and amortize the loan over the whole fifteen years. To do this, we first need to know the outstanding principal by the end of the next twenty-four months. As you know from before, it is the present value of the remaining payments; that is,

$$2{,}136.5653 \cdot \mathbf{PVA}(0.004939, 180) = 2{,}136.5653 \cdot 119.0642 = 254{,}388.51.$$

This amount will be the principal to be amortized over the remaining fifteen years (i.e., months 61-240) at the rate of 5% p.a., semi-annual compounding (or, equivalently, 0.4124% per month). The monthly mortgage payment during that period will be:

$$\frac{254{,}388.51}{\mathbf{PVA}(0.004124, 180)} = \frac{254{,}388.51}{126.8836} = \$2{,}004.90.$$

To summarize, if you stay with your existing lender, your monthly mortgage payment will be $2,136.57 (which is what you are now paying) for the next twenty-four months, and then $2,004.90 for the next fifteen years.

Case 2: Refinance the Loan

Next, we calculate the monthly payments in case you refinance the loan now. The amount of money that you need to get from the new bank is the current outstanding principal plus the prepayment penalty. Recall that in the previous example, we calculated this amount to be $282,316.24. The new bank will give you a five-year mortgage loan at the rate of 5% p.a., semi-annual compounding, which has to be renewed once it is over (remember that there are seventeen years left in the amortization period). We will

Table 5.5. *Comparison of monthly mortage payments*

Time period	Monthly mortgage payment		
	Not refinance	Refinance	Difference
Months 37–60	$2,136.57	$2,049.39	$87.18
Months 61–240	$2,004.90	$2,049.39	−$44.49

Source: Author Calculations.

assume that all the required renewals will be done at this rate. Accordingly, the monthly payment for the next seventeen years will be:

$$\frac{282,316.24}{\textbf{PVA}(0.004124, 204)} = \frac{282,316.24}{137.7561} = \$2,049.39.$$

Table 5.5 summarizes your monthly mortgage payments over the remaining seventeen years under the two choices.

As seen from the table, if you refinance, the savings are positive for the next twenty-four months, and negative for the remaining time. The present value of this sequence of savings is:

$$= 87.18 \cdot \textbf{PVA}(0.004124, 24)$$
$$+ \textbf{PV}(0.004124, 24) \cdot [-44.49 \cdot \textbf{PVA}(0.004124, 180)]$$
$$= 1,988.21 - 5,114.14$$
$$= -3,125.93,$$

where the first term (i.e., $1,988.21) is the sum of the present value of the savings over the next twenty-four months, and the second term (i.e., −$5,114.14) is the present value (as of now) of the present value (as of two years from now) of the savings after month 60. Because the value of the savings is negative, you should not refinance the loan. The prepayment penalty is higher than the benefits from a lower mortgage rate.

5.1.4 Fixed-Rate vs. Floating-Rate Loans

Now that we know how a fixed-rate mortgage works, let us turn our attention to a floating-rate mortgage. Under a floating-rate mortgage (which is also known as adjustable-rate mortgage or variable-rate mortgage), the interest rate is adjusted periodically to correspond to the movements of market rates, as proxied by some benchmark rate. The benchmark rate is typically the bank's prime lending rate, but other rates can also be used (especially in the United States) such as the London Interbank Offered Rate (LIBOR) and a one-year constant-maturity Treasury rate.

Because the mortgage rate can change often, the mechanics of the loan amortization is somewhat different. This is because changes in the rate affect the interest and principal portions of your monthly payments. After a rate change, the old amortization schedule (calculated based on the old mortgage rate) will no longer work. For example, if the rate increases, the interest portion becomes bigger and the principal portion smaller. Consequently, the old mortgage schedule will no longer pay off the loan by the end of the amortization period.

There are generally two ways banks handle rate changes. First, they calculate a new amount of monthly payment that will pay off the loan in the original time frame. Secondly, they let you maintain the current payment amount with the understanding that the length of time until the loan is fully paid off will now be different. In this case, you will continue to make the same monthly payment until the term of the current mortgage is over, at which point it will be renewed with a new amount of payment.

To illustrate the second approach, consider the following example.

Practice Question *Suppose that two years ago, you took out a floating-rate mortgage for $200,000. The mortgage was to be amortized over twenty-five years. The mortgage rate for the past two years was 4.50% APR (or 0.375% per month). Suppose the rate has just increased to 5.50% APR (or 0.4583% per month). If you keep paying the same monthly amount as before, how much longer will it take you to pay the mortgage off?*

To answer this question, we first need to figure out what the current outstanding principal is. As before, the outstanding principal at any time is the present value of the remaining mortgage payments. The current monthly payment is:

$$\frac{200{,}000}{\textbf{PVA}(0.003750,\ 300)} = \frac{200{,}000}{179.9103} = 1{,}111.6650.$$

Because you have been making monthly payments for two years, the principal has been reduced to:

$$1{,}111.6650 \cdot \textbf{PVA}(0.003750,\ 276) = 1{,}111.6650 \cdot 171.7561 = 190{,}935.23.$$

This is the amount that has to be paid off by your future monthly payments. Because the mortgage rate has just increased to 5.50% APR (or 0.4583% per month), a bigger portion of your future payments will go toward interest, and the principal will be reduced at a slower rate. Let N be the new length of time that it takes you to pay off this loan. The PVA factor based on the new rate and the new length of time is:

$$\mathbf{PVA}(0.004583, \, N) = \frac{1 - (1.004583)^{-N}}{0.004583}.$$

This PVA factor multiplied by the current monthly payment must equal the current outstanding principal for the loan. That is,

$$\frac{1 - (1.004583)^{-N}}{0.004583} \times 1{,}111.665 = 190{,}935.23.$$

Solving for N, we get $N = 338.40$ months (or about twenty-eight years and two months). So, instead of twenty-three years of mortgage payments remaining, a rate increase of 1% APR at this point translates to twenty-eight years and two months, or over five additional years. This is the risk that floating-rate borrowers face. Note, however, that a rate decrease would have the opposite effect, and you would be able to pay off the loan more quickly.

Note that if your monthly payment remains the same when the rate increases, it is possible to have negative amortization, which happens if the rate increases to the point where your monthly payment is not enough to cover even the interest accrued on the loan. This means that the unpaid amount will be added back to the principal of the loan, where it generates even more interest. A lot of lenders do not allow this to happen, so they will immediately ask you to pay a higher monthly amount to avoid it.

With floating-rate mortgages, borrowers take the risks of interest-rate movements. One potential reward is that the mortgage rate is typically lower than under fixed-rate loans. This is because floating rates are based on benchmark short-term rates, while fixed rates are based on longer-term rates. Generally, the term structure of interest rates is upward-sloping, and so short-term rates are lower than long-term rates. As a result, floating-rate mortgages should generally be cheaper than fixed-rate mortgages, every-thing else being the same. Indeed, one research study compares the cost of the two types of mortgages using interest-rate data from 1950 to 2006. Assuming mortgage loans originated at the beginning of each month during the period from 1950 to 1992 with fifteen-year amortization period (so that the last mortgage matured at the end of 2006), the study finds that floating-rate mortgages cost less than fixed-rate mortgages (five-year term and then renewed) about 90% of the time. The 10% where fixed-rate mortgages did

better is primarily from mortgages originated in the late 1970s when inflation was very high and short-term interest rates were higher than long-term
rates (i.e., downward-sloping term structure of interest rates).

So, which type of mortgage should you choose? This is basically a risk-
return trade-off decision. If you go for floating-rate loans, you take the risk
of interest-rate movements. You should make sure that your budget can
handle the increase in payments if the rate turns against you. You also need
to be able to handle the stress associated with the uncertainty. The reward, of
course, is the potential savings in interest cost. It should be noted, however,
that in recent years, the gap between short-term and long-term rates has
narrowed (i.e., the term structure, while still upward-sloping, is not as steep
as before). As a result, the potential reward is not as great as it used to be.

Perhaps realizing that it is difficult for borrowers to choose between fixed
and floating rates, several lenders have offered a **split mortgage**, where
one part of the loan carries a fixed rate and the other a floating rate. You
can decide how much of the total loan to be in one kind or the other.
Practically, it is a combination of two separate loans, each of which is
handled independently.

5.2 Borrowing to Invest

When you borrow to invest, the leverage can magnify the gains/losses on
your original investment. To see this, assume that you have $1 and borrow
L at an interest rate of i% p.a., annual compounding. Your debt-to-equity
ratio is $L/1 = L$. You then invest the total amount ($1 + L) in a portfolio
of securities. Suppose that over the following year, the value of the portfolio
grows at the rate of G%. At the end of that year, the return on your equity
(RoE) will be:

$$\text{RoE} = (1 + L)(1 + G) - L(1 + i) - 1 \qquad (5.3)$$
$$= G + L(G - i),$$

which can be positive or negative, depending on three factors: (i) the magnitude of G; (ii) whether G is greater or less than i; and (iii) the debt-to-equity
ratio, L.

Note the two terms in equation (5.3). The first term, G, can be thought
of as the return that you would get if you had not borrowed the money,
but had instead invested only your own $1 in the portfolio. The second
term, $L(G - i)$, is the return on the borrowed money. Note that the debt-
to-equity ratio, L, magnifies the difference between G and i. The more

Table 5.6. *Return on equity at various levels of debt-to-equity ratios*

Debt-to-equity Ratio (L)	Investment growth rate (g, % p.a.)	Borrowing rate (i, % p.a.)	RoE (% p.a.)
0	10.00%	8.00%	10.00%
1	10.00%	8.00%	12.00%
2	10.00%	8.00%	14.00%
5	10.00%	8.00%	20.00%
10	10.00%	8.00%	30.00%
20	10.00%	8.00%	50.00%
100	10.00%	8.00%	210.00%

Source: Author Calculations.

leverage you use (i.e., the higher the L), the greater the magnification. If the portfolio has been doing well (i.e., $G > i$), your RoE is boosted by the leverage. In contrast, if the portfolio has performed poorly (i.e., $G < i$), the leverage will intensify that bad performance.

Practice Question *Suppose you saved up $10,000 to invest in the stock market. You also borrow an additional $20,000 from the bank at a rate of 8% p.a., annual compounding so that your total stock investment is worth $30,000. Suppose that over the following year, your investment has grown by 10%. How much money did you make and what is the return on your equity?*

At the end of the year, your investment is worth $30,000 \cdot 1.10 = \$33,000$, while you owe the bank $20,000 \cdot 1.08 = \$21,600$. As a result, you have $11,400 left. This translates to an RoE of 14%. You can also use equation (5.3) to calculate the RoE. Here, your debt-to-equity ratio is $L = 2$, and so:

$$RoE = g + L(G - i)$$
$$= 0.10 + 2 \cdot (0.10 - 0.08)$$
$$= 0.14 \text{ or } 14\%.$$

The more leverage you use, the higher your RoE will be. Table 5.6 displays RoE's for different debt-to-equity ratios.

Note how the RoE can be in tens or hundreds of percent when the investment growth rate is only 10% p.a. Indeed, this is how real estate investors make their money. They borrow enormous sums of money, secured against the physical asset. If the asset's return exceeds the interest cost (even only slightly so), the return is greatly magnified.

Of course, the risk is that if g is less than i, your equity will shrink. It might even disappear completely. Consider the following example.

Practice Question *Suppose you are interested in buying a piece of land for investment. The land costs $500,000. You want to finance this purchase by using $50,000 of your own money and borrowing $450,000 from a bank at the rate of 5% p.a., annual compounding. What is your RoE after one year if the land price increases only by 1% over that time? What if the price drops by 10% over the year?*

In this case, your debt-to-equity ratio is equal to $450,000/\$50,000 = 9$. If the land price increases by 1%, the RoE is:

$$\text{RoE} = 0.01 + 9 \cdot (0.01 - 0.05)$$
$$= -0.35 \text{ or } -35\%.$$

Your equity is now worth $50,000 \cdot (1 - 0.35) = \$32,500$. You have lost $17,500 in one year.

If the land price declines by 10% over the year, then your RoE is:

$$\text{RoE} = -0.10 + 9 \cdot (-0.10 - 0.05)$$
$$= -1.45 \text{ or } -145\%,$$

which means that you have negative equity in this investment. You now owe the bank more than what the land is worth. Your outstanding debt is now $450,000 \cdot 1.05 = \$472,500$, while your land is worth only $500,000 \cdot 0.90 = \$450,000$. Your equity is now $-\$25,000$.

Now that we know both the benefits and risks of leverage, let us consider a case where a prudent use of it can help to achieve financial goals that seem unreachable. Consider the following example.

Practice Question *Suppose you are now fourty-five years old with no savings. You want to retire when you reach sixty-five, and you want to have $1 million at that time. For the next twenty years, you can save $15,000 per year at the end of each year. The expected rate of return on the investment that you have in mind is 9% p.a., annual compounding. Can you reach your goal?*

If you invest $15,000 per year at the rate of return of 9% p.a., annual compounding, by the end of the next twenty years you will get:

$$15,000 \cdot \textbf{FVA}(0.09, 20) = 15,000 \cdot 51.1601 = 767,401.79,$$

which falls far short of your goal of $1 million.

To achieve the goal, you need to invest more than $15,000 per year. You will have to borrow to top up your investment. Let L be the amount that you will borrow per year. So, the investment amount per year becomes $(15,000 + L)$. This amount must be such that in twenty years, you will get the proceeds that, after subtracting the loan repayment, you will be left with $1 million. Suppose that the borrowing rate is $i = 5\%$ p.a., annual compounding. Then,

$$(15,000 + L) \cdot \textbf{FVA}(0.09, 20) - L \cdot \textbf{FVA}(0.05, 20) = 1,000,000$$
$$(15,000 + L) \cdot 51.1601 - L \cdot 33.0660 = 1,000,000.$$

Solving for L, we have $L = \$12,854.87$. Therefore, you will have to borrow $12,854.87 every year to add to your own savings of $15,000. This means that in total, you will invest $27,854.87. You should verify that this investment will get you to your goal. We have ignored risk, obviously.

Finally, another benefit of using an investment loan is that it can create tax shelters. As we will see in the next chapter, interest expenses on investment loans are tax deductible. This is especially beneficial to investors with high income. We discuss this issue in more detail in the next chapter.

5.3 Debt Consolidation

At any one time, you may have more than one type of debt. When you are young, you tend to have student loans, credit card debts, perhaps car loans, and other consumer loans. At older ages, you might have a home mortgage, a line of credit (L.O.C.), and perhaps an investment margin account. The interest rates charged on these various types of debts are typically not the same. Consequently, a "portfolio of debts" is generally not optimal. If you have a choice, you will be better off and will save money if you can consolidate all your debts at the lowest of all the available rates. You borrow one big loan at the lowest possible rate, and use it to repay all of your debts.

For example, suppose you have the liabilities in Table 5.7, where, to avoid working with different quotation conventions used by different types of debt, we express all interest rates by their effective annual rates (EARs). We assume for simplicity that interests on these loans are paid once a year.

Practice Question *Suppose you can obtain a secured line of credit at an effective annual rate of 4% p.a. How much money will you save by consolidating your liabilities?*

Table 5.7. *Example of different types of liabilities*

Type of debt	Amount owed	Effective annual rate
Student Loan	$30,000	6%
Car Loan	$10,000	7%
Credit Card	$3,000	19%
Store Card	$2,000	30%
Total	$45,000	

Source: Author Data.

Before consolidation, the total amount of interest that you pay in a year is:

$$30,000 \cdot 0.06 + 10,000 \cdot 0.07 + 3,000 \cdot 0.19 + 2,000 \cdot 0.30 = 3,670.$$

To consolidate these debts, you will have to borrow $45,000 from your line of credit at the EAR of 4% and use the proceeds to pay back all four loans that you now have. The interest that you have to pay per year under the consolidation is $45,000 \cdot 0.04 = \$1,800$, which results in a saving of $1,870 per year.

This interest rate in this example may seem exceptionally low to you. However, remember that this line of credit is secured against some of your assets. The collateral lowers the risk to the bank, and so interest rates on secured loans are typically lower than rates on unsecured loans.

In practice, there are two issues to keep in mind. First, you might not be able to borrow at the (very) low rate that would allow you to consolidate debts and save money. If that is the case, having several types of debts is indeed your only option. Secondly, certain kinds of debts are not eligible to be consolidated – one example is mortgage debt. So, the best you can do is to try to consolidate your other debts.

5.4 Is Debt Good or Bad?

Most financial commentators consider loans that are used for investment purposes (either in yourself or in assets) at relatively low interest rates as good debts, and discretionary borrowing used for consumption and expenditures at relatively high interest rates as bad debts. According to them, good debts make financial sense and should be encouraged (in moderation), whereas bad debts reflect poor financial control and should be shunned.

In contrast, we argued in Chapter 4 that incorporating human capital (and thus economic net worth) into our financial plans results in a different perspective. We agree that using your credit card to buy yet another gadget you will never use and do not really need is bad financial planning. Individuals who are ignorant of the basics of credit card interest rates and compounding periods are paying more than they should and suffer from these financial mistakes. Yet we believe that perhaps less emphasis should be placed on the purpose of the debt itself or even the absolute rate you are paying. Rather, greater emphasis should be on getting the best possible rate relative to your individual financial condition and the overall standard of living that borrowing creates over the course of your life. In other words, debt is only a tool to achieve the highest possible overall standard of living.

Consequently, the main question that you should ask yourself when contemplating going into debt should not be whether you can afford a particular purchase. Rather, ask yourself whether today's purchase – which might be financed at high cost with long-term debt – reduces your future standard of living by more than it increases your present standard of living. If the answer to this question is yes, or even maybe, then the purchase does not make sense from a consumption-smoothing perspective.

5.5 Questions and Assignments

1. Imagine that you borrowed $M = \$450,000$ and together with an additional $50,000 of personal equity, you purchased a house worth $500,000. To finance the purchase you took out a twenty-five-year mortgage with a term of three years, at an APR of $i = 6\%$. Please create a mortgage schedule that illustrates the monthly payment, interest paid, principal paid, and outstanding balance for each month over the thirty-six-month term of the mortgage. How much do you owe at the end of thirty-six months? How much have you paid in total over the thirty-six months? What fraction was interest and what fraction was principal? For this question ignore mortgage insurance.

2. In the previous question, imagine that at the end of the three-year term, instead of renewing the mortgage you decide to sell the house. Assume that upon sale (and after all real estate fees) you received $550,000, which is $g = 10\%$ more than the purchasing price. Please compute the return on equity (RoE) from this transaction after you pay off the mortgage loan, and explain exactly how you obtained this number. Hint: Do not just plug numbers into an equation. Think about it first.

3. You want to buy a house for $500,000. You plan to make a down payment of only 5% of the home value, and amortize the loan over the maximum allowable thirty-five years. You negotiated a five-year fixed-mortgage rate of 5%; compounded semi-annually and paid monthly. Due to the (high) 95% loan-to-value ratio, you must pay an additional CMHC premium of 3% of the value of the loan. This is added to the loan amount. What is your monthly mortgage payment?

4. In the previous question, what is the outstanding amount of the loan after eighteen months of mortgage payments? Assume you want to pay off your entire (closed, fixed) mortgage after eighteen months. You must pay a penalty of three months' interest to "break" the mortgage (i.e., interest that you would pay in the next three months if the loan continued to exist). What is the total amount needed to pay off the loan?

5. Five years ago, you took out a fixed-rate mortgage for $300,000 at an APR of 6% and with a five-year term and an amortization period of twenty-five years. Now, you are about to renew the loan for another term of five years at the APR of 5%. What is the amount of monthly payment under this new term?

6. One year ago, you took out a variable-rate mortgage for $350,000 at an APR of 3% and with an amortization period of twenty years. Now, the bank has just increased the mortgage rate to 3.5% APR. If you wish to continue to make the same monthly payment as before, how much longer will it take you to pay off the loan compared to the original schedule?

7. Please answer the previous question assuming that you took out a variable-rate mortgage at an APR of 3%, but with monthly payments that are based on a hypothetical rate of APR of 6%. Assume that exactly one year after you bought the house and borrowed the $M =$ $450,000$, the floating rate underlying the variable-rate mortgage jumps from $i = 3\%/12$ to $i = 5\%/12$ and remains at this rate for the remaining two years. Please compute exactly how much money you owe (the outstanding balance) at the end of the three-year term of the mortgage.

8. Kevin is now forty-five years old. He plans to retire in twenty years. He wants to have $2,000,000 when he retires. Currently, he has no savings. However, he can from now on save $10,000 per year. He has done some calculations and discovered that in order to reach his goal, he will need a rate of return of 20.5682% p.a. on his investment. There is a mutual fund in which he wants to invest. However, the expected

rate of return on this fund is only 10% p.a. Therefore, he plans to borrow money to invest in order to increase the rate of return on his investment. The borrowing rate is 5% p.a. How much does he have to borrow for every dollar of his money?

9. Imagine that you have the following debt obligations. You owe $L(1) =$ $10,000 at an APR of $i(1) = 25\%$, which will be paid off in equal monthly payments over $N(1) = 3$ years. You owe $L(2) = \$16,000$ at an APR of $i(2) = 19\%$, which will be paid off in equal monthly payments over $N(2) = 5$ years. You owe $L(3) = \$24,000$ at an APR of $i(3) = 15\%$, which will be paid off in equal monthly payments over $N(3) = 7$ years. You owe $L(4) = \$10,000$ at an APR of $i(4) = 8\%$, which will be paid off in equal monthly payments over $N(4) =$ 13 years. In other words, the total amount of debt that you have outstanding is $60,000. How much more can you borrow – under the same exact payment schedule – if you consolidate your debts into one "basket" in which you are paying a rate of $v = 5\%$? (Note, this is a nominal rate per year.)

10. In the previous question, please compute the total amount of interest you will pay if you DO NOT consolidate your loan (unadjusted for time value of money) and compare it to the total amount of interest you will pay if you DO consolidate your loan by borrowing $60,000 at the lower 5% rate.

SIX

Personal Income Taxes [Canadian Content]

Learning Objectives

In this chapter, we will learn how to calculate personal income taxes. We then talk about different types of investment income and how they are taxed. Finally, we explore a few ways to minimize the amount of taxes that we have to pay.

6.1 The Logic of Income Tax Calculations

In this section, we describe how income taxes are determined in Canada. Generally, income taxes in other countries follow a similar logic. In Canada, income taxes are assessed at both the federal and provincial levels. You are required to file a tax return in a given (tax) year if for that year you are a resident or a deemed resident of Canada with income above a certain level. Whether or not a person is a resident of Canada is determined by many factors. These factors include the amount of time spent in Canada in that year, ownership of a residence in Canada, and having relatives, bank accounts, and/or other social and economic ties to Canada. Except for residents of the province of Quebec, which administers its own personal income tax collection, Canadians file their tax return using a combined form in which both levels of taxes are calculated.

As with most countries, Canadian incomes taxes (both federal and provincial) are determined using the following three steps:

1. Figure out your total income from all sources. In Canada, you have to report income earned from every source, domestic or foreign. From this, you subtract **deductions** that are allowed by the tax laws, to arrive at a **taxable income**.

2. You then apply (federal and provincial) tax rates to your taxable income. The result is the total tax amount.
3. Finally, you subtract **tax credits** from your total tax to arrive at the amount of tax payable.

Typically, there are three major categories of income. The first category is employment income. This includes wages, salary, commissions, bonuses, and other employment benefits (such as the use of your company's car). If you are self-employed, then your employment income is the income that you make from your business minus reasonable expenses. The second category is pension and other social-security income. This includes income from your company's pension plan and from Canada Pension Plan (CPP). It also includes Old Age Security (OAS) payments and employment insurance payments. The third category is investment income. This includes interests, dividends, capital gains, and net rental income from your property. (More on investment income later in the chapter.) Note, however, that most countries will exempt certain types of income from taxes. In Canada, the exemption list includes lottery winnings, inheritances, certain child-support payments, and capital gains on the sale of principal residences.

Allowable deductions include contributions to pension and retirement savings plans, some employment-related expenses (such as moving and childcare expenses), some investment-related expenses (such as interest on investment loans and counsel fees), capital losses, and spousal support payments.

Tax credits are amounts that both the federal and provincial governments allow you to subtract from the amounts of total taxes that you calculate in step 2. There are two categories of tax credits – refundable and nonrefundable. Most tax credits are nonrefundable, which means that you can only use them to reduce your total taxes down to zero. If you happen to have more credits than you can use, the government will not refund the unused portion to you. We discuss tax credits in more detail later (see Table 6.2).

Practice Question *Suppose that for the year 2011, you have a salary income of $90,000, a bonus of $20,000, and no other income. Suppose also that you have deductions totaling $10,000. What is your taxable income for the year?*

Your total income for the year is $90,000 + $20,000 = $110,000. Your allowable deductions are $10,000. As a result, your taxable income is $110,000 − $10,000 = $100,000. This is the amount on which income taxes will be assessed.

Table 6.1. *Canadian federal income tax rates – 2011*

Taxable income	Rate (%)
First $41,544	15%
Next $41,544 (i.e., Over $41,544 up to $83,088)	22%
Next $41,712 (i.e., Over $83,088 up to $128,800)	26%
Over $128,800	29%

Source: http://www.cra-arc.gc.ca/menu-eng.html.

Next, we will look at how much taxes you have to pay on the income. We will separate our discussion between the federal and the provincial cases.

6.1.1 Federal Income Taxes

For the year 2011, the federal income tax rates are as shown in Table 6.1. Note from Table 6.1 that like most countries, Canada has a progressive tax-rate system, where the tax rate increases as your taxable income increases. At the federal level, there are four **tax brackets**. When calculating taxes, you start from the first bracket and work upward until you reach the last dollar of your taxable income.

Practice Question *Based on the previous example, what is your total tax amount at the federal level for the year 2011?*

From the previous example, your taxable income is $100,000. According to Table 6.1, the first $41,544 of your taxable income is taxed at the rate of 15%, the next $41,544 (i.e., $83,088 − $41,544) at 22%, and the remaining (i.e., $100,000 − $83,088) at 26%. Therefore, your total federal tax will be:

$$(41,544 - 0) \cdot 0.15 + (83,088 - 41,544) \cdot 0.22$$
$$+ (100,000 - 83,088) \cdot 0.26 = 19,768.40.$$

For ease of illustration, we will round the calculations to the nearest whole numbers. Subsequent calculations will be based on the rounded figures instead of the exact figures. Therefore, the results shown can be (very) slightly different from the exact results.

The amount calculated (i.e., $19,768) is not yet the amount that you have to pay to the federal government. You have to subtract tax credits from it in order to come up with that amount. Tax credits are amounts that both the federal and provincial governments allow you to subtract from the amounts of total taxes that you have previously calculated. There are many categories of tax credits that you can use (so be sure to research them). A few examples of them are in Table 6.2.

Table 6.2. *Selected federal and Ontario personal tax credits (2011)*

Type	Federal		Ontario	
	Base amount	Credit amount (15% of base amount)	Base amount	Credit amount (5.05% of base amount)
Basic Personal	$10,527	$1,579	$9,104	$460
Spousal (or equivalent)	$10,527	$1,579	$7,730	$390
– reduced when spouse's income exceeds	$0		$773	
– completely eliminated when spouse's income exceeds	$10,527		$8,503	
Age 65 and over	$6,537	$981	$4,445	$224
– reduced when income exceeds	$32,961		$33,091	
– completely eliminated when income exceeds	$76,541		$62,725	
Disability	$7,341	$1,101	$7,355	$371
Eligible pension income	Actual pension received up to $2,000	Up to $300	Actual pension received up to $1,259	Up to $64
Care for infirm adult	$4,282	$642	$4,291	$217
– reduced when dependent's income exceeds	$14,624		$14,681	
– completely eliminated when dependent's income exceeds	$18,906		$18,972	
University tuition fees	Actual amount paid	15% of amount paid	Actual amount paid	5.05% of amount paid
Education (per month)				
– Full-time	$400	$60	$490	$25
– Part-time	$120	$18	$147	$7
Textbooks (per month)				
– Full-time	$65	$10	$0	$0
– Part-time	$20	$3	$0	$0
Interest on student loans	Actual amount paid	15% of amount paid	Actual amount paid	5.05% of amount paid
Others (e.g., medical expenses, charitable contributions, etc.)	See web sites of the Canada Revenue Agency and/or the Ontario government for details			

There are a few things to note from Table 6.2. First, the amounts of tax credits are not specified directly. Rather, the governments specify the base amounts for each category. To arrive at the actual credit amounts, you have to multiply the base amounts by the lowest tax rate (i.e., first bracket) at the federal and provincial levels. For example, the amount of the federal basic-personal tax credit, $1,579, is equal to the base amount $10,527 multiplied by 15%, which is the rate of the lowest bracket on the federal tax rate schedule. Other amounts are calculated in the same way.

Secondly, some categories of tax credits are subject to income-tested reduction (or clawback). For example, if your spouse does not have income, then you get the full $1,579 in federal spousal tax credit. However, if your spouse has some income, you do not get the full credit. The higher your spouse's income is, the less tax credit in this category you will get. Eventually, if his or her income exceeds the base amount (i.e., $10,527), the reduction will be complete (i.e., you will not get any credit in this category).

Thirdly, these tax credits are nonrefundable. If you cannot use them all (i.e., the credits exceed your tax amounts calculated in the previous step), the governments will not refund you the difference. In other words, you can use the credits only to offset the amounts of taxes that you owe. Note, however, that there are a few categories of them (e.g., age, pension, and disability) where unused amounts can be transferred to the spouse (see an example in Tables 6.9 and 6.10).

In Canada, there are very few refundable tax credits available. Generally, these credits are intended to provide additional tax relief for low-income individuals. Examples of this type of tax credits are low-income tax credits and medical expense supplement tax credits.

Practice Question *Suppose you only have tax credits in the basic personal and spousal categories (where your spouse's taxable income for the 2011 tax year is $5,000). What is the amount of your federal tax payable?*

Recall that your federal tax (before tax credits) is $19,768. From Table 6.2, your federal basic personal tax credit is $1,579. As for the federal spousal tax credit, you will not get the full amount (i.e., $1,579) because your spouse has income. You will receive a reduced amount. The reduction is calculated based on your spouse's income relative to the stipulated clawback rule. As explained earlier, this tax credit starts to get reduced as soon as your spouse has an income, and is completely gone when the income exceeds $10,527. In your case, your spouse's income is $5,000, and so the credit will only be partially reduced. The amount of reduction in this case is $750.[1] As a result, the amount of spousal tax credit that you can use is $1,579 − $750 = $829.

Combining the two categories of tax credits, we have that your federal tax credits for the year 2011 is $1,579 (i.e., basic personal) +$829 (i.e., spousal credit) = $2,408. Consequently, your federal tax payable will be $19,768 − $2,408 = $17,360. Throughout the year, federal taxes may have been withheld from your pay. In such a case, you subtract the amount withheld from $17,360 to see whether you still owe money to the federal government or will get a reimbursement from it.

Finally, it is important to recognize the difference between deductions and tax credits. Deductions reduce your taxable income while tax credits directly reduce your tax amounts. Which one is worth more? Note that because deductions are subtracted "off the top" of your total income, they save you taxes at the rate of the highest tax bracket that you would have reached without the deductions. For example, suppose you did not have the $10,000 deductions, your taxable income would have been $110,000, and the total federal tax would have been $22,368 (try to verify this). By having the deductions, your total federal tax is reduced by $2,600. This amount is indeed equal to the amount of deductions (i.e., $10,000) multiplied by the tax rate of third bracket (i.e., 26%), which is your highest bracket.

On the other hand, tax credits are calculated by multiplying the base amounts by the tax rate of the first bracket (i.e., the lowest). As a result, a base amount of, for example, $10,000 translates to a federal tax credit of only $1,500. Therefore, in your case, a deduction of $10,000 is worth more than a $10,000 base amount for tax credits. In contrast, for people with such low income that they fall in the lowest tax bracket (with or without the deductions), a $10,000 deduction and a $10,000 base amount for tax credits are worth the same to them because the tax savings from either are calculated based on the lowest tax bracket.

It is not clear what criteria that the governments used to decide whether a category of tax relief should be in the form of deductions or a tax credit. Our conjecture is that the system that we have now is the result of incremental chops and changes to the income tax rules over the years. Note that if the governments want to introduce a new category of tax relief, it will be less costly for them to offer it as a tax credit rather than a deduction.

---

[1] The amount of reduction can be calculated based on a linear interpolation as follows:

$$\text{Amount of Reduction} = \frac{5,000}{10,527 - 0} \cdot 1,579 = 750.$$

Table 6.3. *Ontario income tax rates – 2011*

Taxable income	Rate (%)
First $37,774	5.05%
Next $37,776 (i.e., Over $37,774 up to $75,550)	9.15%
Over $75,550	11.16%

Source: http://www.cra-arc.gc.ca/menu-eng.html.

6.1.2 Provincial Income Taxes

In Canada, each province has its own tax rate schedule. We will use the province of Ontario as our example. The logic is essentially the same in other provinces. An exception is the province of Alberta, whose tax rate is flat at 10% of income regardless of the level. In addition, because the province of Quebec administers its own personal income tax collection, its definition of income can differ slightly from that of the federal government's.

The Ontario income tax rates are shown in Table 6.3. Similar to the federal government, the province of Ontario employs a progressive tax rate system. Based on our earlier discussion in the federal case, you should have no problem figuring out the amount of your total Ontario tax (before subtracting tax credits).

Practice Question *What is your total Ontario tax amount for the year 2011?*

As your taxable income is $100,000, your total Ontario tax is:

$$(37,774 - 0) \cdot 0.0505 + (75,550 - 37,774) \cdot 0.0915$$
$$+ (100,000 - 75,550) \cdot 0.1116 = 8,093.$$

Now, Ontario does not let you off that easily. It also imposes what they call **surtax**, which by definition, is added-on tax (or tax on tax). The way surtax works is that if your Ontario tax (*after* subtracting tax credits) exceeds certain thresholds, you will be assessed more taxes. So, before we talk more about surtax, let us figure out your Ontario tax credits.

Practice Question *Suppose, as before, that you only have tax credits in the basic personal and spousal categories (where your spouse's taxable income for the 2011 tax year is $5,000). What is the amount of your Ontario tax credits?*

Table 6.4. *Ontario surtax rates – 2011*

Threshold	Rate (%)
If Ontario tax after credits exceed $4,078	20% of the excess
If Ontario tax after credits exceed $5,219	36% of the excess

Source: http://www.cra-arc.gc.ca/menu-eng.html.

From Table 6.2, your Ontario basic personal tax credit is $460. As in the federal case, your Ontario spousal tax credit is reduced because your spouse has income. The full amount of this category of credit is $390, and the clawback rule is that it starts to get reduced when your spouse's income exceeds $773 and is completely gone when the income exceeds $8,503. Because your spouse has a taxable income of $5,000, the Ontario spousal tax credit will be partially reduced by $213, leaving $390 − $213 = $177 for you to use.[2] Combining the two categories of tax credits, your Ontario tax credits for the year 2011 is $637.

Your Ontario tax after subtracting the tax credit is then:

$$8,093 - 637 = 7,456.$$

This is the amount on which Ontario surtax will be determined.

Ontario imposes surtax if the tax amount after tax credits exceeds certain thresholds. The two thresholds and the surtax rates for 2011 are shown in Table 6.4.

As shown in the table, the first threshold is $4,078. If your tax amount after credits exceeds this threshold, you have to pay 20% of the excess as surtax. The second threshold is $5,219. If your tax amount after credits also exceeds this threshold, you have to pay 36% of the excess as surtax. It is important to note that these two thresholds work independently. You have to compare your Ontario tax amount after tax credits to each threshold. If both of them are exceeded, you add up the two amounts of surtax.

Alternatively, you can interpret the surtax rates as follows. If your Ontario tax after tax credits exceeds $4,078 but is below $5,219, your surtax amount is 20% of the excess. On the other hand, if your Ontario tax after tax credits

---

[2] As before, we can use a linear interpolation to calculate the amount of reduction as follows:

$$\text{Amount of Reduction} = \frac{5,000 - 773}{8,503 - 773} \cdot 390 = 213.$$

Table 6.4a. *Alternative interpretation of Ontario surtax rates – 2011*

Ontario tax after tax credits (X)	Amount of surtax
$4,078 < X < $5,219	20% of (X − $4,078)
X > $5,219	$228.20 + 56% of (X − $5,219)

Source: Author Calculations based on Ontario Tax Rates.

exceeds $5,219, your surtax amount is $228.20 plus 56% of the excess over $5,219 (see Table 6.4a). Either approach will give you the same result.

Practice Question *What is your Ontario surtax for the year 2011?*

From the previous calculations, your Ontario tax after tax credits is $7,456. This amount exceeds both thresholds and so you calculate surtax for both thresholds. The amount for the first threshold is:

$$(7,456 - 4,078) \cdot 0.20 = 676,$$

and the amount for the second threshold is:

$$(7,456 - 5,219) \cdot 0.36 = 805.$$

As a result, your total surtax is $1,481.

Note that you can also get the same result using the alternative interpretation of the surtax rates. Here, your Ontario tax after tax credits exceeds $5,219, and so the surtax amount, according to Table 6.4a, is $228.20 + 0.56 \cdot ($7,456 − $5,219) = $1,481.

Finally, we add this total surtax to your Ontario tax after tax credits to arrive at the amount of Ontario tax payable of $8,937 (i.e., $7,456 + $1,481). As before, throughout the year, Ontario taxes may have been withheld from your pay. In such a case, you subtract the amount withheld from $8,937 to see whether you still owe money to the Ontario government or will get a reimbursement from it.

6.1.3 Combining Federal and Provincial Income Taxes

Now that you have calculated both your federal and Ontario income tax payable, you can add them up to arrive at the total tax payable, which is equal to:

$$17,360 + 8,937 = 26,297.$$

Personal Income Taxes [Canadian Content]

Table 6.5. *How to compute your marginal tax rate: Difference in income taxes between taxable income of $100,000 and $100,001*

	Taxable income		
	$100,000	$100,001	Difference
Federal Income Tax Payable	$17,360.40	$17,360.66	$0.2600
Ontario Income Tax after Tax Credits	$7,455.86	$7,455.97	$0.1116
Ontario Surtax	$1,480.84	$1,480.90	$0.0625
Total Ontario Tax Payable	$8,936.70	$8,936.87	$0.1741
Total Tax Payable	$26,297.10	$26,297.53	$0.4341

Source: Author Calculations based on CRA Tables.

In a progressive tax-rate system like one in Canada and the United States, there is a difference between an average tax rate and a marginal tax rate. Because you calculate your income tax by starting from the first tax bracket and working upward until you exhaust your taxable income, the **average tax rate** represents the average rate (across tax brackets) that you pay, and is calculated by dividing total tax payable by taxable income. In your case, your taxable income is $100,000, while your federal and Ontario tax payable are $17,360 and $8,937, respectively. Therefore, your average federal tax rate is 17.36% and your average Ontario tax rate is 8.94%, resulting in a combined average rate of 26.30%.

In contrast, your **marginal tax rate** is the rate that is applied to the next dollar of the taxable income. Given the current amount of your taxable income, if you were to earn one more dollar, how much tax do you have to pay on that additional income? To answer that, we repeat the previous tax calculations under the same assumptions except that the taxable income will now be $100,001. The results are shown in Table 6.5.

Let us look at federal tax first. As shown in the table, if your income increased by $1, your federal tax would be $0.26 higher. In other words, your marginal federal tax rate is 26%. The reason for this is simple. Your current taxable income of $100,000 is such that you have reached the third bracket (i.e., 26%) of the federal tax schedule (see Table 6.1). Therefore, one additional dollar of income would increase your federal tax by:

$$1 \cdot 0.26 = 0.26.$$

From the table, your total Ontario tax payable (i.e., tax plus surtax) increases by $0.1741. This amount is the sum of the increase in Ontario tax after tax credits (an increase of $0.1116) and the increase in Ontario surtax (an increase of $0.0625). In other words, your marginal Ontario tax rate

Table 6.6. *Marginal tax rates (Federal and Ontario combined – 2011)*

Existing taxable income	Federal (%)	Ontario (%)	Combined rate (%)
First $37,774	15.00%	5.05%	20.05%
Over $37,774 up to $41,544	15.00%	9.15%	24.15%
Over $41,544 up to $66,614	22.00%	9.15%	31.15%
Over $66,614 up to $75,550	22.00%	10.98%	32.98%
Over $75,550 up to $78,361	22.00%	13.39%	35.39%
Over $78,361 up to $83,088	22.00%	17.41%	39.41%
Over $83,088 up to $128,800	26.00%	17.41%	43.41%
Over $128,800	29.00%	17.41%	46.41%

Source: Author Calculations.

is 17.41%. Again, this is not difficult to see. Your current taxable income already puts you in the Ontario tax bracket of 11.16% (see Table 6.3). So, an extra dollar of income would incur a tax of $0.1116. In addition, you would also have to pay surtax. Because your existing Ontario tax already exceeds the two surtax thresholds, any increase in your Ontario tax would incur surtax at the rate of 20% + 36% = 56% (remember that the two thresholds work independently). As a result, an increase of $0.1116 in Ontario tax would incur surtax of $0.1116 · 56% = $0.0625. Taken together, one additional dollar of income would increase your Ontario tax payable by:

$$0.1116 + (0.1116 \cdot 0.56) = 0.1116 \cdot (1 + 0.56) = 0.1741.$$

Combining the federal and Ontario taxes together, we see that one additional dollar of income would increase your income tax by:

$$0.26 + [0.1116 \cdot (1 + 0.56)] = 0.4341.$$

Your marginal tax rate for the two levels combined is 43.41%.

Table 6.6 displays marginal tax rates (federal and Ontario combined) for any level of existing taxable income.

There are two things to note about the table. First, it was created under an assumption that there are no tax credits. Obviously, this is not true in practice. However, as you have seen in Table 6.2, different people will have different amounts of tax credits, depending on their situations. It is therefore not practical to create a table for every possible situation. The most neutral choice is to assume no credits, bearing in mind that any tax credits that you have will increase the upper limit of taxable income in each bracket (e.g., the first bracket may cover income up to, say, $40,000 rather than $37,774). Secondly, there are eight different brackets for marginal tax rates. This is the result of combining the federal and Ontario tax brackets (Tables 6.1 and 6.3, respectively) into one table and also factoring in Ontario surtax.

Marginal tax rate is important because it can affect your incentive to increase your income. To decide whether you should get a second job or invest in a security, you should look at the after-tax income that the second job or the security provides. The tax rate to use in making such a decision is your marginal tax rate. This is because the income that you will get from this decision will be *additional to* your existing taxable income. This is why you should use the tax rate that applies to the next dollar of income.

The proper use of marginal tax rate in your decision making is restricted to what economists call "marginal analyses." It should be used when the amount of the additional income is small (or not too large). When the amount is large, the use of marginal tax rate can lead to an incorrect result. To see this, consider the following example. Suppose, as before, that your existing taxable income is $100,000, and that the second job will pay you $10,000 a year. Your taxable income will now be $110,000, which is still within the second-highest bracket of the marginal tax rate schedules (i.e., 43.41%). It does not push you up to the next bracket. Therefore, the marginal tax rate of 43.41% applies. All of the income from the second job will be taxed at the rate of 43.41%.

Next, what if the second job happens to pay you $40,000 instead of $10,000? Your taxable income will then be $140,000, which means that you will cross over into the highest marginal tax bracket (i.e., 46.41%). This means that your total taxable income is now high enough to exhaust the second-highest bracket and have something left for the highest bracket. Therefore, part of the additional income will incur tax at the 43.41% rate, and the remaining at the 46.41% rate. In this case, it would be wrong to use the starting marginal tax rate of 43.41% in the analysis. In other words, the use of the 43.41% rate would implicitly assume that the additional income will not push you up to the next marginal tax bracket.

Finally, in a progressive-tax system, marginal tax rate will always be at least as high as (and typically higher than), the average tax rate. The two rates will be the same for people whose taxable income is low and within the first tax brackets of both federal and Ontario schedules.

6.2 Investment Income

Now that we know how to calculate income taxes, let us turn our attention to a particular type of income – one that you will be receiving once you start saving. We will talk about investment income and its tax treatments.

Most people invest their savings in a portfolio of assets. The assets can be safe assets such as government bonds and guaranteed investment certificates (GICs). They can also be risky assets such as stocks, commodities, and real-estate properties. For tax purposes, it is important to note that different types of assets give you different types of income, and the tax treatment of investment income varies according to their types.

Generally, there are three types of investment income – interests, dividends, and capital gains. We now discuss each of them.

6.2.1 Interest Income

Interest income is what you will receive if you invest in fixed-income assets such as bank deposits, Treasury bills, Treasury bonds, and corporate bonds. The tax treatment of interest income is that you have to include 100% of them in your total income. You get no tax break from investing in assets that generate interest income. In other words, your marginal tax rate for interest income is the same as your marginal tax rate for employment income.

Note that you have to pay tax on the interest that you have earned in that tax year even if it has not been paid. For example, suppose you have just bought a two-year, zero-coupon bond with a face value of $50,000. You paid the purchase price, which was the present value of $50,000. In two years, you will get $50,000. In the meantime, the bond pays you nothing. However, as time passes, interest is being accrued inside the bond. For tax purposes, you have to calculate the amount of accrued interest for each tax year, and then include it in your income.

6.2.2 Dividend Income

Dividend income is what you will receive if you invest in common and/or preferred shares. The tax treatment for **eligible dividends** (generally those received from, and designated as such by, Canadian public corporations) is different from that of interest income. Here, you will get some tax break on them. This is because dividends are paid out by companies from their *after-tax* profits. These Canadian companies have already paid business income taxes on the income that they generated. Therefore, it would be double taxation if shareholders are again required to pay taxes on dividends. To neutralize this, governments typically provide dividend tax credits (as a category of tax credits). The way it works in Canada is that you are required to include a **grossed-up** amount of dividends in your total income. For example, suppose you received a dividend of $1. You then have to gross

Table 6.7. *Dividend gross-up factors and tax credit percentages*

	Federal		Ontario	
Tax year	Gross-up factor	Tax credits (% of grossed-up dividends)	Gross-up factor	Tax credits (% of grossed-up dividends)
2011	41.00%	16.44%	41.00%	6.40%
2012 and beyond	38.00%	15.02%	38.00%	6.40%

Source: Author Calculations.

this amount up by a gross-up factor. This factor is specified by the Canada Revenue Agency (CRA), and varies from one tax year to the next (see Table 6.7). For the tax year 2011, this factor is 41% (for both federal and Ontario taxes). Therefore, the grossed-up dividend amount is $1.41, which will then be added to your total income. You then proceed to calculate income tax in the same manner as before.

Because of the gross up, your total income increases by more than the actual amount of dividend, and you may wonder how this is fair. The answer is that after you have calculated the tax amounts, you will be allowed to subtract dividend tax credits from them. The amount of dividend tax credits that you get is specified as a percentage of the grossed-up dividend. The percentages are given in Table 6.7.

Practice Question   *Given $1 in actual dividend received in 2011, what are the amounts of federal and Ontario dividend tax credits?*

A $1 of actual dividend translates to a grossed-up amount of $1.41. From Table 6.7, the federal dividend tax credits are 16.44% of the grossed-up amount or:

$$0.1644 \cdot 1.41 = 0.2318.$$

The Ontario dividend tax credits are 6.40% of the grossed-up amount or:

$$0.0640 \cdot 1.41 = 0.0902.$$

In total, the dividend tax credits that you get are $0.3220 per every dollar of dividend that you received in 2011.

There are a few things that you should note. First, because the dividend tax credits are intended to overcome the double-taxation problem, dividends paid by foreign companies (which do not pay corporate taxes to the Canadian federal and provincial governments) are not considered eligible dividends, and thus are not taxed in the manner described here. Secondly, the amount of the dividend tax credits on eligible dividends is the same for every taxpayer, regardless of his or her taxable income. This is because the credits compensate you for the amounts of corporate taxes that companies have already paid on their income before they distributed the remaining cash to you as dividends. The amount of the credits (i.e., $0.3220 for 2011) corresponds roughly to the amount of corporate taxes that companies pay to the federal and Ontario governments. As corporate tax rates will be lower in future years, the gross-up factors and the tax credit percentages for future years in Table 6.7 also change.

Thirdly, because the credit amount is the same for everyone, some people will have more credits than they need, and some less than they need. To see this, consider the following example.

Practice Question   *Given $1 in actual dividend received in 2011, calculate the amount of tax that you (whose existing income is $100,000) have to pay on it. What about the amount of tax for someone whose existing taxable income is $35,000?*

We will calculate the federal and Ontario amounts separately. At the federal level, based on your existing income of $100,000, your marginal federal tax rate is 26% (see Table 6.6). The federal tax before applying dividend tax credits is:

$$1.41 \cdot 0.26 = 0.3666.$$

From the previous example, the federal dividend tax credits per one dollar of actual dividend are $0.2318. As a result, the amount of federal tax that you have to pay is $0.1348. In other words, your marginal federal tax rate for dividend income is 13.48%.

For Ontario, we will start with the tax amount before dividend tax credits and surtax. From Table 6.3, your existing income of $100,000 puts you in the 11.16% bracket, and so your Ontario tax before dividend tax credits and surtax is:

$$1.41 \cdot 0.1116 = 0.1574.$$

Next, from the previous example, the Ontario dividend tax credits per \$1 of dividend received are \$0.0902. Subtracting this amount from the Ontario tax, we have:

$$0.1574 - 0.0902 = 0.0672.$$

Finally, you know from before that your income is high enough for your Ontario tax to exceed both surtax thresholds, and so your surtax rate is 56%. Consequently, the Ontario tax payable per \$1 of dividend received is:

$$0.0672 \cdot 1.56 = 0.1048.$$

The amount of Ontario tax that you have to pay is \$0.1048. Therefore, your marginal Ontario tax rate for dividend income is 10.48%. Adding both federal and Ontario taxes together, we have that the total tax amount is \$0.2396 (and so your combined marginal tax rate for dividend income is 23.96%). In your case, the dividend tax credits are not large enough to offset the tax obligation on the dividends. Still, the marginal tax rate (i.e., 23.96%) on it is much lower than the marginal tax rate on interest income (i.e., 43.41%).

Now, let us consider someone whose taxable income is \$35,000. It is easy to verify that this income puts the person in the first tax bracket at both the federal and Ontario levels. Therefore, the federal tax (after applying tax credits) on the dividend is:

$$(1.41 \cdot 0.15) - 0.2318 = -0.0203,$$

while the Ontario tax amount is:

$$(1.41 \cdot 0.0505) - 0.0902 = -0.0190,$$

where we note that there is no Ontario surtax at this income level.

In this case, both amounts of tax are negative. The dividend tax credits are more than required to offset the tax obligation on the dividend. In other words, the marginal tax rates at both the federal and Ontario levels are negative at -2.03% and -1.90%, respectively. The combined marginal tax rate is -3.93%. This means that he will not have to pay any tax on the dividend. Not only that, the excess credit can be used to offset his other taxes payable in that year. So, by investing and getting one more dollar in dividend income, this person manages to reduce his tax payments by 3.93 cents.

The dividend tax credits are **nonrefundable**, which means that they can only be used to reduce federal or provincial taxes payable to zero. If you do not have other taxes payable that you can use the credits to offset, the governments will not refund the portion of the credits that you cannot use.

By now, it should be obvious that because of the dividend tax credits, you will end up paying less taxes on dividend income than on interest income of the same amount, regardless of the levels of your taxable income (except ones so low that you end up paying no tax on either).

6.2.3 Capital Gains/Losses

Capital gains (losses) occur when we sell assets that we bought for income they generate or for personal use, for more (less) than what we paid for them. The distinction between capital gains/losses and ordinary income/losses is not always clear-cut. This is primarily because the Canadian *Income Tax Act* does not explicitly specify what capital assets include. By convention, capital assets include financial securities, investment properties, and real estates. They also include personal-use items such as cottages and boats.

If you have capital gains, they have to be included in your income. However, in Canada, you get a tax break on this type of investment income. You are required to include only half (i.e., 50%) of the capital gains as your income. For example, suppose in 2011 you realized a capital gain of $2,000 from selling shares of some company. Your **taxable capital gains** will only be $1,000. Accordingly, you pay 50% less tax on capital gains than on interest income of the same amount. If your marginal tax rate for interest income is 43.41%, then your marginal tax rate for capital gains will be 21.70%. It is important to emphasize that capital gains are taxed only after you sell a property and make a profit on it. So, as long as you do not sell it, there is no tax accrued regardless of how much its price has gone up.

If you have capital losses, you are allowed to use 50% of them to reduce or eliminate capital gains that you have in that year. If you have more **allowable capital losses** than needed to offset the taxable capital gains, you can carry the losses forward and use them in future years. Alternatively, you can apply the losses against the taxable capital gains that you had in the previous three years (on which you had already paid taxes). Bear in mind, however, that if you carry them forward, it is possible that future changes in tax rules may reduce the usefulness of the losses. For example, suppose that next year the **inclusion rate** is changed to 25% (i.e., only 25% of capital gains are to be included as income). In this case, you will no longer be able to use the losses that you have carried forward to offset capital gains on a one-to-one basis. The offsetting ratio will be adjusted to reflect the change in the inclusion rate.

There are two important exceptions to the tax treatment of capital gains that we described earlier. First, the gains from selling your principal

Table 6.8. *Marginal tax rates (Federal and Ontario combined) on investment income – 2011*

Existing taxable income	Interest (%)	Dividends (%)	Capital gains (%)
First $37,774	20.05%	−3.93%	10.03%
Over $37,774 up to $41,544	24.15%	1.85%	12.08%
Over $41,544 up to $66,614	31.15%	11.72%	15.58%
Over $66,614 up to $75,550	32.98%	12.50%	16.49%
Over $75,550 up to $78,361	35.39%	15.90%	17.70%
Over $78,361 up to $83,088	39.41%	18.32%	19.70%
Over $83,088 up to $128,800	43.41%	23.96%	21.70%
Over $128,800	46.41%	28.19%	23.20%

Source: Author Calculations.

residence will not be taxed. Secondly, the gains on investment that you put inside certain tax-sheltered vehicles will be taxed differently (more on this shortly).

In summary, different types of investment income are taxed differently. Table 6.8 summarizes the marginal tax rates for the three types of investment income, given various levels of existing income.

As can be seen from Table 6.8, interest income is taxed most heavily. It is treated in the same manner as your employment income. Up to a level of taxable income (i.e., $83,088), dividend income is taxed least heavily. Beyond that level, capital gains are the most tax-friendly form of investment income. Keep these in mind when you decide on what type of investment.

We close this section by noting that in practice, banks, mutual fund companies, and brokerage firms will figure out your investment income according to types and then send you tax slips once a year. Examples of these slips are a T3 slip (for mutual fund income) and a T5 slip (for interest and dividends). The numbers on the slips are based on the judgment of those financial institutions. In complex cases, their numbers may not be perfectly consistent with what you think. Note also that you will not get any slip for capital gains/losses generated from your own trading (not to be confused with capital gains/losses generated inside mutual funds by the funds' trading). Therefore, you have to be careful with record-keeping to ensure that you report the correct amounts.

6.3 Income Tax Planning

There are a few things that you can do to minimize the amount of income tax payable. For example, you need to take advantage of deductions and tax credits. Recall that allowable deductions are amounts that you can subtract from your total income to arrive at taxable income, while tax credits are amounts that you subtract from your total tax to come up with tax payable. Both of them help to reduce the income tax that you have to pay.

You can also try to split your income with a family member who is in a lower tax bracket than you are. In addition, you can shelter a portion of your income from tax. This is typically done by investing that portion in tax-efficient investment accounts. These two strategies are discussed next.

6.3.1 Income Splitting

Income splitting refers to an allocation of income from a family member in the higher tax bracket to a member in the lower one. The Canadian *Income Tax Act* contains several measures to prevent obvious income splitting. For example, suppose you ask your employer to do an indirect payment, where they would pay part of your salary to your spouse. That part of income will still be taxed in your hands. There are also attribution rules that apply in case you transfer your properties to your spouse or children in the hope that income subsequently generated by those properties would be taxed in their hands at lower rates. The rules generally require that any income (loss) on the transferred properties be attributed back to you, and thus be taxed at your tax rate. There are a few exceptions to the rules. First, they do not apply if the transfer is done at market value or if you take payment in the form of a loan bearing at least market interest rate or the rate prescribed by law (effectively an investment loan). Secondly, second-generation income (i.e., income earned on income) is never attributed back. Thirdly, if you transfer a property to your children who are under eighteen years old, only income (loss), but not capital gains/losses, is attributed back. This is true for the years in which your children are still under eighteen. Finally, any income earned on a transferred business is not subject to the rules, provided that the transfer recipient (your spouse or children) carry on business on a regular and continuous basis.

Because of the attribution rules, the opportunities to split income are quite limited. There are, however, a few things that people can do. For example, the spouse with a higher income can pay all living expenses and also the tax bills of the lower-income spouse. This allows the lower-income spouse to have more savings that can be invested in his or her name. The higher-income spouse can also make investment loans to the lower-income spouse at an interest rate acceptable by the tax laws. This is a sensible strategy if the investment income is expected to be higher than the interest rate.

Alternatively, if the lower-income spouse obtains investment loans from an outside party, the higher-income spouse can offer to pay interests on those loans. In addition, if you are self-employed, you may consider hiring your spouse or children provided that the salary that you pay is "reasonable."

For people who are receiving pension payments (i.e., generally retirees), they can split **eligible pension income** with their spouse or common-law partner. Eligible pension income includes payments from registered pension plans (RPPs) that employers set up for employees, and (for those sixtyfive years old or older) annuity payments from their registered retirement savings plans (RRSPs).[3] No funds are actually transferred under pension income splitting. Rather, it is a method to allocate part of the pension income to the spouse for tax-reporting purposes. Up to half of the pension income can be allocated to the spouse.

The benefits of pension income splitting are threefold.

1. To reduce the taxpayer's marginal tax rate. Consider, for example, a retired couple where only one spouse receives pension and the other has no income. Without pension income splitting, the pensioner will have to report and pay tax on all of the pension income. If the amount of the income is substantial, several tax brackets will be crossed and the marginal tax rate will be high. With pension income splitting, the pensioner manages to reduce the amount of income to be reported as his or her own, and put the rest in the spouse's name. Consequently, both will have lower reported income, which will each be taxed at a lower rate.

2. To create pension tax credits for the spouse. Recall from Table 6.2 that one category of tax credits is for eligible pension income. People who do not receive pension income cannot take advantage of this category of credits. Therefore, by allocating pension income to the spouse who has no or little pension income, the spouse will get more pension tax credits.

3. To reduce the clawback of income-tested senior benefits. Canadians age sixty-five or older who meet certain criteria are eligible to receive Old Age Security (OAS) pension. The amount of payment is income tested, and will start to get reduced if the recipient's income exceeds $67,668 (for 2011). The ability to split eligible pension income will lessen the impact of the clawback of the OAS pension. (Note that the OAS pension itself is not eligible pension income.)

---

[3] The precise definition of eligible pension income can be found on the website of Canada Revenue Agency at http://www.cra-arc.gc.ca/.

There is, however, one possible downside to pension income splitting. Recall from Table 6.2 that one category of tax credits is spousal tax credits. The amount of the credits is income tested. This is a concern only if the spouse has no or little income of his or her own. However, if the spouse's own income is already higher than the thresholds at which the credits will be completely eliminated ($10,527 at the federal level and $8,503 at Ontario level), then the credits will already have been lost and thus this downside is not a concern.

To get a better idea of the benefits of pension income splitting, consider the following example.

Practice Question *Jack and Diane are a retired couple living in Ontario (both of whom are over sixty-five). Jack receives an annual pension of $60,000, while Diane has no pension but has an investment income of $10,000 per year. Calculate the amounts of income taxes for both of them in case (i) Jack does not split his pension income; and (ii) Jack transfers half of his pension income to Diane.*

The calculations in case of no pension income splitting are shown in Table 6.9. Jack's total tax payable is $10,119, while Diane, due to her low income, does not have to pay tax. Note that Diane indeed has more tax credits (both federal and Ontario) than she can use. Because these tax credits are nonrefundable, she will not get a refund of the unused amount. The only exception is age tax credits whose *unused* amount can be transferred from one spouse to the other. This is why we see in the table that Jack gets a transfer of age tax credits in an amount of $981 at the federal level. This is the maximum amount of federal age tax credits and Diane has no need for the whole amount. At the Ontario level, Jack gets a transfer of age tax credits from Diane in an amount of $179. The maximum amount of Ontario age tax credits is $224, but Diane needs $45 from it so that she can completely offset her Ontario tax bills.

With pension income splitting, Jack's total tax payable is $2,408, while Diane's total tax payable is $4,715 (see Table 6.10). As a result, the combined amount is $7,122, which is lower than in the no-splitting case by $2,997. The savings come from three sources. First, because the splitting removes $30,000 from Jack's taxable income, he drops from the second tax brackets (both federal and Ontario) down to the first. The transferred $30,000 is now being taxed in Diane's hands at a lower rate. Secondly, the transfer enables Diane to take advantage of pension tax credits. Finally, the transfer reduces Jack's taxable income, and so allows him to retain more income-tested tax

Table 6.9. *Income tax calculations without pension income splitting*

	Jack	Diane	Total
Pension income	$60,000	$0	
Other income	$0	$10,000	
Total Taxable Income	$60,000	$10,000	$70,000
Federal Income Taxes before Tax Credits	$10,292	$1,500	$11,792
Federal Tax Credits			
Basic Personal Tax Credits	$1,579	$1,579	
Spousal Tax Credits	$79	$0	
Age Tax Credits	$372	$981	
Eligible Pension Tax Credits	$300	$0	
Age Tax Credits Transferred from Spouse	$981	$0	
Total	$3,311	$2,560	
Federal Tax Payable	$6,981	$0	$6,981
Ontario Income Taxes before Tax Credits	$3,941	$505	$4,446
Ontario Tax Credits			
Basic Personal Tax Credits	$460	$460	
Spousal Tax Credits	$0	$0	
Age Tax Credits	$21	$224	
Eligible Pension Tax Credits	$64	$0	
Age Tax Credits Transferred from Spouse	$179	$0	
Total	$723	$684	
Ontario Income Taxes after Tax Credits	$3,218	$0	$3,218
Ontario Surtax	$0	$0	$0
Total Ontario Tax Payable	$3,218	$0	$3,218
Total Tax Payable	$10,199	$0	$10,199

Source: Author Calculations.

credits than before (i.e., less clawbacks). The amount of savings due to the first source is $2,112 (calculated by comparing the couple's total taxes before tax credits before income splitting to after income splitting), while the rest comes from the second and third sources.

6.3.2 Tax-Deferred Investment Vehicles

To encourage savings, most countries offer some forms of tax relief to tax-payers. Most commonly, the relief is in the form of allowing taxpayers to

Table 6.10. *Income tax calculations with pension income splitting*

	Jack	Diane	Total
Pension Income	$30,000	$30,000	
Other Income	$0	$10,000	
Total Taxable Income	$30,000	$40,000	$70,000
Federal Income Taxes before Tax Credits	$4,500	$6,000	$10,500
Federal Tax Credits			
Basic Personal Tax Credits	$1,579	$1,579	
Spousal Tax Credits	$0	$0	
Age Tax Credits	$981	$822	
Eligible Pension Tax Credits	$300	$300	
Age Tax Credits Transferred from Spouse	$0	$0	
Total	$2,860	$2,701	
Federal Tax Payable	$1,640	$3,299	$4,939
Ontario Income Taxes before Tax Credits	$1,515	$2,111	$3,626
Ontario Tax Credits			
Basic Personal Tax Credits	$460	$460	
Spousal Tax Credits	$0	$0	
Age Tax Credits	$224	$172	
Eligible Pension Tax Credits	$64	$64	
Age Tax Credits Transferred from Spouse	$0	$0	
Total	$748	$695	
Ontario Income Taxes after Tax Credits	$767	$1,416	$2,183
Ontario Surtax	$0	$0	$0
Total Ontario Tax Payable	$767	$1,416	$2,183
Total Tax Payable	$2,408	$4,715	$7,122

Source: Author Calculations.

defer paying taxes on part of income that they save and on any investment income earned on such savings. In Canada, there are retirement savings accounts such as **registered pension plans (RPPs)** and **registered retirement savings plans (RRSPs)**. The logic of these plans is similar, which is that any (pre-tax) income that you save and put inside these accounts (up to the specified limits) in any tax year will not be counted as your taxable income in that year. So, you do not pay income taxes on the (pre-tax) amount that you put in these accounts. In addition, any income earned on the savings will not be taxed until you finally withdraw part or all of your investment from the accounts, at which time the withdrawn amount will have to be declared as income for that tax year.

The benefits of the deferral are twofold. First, by the concept of time value of money, you know that the value of $1 in tax payment that is made some time in the future is smaller than $1 now. Secondly, if you intend to wait until you retire to start withdrawing from the accounts (you do not have to), your tax rates are likely to be lower than your current rates (because you will not have employment income at that time). Therefore, by saving into these plans, you benefit not only from delaying your tax payment, but also from the expectation that the tax amounts themselves will be lower.

The catch here is that any amount that you withdraw from these accounts will be taxed at the ordinary-income (or employment-income) rate. To make this clear, note that in any amount of withdrawal, there are two components – the principal of the investment (which came from your pre-tax income) and investment income that you have earned on that principal. In the tax calculation, there will be no distinction made among the three different types of investment income. So, even if the income that you made was entirely from dividends or capital gains, you will still pay tax on it as if it were employment income or interest income, which, as discussed earlier, is taxed at a higher rate than dividends and capital gains.

We next briefly discuss the registered retirement savings plans (RRSPs), which have become a major investment vehicle in Canada. An RRSP is intended to be a personal retirement plan. It is legally a trust that can be set up at a bank, a trust company, a brokerage firm, a mutual fund company, or a life insurance company. Contributions into an RRSP are deductible from total income for the purpose of calculating taxable income. The contributions will not be considered taxable income for the current tax year as long as they are made in the year or within sixty days after the end of the year. As a result, we can say the contributions are made with pre-tax money.

Anyone (up to age seventy-one) who has **earned income** in Canada can set up an RRSP. Earned income is defined to include (i) gross amount of wages and other employment benefits; (ii) net income from business; (iii) net rental income; and (iv) other income such as royalties, alimony payments, and payments from Canada Pension Plan (CPP). It is important to note that investment income (e.g., interest, dividends, and capital gains) is not earned income. As a result, if all income you have in the current year is from investment, you will not be able to contribute into an RRSP this year.

Earned income is reduced by alimony and child support paid, and union and professional dues.

For 2011, the annual contribution is limited to 18% of the previous year's earned income, up to the maximum of $22,450. If you also have a registered pension plan (RPP) that your employer set up for you, your RRSP contribution limit will be reduced by **pension adjustment**, which is the total contributions made to your RPP plan by you and your employer in the previous year (if your RPP is a defined-contribution plan), or the deemed value of your pension earned in the previous year (if your RPP is a defined-benefit plan). The limit is also reduced by contributions into a deferred profit-sharing plan (DPSP). Any contributions over the limit are nondeductible and there is a penalty of 1% per month if the over-contributions exceed $2,000.

Practice Question   *In 2010, you made $50,000 in wages and $7,000 in overtime pay. You also had interest and dividend income of $1,000 and $750, respectively. You paid $500 in professional dues. Your pension adjustment for the year was $4,500. How much can you contribute to your RRSP for 2011?*

First, we calculate your earned income. According to its definition, your earned income for 2010 is:

$$50,000 + 7,000 - 500 = 56,500,$$

where we note that investment income is not earned income. Next, the contribution limit for 2011 is 18% of previous year's earned income but not exceeding $22,450;

$$\min\{(56,500 \cdot 18\%), (22,450)\} = \min\{(10,170), (22,450)\} = 10,170.$$

From this amount, we will subtract your pension adjustment. As a result, the limit for your 2011 RRSP contribution is $10,170 - $4,500 = $5,670.

If you do not contribute up to your limit, the unused contribution room can be carried forward to later years. In fact, it may not be wise to contribute the maximum if you know that your tax rate next year will be higher (and so your contribution, which reduces your taxable income, will have a greater benefit).

An RRSP can be off-the-shelf or self-directed. **Off-the-shelf** RRSPs are prepackaged plans offered by banks and mutual fund companies where the investment inside the plans are preselected – typically safe assets (e.g., GICs, savings a/c) or mutual funds. In contrast, **self-directed** plans allow you to control the choice of investments in the plans. You can choose to put any of the **eligible investments** in the plans. Eligible investments include (i) cash or near cash (e.g., savings a/c); (ii) government and corporate bonds; (iii) stocks, eligible mutual funds, and exchange-traded funds (ETFs); (iv) life insurance and life annuities; and (v) investment-grade (physical) gold and silver. Assets that are not eligible include jewelry and real estates.

Any income earned on investments inside an RRSP will not be taxed until it is withdrawn. As mentioned before, any amount withdrawn from an RRSP is taxed as ordinary income.

Practice Question   *You have an excess income of $1,000 (pre-tax) that you want to invest in a guaranteed investment certificate (GIC) for five years. If you invest it inside your RRSP and then withdraw all the proceeds after five years, how much will you get after-tax? Assume that your current marginal tax rate for ordinary income is 39% and will remain the same for the foreseeable future. Also, the interest rate is 5% p.a., annual compounding.*

Because investment income earned inside an RRSP is not taxed until the investment is withdrawn from the plan, your investment will grow at the pre-tax rate of 5% p.a., annual compounding. After five years, you will have:

$$1,000 \cdot 1.05^5 = 1,276.28.$$

Then, when you withdraw it from the plan, you will have to pay tax on the whole amount at your marginal tax rate. Hence, the after-tax proceeds will be:

$$1,276.28 \cdot (1 - 0.39) = 778.53.$$

Practice Question   *Based on the previous example, suppose you want to invest your (pre-tax) income in the same GIC, but leave it outside your RRSP. How much will you have after five years?*

Because you are going to invest outside a tax-deferring account, you have to do it with after-tax money. You have to pay tax on the $1,000 pre-tax income that you have first. At your marginal tax rate, the after-tax amount of the income is $610. In addition, you will have to pay tax every year on the income earned on the investment. In other words, your investment will grow at an after-tax rate, which is:

$$5\% \cdot (1 - 0.39) = 3.05\% \text{ p.a.}$$

After five years, you will have:

$$610 \cdot 1.0305^5 = 708.88,$$

which is already free of tax, as you have already paid it along the way.

Note that you get more if you put this investment inside your RRSP. The difference in the proceeds can be attributed to two reasons. First, if you invest inside your RRSP, you can invest the whole pre-tax amount, and so the principal amount of the investment is different between inside and outside your RRSP ($1,000 vs. $610). The larger investment base inside the RRSP allows you to generate more income. Secondly, inside the RRSP, you do not have to pay tax on the investment income, and so the investment is compounded at a higher rate.

As mentioned earlier, the tax treatment on a withdrawal from an RRSP is the same regardless of the type of investment income earned inside the plan. For example, suppose instead that the investment in the previous example is not a GIC, but rather an equity investment whose return is in the form of capital gains. The investment appreciates in value at the rate of 5% p.a., annual compounding. The after-tax amount that you will get after five years if you put this investment inside your RRSP is the same $778.53. On the other hand, if you put it outside your RRSP, the amount that you will get can be calculated as follows.

Practice Question *Suppose the investment in the previous example generates returns (i.e., 5% p.a., annual compounding) in the form of capital gains. How much will you have after five years if the investment is done outside your RRSP?*

As you know from before, only 50% of capital gains are taxed. Note, however, that the gains will not be taxed until you sell the investment, which is after five years. So, the investment will grow at the 5% p.a. rate over five years to yield a pre-tax value of:

$$610 \cdot 1.05^5 = 778.53,$$

which translates to a capital gain of $778.53 − $610 = $168.53. Only half of this gain is taxed, and so the after-tax proceeds are:

$$778.53 - (168.53 \cdot .50 \cdot .39) = 745.67.$$

The difference in the after-tax proceeds between inside and outside an RRSP in this case is not as large as when the investment generates interest income. So, if you are investing in a variety of investments, put those that generate interest income in your RRSP first. The tax-deferring benefit for them is greatest.

Finally, we conclude with one important practical matter. Note from the previous examples that in our comparisons of after-tax investment returns between inside and outside an RRSP, we used the before-tax money to invest inside an RRSP and the after-tax money to invest outside it. Such comparisons are proper and correct. However, you may wonder that in practice, we normally do not have access to pre-tax money. For example, when your employer pays your wages, they will withhold income taxes and pay you the after-tax amount. Only after you contribute some amount into your RRSP (and thus can deduct that amount from your total income when filing a tax return) will you get a refund on the tax withheld on that amount back (and with some time lag). A contribution into an RRSP is also made with after-tax money.

One way to get around the problem is to ask your employer and Canada Revenue Agency to agree to reduce the amount of the income taxes withheld. To do so, you will need to file a form (T1213 – Request to Reduce Tax Deductions at Source), informing them of the intention to make regular contributions into your RRSP. You will also need to submit proof that you have arranged a preauthorized contribution plan with your bank or your broker. In this case, your employer will not withhold the income tax on the amount that you intend to contribute, and the whole before-tax amount will be put into your RRSP under the preauthorized plan by your bank or broker. The effect of this is that you are indeed investing in your RRSP with before-tax money.

For example, suppose your marginal tax rate is 39% and you file the form to indicate that you will contribute $1,000 of your pre-tax income into your RRSP every month. In this case, your employer will not withhold any income tax on that $1,000, and the amount will go directly into your RRSP.

If you somehow choose not to file that form, $390 will be withheld as income taxes by your employer, and you only get the after-tax amount (i.e., $610) that you can contribute into your RRSP. In this case, what you have to keep in mind is that you have to account for all the tax refunds that this $610 can generate. Consider the following thought exercise:

You now have $610. You put it into your RRSP. This entitles you to a tax refund of $610 · 0.39 = $237.90.

Knowing that you have this refund coming, you immediately contribute another \$237.90 into your RRSP. This contribution entitles you to a tax refund of $\$237.90 \cdot 0.39 = \$92.78$.

Again, knowing that you have \$92.78 in refund coming, you immediately contribute another \$92.78 into your RRSP. This contribution entitles you to a tax refund of $\$92.78 \cdot 0.39 = \$36.18$.

Repeat this process *ad infinitum*. The total amount of refunds that you will get is \$390. This amount, together with the original contribution of \$690, means that you are eventually contributing the pre-tax amount of income.

The point is that when you want to make a comparison between investing inside and outside a tax-deferring account, you need to start with the proper amounts of principals for the two choices. This is so that the two principals are consistent with each other. Here is a simple rule based on our discussion.

$$\text{Pre-tax Amount} = \frac{\text{After-tax amount}}{1 - \text{marginal tax rate}}.$$

It is easy to verify that the after-tax amount of \$690 is equal to the pre-tax amount of \$1,000 at the marginal tax rate of 39%.

6.3.3 Tax-Free Savings Accounts (TFSAs)

In addition to tax-deferring accounts such as RRSPs, some countries also offer tax-free savings/investment accounts. For example, the United States has Roth IRAs while Canada has Tax-Free Savings Accounts (TFSAs). The major difference between these accounts and the tax-deferred accounts discussed earlier is that any income put into Roth IRAs and TFSAs in any tax year is not exempted from tax in that year. Contributions into these accounts are made from after-tax income. However, any earnings on the investment inside these accounts will never be taxed. When you withdraw part or all of the money from these accounts, you will not have to pay tax on the withdrawn amount (because you already paid taxes on the principal, and any income on it is not taxed).

A TFSA can be set up through a bank, a credit union, a brokerage firm, and other financial institutions. The maximum annual contribution is \$5,000. This limit is indexed to inflation in \$500 increments. Contributions can be made in cash or in kind, and any unused contribution room can be carried forward indefinitely.

Any resident of Canada aged eighteen and older can open a TFSA account. Note that it is not necessary to have income in order to do so. The types of investment allowed in a TFSA is the same as in an RRSP (e.g., GICs, bonds, publicly traded stocks, mutual funds, etc.).

Withdrawals from the account can be made at any time. Every time you withdraw an amount, your contribution room in the following year will be increased by that amount (see the following example). Withdrawals from a TFSA are not considered an income. Consequently, they will not affect your eligibility for income-tested benefits and tax credits.

Practice Question   *In 2010, Peter contributed $2,000 into his TFSA and used the money to buy a stock. In 2011, Peter does not make a contribution. Rather, he sells the investment for $2,500 and withdraws the proceeds. What is his contribution room for 2012?*

Peter has an unused room of $3,000 from 2010. Therefore, the contribution room for 2011 is $8,000. He does not make any contribution in 2011, and so this contribution room is carried over to 2012. For 2012, he will get an additional contribution room of $5,000. In addition, the $2,500 that he withdraws in 2011 will increase his 2012 contribution limit by the same amount. As a result, the total contribution room for 2012 is $8,000 + $5,000 + $2,500 = $15,500.

6.3.4 RRSPs vs. TFSAs

With the existence of both RRSPs and TFSAs, you may wonder which plan is better. The answer depends primarily on your marginal tax rates when contributing into the plans vs. when withdrawing from the plans. Consider the following example.

Practice Question   *You have an excess income of $20,000 (pre-tax) that you want to invest in a savings account for twenty years (by which time you will have retired). The interest rate is 4% p.a., annual compounding. Should you invest it in your RRSP or TFSA? Assume that your current marginal tax rate for ordinary income is 30%.*

If you use your TFSA, you have to pay tax on the excess income first. At your current marginal tax rate, the after-tax amount of the income is $14,000. After twenty years, this amount will grow to:

$$14,000 \cdot 1.04^{20} = 30,675.72,$$

which is already free from tax.

On the other hand, if you invest it in your RRSP, the pre-tax proceeds after twenty years will be:

$$20{,}000 \cdot 1.04^{20} = 43{,}822.46.$$

How much you will get after-tax depends on what your marginal rate will be twenty years from now. If it will be greater than 30%, you will get less under the RRSP choice (remember that any amount that you withdraw from your RRSP is subject to tax). If it remains the same, the two choices are equivalent. Finally, if it will be lower than 30%, RRSP is a better choice.

On the surface, it seems sensible to assume that people's marginal tax rates should be lower during their retirement. After all, they no longer work and so have no employment income. However, the reality is not as straightforward as that. This is because any amount withdrawn from an RRSP has to be declared as income, while a TFSA withdrawal has no tax implication (because the principal comes from after-tax money and the income earned on it is not taxed). This difference is significant because any income that you have during retirement can trigger clawbacks on income-tested governmental benefits such as Old Age Security (OAS) payments and Guaranteed Income Supplements (GIS). In addition, as you have seen before, age tax credits can also be rolled back. As a result, it is not just the marginal tax rate, as determined by the level of income, that you have to worry about. You also need to think about the amounts of those income-tested benefits and credits that you would lose if you have income.

For this reason, financial planners have come up with the term **marginal effective tax rate** (METR). It is defined as the tax rate that reflects the true effect of an additional dollar of the taxable income. The true effect includes not only the federal and provincial taxes that you have to pay on it, but also the amount of reduction in benefits and tax credits that one dollar of additional income would cause. For example, suppose your pension income during retirement is at such a level that your marginal tax rate (not METR) is 20%. That is, if you get one more dollar of income, you will have to pay $0.20 as tax to the two levels of governments. If that one additional dollar causes your governmental benefits to decline by $0.25, then it means that the true effect of it is $0.45, and thus the METR is 45%. This is the rate that you should use when you compare RRSP with TFSA.

To calculate your METR, you need to know the details of all the income-tested benefits and tax credits and their clawback rules. We will not get into their details in this book. Keep in mind, however, that the decision between RRSP and TFSA can be more involved that it appears.

Practically speaking, we propose that people should hold both an RRSP and a TFSA. This is because there is always a risk that the tax brackets in the future can change substantially from the current ones. If it happens, the decisions that you make based on your current analyses can be far from optimal. By diversifying your tax-sheltering investment, you will be better prepared for any eventualities.

6.4 Questions and Assignments

1. Assume that you live in Ontario and earned $100,000 (in salary income) during the tax year 2011. Assume that you have no deductions or credits other than your basic personal amount. Compute the total amount of federal tax and provincial tax that you owe. What is your average tax rate? What is your marginal tax rate?

2. Based on question 1, assume that you contributed $15,000 to a Registered Retirement Savings Plan (RRSP) and you made charitable contributions (donations) totaling $2,000 in 2011. Assume also that you are married. Your spouse does not work and only has investment income of $3,000 in 2011. What is the total amount you owe in federal and provincial taxes?

3. Your salary income in 2011 is $110,000. Assume for simplicity that you have no deductions and that you only have basic personal tax credits. Assume also that you have a dividend income of $5,000. What is the amount of income tax (federal and Ontario) that you have to pay? How much of that total is due to the dividend income? What is your marginal tax rate on dividend income?

4. Ruth is going to invest $5,000 a year at the end of each year for the next twenty-five years. The investment will be done in a regular investment account (i.e., no tax deferral), and will accrue capital gains at the (before-tax) rate of 6% p.a., annual compounding. Suppose that she will sell her entire investment after twenty-five years (i.e., immediately after the last investment is made). Suppose also that her marginal income tax rate is 30%. How much money (after-tax) will Ruth have after twenty-five years?

5. Consider a couple who are both seventy years old. The husband has a pension income of $20,000 per year, while the wife has a pension income of $60,000 per year. What are the amounts of income taxes (federal and Ontario) that they have to pay? Assume that they have no deductions, but that they are eligible for the categories of tax credits as mentioned in this chapter.

6. Based on question 5, suppose the wife assigns $20,000 of her pension income to her husband (so that they now both have $40,000 in pension income). What are the amounts of income taxes that they have to pay?

7. What would be the total amount of (federal plus provincial) tax savings if you could split your income this way? (Note: You cannot quite do this given current tax law in Canada. This is a hypothetical question.)

8. Assume that you invest $F = \$20,000$ (your financial capital) in a "tax-sheltered" mutual fund that earns $v = 8\%$ (effective) per year where you do not have to pay any income taxes until you withdraw the money from the investment account in $N = 15$ years. It is only when you withdraw the funds (after fifteen years) that you must pay income tax on all your investment gains at the "ordinary income" rate of $TAX_{oi} = 46\%$. Are you better off (i.e., have more money after fifteen years) under a "continuously taxable" structure in which you must pay capital gains taxes at the (lower) rate of $TAX_{cg} = 23\%$ every single year?

9. Based on question 8, what is the break-even horizon (N) at which the tax shelter is better/worse than the continuously taxable structure?

10. What must your marginal tax rate be at the time you retire in order for it to be more worth it to put your savings into RRSP instead of TFSA? Assume you currently earn $100,000, have $10,000 of deductibles each year, and $5,000 of tax credit each year.

SEVEN

Risk, Utility, and Insurance

Learning Objectives

In our day-to-day life, we face many risks. We can get sick or injured. We may get into an accident while we are driving to work. A fire or a flood can damage our houses. If that does not happen, someone may break into our houses and steal our belongings. In addition, we face the risk from not knowing exactly how long we will live. We may live shorter or longer than expected. If the former, our dependents may suffer from lack of financial support. If the latter, we may run out of retirement money. The list goes on. When these unpleasant events happen, their negative effects on our physical and/or financial well-being can be substantial.

Traditionally, there are insurance products that people can buy to manage these risks. In this chapter, we discuss the theoretical foundation of insurance. We look at insurance from both the buyers' and sellers' perspectives. Specifically, we want to determine when insurance should be used and how it is priced. In the process, we formalize the concepts of risks and people's attitudes toward them. The understanding from this chapter will be helpful to our discussion of life insurance in the next chapter.

7.1 The Concepts of Risk and Risk Preferences

7.1.1 Definition of Risk

Although there is no single, universally accepted definition of **risk**, a common one defines it as the variation in possible outcomes of an event that is subject to chance. The greater the variation, the more risky the event is. Risk can be classified into two distinct categories – speculative risk and pure risk. **Speculative risk** involves events in which either a gain or a loss is possible. Generally, people take speculative risk by choice. For example, when you choose to buy a stock or a lottery, you know that you may make money (if the stock price increases or if your lottery numbers come up in the drawing), or you may lose (if the stock price declines or if other lottery numbers are drawn). On the other hand, **pure risk** involves events that can result in either a loss or no change (i.e., there is no possibility of a gain). Examples of pure risk are risk of injury, illness, or premature death, risk of accidents, and risk of property damages. Generally, people do not take pure risk by choice.

The distinction between speculative risk and pure risk is important. This is because traditional insurance products primarily cover pure risk. Because people do not take pure risk by choice, it is easier to have a large enough pool of people so that the **law of large numbers** can be used to estimate future losses. As we will see shortly, insurance companies typically use this law to figure out expected losses and the appropriate premiums to charge. In addition, because people take speculative risk by choice, the chance (i.e., frequency) of losses will be higher than with pure risk (which people would do whatever they can to minimize). Again, as we will see, insurance premiums depend on the frequency of losses. If the frequency is high, the premiums will be too expensive to be economically viable.

7.1.2 Risk Preferences

Different people have different attitudes toward risk. Although the vast majority of people do not like it, there are those who do not care about it or even want to take it. More precisely, economists have classified people according to their attitudes toward risk into three groups – risk-averse, risk-neutral, and risk-loving. **Risk aversion** is formally defined as an unwillingness to accept a **fair gamble**. A fair gamble is typically defined as one whose expected payoff is equal to its cost. Suppose, for example, that we offer you (at no charge) the following coin-tossing game. You toss a fair coin. If it comes out heads, we give you $10,000. However, if it comes out tails, you have to give us $10,000. Because the coin is fair, the chance of heads or tails is 50-50, and so the expected payoff of this game is zero. Because we do not charge you anything to play this game, it is a fair gamble. Would you accept it?

Whenever people are asked this question, virtually everyone would decline the offer. Therefore, based on the definition of risk aversion, we can say that these people are risk-averse. Recall that risk is defined as the variation in possible outcomes. If they do not take the gamble, their wealth will remain the same for sure. If they take the gamble, their wealth will either decline or increase by $10,000, but the expected change is zero. If they take the gamble, there are now two possible outcomes but their wealth is *expected* to remain the same. Basically, these people were asked to choose between a sure wealth and an uncertain wealth whose expected value is the same as the sure wealth. As a result, people who do not like variations in outcomes will decline the offer.

Obviously, there are various degrees of risk aversion among risk-averse people. Some are more averse to uncertain outcomes than others are. As we will see, how risk-averse they are will determine whether they will buy insurance to protect themselves against risks.

Risk-neutral people do not care about risk. All they care about is the expected value of the outcome. The variation in the possible outcomes does not matter to them. If offered this gamble, they would be indifferent between accepting and declining it. The indifference comes from the fact that the gamble results in an expected wealth that is the same as the sure wealth. Finally, **risk-loving** people like to take risk. They will always accept a fair gamble.

In this chapter, we concentrate our attention on risk-averse people (i.e., virtually everyone). We will shortly talk about insurance premiums and whether, given the premiums, risk-averse people should buy insurance.

7.2 The Concept of Insurance

Insurance is based on the premise that a large-enough pool of people who face similar (although not necessarily identical) risk can be created so that the losses incurred by a few can be spread over the entire pool. For example, suppose 10,000 homeowners somehow manage to get together and agree that if anyone's house burns down, the rest of the group will cover the loss to that unlucky homeowner. Suppose also that each house costs $300,000 and based on past occurrences, one out of every 1,000 houses is expected to burn down in a given year (i.e., probability is 0.001). So, every year, ten houses in the group are expected to be lost, and the expected total loss will be $3 million. By forming a pool, this loss can be spread over the entire group, and so each of the 10,000 homeowners will have to pay only $300 per year. Note that $300 per year is also the expected loss per person as can be calculated by multiplying the cost of the house by the probability of a fire.

In practice, insurance companies are intermediaries who form pools of risk-averse people with similar risk. These companies will collect **insurance premiums** from everyone in the pool and pay them out as compensation to those who suffer the loss. To be sustainable, insurance companies must be able to predict future losses with accuracy so that they can charge proper premiums. To this end, they rely on the law of large numbers, which states that as the number of *independent* trials of a random experiment increases, the average of the results obtained from those trials should be closer and closer to the expected value. For example, if you keep tossing a fair coin, the percentage of heads turning up should be closer and closer to 50%. In our context, this means that the number of people in the pool must be large enough that the actual number of houses damaged per year approaches the expected number. Otherwise, large deviations can occur and there may not be enough money in the pool to pay for the losses.

Obviously, deviations can still occur even with a reasonably large pool. There can be years where losses are less than expected, in which case insurance companies will keep the unused premiums. The unused premiums from these years will be paid out in years where losses are larger than expected. Over the long run, insurance companies will learn from experience and adjust the probability of loss (and thus the premiums that they will charge) accordingly.

Practice Question *Suppose an insurance company wants to insure the* 10,000 *homeowners. As before, one out of every* 1,000 *houses is expected to burn down in a given year. Each house costs* $300,000. *The company wants to have a* 15% *charge to cover its expenses and make profit. What will be the premium?*

As discussed before, the insurance company is expected to pay $3 million every year as compensation. Therefore, without factoring in the required profits, the premium must be $300 per person. Otherwise, there would not be enough money in the pool to pay the expected compensation. With the required 15% profit, the total premium collected must be $3.45 million in total or $345 per person. This premium is higher than the expected loss per person, which is $300.

We want to emphasize that the premiums charged by insurance companies will have to be at least equal to the expected loss; otherwise the insurance pool cannot sustain itself. Because insurance companies also have expenses to cover and profits to make, the premiums will always be higher than the expected loss.

For insurance to work, there are three important things to keep in mind. First, the events have to be independent. That is, the occurrence of one does not affect the occurrence of another. If, for example, some of the houses in the insurance pool are located close together and one of them catches on fire, the chance that the others will burn increases. In this case, the occurrences are no longer independent, and the law of large numbers will not work properly.

Secondly, insurance will not work if there is **moral hazard**. Moral hazard refers to the carelessness or an indifference to a loss after the purchase of insurance.[1] Consider, for example, auto insurance. Drivers may drive less carefully once their cars are insured. If moral hazard is not minimized, the frequency and/or the severity of loss can increase to the point where insurance companies can no longer provide coverage. This is why insurance contracts include provisions that cause the insured to regret the loss even with the coverage. For example, the use of **deductible** requires the insured to pay the first specified dollar amount of loss before the insurance coverage begins. Alternatively, insurance premiums can be increased to penalize and discourage carelessness. For example, if a driver receives a speeding ticket, his or her premiums next year will go up. These mechanisms help to control moral hazard.

Thirdly, insurance can fail if there is **adverse selection**. Adverse selection occurs when there is asymmetric information between insurance companies and the insured. Specifically, the insured know more about their own risk than insurance companies do. If it is not possible for insurance companies to separate clients into different pools according to their risk, there will be only one big pool and insurance premiums will be based on the average risk of that big pool. People who know they have a higher risk than the average will buy the insurance, while those who have a lower risk than the average will consider it too expensive. Consequently, the pool will be populated mainly by high-risk people, and the premiums (which are set according to the average risk) will not be sufficient to cover the losses that will occur. Increasing the premiums will not help because it will drive away even more low-risk people.

One way to reduce adverse selection is to screen people. For example, it is common for the insured to be required to undergo a medical exam before getting the coverage. This is so that the insurance companies can have better information about the true state of the insured's health. Another way to handle adverse selection is to make the purchase of insurance mandatory for everyone, so that low-risk people cannot opt out.

---

[1] Our definition of moral hazard follows the conventional usage of the term in the economics literature. In the insurance literature, what we are referring to here is typically termed "morale hazard," while they use the term "moral hazard" to refer to dishonesty on the part of the insured that increases the probability or the severity of the losses (i.e., insurance fraud).

7.3 The Demand for Insurance

7.3.1 When Should People Buy Insurance?

As we alluded to earlier, life is inherently risky. The risks that we face in our daily life can be classified into three groups. They are personal risks, property risks, and liability risks. **Personal risks** include (i) risk of being sick, injured, or disabled; (ii) risk of unemployment; (iii) risk of premature death; and (iv) risk of not having enough income for retirement (which includes risk of living too long). **Property risks** are the risks of having our property (e.g., a car or a house) damaged or lost due to various causes such as theft, fire, flood, and natural disasters. **Liability risks** are the risks of being held legally liable if we do something that results in bodily injury or property damage to someone else (such as crashing a car into a neighbor's house).

Not all of these risks can be or need to be insured. Here are the criteria that must be satisfied for the purchase of insurance to be sensible:

1. The amount of the potential loss is substantial relative to your *liquid* financial capital (or liquid wealth). If the loss occurs, you will suffer economic hardship. For most people, the expenses due to a serious illness and the loss of a house (or even a car) are considered substantial and thus the risk needs to be managed.
2. The probability of a loss is low. As you saw in the previous section, insurance premiums are calculated based on the probability that losses can occur. If that probability is high, the premiums will be too expensive. Consider the earlier home insurance example. If the chance of a fire were one in every ten houses instead of one in every 1,000, the insurance premium per household would be $34,500 per year (expenses and profits included). This would cause the insurance to be beyond the affordability of most people.
3. The insurance premium must not exceed your **reservation price**, which is the maximum that you are willing to pay given the degree of your risk aversion. The more risk averse you are, the more you will be willing to pay to protect yourself.

Note that we use liquid financial capital (or liquid wealth) as a basis to decide whether people should be insured. Liquid financial capital is the portion of your financial capital (i.e., financial assets minus explicit liabilities; see Chapter 3) that can be converted to cash quickly. The reason why liquid financial capital (and not full financial capital or economic net worth, which includes human capital) should be used is that if a loss occurs,

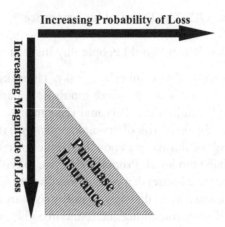

Figure 7.1. Amounts of Losses and Their Probabilities.

you will most likely need to have cash quickly to deal with the problem. In such a situation, assets that cannot be immediately converted to cash (e.g., a house or your human capital) are of little help. Borrowing is not a good option either because the amount of loss can be more than what banks are willing to lend. Also, in practice, the borrowing rate can be punitively high, especially if the loans are not secured. Consequently, for the rest of this chapter, the general term "wealth" or "net worth" will refer to liquid financial capital, unless we specify otherwise.

Figure 7.1 displays the graph between the amounts of losses and their probabilities. The shaded area is the region where getting insurance is recommended. As stated earlier, this is the area where the amounts of losses are high while their probabilities are low. In other words, this is the area where the potential losses are substantial, but their probabilities are low enough to make insurance premiums reasonable.

You should not buy insurance for events that are outside the shaded area. For example, suppose the probability of losses is high, but the amounts of losses are not very large. You would be better off budgeting for the losses by setting money aside (self-insuring). To insure them would require considerable premium payments relative to the sizes of the losses, which effectively means that you would be prepaying those losses.

7.3.2 How Much Should You Pay for Insurance?

In this subsection, we talk about how you can determine your reservation price for insurance. To do so, we need a theoretical framework that can relate the amounts of potential losses, their probabilities, and your degree of risk aversion, to a reservation price. We will use the concept of **utility of wealth**. Utility is a measure of how satisfied (or happy) you are at various levels of wealth. For example, suppose we ask you to give us numbers that reflect how satisfied you will be if your wealth is $1, $10, $100, $1,000, $10,000, and so on. There are no restrictions on what the numbers can be except that they have to be consistent with one another. If you prefer more wealth to less wealth (as virtually everyone does), the number corresponding to a higher level of wealth must be greater than the one for a lower level of wealth. Note that each number by itself is not meaningful. It is when we compare them (i.e., their relative values) that we have a sense of what your preferences are as wealth changes. Based on the numbers that you give us, we can come up with a **utility function** that approximately reflects your preferences. This function relates the different levels of wealth to the numbers that you give.

The exercise that we have described has been done numerous times in the economics literature. Based on their results, economists came up with common functions that represent people's preferences. For risk-averse people, one of the most common functions is the so-called power utility function, which has the following form:

$$u(W) = \begin{cases} \frac{W^{(1-\gamma)}-1}{1-\gamma} & \gamma > 0, \gamma \neq 1 \\ \ln(W) & \gamma = 1, \end{cases} \tag{7.1}$$

where W is the amount of (liquid) wealth and γ is a parameter that reflects your degree of risk aversion. For risk-averse people, the parameter γ takes on a value greater than zero. The more risk-averse you are, the higher is γ.

Note that the function can take on one of two forms, depending on whether or not γ is equal to one. When $\gamma = 1$, the function takes the form of a natural log function. We also want to emphasize that this function is not the only one that can be used to represent preferences of risk-averse people. There are others, but this function is one of the most common ones.[2]

To get an idea of what the function looks like, let us plug some values into it. For the purpose of illustration, we assume that your risk-aversion parameter is $\gamma = 1$. As a result, your utility function is the logarithmic function. Table 7.1 displays your utility at different levels of wealth. Note from the values in the table that while your utility increases with wealth (as it should be because you prefer more to less), the rate of increase is not constant. Rather, the increase is slowing down as you become wealthier.

---

[2] For those who are interested in learning more about various forms of utility functions, please refer to Chapters 13 and 14.

Table 7.1. *Utility at different
levels of wealth,*
$U(W) = \ln(W)$

Wealth	Utility
$100	4.6052
$1,000	6.9078
$5,000	8.5172
$10,000	9.2103
$40,000	10.5966
$50,000	10.8198
$60,000	11.0021
$100,000	11.5129
$500,000	13.1224
$1,000,000	13.8155

Source: Author Calculations.

This means that as you become richer, the satisfaction (or happiness) from getting more money (say, one more dollar) is less and less. Economists term this observation **diminishing marginal utility**. The utility from getting the next dollar is less than from getting the previous dollar. If you plot the relationship between wealth and utility in a graph, you get a picture like the one in Figure 7.2. The line is concave because of diminishing marginal utility.

The property that marginal utility is diminishing is very important and is common to every risk-averse person, regardless of what utility function represents his or her preferences. To see the connection between risk aversion and diminishing marginal utility, recall from earlier that risk aversion is defined as an unwillingness to accept a fair gamble. Consider again the

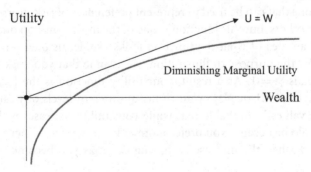

Figure 7.2. Utility of Wealth.

coin-tossing game. You were asked to toss a fair coin. If it comes out heads, we would give you \$10,000. If it comes out tails, you would have to give us \$10,000. Suppose that your current wealth is \$50,000. Suppose also that you are risk-averse and that your preferences can be represented by the natural log utility function (i.e., $\gamma = 1$). If you accept this gamble, your wealth could end up at either \$40,000 or \$60,000 with equal probabilities. If you do not take the gamble, your wealth will remain at \$50,000.

How do you decide? You will compare the utility (or satisfaction) that you will get under the two courses of action. If you do not accept the gamble, you will have a sure \$50,000, which, according to Table 7.1, translates to a utility (or happiness) level of $\ln(50,000) = 10.8198$. On the other hand, if you take the gamble, your wealth can be either \$40,000 (which translates to a utility level of $\ln(40,000) = 10.5966$) or \$60,000 (which translates to a utility level of 11.0021). You can then calculate the expected value of the utility. Because the two possible outcomes have the same chance of happening, the expected utility from taking the gamble is then:

$$0.50 \cdot 10.5966 + 0.50 \cdot 11.0021 = 10.7994.$$

Because the expected utility from the gamble (10.7994) is less than the utility in the case that you do nothing (10.8198), you decline the gamble.

Note that the result is driven by the fact that your marginal utility is diminishing. At your current wealth level of \$50,000, the gain in utility from getting \$10,000 (i.e., if you accept the gamble and heads comes up in the toss) is:

$$11.0021 - 10.8198 = 0.1823.$$

This is less than the loss in utility from losing the same dollar amount (i.e., \$10,000) if tails comes up, which is:

$$10.5966 - 10.8198 = -0.2232.$$

Because the possible gain in utility is less than the possible loss in utility, you decline the gamble.

We want to emphasize that diminishing marginal utility is not specific to the natural log function that we used. As long as people are risk averse, they will have diminishing marginal utility, which will lead them to refuse a fair gamble, regardless of the forms of their utility functions.

Now that you understand how risk aversion affects your decision making, let us apply it to the decisions to buy insurance and the calculations of reservations prices for insurance. The logic of the analysis will be the same as before, which is that you compare the utility from a sure level of wealth to the expected utility from possible outcomes under risk.

Practice Question *You were recently approached by an insurance salesman. He wants to sell you flood insurance at a price (i.e., premium) of $250 per year. The chance of flooding in your area in any given year is about 1%. If a flood occurs, you estimate that the damage to your house will be approximately $20,000. Suppose your current (liquid) net worth is $100,000, and that your risk-aversion parameter is $\gamma = 1$ (i.e., natural log utility function). Should you buy this insurance?*

You are again comparing two courses of action. First, if you do not buy the insurance, your wealth will be uncertain. If a flood does not occur, your wealth will remain at the current level of $100,000. If a flood occurs, you will need to spend $20,000 to fix the damage, and so your wealth will decline to $80,000. Secondly, if you buy the insurance, your wealth will for sure be $100,000 minus the insurance premium of $250. Your wealth will decline to $99,750, and that is where it will remain regardless of whether or not a flood occurs.

Because there is a 1% chance that a flood will occur in any given year, the expected utility in case you do not buy the insurance is:

$$0.99 \cdot \ln(100,000) + 0.01 \cdot \ln(80,000) = 11.5107,$$

while the utility of a sure $99,750 in case you buy the insurance is:

$$\ln(99,750) = 11.5104.$$

Because the expected utility in case you do not buy the insurance is greater than the utility in case you get the coverage, you do not accept the insurance.[3]

There are two important things to note from the example. First, the gamble that you face in this case does not have an upside outcome. In other words, the risk here is pure risk rather than speculative risk. If you do not buy the insurance, you are taking a risk that will lead to either no change or a decline in your wealth. Based on that, we want to know whether you want to pay the insurance premium to get rid of the risk. Although the nature of the gamble is slightly different from the one in the coin-tossing example, the approach that we used is the same as before. Secondly, based on the result of the analysis, you forgo the insurance even though you are risk-averse. This

---

[3] Note the importance of using more than two decimal points in your calculations.

is because the insurance premium is too high considering the potential loss, its probability, your current wealth, and your risk-aversion parameter. We examine the effects of some of these factors on your decision in a moment. For now, we want to know how much the insurance premium has to be in order for you to consider buying the coverage.

Practice Question *Based on the previous example, what is your reservation price (i.e., the maximum that you are willing to pay) for the premium?*

Let I_{max} be the maximum premium that you are willing to pay. I_{max} must be such that the utility of your wealth after subtracting this premium is equal to the expected utility if you do not buy the insurance.

$$\ln\left(100{,}000 - I_{max}\right) = 0.99 \cdot \ln\left(100{,}000\right) + 0.01 \cdot \ln\left(80{,}000\right)$$
$$= 11.5107.$$

To solve for I_{max}, we take the exponential of both sides.

$$\exp\left[\ln\left(100{,}000 - I_{max}\right)\right] = \exp\left[11.5107\right]$$

or

$$100{,}000 - I_{max} = \exp\left[11.5107\right],$$

which leads to:

$$I_{max} = 100{,}000 - \exp\left[11.5107\right]$$
$$= 100{,}000 - 99{,}777.1052 = 222.8948.$$

So, \$222.8948 is your reservation price for the insurance premium. If the premium is less than \$222.8948, you will buy the insurance; otherwise, you take the risk. Note that even though the expected value of the loss is $0.99 \cdot \$0 + 0.01 \cdot \$20{,}000 = \$200$, you will be willing to pay more than that for the insurance. This is because you are risk-averse and so want to get rid of the risk. Also, note from the last step of the calculations that I_{max} is simply your current wealth (\$100,000) minus the exponential of the expected utility in case you do not buy insurance ($\exp[11.5107]$).

7.3.3 The Effect of Current Wealth on Insurance Decisions

We now want to know if your decision whether or not to buy insurance is influenced by your current level of wealth. Consider the next example.

Table 7.2. *Reservation prices at
different wealth levels,*
$U(W) = \ln(W)$

Wealth	Reservation price
$30,000	$327.7799
$40,000	$276.3002
$50,000	$254.7616
$75,000	$232.2558
$100,000	$222.8948
$150,000	$214.4978
$200,000	$210.6101
$300,000	$206.9072
$500,000	$204.0683
$1,000,000	$202.0067

Source: Author Calculations.

Practice Question *Based on the previous example, suppose that your current
wealth is $40,000. What is your reservation price for the premium?*

In this case, your wealth is now $40,000. If you do not insure, your wealth
may remain at the same level (with 0.99 probability) or decline to $20,000
(with 0.01 probability). The equation becomes:

$$\ln(40,000 - I_{max}) = 0.99 \cdot \ln(40,000) + 0.01 \cdot \ln(20,000)$$
$$= 10.5897.$$

As before, taking the exponential of both sides and solving for I_{max}, we have:

$$I_{max} = 40,000 - \exp[10.5897]$$
$$= 276.3002.$$

Note that the maximum premium that you are willing to pay in this case
is $276.3002, which is higher than when your current wealth is $100,000.
Therefore, if the insurance agent wants to charge $250, you will buy the
insurance.

We repeat these calculations at various levels of current wealth. The
reservation prices at those different levels are shown in Table 7.2.

As Table 7.2 shows, the higher your current wealth is, the less you will be
willing to pay for insurance. For example, when your wealth is $1,000,000,
I_{max} is only about $202, which is only slightly higher than the expected
value of the loss (i.e., $200). The reason for this is that as you become more

wealthy, the potential loss of a fixed dollar amount (i.e., $20,000 in this case) becomes less and less significant. The decline in utility from such a loss is smaller and smaller. Again, this is driven by diminishing marginal utility (which, as we have seen, is implied by risk aversion). The richer you are, the smaller the change is in your utility from any change (positive or negative) in wealth. On the other hand, when you do not have a lot, the same amount of potential loss has more impact, and so you are willing to pay more to protect whatever you now have.

7.3.4 The Effect of Risk-Aversion Parameter on Insurance Decisions

Next, we want to know how your degree of risk aversion affects your insurance decisions. So far, we have assumed that your risk-aversion parameter, γ, is equal to one. This is why we have been using the natural logarithmic utility function, which, if you recall, is only a special case of the more general power utility function. We will now repeat the analyses, but this time with other values for γ. Recall that the more risk-averse you are, the higher is the value of γ.

To do so, we use the following, more general form of the function (when $\gamma \neq 1$),

$$u(W) = \frac{W^{(1-\gamma)} - 1}{1 - \gamma}.$$

Practice Question *Suppose once again that you were recently offered flood insurance. The chance of flooding in your area in any given year is about 1%. If a flood occurs, you estimate that the damage to your house will be approximately $20,000. Suppose your current net worth is $100,000, and that your risk-aversion parameter is $\gamma = 2$. What is the maximum premium that you are willing to pay?*

We follow the same logic as before, which is that you compare the utility from a sure level of wealth to the expected utility from possible outcomes under risk. As before, let I_{max} be the maximum premium that you are willing to pay. The utility in case you buy the insurance is:

$$u(100,000 - I_{max}) = \frac{(100,000 - I_{max})^{(1-2)} - 1}{1 - 2}$$
$$= 1 - (100,000 - I_{max})^{-1}$$
$$= 1 - \frac{1}{100,000 - I_{max}},$$

Table 7.3. *Reservation prices at different levels of risk aversion*

Gamma	Reservation price
0.00	$200.0000
0.50	$211.0342
1.00	$222.8948
2.00	$249.3766
5.00	$357.1399
10.00	$692.1564

Source: Author Calculations.

while the expected utility in case you are not insured is:

$$0.99 \cdot u(100,000) + 0.01 \cdot u(80,000)$$
$$= 0.99 \cdot \frac{100,000^{(1-2)} - 1}{1 - 2} + 0.01 \cdot \frac{80,000^{(1-2)} - 1}{1 - 2}$$
$$= 0.99 \cdot \left[1 - 100,000^{-1}\right] + 0.01 \cdot \left[1 - 80,000^{-1}\right]$$
$$= 0.99 \cdot \left[1 - \frac{1}{100,000}\right] + 0.01 \cdot \left[1 - \frac{1}{80,000}\right]$$
$$= 1 - \left[\frac{0.99}{100,000} + \frac{0.01}{80,000}\right].$$

Equating the two, we have:

$$1 - \frac{1}{100,000 - I_{max}} = 1 - \left[\frac{0.99}{100,000} + \frac{0.01}{80,000}\right].$$

Solving for I_{max}, we have $I_{max} = \$249.3766$.

Recall that when $\gamma = 1$ (i.e., logarithmic utility), I_{max} is $222.8948, which is less than in this case. If you are more risk-averse, you are willing to pay more to get rid of risk.

Table 7.3 displays the reservation prices under various values of γ. As the table shows, as long as you are risk-averse (i.e., $\gamma > 0$), your I_{max} will be greater than the expected value of the loss (i.e., $200). The more risk-averse you are, the higher your I_{max}.

If γ is equal to zero, the individuals are not risk-averse. Rather, they are risk-neutral. This is why their reservation price is equal to the expected value of the loss. Because risk-neutral individuals do not care about the variation in the outcomes, they will not pay more than $200 for the insurance.

7.3.5 Generalizations

So far, we have assumed that there are only two possible outcomes if you do not buy insurance – either no loss or some amount of loss. What if there are different degrees of loss that can occur? For example, suppose the damage caused by flooding can be moderate or serious. In this case, the logic of the analysis is still the same. You compare the utility from a sure level of wealth to the expected utility from possible outcomes under risk (regardless of how many outcomes there are).

Let us start with an example where we assume that your risk aversion parameter is $\gamma = 1$ (i.e., logarithmic utility).

Practice Question *Based on the previous example, suppose instead that the chance of serious flooding in any given year is 1%. If it occurs, the damage will be $20,000. In addition, there is a 4% chance of a mild flood, which will result in damage of $5,000. As a result, there is a 95% chance that no flood will occur. Assuming a natural log utility function, what is the maximum premium for you in this case?*

As before, I_{max} must be such that the utility of your wealth after subtracting the premium is equal to the expected utility if you do not buy the insurance, in which case there are now three possible outcomes. Your wealth may remain the same (with 0.95 probability), decline by $5,000 (with 0.04 probability) or decline by $20,000 (with 0.01 probability). As a result,

$$\ln(100,000 - I_{max}) = 0.95 \cdot \ln(100,000) + 0.04 \cdot \ln(95,000)$$
$$+ 0.01 \cdot \ln(80,000)$$
$$= 11.5086.$$

Taking the exponential of both sides and solving for I_{max}, we have:

$$I_{max} = 100,000 - \exp[11.5086]$$
$$= 427.4008.$$

Similar to the two-outcome case, I_{max} is equal to your current wealth ($100,000) minus the exponential of the expected utility in case you do not buy insurance ($\exp[11.5086]$). This enables us to write a general equation for I_{max} when there are m possible outcomes and when $\gamma = 1$ as:

$$I_{max} = W - \exp\left[\sum_{j=1}^{m} p_j \cdot \ln(W - L_j)\right], \qquad (7.2)$$

where L_j is the amount of loss if outcome j occurs and p_j is the probability of outcome j. Note that the amount in the exponential bracket is simply the expected utility over m possible outcomes.

When $\gamma \neq 1$, the more general power utility function is used and the equation for I_{max} takes the form:

$$I_{max} = W - \left(\sum_{j=1}^{m} p_j \cdot \left(W - L_j \right)^{1-\gamma} \right)^{\frac{1}{1-\gamma}}. \qquad (7.3)$$

Practice Question *Suppose instead that your risk-aversion parameter γ is 2. What is the maximum premium for you in this case?*

We will use equation(7.3) to calculate I_{max}.

$$I_{max} = 100,000 - \left(0.95 \cdot (100,000)^{1-2} + 0.04 \cdot (95,000)^{1-2} \right.$$
$$\left. + 0.01 \cdot (80,000)^{1-2} \right)^{\frac{1}{1-2}}$$
$$= 100,000 - \left(\frac{0.95}{100,000} + \frac{0.04}{95,000} + \frac{0.01}{80,000} \right)^{-1}$$
$$= 458.4152.$$

Comparing this premium to the one when $\gamma = 1$, we see again that if you are more risk-averse, the maximum amount that you are willing to pay for insurance is higher.

7.4 Insurance and Consumption Smoothing

Insurance can be used to offset losses if they occur. The purchase of insurance is consistent with the desire to smooth consumption. You do not want severe fluctuations in your standard of living that those potential losses can cause (remember that you should only insure against large losses).[4] This again goes back to the idea of risk aversion. You are willing to pay an insurance premium (and accept a small reduction in consumption/wealth now) to ensure that you would not lose more later.

However, as we have seen, this does not mean that you should always insure. When the amount of the potential loss is small, it will not cause a significant drop in your consumption plan. In addition, if the premium is

---

[4] Strictly speaking, you are smoothing your utility (of wealth) across different states of nature (rather than across time).

too expensive (i.e., the amount of reduction in consumption/wealth is too much), you will forgo insurance and take the risk. Ultimately, you have to consider two aspects of every potential loss. First, what is the probability this event will take place (very small, average, or very high)? Secondly, if the loss occurs, what is the magnitude of the disruption (very large, substantial, small, miniscule) to your smooth standard of living? Our proposition is that you should only insure events that have a potentially disruptive impact on your lifestyle, and only if they have a relatively low probability of occurring. For other events, you can create your own insurance reserve.

For example, consider some trivial risks that will not substantially disrupt your smooth lifestyle such as a snowstorm interfering with your vacation or your TV breaking down after the warranty period. Generally, we do not think that you should buy extended warranties or trip-cancellation insurance. This can save you quite a bit of money. At the same time, we suggest that you consider increasing deductibles (on the insurance that they should have) to the maximum allowed, which means that you will be liable for the first $1,000 (or so) of damage to your cars and the first $5,000 (or so) of damage to your house in the event of a storm, flood, or fire. The savings from this can be significant. For example, the difference between covering the first $500 of damage (the standard deductible on home insurance) and the first $5,000 in damage can be up to half of the usual premium. Most home insurance agents are actually quite reluctant to allow you to do this, and likely will make you sign repeatedly that you understand that the company would not cover the vast majority of the claims they usually receive. However, that is exactly the point. By asking the insurance company to cover only catastrophic losses, you are saving them from paying a claim 90% of the time. This results in a lower premium for you. In addition, you are signaling to them that you take much better care of the property (e.g., by having sufficient working smoke detectors and keeping doors locked). Knowing that you are thus a lower overall financial risk to them, they reduce the premium even further.

Practice Question *You were recently approached by an insurance salesman. He wants to sell you fire insurance (for your home). If a fire occurs, the damage can be either complete (in which case the amount of loss is $300,000) or partial (in which case the amount of loss is $50,000). In either case, you have to spend money equal to the amount of the loss to repair your house.*

You can choose two levels of deductible – either none or $5,000. If you choose no deductible, you will be classified by the insurance company as a "regular" client. According to the company's experience with "regular" customers, the chance that a fire will occur and the whole house will be lost in any given year is 0.05%, while the chance that the damage will be partial is 0.10%. These probabilities are the same as the probabilities for people who choose not to insure. Assume for simplicity that the premium that the company will charge is equal to the expected compensation that they have to pay (i.e., profits not taken into account). The premium in this case will be $200 per year.

If you choose a deductible of $5,000, you will be classified by the insurance company as a "low-risk" client. According to the company's experience with "low-risk" customers, the chance that a fire will occur and the whole house will be lost in any given year is 0.02%, while the chance that the damage will be partial is 0.05%. The premium that they will charge is the expected compensation (after subtracting the deductible), which is $81.50 per year.

Suppose your current (liquid) net worth is $350,000, and that your risk-aversion parameter is $\gamma = 1$ (i.e., natural log utility function). Should you buy the insurance? If so, which deductible would you choose?

First, if you do not buy the insurance, the expected utility is:

$$0.9985 \cdot \ln(350,000) + 0.0005 \cdot \ln(50,000)$$
$$+ 0.001 \cdot \ln(300,000) = 12.7646.$$

If you buy the insurance with no deductible, you have to pay a premium of $200 (and thus your wealth immediately afterwards will be $349,800). If a fire occurs, you will be fully compensated, and so your wealth remains the same. Your expected utility will be:

$$\ln(349,800) = 12.7651.$$

If you choose a $5,000 deductible, you have to pay a premium of $81.50 (and thus your wealth immediately afterwards will be $349,918.50). If a fire occurs, you suffer a loss of $5,000 (i.e., your deductible). Your expected utility will be:

$$0.9993 \cdot \ln(349,918.50) + 0.0002 \cdot \ln(344,918.50)$$
$$+ 0.0005 \cdot \ln(344,918.50) = 12.7654.$$

As a result, you choose to buy the fire insurance with a deductible of $5,000. This is the strategy that gives you the highest expected utility.

The amounts of money that you save can then be deposited in a dedicated account that will act as your "personal insurance reserve fund." This account will be used to cover those small losses if they occur. To do this properly, the fund must only be used for expenditures that would have been covered by insurance that you declined.

7.5 Questions and Assignments

1. You own a house with a market value of $400,000. You have $150,000 in your liquid wealth. Your risk-aversion parameter is $\gamma = 1$. There is a 1% chance that a flood will occur and cause $50,000 in damage in a given year. Assuming that insurance companies make a 15% profit, how much is the insurance premium?
2. Based on question 1, will you buy the insurance? What is the maximum premium that you are willing to pay (i.e., the reservation price)?
3. Again, based on question 1, how will the reservation price change if your liquid wealth is $100,000? Explain why there is a difference between the reservation price in this case and the one in question 2.
4. Repeat the calculations in questions 1 and 2 with an assumption that your risk-aversion parameter is $\gamma = 2$. Compare and contrast the results.
5. Assume that your liquid wealth is $100,000 and you own a car worth $35,000. Every month, there is a 0.10% chance that you will get into a car accident where the car will be totalled and so you need to buy a new car. There is also a 0.50% chance that a damage of $5,000 will occur. How much are you willing to pay for insurance if your risk-aversion parameter is $\gamma = 1$?
6. Suppose that your liquid wealth is $35,000. You have just bought a $5,000 all-inclusive vacation that you plan to take in December. The travel agent is trying to sell you trip-cancellation insurance. This insurance will reimburse all the money that you paid (i.e., $5,000) if it happens to snow heavily on your departure date (and so the plane cannot leave). Suppose that there is a 1% chance that a heavy snow could occur on your departure date, and that you are quite risk-averse ($\gamma = 3$). Will you pay $75 for this insurance?
7. Imagine your liquid wealth is $50,000 and you know that one out of every four (i.e., 25%) of your friends traveling to Thailand gets food poisoning. The breakdown of those unlucky 25% is 10% end up in the hospital with $1,000 of medical expenses. Out of bad luck, 5% not only end up in the hospital with a medical bill, but also miss their returning flight and have to purchase another plane ticket for $1,600. Finally, the remaining 10% do not experience severe food poisoning and need to purchase only $100 worth of medicine. If you are planning to travel

to Thailand, how much are you willing to pay for travel insurance? Assume your risk aversion is $\gamma = 2$.

8. Assume your insurance company offers you a $750 premium for insurance on your house if you are a regular client. Regular clients have a 0.03% chance of having their $350,000 house burnt down, and a 0.6% chance of having $10,000 damage to their home. On the other hand, you can choose to pay a $200 premium if you agree to a $2,000 deductible. Clients who accept the deductible have a 0.02% chance of having their entire house burn down and a 0.3% chance of having $10,000 damage to their home. Which premium should you choose assuming $\gamma = 1$ and your liquid wealth is $400,000?

9. Repeat question 1 assuming the deductible is $6,000 and your risk aversion is $\gamma = 2$.

10. Essay: Please discuss the impact of risk aversion (γ) on the magnitude of the deductible that you would select when insurance is fairly priced.

EIGHT

Mortality Risk and Life Insurance

Learning Objectives

In this chapter, we discuss mortality risk and life insurance. Specifically, we examine the necessity of having life insurance and the appropriate amount of coverage. We then study how the premiums are determined. We also look at different types of life insurance policies.

8.1 Who Needs Life Insurance?

Life insurance is a contract whereby an insurance company promises to pay a sum of money to the designated **beneficiary** if the **insured** passes away. That sum of money is referred to as the **death benefit** or the **face value** of the policy. In exchange, the insured has to pay an insurance premium to the company. Typically, an insurance premium is paid monthly while the insured is still alive. However, the insured can choose to pay it in one lump sum at the start of the policy. In some cases, the person who pays the premiums is not the insured. That person is referred to as the **owner** of the policy. For example, if you purchase life insurance for your spouse, you are the owner while your spouse is the insured.

The primary reason for getting life insurance is to protect against financial problems associated with the insured's premature death. These financial problems include the loss of the insured's future earnings, which could lead to a lower standard of living for his or her family (i.e., dependents). They also include funeral expenses, unpaid medical bills, and outstanding debts. Based on this reason, you should consider purchasing life insurance if you are earning income and you have dependents who rely on your income for financial support. This means that life insurance may not be needed in the following cases. First, you are already past your working years and thus there is no more income to protect. Secondly, you may still be working but have accumulated sufficient wealth to pass to your family members so that they will not suffer financial hardship if you pass away. Thirdly, you are single and have no dependents.

There are, however, other reasons for buying life insurance. For example, as discussed later in this chapter, certain types of life insurance policies allow people to save and shelter income on their savings from taxes (for a period of time). This feature will appeal to people who have already maximized their contributions into their registered plans (e.g., RRSPs). Another reason is that in certain cases, people may be required to have life insurance where the beneficiary is a third party (i.e., nonfamily members). For example, large corporations usually purchase insurance on key employees' lives, with the corporations being the beneficiary. The purpose is to protect the employers against the unexpected death of valuable personnel. Also, a mortgage lender will ask borrowers to have life insurance where the lender is the beneficiary. This is to protect the lender in case the borrower passes away before the mortgage is paid off.

Finally, even if you are still young and do not yet earn any income or have any dependents, you may want to buy life insurance. As you will shortly see when we talk about mortality risk, the probability of death increases with age. As a result, the earlier you buy life insurance, the cheaper it will be. This creates an incentive for young people to buy long-term life insurance as early as they can. If it later turns out that they do not need as much of it, they can then reduce the face value of the policy. In addition, having a policy in place guarantees that you can renew it later (typically without proof of insurability such as a medical exam).

8.2 How Much Coverage Do You Need?

In general, there are two approaches to determining how much life insurance a person requires. The first approach is the human-capital approach, while the second approach is the expense (or needs) approach.

8.2.1 Human-Capital Approach

The human-capital approach is based on the idea that the purpose of life insurance is to protect the insured's future income on which his or her dependents rely. This approach looks at the amount of *after-tax* human capital that you have remaining. The approach calculates your net human capital, H_x (i.e., $GH_x - iL_x$), on an after-tax basis. The reason why the after-tax basis is used is that you want the death benefit to reflect the amounts of wages that you take home after paying income taxes. Because death benefit is not subject to taxes when your beneficiary receives it (although the income subsequently earned on it is), you should not use your pre-tax income in the calculation; otherwise, the resulting net human capital would overstate the value of your future take-home pay.

Recall from Chapter 3 that there are two ways to handle income taxes when calculating net human capital. You can use after-tax salary in the calculation (together with your subsistent consumption). In this way, the resulting number is after-tax net human capital. Alternatively, if you prefer to use pre-tax salary in the calculation, you have to calculate separately the present value of future income taxes that you will have to pay, and then subtract it from the pre-tax net human capital. Either approach will give you the same result.

To make sure that you get the idea, let us look at a numerical example. As we did in Chapter 4, we will do the following calculation on real (rather than nominal) terms. We will work with real values of the cash flows. This also means that all the rates are expressed in real terms.

Practice Question   *You turned thirty years old today. Your next pre-tax annual salary (payable at the end of this year) is $50,000. It is growing at a real rate of 0.5% per year. You plan to work until you are sixty-five years old. You are married with two children. You expect to live until eighty-five years old, and estimate your subsistent consumption to be about $12,000 per year. Assume that the after-tax real valuation rate is $v = 2\%$ per year, and that your average tax rate will be approximately 25% for the rest of your working years. What is the amount of life insurance coverage that you need?*

We will use the after-tax salary in the calculation. At the average tax rate of 25%, your pre-tax salary translates to an after-tax amount of:

$$50,000 \cdot (1 - 0.25) = 37,500.$$

Based on this information, your after-tax gross human capital is:

$$\mathbf{GH}_{30} = 37,500 \cdot \mathbf{PVA}(\overline{g}_w, v, R - x)$$

$$= 37,500 \cdot \left[\frac{1 - \left[(1.005)^{35} \cdot (1.02)^{-35} \right]}{0.02 - 0.005} \right] = 1,011,509.$$

Next, we calculate your implicit liabilities:

$$\mathbf{iL}_{30} = 12,000 \cdot \mathbf{PVA}(v, D - x) = 12,000 \cdot \left[\frac{1 - (1.02)^{-55}}{0.02} \right] = 398,097.$$

Therefore, your net human capital is:

$$H_x = 1{,}011{,}509 - 398{,}097 = 613{,}412.$$

This is the amount of life insurance coverage that you need.

The human-capital approach has two important limitations. First, it is dependent on the assumptions about your wages and the valuation rate. As you have seen in Chapter 3, the value of human capital is highly sensitive to the assumptions on the valuation rate and the salary growth rate. Secondly, it does not take into account your current wealth. As mentioned earlier, you may need little or no life insurance if you are already wealthy enough that your family will not suffer financial hardship if you pass away. Therefore, the approach may lead people to buy more life insurance than they need.

8.2.2 The Expense (Needs) Approach

The expense approach looks at the expenses your family members will incur that cannot be covered by your current wealth and their own income over the course of their lives. You then buy insurance to cover those expenses rather than to replace your income. The approach is based on the idea that the purpose of life insurance is to maintain the standard of living of your family members after you pass away.

To use this approach, you need to create two financial statements. The first is a balance sheet of your current financial capital (i.e., $F_x = M_x - eL_x$). In addition, this balance sheet will also include items that will occur if you were to pass away. For example, you should include the amounts of death benefits that your estate can get from your employer or the governments such as Canada Pension Plan (CPP) Death Benefits. On the liability side, although there is no estate tax in Canada, your assets will be considered disposed of at the time of death. This creates income tax liability that has to be paid before the remaining assets can be passed on to your family.[1] In addition, if there are expenses related to your death such as funeral expenses, transition funds, and legal costs, they should be deducted from your financial wealth. The result is the amount of wealth that can be transferred to your family.

The second financial statement that you need to create is a cash flow statement of your surviving family members. The inflows should include

---

[1] The exception is if the assets are passed to the surviving spouse or to a trust for the spouse (spousal trust). The spouse or the spousal trust will then take ownership of the assets at the deceased's original costs. Taxes on the assets are deferred until they are either disposed of by the spouse or the spousal trust, or until the spouse dies.

your spouse's income and CPP survival benefits (i.e., CPP pension paid to the spouse of a deceased contributor), and your children's CPP benefits (i.e., CPP benefit for dependent children of a deceased contributor). The outflows should include income taxes and an estimate of the expenses required for your children to have necessary education and for all your dependents to enjoy the same standard of living during the dependency period. The dependency period can be different among family members. For example, your spouse may have only been working part-time in order to take care of your children. In this case, your spouse would be counting on your income for support into the retirement years. On the other hand, when your children finish university, they will no longer be dependent.

The difference between inflows and outflows is the net cash flows. You then calculate their present value. This result is the amount that has to be financed by your existing wealth (from the balance sheet that you have just created) and the life insurance that you are going to buy. The amount of life insurance that you need is equal to the difference between the present value of the net cash flows and your existing wealth.

Unlike the human-capital approach, the expense approach does take into account your current wealth. Still, it requires you to make assumptions about your dependents' income and expenses. Therefore, the determination of the amount of life insurance that you need is never an exact procedure. As you can imagine, there can be a substantial difference in the amounts between the human-capital and the expense approaches. We believe that the human-capital approach establishes the upper bound for the coverage while the expense approach sets the lower bound, and anything in between is acceptable.

Note that your insurance needs will change over time. Families' expenses will decline substantially as their children grow up and leave the nest. Likewise, the discounted value of wages and other income will decline with time. On the other hand, family members may suffer deteriorating health conditions, which requires more expenses. As a result, from time to time, you need to reevaluate your insurance needs, and, if possible, adjust the face value of the policy accordingly.

8.3 Types of Life Insurance

There are two major types of life insurance – term insurance and cash-value insurance. **Term life insurance** is the most basic type of life insurance. It provides protection for a specific term and has no savings components (and thus no cash value). In contrast, **cash-value life insurance** has a savings component (and thus cash value). There are many variations of these two types of life insurance available.

8.3.1 Term Life Insurance

Term life insurance covers the insured for a specific period. The period can be, for example, one, five, ten, or twenty years. It will pay the death benefit to the beneficiary if the insured dies within the period. Otherwise, the policy will expire worthless. Commonly, the (monthly) premiums remain constant throughout the term.

Most term insurance policies have a renewable option. The option allows the insured to renew the policy for an additional period without proof of insurability (e.g., a medical exam). There are, however, some limitations on renewability. For example, the face value of the new policy typically cannot be greater than the previous face value, while the length of the new period cannot be longer than the previous period. In addition, insurance companies generally do not allow renewals if the insured is beyond a certain age (typically sixty-five or seventy), or if the number of renewals has reached the stated maximum (e.g., three times).

The premiums for the new term will increase to reflect the insured's higher mortality risk as he or she gets older. As you will see, people's mortality risk increases at a faster rate as they age. Consequently, there will be a point where the premiums for the next renewal are prohibitively expensive.

Other options on term life policies include decreasing coverage amounts where the face values gradually decline each year, and convertibility into cash-value policies without a medical exam (up to a certain age). The decreasing-coverage option allows for the insured's declining insurance needs, which may be due to fewer remaining working years, lower outstanding debt obligations, or smaller financial support required by dependents. The convertibility option is useful for people who, for some reasons, want to maintain the insurance coverage beyond the age where term policies can no longer be renewed or can be renewed but at a very high rate.

Term life insurance does not have a savings element. Therefore, it is a pure form of life insurance, and its premiums mainly reflect the insured's mortality cost. We will now look at how the premiums are determined. After it is done, we will return to the second type of life insurance, which is cash-value life.

Mortality Risk

To understand how life insurance is priced, we first need to understand mortality risk, which is the risk (or chance) that the insured will die within a certain period of time. One way to estimate that risk is to look at historical death rates. Most countries collect death rates of their citizens according to various characteristics (such as age, gender, health condition, etc.). These rates are typically reported in the form of tables. In Canada, Statistics Canada compile such statistics every ten years. Their latest tables contain data collected from 2000 to 2002. The death rates are reproduced as probabilities in Table 8.1.

The table displays the probability that a Canadian female or male who is currently x years old will die within one year (i.e., before he or she reaches age $x + 1$). The ages x shown in the table range from 0 (i.e., just born) to 109. For example, the probability that a twenty-five-year-old person will die within a year is 0.00033 for females and 0.00083 for males.

There are a few things to note about Table 8.1. First, the probabilities displayed are averages of the entire population of Canada, without regard for their home provinces, socioeconomic status, health condition, education, or race. All of these factors can make a difference and lead to their own (different) mortality tables. Secondly, the probability of death (within a year) at any age is lower for women than men. Thirdly, due to limited data availability, the table only goes up to age 109. This does not mean that the table assumes that everyone will be dead before age 110. This is why the probability that a 109-year-old person will die within the next year is not equal to one. (The oldest Canadian ever passed away at age 117.) Finally, the probabilities of death (within one year) shown in the table are not always increasing with age. For example, between ages zero and nine, the probabilities are declining. This is consistent with the observation that the first few years of life are very precarious for children. The probabilities are also declining between ages twenty-four and twenty-seven. This is the result of the fact that the death rates of males between the ages of eighteen and twenty-three are unduly high as a result of motor vehicle accidents. The rates start to move back to normal starting from age twenty-four, thus the observed decline. Besides these two exceptions, however, the probabilities *should* increase with age.

Following actuarial notations, we will denote by q_x the probability that an x-year-old person will die within one year, and by p_x the probability that he or she will survive for *at least* one more year. Obviously,

$$p_x = 1 - q_x.$$

Similarly, we denote by $_nq_x$ the probability that an x-year-old person will die within n years, and by $_np_x = 1 - (_nq_x)$ the probability that he or she will survive for *at least* n more years.

Table 8.1. *Mortality probability*

	Probability of death before reaching the next birthday ($1q_x$)			Probability of death before reaching the next birthday ($1q_x$)	
Age (x)	Female	Male	Age (x)	Female	Male
0	0.00467	0.00577	38	0.00079	0.00132
1	0.00035	0.00035	39	0.00085	0.00141
2	0.00020	0.00021	40	0.00092	0.00152
3	0.00015	0.00021	41	0.00099	0.00164
4	0.00012	0.00020	42	0.00109	0.00178
5	0.00010	0.00017	43	0.00120	0.00195
6	0.00008	0.00013	44	0.00132	0.00213
7	0.00007	0.00009	45	0.00145	0.00233
8	0.00007	0.00008	46	0.00160	0.00255
9	0.00007	0.00008	47	0.00176	0.00279
10	0.00009	0.00010	48	0.00193	0.00304
11	0.00009	0.00010	49	0.00210	0.00331
12	0.00013	0.00015	50	0.00229	0.00360
13	0.00016	0.00023	51	0.00251	0.00394
14	0.00020	0.00034	52	0.00276	0.00434
15	0.00024	0.00046	53	0.00305	0.00481
16	0.00028	0.00057	54	0.00337	0.00533
17	0.00031	0.00066	55	0.00372	0.00590
18	0.00033	0.00072	56	0.00410	0.00654
19	0.00034	0.00078	57	0.00451	0.00726
20	0.00034	0.00082	58	0.00494	0.00805
21	0.00034	0.00085	59	0.00538	0.00890
22	0.00034	0.00087	60	0.00587	0.00982
23	0.00033	0.00087	61	0.00641	0.01085
24	0.00033	0.00085	62	0.00704	0.01198
25	0.00033	0.00083	63	0.00774	0.01321
26	0.00033	0.00081	64	0.00850	0.01451
27	0.00033	0.00080	65	0.00933	0.01593
28	0.00035	0.00082	66	0.01026	0.01752
29	0.00037	0.00084	67	0.01131	0.01930
30	0.00039	0.00088	68	0.01243	0.02124
31	0.00042	0.00091	69	0.01362	0.02329
32	0.00046	0.00096	70	0.01493	0.02555
33	0.00050	0.00100	71	0.01645	0.02810
34	0.00055	0.00105	72	0.01823	0.03104
35	0.00061	0.00110	73	0.02019	0.03429
36	0.00067	0.00116	74	0.02230	0.03779
37	0.00073	0.00123	75	0.02467	0.04165

Age (x)	Probability of death before reaching the next birthday ($1q_x$)		Age (x)	Probability of death before reaching the next birthday ($1q_x$)	
	Female	Male		Female	Male
76	0.02742	0.04599	93	0.17087	0.22086
77	0.03066	0.05091	94	0.18680	0.23867
78	0.03424	0.05631	95	0.20376	0.25754
79	0.03807	0.06210	96	0.22177	0.27751
80	0.04240	0.06846	97	0.24083	0.29858
81	0.04748	0.07555	98	0.26094	0.32077
82	0.05354	0.08353	99	0.28209	0.34406
83	0.06068	0.09214	100	0.30425	0.36846
84	0.06872	0.10129	101	0.32740	0.39396
85	0.07755	0.11135	102	0.35151	0.42053
86	0.08703	0.12268	103	0.37651	0.44815
87	0.09704	0.13566	104	0.40237	0.47678
88	0.10767	0.15005	105	0.42902	0.50637
89	0.11899	0.16558	106	0.45638	0.53687
90	0.13088	0.18264	107	0.48439	0.56822
91	0.14322	0.20160	108	0.51296	0.60036
92	0.15588	0.22283	109	0.54200	0.63320

Source: Statistics Canada.

The probabilities in Table 8.1 can be used in various ways. For example, suppose you want to make a prediction about the probability that someone will be alive after a period of time.

Practice Question *What is the probability that a thirty-five-year-old woman will be alive after two years?*

The question asks for the probability that a thirty-five-year-old woman will survive for at least two more years, $_2p_x$. To do that, she will have to survive the first year, and then survive the second year.

The probability of surviving the first year is one minus the probability that a thirty-five-year-old woman will die within a year;

$$p_{35} = 1 - q_{35},$$

which, according to Table 8.1, is:

$$p_{35} = 1 - 0.00061 = 0.99939.$$

After she survives the first year, she will be thirty-six years old. The probability of surviving the second year is one minus the probability that a

36-year-old woman will die within a year;

$$p_{36} = 1 - q_{36},$$

which, according to Table 8.1, is:

$$p_{36} = 1 - 0.00067 = 0.99933.$$

Consequently, the probability of surviving at least two more years is:

$$\begin{aligned}
{}_2p_{35} &= (p_{35}) \cdot (p_{36}) \\
&= (1 - q_{35}) \cdot (1 - q_{36}) \\
&= 0.99939 \cdot 0.99933 \\
&= 0.9987204.
\end{aligned}$$

Practice Question *What is the probability that a thirty-six-year-old woman will die within the next two years?*

Because we already know the chance that she will survive the next two years, the probability that she will die within two years is simply:

$$\begin{aligned}
{}_2q_{35} &= 1 - ({}_2p_{35}) \\
&= 1 - 0.9987204 \\
&= 0.00127959.
\end{aligned}$$

Note that this probability is not the same as the sum of q_{35} and q_{36}, which is equal to:

$$\begin{aligned}
q_{35} + q_{36} &= 0.00061 + 0.00067 \\
&= 0.00128000.
\end{aligned}$$

Although the difference between the two amounts is very small, the second amount (i.e., 0.00128000) is incorrect. To get the probability of death within the next two years, you cannot add up the probabilities q_{35} and q_{36} from Table 8.1. This is because these probabilities are age-dependent. In other words, each of these probabilities is conditional upon the person reaching a certain age. For example, q_{36} is the probability of death within one year conditional upon the person being thirty-six years old. Consequently, the proper way to find the probability of death within a given time period is to first find the probability of survival over that period and then subtract it from one.

Practice Question *What is the probability that a thirty-five-year-old woman will survive the next two years (i.e., to reach thirty-seven years old) and then die within the following year (i.e., before turning thirty-eight)?*

We know from before that the probability of surviving the next two years is $_2 p_{35} = 0.9987204$. By then, she will be thirty-seven years old. The probability that she will then die in the following year is q_{37}, which, from Table 8.1, is 0.00073. As a result, the probability that we want to find is:

$$(_2 p_{35}) \cdot (q_{37}) = 0.9987204 \cdot 0.00073 = 0.0007291.$$

To summarize what we have discussed so far, the probability that an x-year-old person will survive for at least n more years is:

$$\begin{aligned}
_n p_x &= (p_x) \cdot (p_{x+1}) \cdot \ldots \cdot (p_{x+n-1}) \\
&= (1 - q_x) \cdot (1 - q_{x+1}) \cdot \ldots \cdot (1 - q_{x+n-1}) \\
&= \prod_{i=0}^{n-1} (1 - q_{x+i}).
\end{aligned}$$

The probability that an x-year-old person will die within the next n years is:

$$\begin{aligned}
_n q_x &= 1 - (_n p_x) \\
&= 1 - \prod_{i=0}^{n-1} (1 - q_{x+i}).
\end{aligned}$$

Finally, the probability that an x-year-old person will survive for the next n years and then die in the following year is:

$$(_n p_x) \cdot (q_{x+n}) = \prod_{i=0}^{n-1} (1 - q_{x+i}) \cdot (q_{x+n}).$$

Before we move on to the calculations of life insurance premiums, we want to mention one more statistic that you can obtain from using the probabilities in Table 8.1. Suppose you want to know the life expectancy of yourself or someone else. **Life expectancy** is the expected number of years of life remaining at a given age. Similar to the calculation of any expected value, you calculate life expectancy by multiplying each possible outcome by its probability and then sum the results up. In this case, the possible outcomes are the number of years that you will continue to live. You may live for one more year, two more years, three more years, and so on. The associated probabilities can be obtained based on our discussion previous.

Practice Question *How many more years can a sixty-five-year-old Canadian male expect to live?*

To answer this question, we make two assumptions regarding Table 8.1. First, we assume that no one will live to age 111. Once people turn 110 years old, we assume that they will survive for only one more year. In other words, the probability that a 110-year-old will die within one year, q_{110}, is one. With this assumption, we augment Table 8.1 to include the last line for age 110. Secondly, we assume that all the deaths in a given year occur at the end of that year. This is to simplify the calculations. In reality, people can die at any time during the year. Therefore, this assumption will slightly overstate the resulting life expectancy.[2]

Table 8.2 displays the calculation of life expectancy. Column 2 of the table lists all the possible outcomes (i.e., number of years to live). Column 3 display the probabilities associated with those outcomes. For example, the probability that a sixty-five-year-old man will live for exactly one more year is equal to the probability of him dying within one year, which, from Table 8.1, is $q_{65} = 0.01593$. The probability that a sixty-five-year-old man will live for exactly two more years is equal to the probability that he will survive the first year and then die in the second year, which, based to our earlier discussion, is equal to:

$$p_{65} \cdot q_{66} = (1 - q_{65}) \cdot (q_{66})$$
$$(1 - 0.01593) \cdot 0.01752$$
$$= 0.017241.$$

Other probabilities are obtained in the same manner.

Column 4 of the table displays the products of columns 2 and 3 (i.e., each possible outcome multiplied by its probability). Summing up these products, we have the expected value of the number of years to live, which is 17.4811 years.

Table 8.3 displays life expectancy *at birth* (averaged over the whole population) of the top ten and bottom ten countries in the world as of 2005. The numbers in the table were obtained from Towers Watson & Co., Ltd.

---

[2] For a continuous-time model where death can occur at any instant in time, please refer to Chapter 13.

Table 8.2. *Calculation of conditional life expectancy of a 65-year-old Canadian*
Male

Age (x)	Number of years to live (i)	Probability of living exactly i more years	Number of years multiplied by probability
65	1	0.015930	0.015930
66	2	0.017241	0.034482
67	3	0.018660	0.055979
68	4	0.020139	0.080556
69	5	0.021614	0.108069
70	6	0.023159	0.138954
71	7	0.024820	0.173737
72	8	0.026646	0.213167
73	9	0.028522	0.256699
74	10	0.030356	0.303556
75	11	0.032192	0.354111
76	12	0.034066	0.408790
77	13	0.035976	0.467687
78	14	0.037766	0.528724
79	15	0.039304	0.589560
80	16	0.040639	0.650217
81	17	0.041777	0.710210
82	18	0.042700	0.768602
83	19	0.043167	0.820175
84	20	0.043081	0.861629
85	21	0.042563	0.893826
86	22	0.041672	0.916791
87	23	0.040428	0.929848
88	24	0.038650	0.927607
89	25	0.036251	0.906271
90	26	0.033365	0.867489
91	27	0.030102	0.812760
92	28	0.026565	0.743807
93	29	0.020463	0.593417
94	30	0.017229	0.516868
95	31	0.014154	0.438773
96	32	0.011324	0.362355
97	33	0.008802	0.290478
98	34	0.006633	0.225522
99	35	0.004832	0.169136
100	36	0.003395	0.122205
101	37	0.002292	0.084811
102	38	0.001483	0.056348
103	39	0.000916	0.035712
104	40	0.000538	0.021505

(continued)

Table 8.2 *(continued)*

Age (x)	Number of years to live (i)	Probability of living exactly i more years	Number of years multiplied by probability
105	41	0.000299	0.012249
106	42	0.000156	0.006567
107	43	0.000077	0.003296
108	44	0.000035	0.001538
109	45	0.000015	0.000663
110	46	0.000009	0.000393
Expected Number of Years to Live			**17.4811**

Source: Author Calculations based on Statistics Canada data in Table 8.1 (assuming death at year-end).

Table 8.3. *Life expectancy in various countries*

Top 10 country	Life expectancy
Japan	82.40
Sweden	80.70
Hong Kong	80.60
Macoa	80.07
Israel	79.97
Iceland	79.91
Norway	79.73
France	79.69
Australia	79.64
Belgium	79.59

Bottom 10 country	Life expectancy
Rwanda	43.33
Burandi	42.66
South Africa	42.44
Sierra Leone	42.37
Malawi	40.52
Mozambique	38.40
Botswana	38.20
Djibouti	37.60
Lesotho	36.30
Swaziland	35.30

Source: The Calculus of Retirement Income (2006), Cambridge Unversity Press.

As you can see, there are significant differences between the top ten and bottom ten countries. This is due primarily to their socioeconomic conditions.

Life Insurance Premiums
We can now calculate life insurance premiums. As with any other kinds of insurance, life insurance works by pooling risks. For example, consider a one-year term life insurance for an x-year-old individual. The policy will pay $\$M$ (at the end of the year) if the insured dies at any time during the year. As previously defined, the mortality probability (i.e., the chance that the payment has to be made) is q_x. If the insurance company sells N of these policies where N is very large, it will have to pay compensation on approximately $N \cdot q_x$ policies, and so the total expected payment is $\$M \cdot N \cdot q_x$. Because this payment will be made at the end of the year (i.e., we assume that all the deaths in a given year occur at the end of that year), its present value is:

$$\frac{M \cdot N \cdot (q_x)}{1 + v}, \tag{8.1}$$

where v is the valuation rate. Without considering the required expenses and profits, this is the amount that the insurance company has to collect from those N individuals at the start. In other words, it must collect:

$$A_{x:1} := \frac{M \cdot (q_x)}{1 + v} \tag{8.2}$$

from each individual up front. This is the **actuarially fair net single premium** for this one-year term life policy. The term net single premium (NSP) is to remind the reader that this premium is paid up front in one lump sum. The term actuarially fair is meant to suggest that the only thing the premium covers is the pure death benefit. It does not account for profits or anything nonactuarial.

The numerator of equation (8.2) is the expected compensation per person. We will from this point on refer to this quantity as the **expected loss** or **expected mortality cost**. It should be noted that we assume here that the insurance company can invest the collected premium at the valuation rate.

The higher the valuation rate, the lower the NSP is. The intuition is that insurance companies collect the NSP up front. They then invest it at the valuation rate to prepare to pay it out as compensation at the end of the year. Therefore, the higher the rate of return that they can get from the investment, the lower the amount is that they need to start off with.

Also, in practice, insurance companies will also include their expenses and required profits into the premiums. Let Λ be the expenses and required profits, expressed as a percentage of the actuarially fair net single premium. The premium for the one-year term life policy is then:

$$(1 + \Lambda) \cdot A_{x:1}. \tag{8.3}$$

Practice Question *What is the actuarially fair net single premium for a one-year term life policy with a \$100,000 death benefit for a thirty-year-old Canadian man? What is the same premium for a thirty-year-old Canadian woman? Assume that the valuation rate is 5% p.a., annual compounding.*

Based on Table 8.1, the probability that a thirty-year-old man will die within one year is $q_{30} = 0.00088$. So, the expected mortality cost of this one-year term policy is:

$$(100{,}000) \cdot (0.00088) = 88,$$

and so the actuarially fair premium is:

$$\frac{88}{1.05} = 83.81.$$

For a thirty-year-old woman, $q_{30} = 0.00039$, and so the mortality cost is \$39. The actuarially fair premium is then:

$$\frac{39}{1.05} = 37.14.$$

Note that the actuarially fair insurance premium is simply the present value of the expected mortality cost. Note also that in practice, insurance premiums are not paid in one lump sum up front. Rather, they are normally paid in installments. This requires that we amortize the net single premium into periodical premiums. We will come back to address this procedure shortly. For now, let us consider insurance policies for longer terms.

Practice Question *What is the actuarially fair net single premium for a two-year term life policy with a \$100,000 death benefit for a thirty-year-old Canadian man? Assume that the valuation rate is 5% p.a., annual compounding.*

To calculate the fair premium, we need to calculate the expected mortality costs for the two years, discount them by the valuation rate, and then sum them up. The expected mortality cost for the first year has already been calculated in the previous example (i.e., $88). The expected mortality cost for the second year can be calculated as follows. For the compensation to be paid at the end of the second year, the insured must survive the first year and then die some time in the second year. The probability of this is:

$$(p_{30}) \cdot (q_{31}) = (1 - q_{30}) \cdot (q_{31})$$
$$= (1 - 0.00088) \cdot 0.00091$$
$$= 0.0009092.$$

As a result, the expected mortality cost for the second year is:

$$100,000 \cdot 0.0009092 = 90.92.$$

The actuarially fair NSP is then:

$$\frac{88}{1.05} + \frac{90.92}{1.05^2} = 166.28.$$

As before, the actuarially fair insurance premium is the present value of the expected mortality cost. To generalize, the actuarially fair NSP for a two-year term life insurance with a face value of M for an x-year-old is:

$$A_{x:2} := \frac{M \cdot (q_x)}{1 + v} + \frac{M \cdot (p_x) \cdot (q_{x+1})}{(1 + v)^2} \tag{8.4}$$

$$= M \cdot \left[\frac{(q_x)}{1 + v} + \frac{(p_x) \cdot (q_{x+1})}{(1 + v)^2} \right].$$

Based on the same logic, the actuarially fair NSP for a n-year term life insurance with a face value of M for an x-year-old is:

$$A_{x:n} := M \cdot \left[\frac{q_x}{1 + v} + \frac{(p_x) \cdot (q_{x+1})}{(1 + v)^2} + \frac{(_2 p_x) \cdot (q_{x+2})}{(1 + v)^3} + \cdots \right.$$

$$\left. + \frac{(_{n-1} p_x) \cdot (q_{x+n-1})}{(1 + v)^n} \right] \tag{8.5}$$

$$= M \cdot \sum_{j=0}^{n-1} \frac{(_j p_x) \cdot (q_{x+j})}{(1 + v)^{j+1}},$$

Mortality Risk and Life Insurance

Table 8.4. *Actuarially fair net single premium on a 10-year term life insurance with a face value of $100,000 for a 30-year-old Canadian male*

Age (x)	j	Probability that an x-year-old male will die within one year ($1q_x$)	Probability that a 30-year-old male will survive at least j more years (jp_{30})	Expected compensation	PV of expected compensation
30	0	0.00088	1.000000	$88.00	$83.81
31	1	0.00091	0.999120	$90.92	$82.47
32	2	0.00096	0.998211	$95.83	$82.78
33	3	0.00100	0.997253	$99.73	$82.04
34	4	0.00105	0.996255	$104.61	$81.96
35	5	0.00110	0.995209	$109.47	$81.69
36	6	0.00116	0.994114	$115.32	$81.95
37	7	0.00123	0.992961	$122.13	$82.67
38	8	0.00132	0.991740	$130.91	$84.39
39	9	0.00141	0.990431	$139.65	$85.73
Actuarially Fair Net Single Premium					$829.49

Source: Author Calculations (all cash flows at year-end).

where the numerator of each term is the expected mortality cost for each of the *n* years.

Practice Question *What is the actuarially fair net single premium for a ten-year term life policy with a $100,000 death benefit for a thirty-year-old Canadian man? Assume that the valuation rate is 5% p.a., annual compounding.*

The logic of the calculation is the same as before. Here, we need the expected mortality costs for all ten years. We have calculated the first two in the previous examples. The expected mortality costs for the other eight years can be similarly calculated. We present the results in Table 8.4. The fair NSP in this case is $829.49.

Now, because insurance premiums are normally paid in equal installments at the beginning of each period, we have to amortize the NSP into periodic premiums. In Chapter 5, you learned how to amortize mortgage principals. However, there is an important difference between mortgage amortization and insurance premium amortization. In mortgage amortization, there is a fixed, known number of payments (e.g., over twenty or twenty-five years). For insurance amortization, we cannot make such an assumption. This is because insurance companies can collect premiums only as long as the insured is alive. If the insured dies before the end of the insurance term, the insurance company will have to pay the death benefits, and there will be no more future premiums to collect.

As a result, we need to use an amortization technique that takes into account mortality probability. In other words, we need a technique to convert a lump sum into a sequence of mortality-contingent payments. To have a good understanding of this technique, consider the following example.

Practice Question *Suppose there is an annuity-like product that will pay $1 every year (at the start of each year). The payment will continue as long as the recipient is alive up to ten years. Suppose that the valuation rate is 5% p.a., annual compounding. How much should insurance companies charge a thirty-year-old Canadian man for this product?*

In this case, the payments from the annuity are not guaranteed for ten years. Rather, they will stop if the recipient passes away. As a result, the number of payments is uncertain, and we cannot use the PVA factors that we saw in Chapter 2 to discount the payments. Instead, we have to use mortality probabilities to calculate expected payments before we can discount them.

There are ten possible payments from the product (i.e., if the recipient is alive throughout the ten years). We will apply mortality probability to each payment. The first payment occurs at the start of the first year (i.e., now), and so there is no uncertainty about it. Also, because it occurs now, we do not need to discount it.

The second payment occurs a year from now. From Table 8.1, the probability that a thirty-year-old man will survive for at least one year (and so he will be around to receive this payment) is $1 - q_{30} = 1 - 0.00088 = 0.99912$. Therefore, the expected value of the second payment is:

$$1 \cdot 0.99912 = 0.99912,$$

and so the present value of it is:

$$\frac{0.99912}{1.05} = 0.95154.$$

The expected values of the other payments can be calculated in the same manner. We multiply each payment by the probability that the recipient will survive at least long enough to receive it. We then discount all those expected values back to the current time. The results are shown in Table 8.5.

The sequence of the ten mortality contingent payment of $1 per year translates to a present value of $8.075 now. Note that if you simply used the

Table 8.5. *Price of a mortality-contingent annuity that pays $1 per year (at the start of each year) up to 10 years*

s	j	Probability that a 30-year-old male will survive at least j more years (jp_{30})	Expected value of $1 payment	PV of expected value
30	0	1.00000	$1.00000	$1.00000
31	1	0.99912	$0.99912	$0.95154
32	2	0.99821	$0.99821	$0.90541
33	3	0.99725	$0.99725	$0.86146
34	4	0.99626	$0.99626	$0.81962
35	5	0.99521	$0.99521	$0.77977
36	6	0.99411	$0.99411	$0.74182
37	7	0.99296	$0.99296	$0.70568
38	8	0.99174	$0.99174	$0.67125
39	9	0.99043	$0.99043	$0.63844
		Actuarially Fair Net Single Premium		$8.07500

Source: Author Calculations.

PVA factor for an annuity due without thinking about mortality probability, you would get a present value of $8.1078, which is higher because the factor assumes that all ten payments would be made. In contrast, the technique that we have just described weight-averages the present value of each of the ten payments by the probability that the recipient will be alive long enough to receive that payment.

Now that we know the technique to convert a sequence of mortality-contingent payments into a lump sum, it is straightforward to apply it in the amortization of the actuarially fair NSP from the previous example.

Practice Question *Recall the ten-year term life policy with a $100,000 death benefit for a thirty-year-old Canadian man in a previous example. Suppose the insurance company requires the premium to be paid once a year at the beginning of each year. How much is the annual premium?*

Recall that the fair NSP for a ten-year term life policy with a $100,000 death benefit for a thirty-year-old Canadian man in this case is $829.49. Recall also that we know that a sequence of $1 mortality-contingent payments for up to ten years translates to $8.075 (and, by logic, vice versa). As a result, the annual premium must be:

$$\frac{829.49}{8.075} = 102.72.$$

Table 8.6. *Monthly premium on a $100,000 term life insurance policy*

	Age					
	30		40		50	
Term	Male	Female	Male	Female	Male	Female
5 years	$12.71	$11.53	$19.65	$15.30	$105.65	$59.27
10 years	$8.21	$7.68	$17.95	$14.57	$102.51	$55.96
20 years	$11.01	$9.68	$27.56	$21.19	$207.54	$128.07
30 years	$15.47	$12.88	$46.23	$33.15	$307.33	$259.50
To-100	$33.51	$27.27	$103.60	$81.51	$373.83	$299.07

Source: Data compiled by the IFID Centre (www.ifid.ca).

Formally, the annual premium for an n-year term life insurance with a face value of $\$M$ for an x-year-old individual is:

$$\frac{A_{x:n}}{\sum_{j=0}^{n-1} \frac{(_j p_x)}{(1+v)^j}}$$

where $A_{x:n}$ is as defined in equation (8.5).

Finally, we note that in practice, the premiums are paid once a month at the start of each month rather than once a year. We can approximate the amount of monthly premium by dividing the annual premium by twelve. For the earlier example, the monthly premium would be $102.72/12 = \$8.56$.

Life Insurance Premium Quotes
Now that you understand how theoretical insurance premiums are determined, let us take a look at some sample insurance premium quotes for term life policies. Table 8.6 displays the monthly premiums that males and females of various ages would have to pay to obtain a $100,000 death benefit coverage for different coverage terms. These numbers were calculated by averaging the three to four best quotes in the market (in early 2006). Note that these premiums are constant throughout the terms of the policies.

Many obvious – and some not so obvious – observations emerge from Table 8.6. First, for any given term of coverage, a male, of any age, has to pay a higher monthly premium than a female does for the same amount of coverage. Of course, the differences between male and female mortality probabilities account for this observation. Next, both males and females of any age pay more for twenty years of coverage than they would pay for

Table 8.7. *Monthly premium on a $100,000 term life insurance policy for a 50-year-old male according to health status*

| | Health condition | | | | | |
| | Average | | Excellent | | Exceptional | |
Term	Male	Female	Male	Female	Male	Female
5 years	$27.61	$20.68	$19.65	$15.30	$15.37	$12.11
10 years	$23.54	$18.38	$17.95	$14.57	$14.86	$12.48
20 years	$38.69	$28.65	$27.56	$21.19	$23.85	$17.90

Source: Data compiled by the IFID Centre (www.ifid.ca).

ten years of coverage. This is to be expected because longer-term policies involve higher mortality risks for the years that are not covered by shorter-term policies.

However, what may appear counterintuitive is that a five-year policy is actually more expensive than a ten-year and, in certain cases, even a twenty-year policy. This slight irregularity is likely due to a combination of several factors. First, not many insurance companies offer five-year policies, as consumers in general tend to be more interested in longer-term insurance. The lack of competition may result in higher premiums for these policies. In addition, the insurers may be trying to amortize all of the costs associated with offering these policies over a shorter period of time. Either way, it does remain a bit of a puzzle.

In practice, life insurance prices also depend on your health status. Table 8.7 illustrates the impact of health status on the premium that a fifty-year-old male would pay. For example, a fifty-year-old male who is in exceptional health would only have to pay $23.85 per month for a twenty-year policy, with a death benefit of $100,000. In contrast, a fifty-year-old male in average health would have to pay $38.69 for the same contractual terms. As you can see, the 62% markup or premium (over the exceptional-health case) is quite a substantial incentive to "prove" that you are in exceptional health (if you are) when purchasing life insurance. In our notations, the $_nq_x$ for a very healthy individual is lower than the $_nq_x$ for a less healthy individual for any n. You can imagine a whole family of mortality tables that reflect the health of different individuals.

While we are on the topic of health status, it is important to be aware that adverse selection can be a problem. Applicants who are affected by or predisposed to a health condition may withhold this information from the insurers. In fact, potential evidence of adverse selection is observed in the number of deaths resulting from cancer, which is higher during the early years in the term of life insurance policies than during the later years.

8.3.2 Cash-Value Life Insurance

In contrast to term life insurance, which covers the insured for a specific term, cash-value life insurance provides lifelong insurance protection. The death benefit is paid whenever the insured dies. In addition, they have cash value (sometimes referred to as **cash surrender value** or **savings component**). Basically, cash value is the amount that the policyholder would get if he or she cancels the policy.

There are two major types of cash-value policies. They are **whole life** and **universal life** insurance. Within each type, there are several variations. We will not get into details about each variation. Rather, we will discuss the primary characteristics of each of the two types.

Whole Life Insurance

In its most common variation, whole life insurance pays the death benefit when the insured dies or reaches 100 years old, whichever is earlier.[3] Its monthly premiums are the same (i.e., level) throughout the premium-paying period, which can, for example, be for life, for twenty years, or until age sixty-five. Obviously, the premiums charged will be adjusted to reflect the length of the premium-paying period chosen.

Insurance premiums for whole life policies are far higher than premiums for term life policies. This is because under whole life insurance, the death benefit will be paid for sure at some point. In contrast, term life policies only pay compensation if the insured dies before the end of the term. Therefore, the expected mortality cost under whole life is higher, resulting in higher premiums.

The fact that premiums are level throughout the premium-paying period lead to the cash value or savings component. To see why, note from the previous subsection that the expected mortality costs increase with age because the older you are, the higher the mortality probability is. Therefore, level premiums mean that premiums are higher than the expected mortality costs in the early years. The reverse is true for the later years (see Figure 8.1).

The excess premiums during the early years are invested by the insurance company (typically in low-risk assets). This is why savings (or cash value)

---

[3] In the past few years, there has been a shift from 100 years old toward 121 years old in new policies.

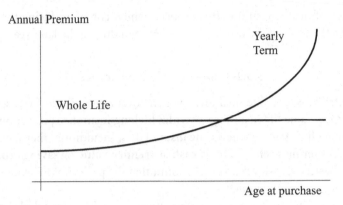

Figure 8.1. Premiums.

are built up inside the policy. The savings are intended to compensate for the shortfalls in the later years. However, if policyholders decide to cancel their policy, they can withdraw all their cash value. Alternatively, they can borrow against it or use it to pay for future premiums in case they do not want to make any more premium payments (which will result in the face value of the policy being adjusted downward accordingly).

Insurance companies usually promote the benefits of the savings component. One obvious advantage of saving inside an insurance policy is that the savings will earn investment income on a tax-deferred basis. However, remember that this advantage comes at a cost. Whole life premiums generally include much higher expenses (such as commissions to insurance agents) than term life premiums do. For some people (such as those who have already maximized their contributions into their registered savings plan such as their RRSPs), the additional room for tax-deferred savings provided by whole life policies can be worth the increase in the premiums. For others, they would be better off buying term life insurance and invest the difference in premiums themselves. This is particularly true if they do not have a need for lifelong insurance protection.

A whole life insurance policy can be either a participating policy or a nonparticipating policy. A **participating policy** gives the policyholder the right to share in the surplus of the insurance company. In some years, the insurance company has higher returns than expected. This may be due to lower-than-expected mortality costs and expenses. It may also be due to better-than-expected earnings on their investment. The surplus will be distributed to holders of participating policies in the form of "dividends." The policyholders can choose to receive them in cash, apply them against future premiums, use them to buy more coverage, or invest them with the insurance company. Note that the "dividends" are, in effect, a refund of part of the premiums that have been paid. In contrast, a **nonparticipating policy** does not allow policy holders to share in the surplus. As a result, its premiums are generally lower than those of participating policies.

Universal Life Insurance

Universal life insurance is a newer, more flexible form of whole life insurance. It explicitly separates the insurance element from the cash-value component and the policy expenses. It is as if the insured were buying a pure life insurance and an investment at the same time. Policyholders can determine the amount and frequency of the premium within limits. The minimum premium is the amount required to keep the insurance protection in force. The maximum premium is determined by the tax authority. This is because income on the investment inside a cash-value policy is tax deferred. Because the difference between the maximum and the minimum level of premiums is simply the savings component, the tax authority does not allow people to have as much tax-deferred investment inside a policy as they want.

A universal life insurance policy is in force as long as the policyholder maintains the insurance portion of the premium (or uses the existing cash value to do so). There are two options for death benefit. Under the first option, the death benefit starts from an initial amount that is based on the pure life insurance protection that the insured chooses at the start. It is then "added" by the amount of cash value accumulated along the way. Note that this does not mean that the death benefit will keep increasing. The cash value can fluctuate, especially if the insured chooses to forgo some premium payments and apply the existing cash value toward the minimum premium.

Under the second option, the death benefit remains constant until the accumulated cash value exceeds a certain threshold. Beyond the threshold, the excess is added to the death benefit. The reason why the death benefit (which, remember, determines how much of the premium payment is for the pure insurance purpose) has to increase is that the savings component cannot grow too large as to violate the allowed tax-deferred limit.

Although universal life insurance provides considerable flexibility in terms of the amount and frequency of the premium, the amount of the death benefit, and full or partial withdrawals of the cash value, it has a few drawbacks. First, the expenses can be high, typically between 5% and 10% of each premium payment. Secondly, there can be charges if the policy is terminated early or if a partial withdrawal of the cash value is made. Finally, insurance companies have a right to increase the mortality charge (i.e., the cost of the pure insurance component) up to some stated limit.

8.4 Questions and Assignments

1. You are forty-five years old and will receive a salary of $70,000, which is expected to grow at 1%. Your taxes are at 35% and will continue to be for the rest of your life. You will retire at sixty-five and expect to live until you are ninty years old. You have estimated your subsistent consumption to be about $20,000 per year. Assuming that the after-tax real valuation rate is $v = 2\%$ per year, what is the amount of life insurance coverage that you need if you use the human-capital approach?

2. How and why will your answer to question 1 change if you used the expense approach?

3. Susan is now sixty-five years old. What is her life expectancy? What is the probability that she will live to at least eighty years old?

4. Daniel is also sixty-five years old. What is his life expectancy? What is the probability that he will not live to see his eightieth birthday?

5. What is the probability that a seventy-year-old man will live for exactly three more years?

6. Katie is thirty-five years old. She is considering purchasing a five-year term life insurance. She wants the death benefit to be $200,000. Assume that the valuation rate is 4%. What is the actuarially fair net single insurance premium?

7. Based on question 6, if the premiums are to be paid once a year at the start of each year, how much will the annual premium be?

8. How much should insurance companies charge a fifty-year-old woman for an annuity-like product that will pay her $25,000 every year (at the beginning of each year) until she dies?

9. Based on question 8, what if the annuity has a guarantee period of ten years? Even if she passes some time in the next ten years, her estate will still get the yearly payment until the ten-year period is over.

10. How would you price/value a life annuity in which your beneficiary gets a refund of the unpaid premium if you die before you get your money back? In other words, assume an annuity that pays you income of C dollars per year, for which you must pay a premium of M up front. Assume this annuity will pay a death benefit of $\max[0, M - TC]$, where T is the number of years you live (and get payments) after the purchase. Compute a fair premium for M.

NINE

Investment and Diversification

Learning Objectives

People invest their savings in order to attain some specific objectives. The objectives can be short term (such as for education or for a down payment on a house) or long term (such as for retirement). The goal of an investment decision is to choose a portfolio that is optimal for the investor's objective and risk preference.

In this chapter and the next, you will learn about investment decisions – how you should invest your savings and what factors you have to take into consideration when making an investment decision. Because investment is now a very large topic, it is not possible to cover every aspect of it in detail in this book. We concentrate on the most important issues and also on how investment decisions are related to the concept of consumption smoothing.

This chapter discusses the basic principles of investment. It starts by identifying the investment choices that are available to you. We classify these choices into five categories (or asset classes), and examine the risk and return of each asset class. Finally, you learn the concept of asset allocation and diversification.

9.1 Investment Decisions and Consumption

Saving and investing for retirement is what most people have to do. Recall from Chapter 4 that under the consumption-smoothing framework, you choose a consumption pattern that maximizes your total standard of living over your lifetime. One factor that determines the pattern of your optimal discretionary consumption is the rate of return that you can get on your savings. The higher the rate of return, the more consumption you can have.

So far in this book, we have used one so-called valuation rate v to discount and grow all cash flows. We used v to discount your future wages to arrive at the number for your gross human capital. We used v to calculate the present value of your consumption. In addition, we assumed that your investments (i.e., financial capital) would grow at the same rate v. We were deliberately vague about how to arrive at v, and why all these valuation exercises should be done at the same rate. In reality, of course, the omission of any randomness or uncertainty in v, or the fact that v can be different depending on context, is quite serious. In this chapter, we take the opportunity to chip away at this assumption.

More specifically, recall from Chapter 4 how we derived your optimal consumption rate at age x and your optimal "smooth" lifelong consumption plan. The following equation should refresh your memory:

$$c_x^* = \frac{W_x}{\text{PVA}(\overline{g}_c, v_c, D - x)} \qquad (9.1)$$
$$= \frac{F_x + w_x \cdot \text{PVA}(\overline{g}_w, v_w, R - x) - b_x \cdot \text{PVA}(\overline{g}_b, v_b, D - x)}{\text{PVA}(\overline{g}_c, v_c, D - x)},$$

where we assume that all cash flows occur at the end of the year.

In the numerator of the last equality, the value of your gross human capital $\mathbf{GH}_x$ is written explicitly as the present value of your wages (from now until retirement age R), while the value of your implicit liabilities is expressed as the present value of your subsistent consumption (from now until age of death D). The denominator is the present value factor PVA from now until age of death D.

Notice, however, that in this equation – and for the first time – we have used three different valuation rates v_w (to discount wages), v_b (to discount nondiscretionary consumption), and v_c (to discount discretionary consumption). Until now, we have assumed all the three rates are the same but there is a strong rationale for (possibly) using different rates, especially between v_w and v_c. The rate v_w is a valuation rate that takes into account the riskiness of your human capital. Individuals with safe jobs will discount wages at lower rates, whereas those in riskier jobs (from a volatility of wages perspective) will discount their expected wages at higher rates.

In contrast, the rate v_c that is used to value discretionary consumption is related to the investment rate of return on your portfolio. To see why, consider, for example, that you invest your financial capital plus your net human capital (i.e., your economic net worth) in a (risky) asset. Obviously, you do not know what the actual (i.e., realized) rate of return on it will be. You may end up with a high or low rate of return. As a result, when you choose to invest in a risky asset, your discretionary consumption will also be risky because it depends on what the realized returns on the investment will be. It then follows that the rate v_c that you should use to discount your consumption should be equal to the rate of return realized on your chosen investment.

Your choice is to decide how to invest. To make this choice clear, consider the following example. You are now thirty years old. You have a relatively safe job and make $50,000 per year. Your wage will remain the same (i.e., $g_w = 0$) until you retire at age sixty-five. You now have $100,000 in saved-up financial capital. You will live until ninety years old. Suppose that the appropriate discount rate for your wages is $v_w = 5\%$ p.a. Also assume for the sake of this illustrative example that there are no implicit liabilities (the logic of the example is not affected by this assumption).

Based on the discussion in Chapter 4, you can calculate the value of your gross human capital (which is also your net human capital because we assume that the implicit liabilities are zero). That value is $\mathbf{H}_{30} = \$818,710$. Therefore, your economic net worth (ENW) is $\mathbf{W}_{30} = \$918,710$, which is also your lifetime budget constraint that you can use to finance consumption for the rest of your life. Stated differently – and this is critical – if you wanted to, you could borrow against your human capital (at the borrowing rate of 5%, which reflects the risk of your wages) and invest the entire $918,710 anywhere you like.

Now assume that you face an **investment asset allocation** choice. To finance the consumption for the next $D - x = 60$ years of your life, you can invest the entire W_{30} in one of two ways. Route A is to invest in a relatively safe investment that (also) earns 5% p.a. for the rest of your life. In this case, the rate that you will use to discount your consumption is $v_c = 5\%$ p.a. If we assume no consumption growth ($g_c = 0$), the PVA factor will be $\mathbf{PVA}(0, 0.05, 60) = 18.9293$, and the optimal consumption will be $48,534 for the rest of your life.

Next consider route B. In contrast, imagine that your investment advisor (or Ms. Market) tosses a fair coin. Based on the outcome the advisor will grant you a specific investment return. If the coin lands on heads, you will be entitled to invest your entire economic net worth $\mathbf{W}_{30}$ at the rate of 8% p.a. for the rest of your life. On the other hand, if the coin lands on tails, your advisor (or the market) will only grant you a 2% p.a. return for the rest of your life.

If you are lucky enough to earn 8%, then the PVA factor to be used for consumption purposes – the denominator of equation (9.1) – would be $\mathbf{PVA}(0, 0.08, 60) = 12.3766$, in which case the optimal consumption becomes \$74,230 per year for the rest of your life. However, if you lose the bet, the PVA factor would be **PVA**$(0, 0.02, 60) = 34.7609$ and you would be forced to consume a mere \$26,429 per year for the rest of your life. Note that both possible paths are smooth and consistent with lifecycle principles. They both satisfy the budget constraint under each possible outcome, but the former outcome leads to much higher actual consumption compared to the latter.

Would you be willing to take such a bet? That is the investment asset allocation decision and the impetus for this chapter and the next. You have to decide if you want to earn the safe v_c and enjoy an intermediate level of consumption \$48,534, or take your chances and subject yourself to a 50% chance of \$74,230 and 50% chance of \$26,429.

Of course, real life – as opposed to the textbook world – is much more complicated because you can revise your decision (asset allocation) every instant in time, but the big picture is exactly the same. As you might conclude, those of you who are risk tolerant might be willing to take this chance and those of you who are risk averse – in the same context as the insurance discussed in the previous chapter – might decide to play it safe.

9.2 Major Asset Classes

There are numerous investment choices available in the market. We will group them into five asset classes. An **asset class** is a group of assets that possess similar risk/return characteristics and generally behave in the same manner in response to changes in economic factors. It is widely accepted that there are five major asset classes that people can invest in. They are (i) cash equivalents; (ii) fixed income (bonds); (iii) equity; (iv) commodities; and (v) real estate. We briefly discuss each of these asset classes. Note that our discussion applies to both Canadian and international assets.

9.2.1 Cash Equivalents

Cash equivalents are assets or securities that are short term in nature and can be quickly converted into cash with no (or very minimal) loss of principals. These assets are mainly short-term debt instruments and their returns are in the form of interest. Examples are bank deposits, guaranteed investment certificates (GICs), Treasury bills (i.e., short-term debt instruments issued by governments), and money-market mutual funds (i.e., mutual funds that invest in short-term debt securities).

Because of their liquidity, they have low risk (of not paying back the original investment). This characteristic appeals to people who want to set aside some funds for emergency purposes or for a short-term goal. It also appeals to conservative investors who want to preserve their capital. Their returns, however, are also low, especially on an after-tax basis. As you recall from Chapter 6, interest is the most-heavily taxed form of investment income. The after-tax rates of return from these assets are typically barely enough (and lately not even enough) to keep up with inflation. For example, between January 2005 and December 2009 (i.e., sixty months), the after-tax one-year Canadian Treasury bill rates, assuming a marginal tax rate of 30%, exceeded the inflation rates (in the subsequent twelve-month period) in only thirty-six of the sixty months. Therefore, this asset class can actually reduce your wealth in real terms.

Because of their heavy tax treatment, people who want to hold these assets for a long period of time should put them into a tax-sheltering account such as a TFSA and an RRSP.

9.2.2 Fixed Income (Bonds)

Bonds are medium term (i.e., 2 to 5 years) and long term (greater than five years) debt securities issued by governments and corporations. When you buy a bond, you are lending money to the issuer of the bond. In return, the issuer promises to pay interest and pay back the principal at the bond's maturity. To invest in this asset class, you can buy individual bonds directly. Alternatively, you can invest through mutual funds or exchange-traded funds (ETFs) that hold portfolio of bonds. We discuss these funds later in the chapter. As before, because the returns will be mainly in the form of interest, bonds and bond funds are better held inside a tax-sheltering account.

There are primarily two types of risks associated with bond investment. The first type is **default risk** or the risk of not getting the promised interest payments and/or principal repayment. If the bond's issuer is the government of a major country, the default risk is practically nonexistent. Bonds issued by other countries, other levels of government (e.g., provincial and municipal), and corporations have default risk. The amount of risk depends on the fiscal conditions of the issuers. Bond-rating agencies such as *Moody's, Standard & Poor's*, and *Dominion Bond Rating Service (DBRS)* regularly publish the credit ratings of these bonds that investors can use when making purchase decisions.

The second type of risk is **interest-rate risk**. Most of the bonds available in the market are fixed-rate bonds (and so their cash flows are known and fixed). When market interest rates fluctuate, the prices of the bonds will change. This is because bonds are priced by discounting their cash flows using the current interest rates. If, for example, the market rates increase, the prices of the bonds will decline, and vice versa. The longer the maturity of the bond, the larger the effect of changes is in market interest rates.

Interest-rate risk is important to you if you plan to sell your bonds before their maturity. Because of this risk, the prices that you will get for them are uncertain. However, if you plan to hold the bonds until their maturity, you are sure to receive the face values of the bonds back (assuming no default risk).

9.2.3 Equities

Equity securities include stocks and stock indices. Stocks represent an ownership of the companies that issue them. These companies can be public or private. Public companies are companies that have at one time (or more) sold their shares to the public, and now their shares are traded on stock exchanges. Therefore, it is easy to buy or sell shares of public companies. In contrast, shares of private companies are not listed on stock exchanges (and thus are not liquid).

Stock indices are portfolios of publicly traded stock constructed according to some pre-specified criteria. For example, there are broad-based indices such as the TSX composite and the S&P/TSX 60 in Canada and the S&P 500 in the United States. These indices cover most of the market in terms of market capitalization (i.e., the values of the stocks that are in the market). There are also sector indices that cover companies in specific industry sectors such as the financial and energy sectors. Typically, investors invest in stock indices through mutual funds and ETFs.

As an owner (or a shareholder), you are entitled to the company's residual cash flows after lenders have been paid. Therefore, when you buy a stock, you are taking more risk than if you are buying a bond issued by the same company. When the company does well, you can expect to share in the profits. When the company does poorly, you will get nothing or even lose part of your initial investment. This is the primary source of risk that equity investors face. Because the risk is higher, their *expected* returns are also higher. We will shortly talk about equity's historical rates of return and compare them to those of other asset classes.

Returns from an equity investment comes in the form of dividends and/or capital gains. As you know from Chapter 6, these forms of investment income receive more favorable tax treatment than interest income does.

9.2.4 Commodities

Commodities are assets that are used for consumption or as raw materials in the production of goods and services. There are three major groups of commodities. They are (a) energy such as crude oil and natural gas; (b) metals such as gold, copper, and aluminum; and (c) agricultures such as wheat, corn, and cotton.

There are a few ways to invest in commodities. First, you can buy them directly. This is feasible for certain commodities such as gold. Still, it will require that you find a storage facility for them. For other commodities such as perishable agricultural products, this strategy would not work. Secondly, you can buy stocks of companies that produce commodities such as mining or oil companies. This approach has traditionally been common for most investors, especially retail ones. However, it is an indirect way to gain exposure to commodity price movements because the returns from investment are dependent not only on commodity prices, but also on the companies' management ability. Thirdly, you can trade futures contracts on commodities. A futures contract is an agreement to buy or sell an asset in the future at a predetermined price. These contracts are risky because they contain substantial leverage and, as a result, are traded primarily by sophisticated investors. Finally and most recently, you can buy mutual funds and ETFs that hold physical commodities, shares of commodity firms, or futures contracts.

During the past few years, commodity mutual funds have become very popular. This, together with the fact that institutional fund managers have moved their money into commodities in search for higher returns, has brought commodities to mainstream attention.

Historically, the major benefit of commodity investment has come from the fact that commodities act as a hedge against the increase in the prices of consumption baskets. Because commodities are used as raw materials in the production of goods and services, commodity prices are correlated with prices of finished products. Investors who are concerned about inflation eroding the purchasing power of their investments can invest in commodities to protect against it.

In addition, returns on commodities are not highly correlated with the returns of other asset classes. As we will see in the next chapter, assets that are not highly correlated with others can provide diversification benefits to investment portfolios.

As for their risk, it does depend on the types of commodity that you want to invest in. Generally, however, commodities are more risky than an average equity asset.

9.2.5 Real Estate

Real estate refers to both residential (e.g., a house and a cottage) and commercial (e.g., a shopping plaza and an office building) properties. There are two approaches to real-estate investment – direct and indirect. With direct investment, you invest in physical real-estate properties. Typically, the properties are residential rather than commercial (which requires considerable knowledge and active involvement). Direct investment requires substantial amounts of money, and so has traditionally been done by wealthy individuals. Lately, however, small investors were lured by the housing price boom in the early part of the twenty-first century, especially in the United States. They took out mortgage loans to invest in residential properties in the hope that prices would continue to move up. Unfortunately, the housing market in the United States and a few other countries suffered a steep downturn in 2008, and many investors lost money from it.

With indirect investment, you can invest in real estate investment trusts (REITs), which are publicly traded funds that invest in real-estate properties. Indirect investment is more appropriate for individual investors because REITs are managed by professionals who have knowledge of real-estate markets and know how to manage properties.

Real estate prices typically move with economic conditions. As a result, the risk of real-estate investment comes from the underlying risk in the economy (e.g., growth, unemployment, etc.). In addition, direct investment has liquidity risk, as it is costly and time-consuming to buy and sell real estate. In contrast, REIT investors can easily buy and sell their investment units in the market, and so liquidity risk is not as significant.

One benefit of an investment in real estate is that it can provide you with a hedge against your sheltering needs. For example, suppose you do not yet own a house (i.e., you are renting a place). If house prices are to go up, it will be more expensive for you to buy a house. Even if you plan to continue to rent, the rental payment may increase to reflect the higher price of the house that you are renting. To protect against this risk, you can buy a house right now. Alternatively, you can buy a REIT that invests in residential properties. If house prices do indeed increase, you will get positive returns from the

Table 9.1. *Annual rates of return and standard deviations of different asset classes*

Year	Cash equivalents (% p.a.)	Fixed-income (% p.a.)	Equity (% p.a.)	Commodities (% p.a.)	Real estate (% p.a.)
1991	8.70%	9.36%	12.02%	−6.08%	
1992	6.60%	8.16%	−1.43%	10.14%	
1993	5.15%	7.24%	32.55%	−0.05%	
1994	6.09%	8.26%	−0.18%	18.38%	
1995	7.04%	7.93%	14.53%	6.01%	
1996	4.44%	6.86%	28.35%	17.36%	
1997	3.64%	5.87%	14.98%	−4.26%	
1998	4.92%	5.26%	−1.58%	−25.59%	
1999	4.92%	5.56%	31.71%	12.59%	2.88%
2000	5.70%	5.96%	7.41%	28.25%	8.38%
2001	3.77%	5.32%	−12.57%	−17.53%	17.84%
2002	2.77%	5.08%	−12.44%	22.85%	−1.82%
2003	2.94%	4.54%	26.72%	0.36%	15.83%
2004	2.32%	4.34%	14.48%	0.46%	5.39%
2005	2.87%	3.89%	24.13%	13.62%	16.95%
2006	4.11%	4.18%	17.26%	−2.76%	17.60%
2007	4.26%	4.25%	9.83%	−5.81%	−10.83%
2008	2.52%	3.36%	−33.00%	−21.44%	−43.05%
2009	0.44%	2.84%	35.05%	1.46%	42.44%
2010	0.78%	2.88%	17.61%	10.88%	15.07%
Mean	4.20%	5.56%	11.27%	2.94%	7.22%
Standard Deviation	1.81%	1.71%	17.96%	14.57%	20.56%

Source: All return series were calculated by the authors based on data from Bloomberg and Dow Jones Indexes.

REIT investment, which you can then use to help pay for a house or a higher rent.

9.3 Historical Returns

We now look at the historical returns of the five asset classes. Because each asset class covers many securities from many countries, we need to choose a representative for each class. For the purpose of this discussion, each class will be represented by a specific Canadian security/index. Keep in mind, however, that there are many other securities outside of Canada that you can also (and should) invest in.

Table 9.1 displays the rates of return of each asset class from 1991 to 2010. The returns on cash equivalents are represented by the interest rates on

Canadian six-month Treasury bills. For fixed-income securities, the returns
are the yields on Canadian long-term (five to ten years) marketable bonds.
For these two asset classes, the rates shown for each year are the averages
of the rates in the twelve months of that year. For equity, we use the TSX
Composite Total Return Index. This index represents approximately 70%
of the total market capitalization of all companies listed on the Toronto
Stock Exchange. Its returns consist of both the dividends and capital gains
on the stocks comprising the index. Commodities are proxied by the Dow
Jones-UBS Commodity Index. The index tracks the price movements of a
portfolio of nineteen commodities weighted by their economic significance
and market liquidity. We present the index returns in Canadian dollar terms
by converting their returns in U.S. dollar (which is the currency in which
most commodities are priced) into Canadian dollar using the exchange
rate at the end of each year. Finally, we use TSX Capped REIT Index for
real estate. This index captures the returns on a portfolio of real-estate
investment trusts listed on the Toronto Stock Exchange. The data for this
index start from 1999.

Over the past twenty years, the average rates of return on cash equivalent
and fixed-income asset classes were 4.20% p.a. and 5.56% p.a., respectively.
On the other hand, equity yielded an average rate of return of 11.27% p.a.
Note, however, that while the returns of these three asset classes varied
from year to year, the variation, as measured by standard deviation, was
much less for cash equivalents and fixed-income securities than for equity.
Cash equivalents and fixed-income assets had lower risks than equity did.
However, their returns were also lower.

For commodities, their returns fluctuated substantially from year to year.
In the past twenty years, their annual returns were as high as 28% and as
low as −26%. The standard deviation was 14.57%, which is much higher
than those of cash equivalents and fixed-income asset classes. Because of
the considerable variation in commodities' annual returns, the average rate
of return was small. It was indeed lower than the average cash equivalents
and fixed-income returns over the same time period.

It thus appears that commodities had lower average returns and higher
risk than fixed-income securities, and so they would not be useful as part of
your portfolio. However, as mentioned earlier, commodities may provide
diversification benefits if their returns are not highly correlated with those
of other asset classes (a subject that we examine shortly). We want to also
emphasize that the returns shown in Table 9.1 were from the portfolio of
nineteen commodities belonging to and weighted as specified by the Dow
Jones-USB Commodity Index. Obviously, each individual commodity has

its own risk/return profile. As a result, a different mix of commodities can yield a different outcome.

9.3.1 Arithmetic Average vs. Geometric Average

It is important to note that the average rates of return shown in Table 9.1 are simple (or arithmetic) averages of the returns over the twenty-year period. This is not the average annual rate at which your investment would grow during that period. For that, you need to take into account the compounding effect of your investment (which arithmetic averages do not). For example, if you invested $100 in the TSX Composite Total Return Index at the start of 1991, your money will grow each year at the rate of return of that year (which can be positive or negative). This means that by the end of 1991, you would have $100 \cdot (1 + 0.1202) = $112.02. Then, by the end of 1992, the investment would become $112.02 \cdot (1 - 0.0143) = $110.42, and so on. By the end of 2010 you would end up with $649.47, which means that over twenty years, your investment would have grown by 649.47%. The average annual growth rate over the period is then:

$$\left[\frac{649.47}{100}\right]^{\frac{1}{20}} - 1 = 0.098065 \text{ or } 9.8065\% \text{ p.a.}$$

This average is the so-called geometric average (also known as the compound annual growth rate (CAGR)). It takes into account the compounding effect. Note that it is lower than the arithmetic average (which is 11.27% p.a.). In fact, it is well known that the arithmetic average of any series of numbers will always be at least as high as the geometric average of the series. The more variable the numbers in the series are (i.e., in our context, the more volatile the returns during the period are), the greater the difference will be between the two averages. Therefore, when it comes to rates of return, the use of an arithmetic average can be misleading because it will tend to overstate the actual average growth rate of your investment, especially over a volatile period.

Formally, let R_t be the realized return on an asset during period t. The geometric average rate of return over T periods (i.e., period 1 to period T) is:

$$\left[\prod_{t=1}^{T}(1 + R_t)\right]^{\frac{1}{T}} - 1. \tag{9.2}$$

Table 9.2. *Correlation coefficients among asset classes*

	Cash equivalents	Fixed-income	Equity	Commodities (In C$)	Real estate
Cash equivalents	1.00				
Fixed-income	0.91	1.00			
Equity	−0.08	−0.01	1.00		
Commodities (In C$)	0.07	0.20	0.32	1.00	
Real estate	−0.26	−0.08	0.72	0.30	1.00

Source: Author Calculations.

Note that the calculation in equation (9.2) involves multiplying (one plus) each period's return together. This is why a geometric average rate of return takes into account the compounding effect of investment (i.e., how your investment will grow given each period's realized return).

9.3.2 Correlations of Returns

Next we look at the correlation coefficients among the returns of the five asset classes. Correlation coefficients measure the extent to which one random variable co-moves with another random variable. The theoretical maximum for the value of correlation coefficients is +1 (i.e., the two random variables co-move perfectly positively with each other), while the theoretical minimum is −1 (i.e., the two random variables co-move perfectly negatively with each other). A coefficient of zero implies that the two variables are not related.

The correlation coefficients are displayed in Table 9.2. There are a few things to note from the table. First, the returns on cash equivalents and fixed income securities were almost unrelated to the returns on equity and commodities. The correlation coefficients are very close to zero. Secondly, commodities' returns (in either currency) are positively correlated with equity's returns. However, the correlations are not very strong. The coefficient between commodities' returns and equity's return is only 0.32. In other words, commodities and equity tended to move in the same direction, but not very frequently. Finally, real estate and equity had a strong correlation (i.e., 0.72). This is not that surprising considering that the two asset classes depend on most of the same economic factors.

9.4 Asset Allocation and Diversification

Now that we know the risk/return profiles of the five asset classes, one very important investment decision that you have to make is how to allocate your investment among these asset classes. Essentially, we are talking about the concept of diversification (which will be formally discussed in the next chapter). You want to spread your wealth among different asset classes to take advantage of the imperfect correlations among them. In some years, some asset classes may do well while the others may not. On average, you balance the good with the bad, and hopefully you come out ahead (or not having a heavy loss) every year.

For example, consider the year 2002. If you had put all of your investment in Canadian equity, the rate of return on your investment, according to Table 9.1, would have been -12.44%. If, however, you had spread your investment evenly among all the five asset classes (i.e., 20% in each), your return would have been:

$$0.2 \cdot 2.77 + 0.2 \cdot 5.08 + 0.2 \cdot [-12.44] + 0.2 \cdot 22.85 + 0.2 \cdot [-1.82]$$
$$= 3.29\% \text{ p.a.,}$$

which, while not great, would still have been acceptable in such a year.

Your allocation decision will depend primarily on two factors. The first factor is your risk preference. If you are risk-averse (like most people are), you will perform a trade-off between returns and risks and choose the asset mix (i.e., how much in safe assets and how much in risky assets) with the overall risk/return profile that you are most comfortable with. The second factor is the nature of your economic balance sheet. In particular, you should take into consideration the two biggest assets that you have, which are your gross human capital, $\mathbf{H}_x$, and your house (if you own one).

Let us consider first your gross human capital. As discussed in Chapter 3, your gross human capital has its own risk/return profile because different occupations have different inherent risks. For example, an investment banker or a stockbroker has income that is highly dependent on stock market conditions. When the market is doing well, he will likely earn a substantial bonus. On the other hand, when there is a recession (like the one in late 2008), he will not make as much money or might even get laid off. Consequently, his gross human capital has a risk/return profile that is similar to equity, and so it may not be wise for him to put a lot of his savings into equity. Rather, he should diversify into other asset classes such as fixed income. In contrast, consider a tenured university professor. Her job is stable and her salary does not depend (at least directly) on stock market movements. As a result, her gross human capital has a risk/return profile that is similar to fixed-income assets. In this case, she can afford to take more investment risk.

We want to emphasize that the determination of the risk/return profile of your human capital can be a difficult task, especially if your job falls somewhere between the two extremes (i.e., fixed-income vs. equity). The profile will only become evident over time.

To make this point clear, consider the following example.

Practice Question   *Consider a fifty-year-old professional whose job is relatively safe (such as a quasi-government job). Her net human capital is $600,000. She has a risk/return profile similar to a portfolio of $400,000 in bonds and $200,000 in stocks. In addition, she has managed to accumulate $500,000 in financial capital. If she wants the risk/return profile of her whole economic net worth to be 50% risky and 50% safe, how should she allocate her financial capital?*

Her economic net worth is now $600,000 + $500,000 = $1,100,000. To split this evenly between risky and safe assets, she needs to have $550,000 in each. Because her net human capital already represents $400,000 worth of safe assets, she should invest only $150,000 of her financial capital in safe assets. The rest should be invested in risky assets. In other words, her financial capital should consist of $150,000 (or 30%) in safe assets and $350,000 (or 70%) in risky assets. Note that anyone who only looks at her financial capital may mistakenly conclude that she is taking too much risk. However, she has achieved her overall desired asset mix. Her relatively safe human capital allows her to take more investment risk.

Next, consider the role of a house in making investment decisions. Most Canadian households already have an investment in real estate in the form of their houses. According to Statistics Canada, the home ownership rate (i.e., the proportion of households who own their home, either outright or with a mortgage) was about 68% in 2006 (the next census will come out in 2011). For these people, their overall portfolios are already significantly overweighed in real estate. Consequently, it may be a good idea for them to direct their future savings away from this asset class. For people who are renting, however, they will not have this constraint, and so they can afford to have more exposure to real estate. As we mentioned earlier, an investment in real estate (such as owning a REIT) can help these people to hedge their sheltering needs.

In summary, when you make an allocation decision, you want to diversify your whole economic balance sheet, and not just your investment portfolio. Obviously, it can be a long, gradual process to achieve diversification. This is especially true when you are young and most of your assets are in the form of your human capital and house. As time passes, you gradually convert your human capital into financial capital. It is during this period that you should move your allocation toward the desired combination.

9.5 Mutual Funds and Exchange-Traded Funds

The most efficient way to invest in a large portfolio of securities is to buy mutual funds and/or exchange-traded funds. Although the underlying idea is the same for the two kinds of funds, there are important differences between them that investors should be aware of.

9.5.1 Mutual Funds

A mutual fund is a investment pool that accepts money from many investors and invests that money in a portfolio of securities. Depending on the stated objectives of the fund, the securities in the portfolio can be anything from the five asset classes mentioned earlier. The funds can either be actively or passively managed. In an **actively managed fund**, the fund manager attempts to generate good returns by choosing which securities to hold given the fund's mandate. In contrast, a **passively managed fund** simply attempts to mimic the movements of some bond or equity index (and thus it is sometimes referred to as an **index fund**). There is no significant managerial input on the composition of the underlying portfolio. In addition, the portfolio is not frequently revised.

Types of Mutual Funds
There are now (as of 2011) approximately 200 mutual funds companies in Canada. Altogether, they offer close to 10,000 mutual funds to investors. These funds can be categorized into various types, the most common of which are as follows:

- Money market funds: The goal of these funds is to generate stable income with good liquidity. They invest in securities that belong to the cash equivalents asset class such as T-bills and high-quality commercial papers (unsecured, short-term instruments issued by corporations). They are relatively low risk.
- Bond funds: These funds generally invest in government bonds and investment-grade corporate bonds. As a result, they keep the default risk low, and so the main risk is interest-rate risk. There are, however, some bond funds that invest in noninvestment-grade bonds

(i.e., junk bonds). These funds aim to generate higher yields in exchange for taking on default risk. Consequently, they are more speculative in nature. The advantages of bond funds are that they are diversified and more liquid than individual bonds.

- Dividend funds: These funds aim to generate dividends with a small possibility for capital gains. They invest in preferred stocks and common stocks that have good records of consistent dividend payments.
- Growth funds: These funds intend to maximize capital appreciation. Investing primarily in common stocks of high-growth firms, they are riskier than dividend funds.
- Balanced funds and asset allocation funds: These type of funds are very popular in Canada. They aim for a mixture of income, growth, and safety. They hold both stocks and bonds, and usually have guidelines for the weight in each asset class.
- International funds: These funds invest in stocks and stock indices of foreign countries. They may concentrate on a specific region of the world (such as Europe or Asia). They provide diversification benefits to investors who have a high percentage of their wealth invested in Canadian stocks.

Mutual Funds Expenses

A fund's expenses come in two categories – sales commissions and management fees. With respect to sales commissions, mutual funds can be classified as load funds or no-load funds. A **load fund** is a mutual fund where investors pay a commission when they buy (front-end load) or redeem (back-end load) fund units. The commissions are intended to compensate the fund's sales force (e.g., brokers, advisors, and financial planners) for the explanations and advice that they give to investors. Generally, the commissions are a few percentages (e.g., 2% to 5%) of the value of the investment (though higher rates exist). Front-end loads also depend on the size of the investment. The higher the amount of the investment, the lower the rates are. The rates of back-end loads depend on how long the funds are held before you redeem them. The longer the holding period, the lower the rates are. Both front-end and back-end loads have the effect of discouraging short-term investment in the funds.

The front-end loads are deducted from the value of your investment when you purchase the funds. For example, suppose you decide to invest $10,000 in a fund that charges a 3% front-end load. You make a payment of $10,000, and $300 will be deducted from it, which means that the amount available for investment is $9,700. The back-end loads, on the other hand, are subtracted from the proceeds when you redeem your investment. For example, suppose you want to withdraw $5,000 from a fund that charges a 4% back-end load. You will end up with $5,000 − $200 = $4,800.

A **no-load fund**, on the other hand, does not charge commissions and is available from mutual fund companies and banks that sell their products directly to the public. You can also buy a no-load fund through a discount broker.

The second category of mutual funds expenses is management fees. Management fees (or management expenses) are intended to compensate the fund companies for their operating costs (e.g., bookkeeping costs), investment management costs, marketing costs, and other administrative expenses. They are charged as a percentage of the fund's total assets and therefore are typically referred to as **fund management expense ratios (MERs)**. MERs typically range from 0.25% to 3% per year, and are deducted directly from the funds' values before the funds' performance is calculated. MERs usually depend on the types of assets held by the funds. For example, funds that invest in foreign countries usually have higher MERs than funds that invest domestically.

One important component of MERs is service fees (or trailers). Service fees are ongoing compensation that mutual funds companies pay to financial planners/advisors for ongoing services that they provide to investors. Trailer fees typically range from 0.5% to 1% per year. Obviously, trailer fees increase the funds' MERs (but this does not necessarily mean that funds with no trailer fees will always have low MERs). People who need investment advice will usually end up with funds whose MERs contain trailer fees.

The following example illustrates the effect of MERs on funds' performance.

Practice Question *You are now thirty years old. You want to invest $10,000 per year (at the end of each year) in a mutual fund. The fund invests in a portfolio of securities whose expected return is 8% p.a. The fund charges a MER of 0.50%. You will retire at sixty-five. How much money will you have at the start of your retirement? What if the fund's MER were 1.50%?*

If the fund's MER is 0.50%, the expected return on the investment after MER is then 7.50% p.a. The amount of money that you will have after thirty-five years of investment is:

$$10,000 \cdot \textbf{FVA}\,(0.075,35) = 10,000 \cdot \left[\frac{(1.075)^{35} - 1}{0.075} \right] = 1,542,516.$$

On the other hand, if the fund's MER were 1.50%, the expected return after MER is then 6.50% p.a. In this case, you have:

$$10,000 \cdot \textbf{FVA}\,(0.065,35) = 10,000 \cdot \left[\frac{(1.065)^{35} - 1}{0.065} \right] = 1,240,347,$$

which is lower by more than 300,000, so beware of the fund's expenses. A difference of only 1% per year can translate into a substantial amount of money over a long period.

Note that trading costs (i.e., brokerage fees that the funds have to pay when they trade) are typically not included in MERs. This adds another layer of costs to the funds. Actively managed funds will have higher MERs and trading costs than index (i.e., passively managed) funds. This is because actively managed funds require regular investment input from the funds' management. They also trade more frequently and so incur more brokerage fees.

Benefits of Mutual Funds
Mutual funds have three major benefits. First, because they accumulate a lot of money, they have economies of scale, which enable them to buy and sell securities in large lots and save investors transaction costs. They also allow small investors to achieve diversification. Rather than having to buy many individual securities to form a diversified portfolio by themselves, small investors can buy units of a mutual fund and get to own part of the underlying portfolio of many stocks. Secondly, they simplify your decision-making process. Instead of having to evaluate individual securities, you now only need to decide based on the risk/return profiles of the funds in which you are interested. As a by-product, the record-keeping process is also less demanding, because you regularly receive a statement listing the values of the funds that you own. Thirdly, mutual funds are a liquid investment. Investors can convert their holdings into cash quickly.

Disadvantages of Mutual Funds
There are a few disadvantages to mutual funds. First, because of the commissions and MERs, they can be costly. The second disadvantage of mutual funds is the below-par performance of most actively managed funds. Studies have shown that actively managed funds, on average, underperform market indices. This is due in large part to their high management expenses. For example, if a fund charges management fees of 3% per year, then it has to beat the market every year by that much just to stay even with the market.

The third disadvantage is the tax impact of distributions from mutual funds. Mutual funds are required to distribute the income that they receive from the securities that they hold to the unit holders every year. At the end of each year, fund companies will send investors a report detailing the types and amounts of income. The income includes interest, dividends, and capital gains (from the funds' trading). You will then have to pay taxes on the income. Note that you have to pay taxes on the capital gains that the funds generate even if you do not sell your fund units. Funds that buy and sell securities frequently have substantial capital gains distributions.

9.5.2 Exchange-Traded Funds (ETFs)

An exchange-traded fund (ETF) is an investment pool that is similar in concept to a mutual fund. The major difference is that units of an ETF are traded on stock exchanges (like stocks). Investors who want to invest in an ETF will buy its units in the market at the prevailing market price. This is different from the case of mutual funds where investors buy them from the funds or their salespeople, and the price is equal to the net asset value (NAV) per unit at the end of that day. Investors who no longer wish to hold an ETF will sell its units in the market during trading hours. Again, this is different from the case of mutual funds where investors redeem their units from the fund companies at the redemption price equal to the NAV per unit at the end of that day. The fact that you can trade an ETF at any time during trading hours at the prevailing market price gives you greater control over the price at which you want to trade.

Traditionally, ETFs are passively managed. Their investment objectives are simply to track the performance of bond or equity indices. As a result, ETFs have low portfolio turnovers and their trading costs and MERs are generally very low (e.g., 0.15% to 0.50%). Keep in mind, however, that because ETFs are traded in the market, you will incur brokerage fees every time you buy or sell them. To avoid brokerage fees negating the benefits of low MERs, you should use a discount broker (who may charge as little as $10 per trade). You should also avoid buying ETFs in small increments.

9.6 Summary

In this chapter, we introduce the topic of investment. We look at the five asset classes and their risk/return profiles. Relatively safe assets such as cash equivalents and fixed-income securities have lower returns but also lower risks than risky assets such as equity, commodities, and real estate. In an investment decision, you allocate your savings across these asset classes such that you achieve the desired risk/return profile for your *overall* wealth. This means that you take the risk/return profile of your net human capital into consideration when you make an investment decision.

Diversification is an important concept. As shown in Tables 9.1 and 9.2, different asset classes do not move in tandem. In some years, one asset class does better than others. Therefore, you can reduce your investment risk by spreading your investment over different asset classes. You should also diversify your investment within each class. To this end, mutual funds are a great tool to gain exposure to large portfolios of securities. People no longer need a lot of money to have investment portfolios that are well diversified both across and within asset classes. The benefits of diversification will be explored in more detail in the next chapter.

9.7 Questions and Assignments

1. If you put in $20,000 into a real-estate investment trust in 1999 (whose returns mimic the TSX Capped REIT Index in Table 9.1), what did your money grow to at the end 2010?

2. Suppose that you decide to split your investment evenly among the five asset classes in Table 9.1. Calculate the weighted average returns that you would get each year between 2000 and 2010. Also, calculate the standard deviation of those weighted average returns.

3. Consider a thirty-five-year-old investment banker. Her net human capital is $1,000,000. She has a risk/return profile similar to a portfolio of $200,000 in bonds and $800,000 in stocks. In addition, she has managed to accumulate $100,000 in financial capital. If she wants the risk/return profile of her whole economic net worth to be 50% risky and 50% safe, how should she allocate her financial capital?

4. How much of $100,000 financial capital should a hair dresser allocate toward bonds vs. stocks? State and explain your assumptions.

5. Please refer to question 4. How will your answer change if you found out that he owned a condo?

6. How does the person's age affect which asset class they invest in? Please explain.

7. You are considering investing in a mutual fund. The fund is a loaded fund, and it offers you a choice. You can choose to pay a front-end load of 5% or a back-end load of 3%. If you choose the front-end load, the fund's MER will be 2% per year. If you choose the back-end load, the fund's MER will be 2.25% per year. Assume that the

fund expects to generate a return of 10% per year (before expenses), and that you intend to invest in this fund for five years. Which choice will you choose?

8. Based on question 7, will your decision change if you intend to invest in the fund for ten years? If so, find out the break-even holding period where you will feel indifferent between the two choices.

9. You are now twenty-five years old. You want to invest $15,000 per year (at the end of each year) in a mutual fund. The fund invests in a portfolio of securities whose expected return is 9% p.a. The fund charges a MER of 1%. How much money will you have thirty years from now?

10. Refer to question 9. What if the MER was 2%?

TEN

The Mathematics of Portfolio Diversification

Learning Objectives

In this chapter, you will formally learn the concept of diversification. In the process, you will become mindful of investment-performance claims and the roles of chance in obtaining above-average returns. You will also learn how you can construct an investment portfolio that is optimal for you given your risk preference and risk/return trade-off.

10.1 Impressive Investment Performance: Real or Fake

In the mid-1980s, a clever investment broker at a large American brokerage firm (in its Baltimore, Maryland branch) devised the following strategy in publishing his newsletters. He obtained a list of 2,000 high-net-worth individuals from a local golf club. In early January, he sent a letter to 1,000 of them (chosen at random) suggesting that they buy (i.e., long) soybean futures contracts. At the same time, he sent a different letter to the other 1,000, suggesting that they sell (i.e., short) soybean futures. By late January, soybean futures price dropped by about 10%, and so anyone in the second group who took his advice earned 10% in one month.

In early February, he sent follow-up letters to 500 of the "winners" (i.e., those who were told to short soybean futures contracts), advising them to buy German Deutschmark futures (at the time, Germany had not yet adopted the euro as their currency). The other 500 "winners" were sent a letter advising them to short Deutschmark futures. It turned out that the Deutschmark went up by 5% in February. So, 500 people got letters that correctly predicted the future two months in a row.

Then, in early March, he sent another letter to 250 of those two-time winners and suggested that they buy S&P stock index futures contracts while the other 250 were told to short the contracts. In that month, the S&P

Table 10.1. *Random investment advice to 2,000 people*

Month	Return (%)	Probability of consecutive correct predictions	No. of winners by the end of each month
January	10%	0.500000	1,000
February	5%	0.250000	500
March	4%	0.125000	250
April	7%	0.062500	125
May	5%	0.031250	62
June	8%	0.015625	31
July	6%	0.007813	15
Compound Return	54%		

Source: Author Calculations.

index fell by about 3%, and there were now 250 people who received correct predictions for three consecutive months.

He continued this process of sending contradictory predictions to the groups. Each month, the number of winners is halved. There were 125 winners in April, 62 in May, 31 in June, and 15 in July. By the end of July, the fifteen winners had been receiving correct prediction seven months in a row. If any of them had taken action based on the advice every month, he or she would have earned compounded return of about 54% over seven months, which would have been extraordinary by most measures.

Table 10.1 summarizes the outcomes of the strategy together with the probabilities of consecutive correct predictions. Obviously, the strategy did not rely on the broker's predictive power. Rather, the outcomes (i.e., who would get the right predictions) were determined by chance. Because the broker split the group in half every month, the probability of receiving a correct prediction is 0.50 per month. After seven months (i.e., in July), the probability of receiving seven correct predictions in a row is $0.50^7 = 0.007813$. As a result, out of the 2,000 people that the broker started off with, about 15 ended up being seven-time winners.

In fact, at the end of the seventh month, the broker sent a letter to each of the fifteen seven-time winners, congratulating them and asking each of them for $1 million. It turned out that about two-thirds of the winners did give money to the broker, who subsequently disappeared, never to be seen again.

Now, if you had been one of those people who had been receiving a series of correct investment predictions, what would you have thought? Would you not have been inclined to believe that the broker did indeed possess an extraordinary predictive ability? Would you not have been tempted to follow his recommendations?

The message of the story is that claims of good investment performance may have nothing to do with ability, and everything to do with chance. In addition, it can be very difficult to distinguish ability from chance. Mutual fund and hedge fund companies introduce many funds with different risk levels and slants on the market. For example, there are currently more than 200 fund companies in Canada, offering more than 10,000 funds to investors. As time passes, they shut down the funds that did not do well and keep only the good ones. In their advertisements, you will only see good performance. This creates survivorship biases in performance measurements. As a result, you need to be careful with performance claims.

10.2 Portfolio Diversification

In this section, you are introduced to the mathematics of risk and returns, which will then lead to the formal discussion of portfolio diversification.

10.2.1 Preliminaries

Let us start with a very simple risk-taking example. Suppose you are at a roulette table in a casino. You place a $10,000 bet (for red or black). If the color that you bet on comes up, you double your money, or $20,000. Otherwise, you will get nothing. How much money do you *expect* to have after the wheel stops spinning? Obviously, the answer is $10,000. The reason is quite simple. The chance of getting red or black is 50–50. So, regardless of the color that you choose, your chance of winning is 50%, and so the expected payoff of the bet is $10,000 (which is the same as the amount of your bet). Note that $10,000 is the expected payoff, which is a mathematical concept. The actual payoff that you will get does not have to be the same as the expected payoff. In this case, the actual payoff will be either $20,000 or zero (i.e., only two possible outcomes). You will either double your money or lose it all.

Now suppose you bet $5,000 each on two tables (let us call them Table A and Table B). Your total bet (or investment) is again $10,000. What are the possible outcomes and the expected payoff? Think of the combinations of outcomes that can occur.

You can win on both tables, which means you will get $10,000 per table or $20,000 in total. Because the two tables operate independently of each other, the probability of winning at each table is 0.50 (i.e., the fact that you win at one table does not affect the chance that you will win at the other), and thus the probability of this outcome is $0.50 \cdot 0.50 = 0.25$. You can win on one table and lose on the other. If this happens, you get $10,000. There are two ways that this outcome can occur. You win on Table A but lose on Table B (and vice versa). The chance of each way happening is $0.50 \cdot 0.50 = 0.25$ (again, the two tables are independent of each other). So, the probability of this outcome is twice that, or 0.50. Finally, you can lose on both tables, in which case you get zero. The probability of this outcome is $0.50 \cdot 0.50 = 0.25$.

Therefore, the expected payoff from betting $1 each on two tables is:

$$(0.25 \cdot 20{,}000) + (0.50 \cdot 10{,}000) + (0.25 \cdot 0) = \$10{,}000.$$

Note that by spreading your money over two tables, there are more possible outcomes than before (i.e., four different win-lose combinations and three different dollar outcomes). Note also that the chance that you will lose all your investment is now 0.25.

Next, let us take it a step further. Suppose you bet $100 each on 100 tables. Your total investment is again $10,000. There are now too many possible outcomes to write out – from winning on only one table to winning on all 100 tables. The expected payoff in this case is, as before, $10,000. (You can simply note that the expected payoff per table is $100, and so with 100 independent tables, the total expected payoff must be $10,000.) However, what about the chance of losing money or the chance of getting less than a certain dollar amount?

Table 10.2 displays selected possible outcomes and their probabilities (you will shortly learn how these probabilities are calculated). For example, the probability of getting a payoff that is less than $9,500 (i.e., a loss of 5% or more) is 0.3085, while the probability of getting less than $9,000 (i.e., a loss of 10% or more) is 0.1587. In addition, the chance of getting a payoff below $5,000 (i.e., a loss of 50% or more) is negligible.

Now, let us see what happens if you spread your money even further. Suppose you bet $1 each on 10,000 tables. Your total investment is still $10,000, and the expected payoff is again $10,000. Let us compare the probabilities of losses in this case to the previous case. The probabilities are shown in Table 10.3.

As you can see, the probability of losing 5% or more is now negligible (compared to 0.3085 in the previous case), while the chance of losing 1% or more is also substantial lower.

Table 10.2. *Probability of outcomes being less than a certain dollar amount — 100 tables*

Outcome	Return on investment	Probability
Less than or equal to $5,000	<= 50%	0.0000%
Less than or equal to $7,500	<= 25%	0.6210%
Less than or equal to $9,000	<= 10%	15.8655%
Less than or equal to $9,500	<= 5%	30.8538%
Less than or equal to $9,900	<= 1%	46.0172%
Less than or equal to $10,000	<= 0%	50.0000%

Source: Author Calculations.

Now, having seen the probabilities of losses under both strategies (i.e., 100 tables vs. 10,000 tables), which one would you choose? Both strategies have the same expected payoff, but the second strategy has much less risk (i.e., the outcomes are closer to the mean than under the first strategy).

Here is an important point of the exercises that you have done so far. When you bet all your money on one table, the chance of losing it all is greater than when you spread it over 100 tables. In turn, if you spread your investment over 10,000 tables, the chance of getting high losses are even lower. There are two things that drive this outcome. First, the roulette tables are independent (i.e., their outcomes are not correlated). Secondly, as you spread your bet over more and more tables, the outcome will be closer and closer to the expected outcome (remember that the expected payoff is always $10,000). This is indeed the result of the law of large numbers, which we touched on in Chapter 7. If you recall, the law of large numbers states that as the number of *independent* trials of a random experiment increases, the

Table 10.3. *Probability of outcomes being less than a certain dollar amount — 10,000 tables*

Outcome	Return on investment	Probability
Less than or equal to $5,000	<= 50%	0.0000%
Less than or equal to $7,500	<=25%	0.0000%
Less than or equal to $9,000	<= 10%	0.0000%
Less than or equal to $9,500	<= 5%	0.0000%
Less than or equal to $9,900	<= 1%	15.8655%
Less than or equal to $10,000	<= 0%	50.0000%

Source: Author Calculations.

average of the results obtained from those trials should be closer and closer to the expected value.

What we have illustrated is exactly the concept of diversification. When you spread your investment over many securities, the outcome will become less risky and the chances of large losses are reduced. So far, we have seen only the case where there are no correlations among those securities. We next move to the case where correlations are no longer zero. Before we do so, let us formally derive the expressions for all the expected payoffs and probabilities that we have discussed so far.

10.2.2 From Bernoulli to Binomial

In all of the previous examples, we assumed that the result of a bet at each table can be only one of two things – either you win the bet and double your money, or you lose the bet and get nothing. In cases like this, we say that the possible outcomes follow a Bernoulli distribution. We now define the expected value and the variance of a Bernoulli random variable *based on our context of a roulette bet* (the definitions will be different from the standard ones because the bet doubles your money if you win).

Consider a $M bet on a roulette table. Suppose that the probability of winning is p, and so the probability of losing is $1 - p$. Let w_i be the (random) outcome from your bet at the ith roulette table. If you win, you will get $w_i = \$2M$. If you lose, you will get nothing (i.e., $w_i = 0$). The expected value of the payoff is then:

$$E[w_i] = p \cdot 2M + (1 - p) \cdot 0 = 2pM. \tag{10.1}$$

The variance of the payoff is:

$$\begin{aligned} VAR[w_i] &= p(2M - 2pM)^2 + (1 - p)(0 - 2pM)^2 \\ &= 4p(1-p)M^2, \end{aligned} \tag{10.2}$$

and so the standard deviation is:

$$SD[w_i] = M\sqrt{4p(1-p)}. \tag{10.3}$$

It is straightforward to use equations (10.1) and (10.3) to verify that the expected payoff of a $1 bet (i.e., $M = 1$) at a fair table (i.e., $p = 0.50$) is $1, while the standard deviation of the payoff is $1.

Practice Question *What is the expected payoff and the standard deviation of the payoff for a $1 bet at a roulette table where the odds of winning are in your favor (say, $p = 0.55$)?*

The expected payoff in this case is:

$$E[w_i] = 2 \cdot p \cdot 1 = 2 \cdot 0.55 \cdot 1 = 1.10,$$

which is greater than in the case of a fair table (because the odds are in your favor). The standard deviation is:

$$SD[w_i] = 1 \cdot \sqrt{4p(1-p)} = 1 \cdot \sqrt{4 \cdot 0.55 \cdot (1-0.55)} = 0.994987.$$

Now, suppose you bet $\$M$ per table at N tables simultaneously. In this case, your gamble is indeed a series of N independent bets (or N Bernoulli trials). If you add up all the N payoffs, the total payoff (i.e., the payoff of the portfolio of bets over N tables), denoted by **W**, is:

$$\mathbf{W} = \sum_{i=1}^{N} w_i. \tag{10.4}$$

The total payoff follows a binomial distribution with the expected value of:

$$E[\mathbf{W}] = E\left[\sum_{i=1}^{N} w\right] = N \cdot E[w_i] = N2pM, \tag{10.5}$$

and the variance of:

$$VAR[\mathbf{W}] = \sum_{i=1}^{N} VAR[w_i] = N \cdot VAR[w_i] = N4p(1-p)M^2. \tag{10.6}$$

As a result, the standard deviation is:

$$SD[\mathbf{W}] = M\sqrt{N4p(1-p)}. \tag{10.7}$$

Note that in deriving the portfolio variance in equation (10.6), we use the fact that all the N roulette tables operate independently of one another. There is no correlation among their payoffs. That is why there are no covariance terms in the equation.

Practice Question   *You have $10,000 to bet on roulette tables. Suppose you decide to bet $100 per table over 100 fair tables. What is the portfolio's expected payoff and standard deviation?*

Here, $M = \$100$, $N = 100$, and $p = 0.50$. Using equations (10.5) and (10.7), we have:

$$E[\mathbf{W}] = N2pM = 100 \cdot 2 \cdot 0.5 \cdot 100 = 10,000,$$

and

$$SD\left[\mathbf{W}\right] = M\sqrt{N4p\left(1 - p\right)} = 100 \cdot \sqrt{100 \cdot 4 \cdot 0.50 \cdot \left(1 - 0.50\right)} = 1,000.$$

Practice Question *Suppose instead that you decide to bet $1 per table over 10,000 tables. What is the portfolio's expected payoff and standard deviation?*

Here, $M = \$1$, $N = 10,000$, and $p = 0.50$. Again, using equations (10.5) and (10.7), we have:

$$E\left[\mathbf{W}\right] = N2pM = 10,000 \cdot 2 \cdot 0.5 \cdot 1 = 10,000$$

and

$$SD\left[\mathbf{W}\right] = M\sqrt{N4p\left(1 - p\right)} = 1 \cdot \sqrt{10,000 \cdot 4 \cdot 0.50 \cdot \left(1 - 0.50\right)} = 100.$$

The standard deviation of the payoff from placing a $1 bet per table over 10,000 tables is $100. You should note one interesting fact here. Despite the fact that each $1 bet has a standard deviation of $1, taking 10,000 of them simultaneously does not lead to a standard deviation of $10,000. Rather, the standard deviation is $100. This is the result of the fact that all of the tables are independent of one another.

Note from the two examples that while the two betting strategies have the same expected payoff, the latter has a much lower standard deviation. As you may recall, standard deviation measures the dispersion of possible outcomes around the expected value (i.e., the chances that the realized outcome will be higher and lower than the expected outcome). This is why it can be used as a measure of investment risk. The smaller the standard deviation, the higher the chance is that the realized outcome will be closer to what you expect.

This is precisely the reason why the probabilities of losses that you saw in Table 10.2 and 10.3 are different. Recall that in Table 10.2, you bet $100 per table over 100 tables, while in Table 10.3, you bet $1 per table over 10,000 tables. Because the dispersion of possible outcomes in the latter case is smaller, the probability that you will suffer a large loss is also smaller.

10.2.3 The Central Limit Theorem

To be precise, let us calculate some of the probabilities reported in Tables 10.2 and 10.3. To do so, we will introduce the concept of the **central limit theorem**, which states that if you add up a sufficiently large number of independent random variables (which are identically distributed), the resulting sum (which will also be a random variable) will approximately be normally distributed. In our context, we are adding together the random payoff per table, w_i, to get the random payoff of the portfolio, W. The central limit theorem says that W will follow a normal distribution with mean $E[W]$ and standard deviation $SD[W]$.

Once you have this normal property, you can then use a common statistical technique to calculate the probability of W being below a certain dollar amount, Y. You might recall from your statistics courses that in order to calculate the cumulative probability that W will take on a value of at most Y (i.e., the area under the normal curve from the left tail to point Y), you need to calculate the z-score for the value of Y. That is,

$$\Pr[W \le Y] = \Pr\left[\frac{W - E[W]}{SD[W]} \le \frac{Y - E[W]}{SD[W]}\right] \quad (10.8)$$
$$= \Pr\left[z \le \frac{Y - N2pM}{M\sqrt{N4p(1-p)}}\right],$$

where z is a standard normal random variable (i.e., one with mean of 0 and standard deviation of 1). You then look up the value corresponding to that z-score from normal cumulative probability tables.

Practice Question   *You decide to bet $100 per table over 100 fair roulette tables. What is the probability that the total payoff will be less than $9,500?*

This is indeed the betting strategy that you use in Table 10.2. From the table, the probability of getting less than $9,500 is 0.308538. It can be calculated as follows. First, we recall from the earlier examples that this strategy has an expected payoff of $10,000 and a standard deviation of $1,000. So, the probability that we want is:

$$\Pr[W \le 9{,}500] = \Pr\left[z \le \frac{9{,}500 - 10{,}000}{1{,}000}\right]$$
$$= \Pr[z \le -0.50].$$

You can then look the value of this z-score up from the normal tables. Alternatively, you can use the function NORMSDIST in Excel. Either way, you will get:

$$\Pr[z \le -0.50] = 0.308538.$$

Practice Question   *What if you bet $1 per table on 10,000 tables? What is the probability that the total payoff will be less than $9,500?*

This is the betting strategy that you use in Table 10.3. From the table, the probability of getting less than \$9,500 is negligible. To calculate this, recall from the previous examples that this strategy has an expected payoff of \$10,000 and a standard deviation of \$100. So, the probability that we want is:

$$\Pr\left[W \le 9,500\right] = \Pr\left[z \le \frac{9,500 - 10,000}{100}\right]$$
$$= \Pr\left[z \le -5.00\right].$$

You can then look the value of this z-score up from the normal tables. Alternatively, you can use the function NORMSDIST in Excel. Either way, you will get:

$$\Pr\left[z \le -5.00\right] = 0.000000287.$$

Just to make sure that you understand this idea, consider another example.

Practice Question *You have \$500 and will allocate it evenly across fifty tables (i.e., \$10 per table). Suppose that the probability of winning at each table is 0.53. What is the probability that you will end up with less than \$500 at the end of the round?*

In this case, $p = 0.53$, $M = \$10$, and $N = 50$. Consequently, the expected portfolio payoff is:

$$E\left[W\right] = N2pM = 50 \cdot 2 \cdot 0.53 \cdot 10 = 530$$

and the standard deviation is:

$$SD\left[W\right] = M\sqrt{N4p\left(1 - p\right)} = 10 \cdot \sqrt{50 \cdot 4 \cdot 0.53 \cdot \left(1 - 0.53\right)} = 70.5833.$$

So, the probability that you will end up with less than \$500 is:

$$\Pr\left[W \le 500\right] = \Pr\left[z \le \frac{500 - 530}{70.5833}\right]$$
$$= \Pr\left[z \le -0.42503\right]$$
$$= 0.335408.$$

Practice Question *How many tables do you have to split the \$500 across so that the probability of losing money (i.e., ending up with less than \$500) is no more than 0.15?*

Let N be the minimum number of tables that you need in order for the probability of losing money to be less than 0.15. The amount of bet per table is then $500/N$. The expected portfolio payoff is then:

$$E\,[\mathbf{W}] = N2pM = N \cdot 2 \cdot 0.53 \cdot \frac{500}{N} = 530$$

while the standard deviation is:

$$SD\,[\mathbf{W}] = M\sqrt{N4p\,(1-p)}$$
$$= \frac{500}{N} \cdot \sqrt{N \cdot 4 \cdot 0.53 \cdot (1-0.53)} = \frac{499.0992}{\sqrt{N}}.$$

As a result, the probability that you will end up with less than $500 is:

$$\Pr\,[\mathbf{W} \le 500] = \Pr\left[z \le \frac{500-530}{499.0992} \cdot \sqrt{N}\right]$$
$$= \Pr\left[z \le -0.601083\sqrt{N}\right].$$

You want this probability to be 0.15. From using the NORMSDIST function (by trial and error), the z-score that corresponds to the cumulative probability of 0.15 is -1.0364. Therefore,

$$-0.601083\sqrt{N} = -1.0364.$$

Solving for N, you will have $N = 297.2939$. You need to spread your bet across at least 298 tables to make sure that the chance of losing money is less than 15%.

10.3 Portfolio Construction

In the previous subsection, you have seen the effect of diversification when the payoffs are independent of one another (i.e., there are no correlations among the payoffs from the roulette tables). In actual investment, you will spread your savings across different asset classes (and also across different securities in each class). As you have seen in Table 9.2 in Chapter 9, the correlations among the five asset classes can be positive or negative. In addition, the correlations among securities in each class are likely to be nonzero. We now want to know the effect of nonzero correlations on diversification.

We start with a very simple example. Suppose there are only two assets in the world, A and B. You can think of them as two asset classes or two different funds or securities. Asset A has an expected return of 8% p.a. and a standard deviation (of returns) of 15% p.a. Asset B has an expected return of 12% p.a. and a standard deviation of 25% p.a. Suppose that you want to divide your savings *evenly* between the two assets. What will be the expected return and the standard deviation of the investment portfolio?

Let us calculate the portfolio's expected return first. Because half of your money will be in Asset A and the other half in Asset B, the expected return of the portfolio is simply:

$$0.50 \cdot 0.08 + 0.50 \cdot 0.12 = 0.10 \text{ or } 10\% \text{ p.a.}$$

The portfolio's expected return is just the weighted average of the two assets' returns. In this case, the weight in each asset is 0.50 because your money is divided evenly between the two assets.

What about the risk (or standard deviation of the returns) of the portfolio? To figure it out, we need one more piece of information, which is how the returns on the two assets correlate. Denote by $\rho_{A,B}$ the correlation coefficient between the return on Asset A and the return on Asset B (i.e., how the two returns co-move with each other). The correlation coefficient can range in value from $+1$ to -1. If $\rho_{A,B} = +1$, then the two returns have a perfect positive (increasing) linear relationship. If $\rho_{A,B} = -1$, then the two returns have a perfect negative (decreasing) linear relationship. If $\rho_{A,B} = 0$, then there is no correlation between the two assets (just like in the earlier examples of the roulette tables). In addition, $\rho_{A,B}$ can take on any value within the range.

Let σ denote standard deviation. If you recall from your statistics courses, the standard deviation of a sum of two random variables, X and Y, is calculated by:

$$\sigma_{X+Y} = \sqrt{VAR(X) + VAR(Y) + 2COV(X,Y)} \qquad (10.9)$$

where $COV(X,Y)$ is the covariance between X and Y and can also be expressed as:

$$COV(X,Y) = \rho_{X,Y} \cdot \sigma_X \cdot \sigma_Y.$$

As a result, equation (10.9) can be rewritten as:

$$\sigma_{X+Y} = \sqrt{\sigma_X^2 + \sigma_Y^2 + 2 \cdot \rho_{X,Y} \cdot \sigma_X \cdot \sigma_Y}. \qquad (10.10)$$

In our case, your portfolio is the sum of $0.50\,A$ and $0.50\,B$. Therefore, its standard deviation is:

$$\sigma_{\text{Port}} = \sigma_{0.50A + 0.50B}$$

$$= \sqrt{\sigma_{0.50A}^2 + \sigma_{0.50B}^2 + 2 \cdot \rho_{A,B} \cdot \sigma_{0.50A} \cdot \sigma_{0.50B}}$$

$$= \sqrt{0.50^2 \cdot \sigma_A^2 + 0.50^2 \cdot \sigma_B^2 + 2 \cdot 0.50 \cdot 0.50 \cdot \rho_{A,B} \cdot \sigma_A \cdot \sigma_B}.$$

Now, let us assume a few values for $\rho_{A,B}$ and see what we get as standard deviation for the portfolio.

Case 1: Perfect Positive Correlation ($\rho_{A,B} = +1$)

Suppose that $\rho_{A,B} = +1$. From earlier, $\sigma_A = 0.15$ and $\sigma_B = 0.25$, and so the standard deviation of your portfolio is:

$$\sigma_{\text{Port}} = \sqrt{0.50^2 \cdot 0.15^2 + 0.50^2 \cdot 0.25^2 + 2 \cdot 0.50 \cdot 0.50 \cdot 1 \cdot 0.15 \cdot 0.25}$$

$$= 0.2000 \text{ or } 20\% \text{ p.a.}$$

Note one important point here. When the correlation coefficient is $+1$, the resulting portfolio's standard deviation is 20% p.a., or simply the weighted average between the two standard deviations (i.e., 15% and 25%). In cases like this, we say that there is no benefit from diversification. The risk of the portfolio is still proportional to the weights that you put in the two assets. In other words, you are simply averaging the risks according to the weights.

Case 2: Zero Correlation ($\rho_{A,B} = 0$)

Next, suppose that $\rho_{A,B} = 0$. The portfolio's standard deviation is then:

$$\sigma_{\text{Port}} = \sqrt{0.50^2 \cdot 0.15^2 + 0.50^2 \cdot 0.25^2 + 2 \cdot 0.50 \cdot 0.50 \cdot 0 \cdot 0.15 \cdot 0.25}$$

$$= 0.1458 \text{ or } 14.58\% \text{ p.a.}$$

Now you can see the benefit of diversification. While the portfolio's expected return is still the same as before (i.e., 10% p.a.) because the calculation of it is not dependent on the value of $\rho_{A,B}$, the portfolio's standard deviation is now only 14.58% p.a. The risk of the portfolio is now less than proportional to the weights that you put in the two assets. As a result, when there is no correlation between the two assets, you get the same portfolio's expected return but with lower risk.

Case 3: Perfect Negative Correlation ($\rho_{A,B} = -1$)
Next, suppose that $\rho_{A,B} = -1$. The portfolio's standard deviation is then:

$$\sigma_{\text{Port}} = \sqrt{0.50^2 \cdot 0.15^2 + 0.50^2 \cdot 0.25^2 + 2 \cdot 0.50 \cdot 0.50 \cdot (-1) \cdot 0.15 \cdot 0.25}$$
$$= 0.0500 \text{ or } 5\% \text{ p.a.}$$

Now the benefit of diversification is even greater than before. The standard deviation of the portfolio is only 5% p.a. Because the lowest possible value for correlation coefficients is -1, this is where the greatest benefit of diversification occurs.

Case 4: Real-World Correlations
In the real world, the correlations among different assets fall somewhere between the two boundaries (as you have already seen in Table 9.2). To continue with our example, suppose that $\rho_{A,B} = 0.60$. The standard deviation of the portfolio in this case is:

$$\sigma_{\text{Port}} = \sqrt{0.50^2 \cdot 0.15^2 + 0.50^2 \cdot 0.25^2 + 2 \cdot 0.50 \cdot 0.50 \cdot 0.60 \cdot 0.15 \cdot 0.25}$$
$$= 0.1803 \text{ or } 18.03\% \text{ p.a.,}$$

which means that some diversification benefit exists becuase the risk of the portfolio is less than proportional to the weights. As long as the $\rho_{A,B}$ is not equal to $+1$, you will get some diversification benefit by combining different assets into your portfolio.

10.3.1 Efficient Frontier for Two Assets

So far, we have assumed that you split your savings evenly between the two assets. If $\rho_{A,B} = 0.60$, this set of portfolio weights will give you an expected portfolio return of 10% p.a. and the standard deviation of 18.03% p.a. This is the risk/return profile of the portfolio with equal weighting. Another set of weights will give you a different risk/return profile for the portfolio. To generalize, denote by f_A and f_B the weights that you want to put in Asset A and Asset B, respectively. The general equation for portfolio's standard deviation is:

$$\sigma_{\text{Port}} = \sqrt{f_A^2 \cdot \sigma_A^2 + f_B^2 \cdot \sigma_B^2 + 2 \cdot f_A \cdot f_B \cdot \rho_{A,B} \cdot \sigma_A \cdot \sigma_B}. \qquad (10.11)$$

Practice Question *Assume, as before, that $\rho_{A,B} = 0.60$. Suppose you want to put 70% of your money in Asset A and 30% in Asset B. What is the expected return and standard deviation of the portfolio?*

Table 10.4. *Portfolio's risk and return under different weight combinations:*
correlation = 0.60

Fraction in A	Fraction in B	Portfolio's expected return (% p.a.)	Portfolio's standard deviation (% p.a.)
1.00	0.00	8.00%	15.00%
0.90	0.10	8.40%	15.13%
0.80	0.20	8.80%	15.52%
0.70	0.30	9.20%	16.16%
0.60	0.40	9.60%	17.00%
0.50	0.50	10.00%	18.03%
0.40	0.60	10.40%	19.21%
0.30	0.70	10.80%	20.52%
0.20	0.80	11.20%	21.93%
0.10	0.90	11.60%	23.43%
0.00	1.00	12.00%	25.00%

Source: Author Calculations.

In this case $f_A = 0.70$ and $f_B = 0.30$. The expected return of the portfolio is:

$$0.70 \cdot 0.08 + 0.30 \cdot 0.12 = 0.0920 \text{ or } 9.20\% \text{ p.a.},$$

while the standard deviation is:

$$\sigma_{\text{Port}} = \sqrt{0.70^2 \cdot 0.15^2 + 0.30^2 \cdot 0.25^2 + 2 \cdot 0.70 \cdot 0.30 \cdot 0.60 \cdot 0.15 \cdot 0.25}$$
$$= 0.1616 \text{ or } 16.16\% \text{ p.a.}$$

As you see, when you put more weight into Asset A (which has a lower standard deviation than Asset B does), the resulting portfolio has a lower risk than the equal-weight portfolio. However, the expected return on the portfolio is also lower. This is the risk-return trade-off that you have to make.

If you repeat the previous calculations for all possible combinations of weights, you will get a different risk/return profile for each weight combination. Table 10.4 displays the profiles for selected weight combinations.

Note that regardless of the weight combinations (except 100% in Asset A or 100% in Asset B), you will get diversification benefits. The portfolio's standard deviations are all less than proportional to the weights in the two assets. For example, with 30% of your wealth in Asset A and 70% in Asset B, the portfolio's standard deviation is 20.52% p.a., which is less than the weighted average of the two assets' standard deviations (i.e., $0.30 \cdot 0.15 + 0.70 \cdot 0.25 = 0.22$ or 22% p.a.).

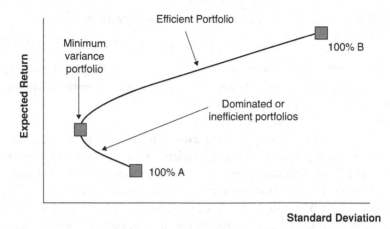

Figure 10.1. Investment Opportunity Set.

If you plot all the possible risk/return profiles in a graph between expected return and standard deviation, you will get a hyperbolic line as shown in Figure 10.1. Every point on the line is a portfolio with a unique weight combination and risk/return profile. The whole line is called the **portfolio frontier**. The top portion of the line (i.e., the upward-sloping portion) is referred to as the **efficient frontier**. It is called this because each point on it is a portfolio with the highest return for a given standard deviation (or risk).

Obviously, you will only choose to invest in a portfolio that is on the efficient frontier. However, exactly which point on the frontier you choose depends on your risk preference (i.e., the degree of your risk aversion). This decision requires that you do a trade-off between return and risk. If you are more tolerant of risk, you choose a point higher on the frontier. You accept more risk in exchange for a higher expected return. If you are more risk-averse, you will choose a point lower in the frontier, and accept a lower expected return in exchange for a lower risk.

10.3.2 Efficient Frontier for More Than Two Assets

This idea can be extended into a case where there are more than two assets. We will not get into much detail here. We only want to show that the logic of the portfolio frontier is still the same.

Suppose, for example, that there are three assets: A, B, and C. The expected return of the portfolio is calculated in the same way as before, which is the weighted average of the expected returns on the three assets. That is,

$$E[R_P] = f_A \cdot E[r_A] + f_B \cdot E[r_B] + f_C \cdot E[r_C] \qquad (10.12)$$

where R_P is the return on the portfolio, and r_A, r_B, and r_C are the returns on assets A, B, and C, respectively. Also, f_A, f_B, and f_C are the portfolio's weights of assets A, B, and C respectively.

The portfolio's standard deviation is also calculated in the same manner as before (i.e., as in equation (10.11), except that now there are three variance terms (one per asset) and six covariance terms. Why are there more covariance terms than the variance terms? It is because you have to account for all the covariances between each asset and the other two assets (i.e., between A and B, B and A, A and C, C and A, B and C, C and B). Note that because the covariance between A and B is the same as the covariance between B and A, we can group the six covariances into three pairs.

The equation for the portfolio's *variance* is:

$$\sigma^2_{\text{Port}} = f_A^2 \cdot \sigma_A^2 + f_B^2 \cdot \sigma_B^2 + f_C^2 \cdot \sigma_C^2 + 2 \cdot f_A \cdot f_B \cdot \rho_{A,B} \cdot \sigma_A \cdot \sigma_B$$
$$+ 2 \cdot f_A \cdot f_C \cdot \rho_{A,C} \cdot \sigma_A \cdot \sigma_C + 2 \cdot f_B \cdot f_C \cdot \rho_{B,C} \cdot \sigma_B \cdot \sigma_C, \qquad (10.13)$$

and, as a result, the standard deviation of the portfolio is:

$$\sigma_{\text{Port}} = \sqrt{\sigma^2_{\text{Port}}}. \qquad (10.14)$$

The first three terms on the right-hand side of equation (10.13) are the three individual variances, while the last three terms are the three pairs of covariances.

We can use the same logic to extend the setup to the case where there are N assets. The portfolio's expected return becomes:

$$E[R_P] = \sum_i f_i \cdot E[r_i] \qquad (10.15)$$

where r_i is the return on asset i, and f_i is the weight of asset i in the portfolio.

The equation for the portfolio's standard deviation now has N variance terms (one per asset) and many more covariance terms ($N \cdot [N-1]$ terms, to be precise):

$$\sigma_{\text{Port}} = \sqrt{\sum_i f_i^2 \cdot \sigma_i^2 + \sum_i \sum_{j \neq i} f_i \cdot f_j \cdot \rho_{i,j} \cdot \sigma_i \cdot \sigma_j}. \qquad (10.16)$$

The first term in the square root on the right-hand side of equation (10.16) is the sum of N individual variances, while the second term is the sum of all covariances. It is important to note that when N is large, the risk (i.e., standard deviation) of the portfolio is no longer driven by the individual variances. Rather, it is driven by the covariance terms. To see this, suppose that $N = 100$, and you will divide your investment evenly among the 100 assets. In this case, the weight given to each asset is $f_i = 0.01$, and so f_i^2, which is multiplied to each variance, is only 0.0001. This substantially reduces the importance of the individual variances in determining the portfolio's risk. In contrast, the sum of the covariances becomes more important because there are many more covariance terms in the equation.

What we have just said is indeed the essence of the **modern portfolio theory**. According to the theory, as long as the correlations among the assets are not all equal to $+1$, the only risk that matters in the portfolio context is the covariance risk or the risk of the co-movements among assets. Individual risks (i.e., variances or standard deviations) become less and less important as you increase the number of assets in your portfolio. This is indeed the benefit of diversification.

Figure 10.2 displays the benefit of forming a portfolio of assets to obtain diversification. If you hold only a few assets, the risk of your portfolio still contains a sizable contribution from individual risk (also known as diversifiable risk, unsystematic risk, or company-specific risk). As you keep adding assets (that are not perfectly correlated with one another) into your portfolio, the unsystematic risk gets diversified away, and you are left with the portion of the risk that is caused by the covariances among the assets. This portion of the risk cannot be diversified away because it is generated by how the assets co-move with one another. This portion is called nondiversifiable risk (also known as systematic risk or market risk).

Studies have shown that when forming a portfolio of stocks, it generally takes between thirty and fifty stocks for the diversifiable risk to become negligible.

The portfolio frontier and the efficient frontier also follow the same logic as in the two-asset case. Now, every point on the efficient frontier is a portfolio of N assets that has the highest expected return for a given variance. Obviously, which portfolio you choose depends on your own risk/return trade-off.

10.4 Summary

In this chapter, you learned that extraordinary investment performances are not necessarily due to ability, but rather to chance or to some clever schemes.

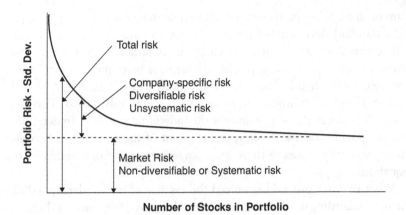

Figure 10.2. Lingo of Modern Portfolio Theory.

You then learned the concept of diversification. By forming a portfolio and spreading your investment across many assets, you can take advantage of the fact that the correlations among them are not perfectly positive. As a result, you can diversify away asset-specific risk. The only risk that matters in the portfolio context is the covariance risk or the risk of the co-movements among assets. The lower the correlations among the assets, the lower the risk of the portfolio is. Finally, you also learned how to calculate the probability that a given amount of loss will occur.

10.5 Questions and Assignments

1. You have $100,000 to bet on roulette tables. Suppose you decide to bet $1,000 per table. If you land on a red, you double your money but if you land on a black, you lose your money. What is the portfolio's expected payoff and standard deviation? Assume that the tables are fair and independent of one another.

2. Refer to question 1. Now suppose instead that you decide to bet $10 per table over 10,000 tables. What is the portfolio's expected payoff and standard deviation?

3. Explain why there is a difference between the standard deviation of the two previous answers.

4. You have $200,000 on 200 fair roulette tables. What are the chances that you will end up with less than $100,000 payoff?

5. How many fair tables do you have to split the $200,000 across so that the probability of losing money (i.e., ending up with less than $200,000) is no more than 10%?

6. Assume you have $100,000 split on 100,000 tables. The expected payoff is $120,000 and the standard deviation is 30,000. What are the chances that you will end up with *more* than $150,000?

7. Assume you have two asset classes A and B. Asset A gives you a return of 7% and has a standard deviation of 18%. Asset B gives you a return of 13% and a standard deviation of 27%. The $\rho_{A,B} = 0.65$. Suppose you divide your money equally among these two assets. What is the expected return and standard deviation of the portfolio?

8. Based on question 7, suppose you invest $10,000 in a portfolio of assets A and B (with money split evenly between them). What is the probability that, after one year, you will lose money? What about the probability of ending up with less than $9,000?

9. Refer to question 8. Now suppose you want to put 65% of your money in Asset A and 35% in Asset B. Recalculate the expected return and the standard deviation. Also recalculate the probabilities.

10. Essay: Please discuss how you might go about calibrating the value of $\rho_{A,B}$ in "real life" and what sort of data you might need to do this properly.

ELEVEN

Housing Decisions

Learning Objectives

You will recall from Chapter 3 that for most people during most of their lives, human capital is the most valuable asset on their personal balance sheets. Have you ever thought about what asset is next in line – what your second most valuable asset is? It probably would not surprise you to learn that for homeowners, this spot is occupied by their personal residences. Although home-ownership rates (as percentages of households) vary from one country to the next, they currently exceed 60% in many countries such as the United States, Canada, Great Britain, Singapore, and Spain.[1] For homeowners, the value of their houses represents a sizable portion of their total assets.

In this chapter, we examine housing decisions. Specifically, you will learn how to decide between buying and renting a house.

11.1 Buying or Renting?

The decision between buying and renting a house is a difficult one because it depends not only on financial considerations, but also on lifestyle choices and personal circumstances. We will start from a purely financial perspective.

11.1.1 From a Purely Financial Perspective

To make a decision based strictly on financial considerations, you need to consider the cost and payoff of each alternative. If you rent, the only expenses that you have are the rental expense and tenant's insurance expense. Tenant's

---

[1] The data are from Statistics Canada and the March 3, 2011, issue of the *Economist*.

insurance covers your possessions (which can be lost due to theft, fire, or water damage) and liability from any damage that you cause to your building or other people who live there. Both of these expenses are recurring monthly expenses that you have to pay as long as you rent the property.

On the other hand, there are many costs associated with buying a house. They are:

- Closing costs: These costs include appraisal fees, home inspection fees, land transfer tax, and legal fees. Typically, the costs are between 1% and 3% of the house price.
- Mortgage insurance fees: Recall from Chapter 5 that if you make a down payment of less than 20% of the house price, you will need to get mortgage insurance. Current insurance premiums range from 1% to 2.75% of the loan principal, depending on the percentage of your down payment. You can choose to pay the premium in cash up front. Alternatively, you can add the premium onto the principal of the mortgage loan (that is to be amortized).
- Mortgage payments
- Property taxes
- Home insurance premium
- Condominium fees (if applicable).

As you can see, buying a house involves a substantial outlay of expenses up front (i.e., closing costs and mortgage insurance premium). It also requires greater monthly expenses than renting does. As a result, if you rent, you will have more cash left that you can invest. On the other hand, if you buy, you are building up your equity in your house with each mortgage payment (i.e., you are investing in the form of a house). Consequently, you will have to compare the payoff from the investment under each choice. This will require that you come up with estimates of expected rates of return on the cash investment and on the house.

The expected return on the cash investment will depend on the assets that you put the money into. In Chapter 9, you saw examples of *historical* rates of return on different asset classes. Although there is no guarantee that those returns will repeat in the future, they at least provide some guideline for what you can expect to get.

The expected return on the house will come in two forms. First, you expect the house to appreciate in value. The expected rate of appreciation will depend primarily on the economic condition (of the country as a whole and in your region in particular). For example, based on the data from Teranet and the National Bank of Canada, the compound rate of changes in house prices from 2000 to 2010 is approximately 6.59% p.a. for the whole country. Over the same period, the compound rates of changes in specific locations such as Toronto and Calgary are 5.21% p.a. and 7.24% p.a., respectively.

The second form of expected return on the house is rental income. This is if you rent some part of the house to someone else. The rental income that you get should be based on the market rate for a comparable rental unit in your location.

Practice Question *You are considering buying a $400,000 condominium. You have saved $80,000 for the down payment and $10,000 for the closing costs. The mortgage rate is 4.50% p.a., monthly compounding. The mortgage is to be amortized over twenty-five years. In addition, the following is the information that you have and the assumptions that you have made.*

- *Expected growth rate of condo price: 5% per year*
- *Property tax: 1.50% of the price of the condo at the beginning of the year, payable at the end of each year*
- *Condo fees: $7,000/year (which is expected to grow by 2% per year), payable at the end of each year*
- *Home insurance premium: $800/year (which is expected to grow by 2% per year), payable at the end of each year*

Alternatively, you can rent the same condo for $1,800/month (inclusive of tenant's insurance premium). Assume (again) that the rent for the whole year is paid at the end of each year. The rent will increase by 2% per year. The after-tax rate on return on cash investment is 5% p.a., annual compounding. Which alternative would you choose?

The analysis is presented in Table 11.1. In Panel A of the table, we calculate the recurring expenses under the two alternatives for the first ten years. If you buy the condo, you will have four recurring expenses.

1. Mortgage payments: The mortgage principal ($320,000) is to be amortized over 300 months at the interest rate of 4.50% p.a., monthly compounding (or 0.375% per month). The monthly payment is:

$$\frac{320,000}{\text{PVA}(0.00375,300)} = \$1,778.6639,$$

which translates to $21,343.97 per year.

2. Property tax: For the first year, property tax is 1.50% of $400,000, or $6,000. For future years, the amounts are 1.50% of the condo prices at the start of the year. For example, given that the condo price is

Table 11.1. *Buying vs. renting a house: A financial perspective*

Panel A – Recurring expenses

	Year 1	Year 2	Year 3	Year 4	Year 5	Year 6	Year 7	Year 8	Year 9	Year 10
Buy										
Mortgage payments	21,344	21,344	21,344	21,344	21,344	21,344	21,344	21,344	21,344	21,344
Property tax	6,000	6,300	6,615	6,946	7,293	7,658	8,041	8,443	8,865	9,308
Condo fees	7,000	7,140	7,283	7,428	7,577	7,729	7,883	8,041	8,202	8,366
Home Insurance premium	800	816	832	849	866	883	901	919	937	956
Total	35,144	35,600	36,074	36,567	37,080	37,613	38,169	38,746	39,348	39,974
Rent										
Rental expenses and tenant's insurance premium	21,600	22,032	22,473	22,922	23,381	23,848	24,325	24,812	25,308	25,814
Difference	13,544	13,568	13,601	13,645	13,699	13,765	13,843	13,935	14,040	14,160

Panel B – Investment of up-front outlay and yearly differences (If you rent)

	Year 1	Year 2	Year 3	Year 4	Year 5	Year 6	Year 7	Year 8	Year 9	Year 10
Investment of down payment and closing costs	94,500	99,225	104,186	109,396	114,865	120,609	126,639	132,971	139,620	146,601
Investment of yearly differences in recurring expenses	13,544	27,789	42,780	58,564	75,192	92,717	111,196	130,690	151,265	172,988
Total amount that you will have if you rent	108,044	127,014	146,966	167,960	190,057	213,325	237,835	263,661	290,884	319,588

Panel C – Equity that you will have built up in your condo (If you buy)

	Year 1	Year 2	Year 3	Year 4	Year 5	Year 6	Year 7	Year 8	Year 9	Year 10
Condo price	420,000	441,000	463,050	486,203	510,513	536,038	562,840	590,982	620,531	651,558
Outstanding mortgage principal	312,911	305,496	297,741	289,629	281,145	272,271	262,990	253,282	243,128	232,507
Equity in Your Home	107,089	135,504	165,309	196,573	229,367	263,767	299,850	337,701	377,404	419,051

Source: Author Calculations.

227

expected to increase by 5% per year, your condo is expected to be worth $420,000 at the start of next year, and so the property tax will be $6,300.

3. Condo fees: The fees are $7,000 for the first year, and 2% higher per year for each of the following years.
4. Home insurance premium: The premium is $800 for the first year, and 2% higher per year for each of the following years.

Adding up all these recurring expenses, you will have $35,143.97 ($\approx$ $35,144) for the first year, $35,600 for the second year, and so on. On the other hand, if you rent, your monthly expenses will be $1,800 per month or $21,600 for the first year, and 2% higher per year in each of the following years.

The difference between the expenses under the two choices are the amounts that you can invest if you rent. The value of this investment at the end of each year is shown in Panel B of the table. Because we assume that these recurring expenses are paid at the end of the year, the value for the first year (i.e., $13,544) is simply the difference in the first year from Panel A. The value for the second year is equal to the value for the first year plus earnings on it (at 5% p.a.) and the difference in the second year; that is,

$$13,544 \cdot (1.05) + 13,568 = 27,789.$$

The value for each of the following years can be calculated in the same manner.

Panel B also shows the value of the investment of the up-front costs, which you do not have to pay if you rent. Recall that the up-front costs are the down payment ($80,000) and the closing costs ($10,000). In total, this $90,000 can be invested right away (i.e., from the start of the first year). By the end of the first year, this amount will grow to:

$$90,000 \cdot 1.05 = 94,500,$$

which is the amount shown in the table for the first year. The amounts for the following years are based on the rate of return of 5% p.a.

Panel C shows the amount of equity that you will have built up in your condo if you buy it. This is equal to the expected condo price minus the outstanding mortgage principal. For example, the condo price at the end of the first year is expected to be $400,000 \cdot 1.05 = $420,000. As for the outstanding principal of your mortgage at the end of the first year, it is equal to:

$$\$1,778.6639 \cdot \mathbf{PVA}(0.00375,288) = 312,911.$$

Therefore, by the end of the first year, the equity that you will have built up in your condo if you buy it now is:

$$420,000 - 312,911 = 107,089.$$

The numbers for future years can be calculated similarly.

As you can see from the table, the investment value if you rent exceeds the equity in your condo only in the first year. From the second year on, the reverse is true. Therefore, if you intend to remain in the present location only for a short period of time (e.g., you plan to move or want to remain mobile), you will be better off renting. This result is driven by the initial cash outlay for the closing costs in purchasing the condo. For the first year, the condo price has not gone up sufficiently to overcome these costs.

There are, however, a few important points to note about this comparison. First, the comparison is not completely fair. This is because the purchase alternative is indeed a *leveraged* investment in the house, but we did not assume that you will borrow to invest if you rent. While this is consistent with practice, it biased the results in favor of the purchase alternative. In fact, this *partly* explains why homeowners become wealthier than renters. For example, based on the data that Statistics Canada collected in 2005 (latest survey available), the median net worth of homeowners was $327,000, while the median net worth for renters was a paltry $14,000. Note, however, that the relationship between home ownership and net worth can work both ways. Owning a home can make you more wealthy, especially in a rising housing market. At the same time, it is easier for people with more wealth to buy a home. Note also that using leverage to buy a house is a risky transaction. In our earlier example, the numbers are based on the expected rate of increase in the condo price. In reality, the condo price may not go up as highly as anticipated, or it may even fall.

For example, suppose the condo price remains the same over the ten-year comparison period. In this case, the results will be as shown in Panel A of Table 11.2. You can see that you will always be better off with renting because you can invest the unused cash at 5% p.a. while there are no capital gains on the condo. In an extreme case, the condo price might drop sharply, which could lead to the situation where you ended up owing more on your mortgage than the condo is worth. In other word, your equity on the condo becomes negative. This is indeed what has been occurring in the United States as a result of the subprime crisis. Many homeowners decided to walk away from their houses because they did not want to continue to repay their mortgage loans. (In Canada, homeowners cannot walk away without declaring bankruptcy.)

Table 11.2. *Buying vs. renting a house: Alternative assumption*

Panel A – Rate of condo price increase = 0% p.a.

	Year 1	Year 2	Year 3	Year 4	Year 5
Total amount that you will have if you rent	108,043.97	126,714.13	146,036.29	166,037.40	186,745.67
Equity in Your Home	87,088.99	94,503.65	102,258.94	110,370.50	118,854.71

	Year 6	Year 7	Year 8	Year 9	Year 10
Total amount that you will have if you rent	208,190.61	230,403.06	253,415.32	277,261.15	301,975.90
Equity in Your Home	127,728.68	137,010.32	146,718.35	156,872.38	167,492.87

Panel B – With sale commission of 4.50%

	Year 1	Year 2	Year 3	Year 4	Year 5
Total amount that you will have if you rent	108,043.97	127,014.13	146,966.29	167,959.65	190,057.07
Equity in Your Home	88,188.99	115,658.65	144,471.69	174,693.89	206,394.27

	Year 6	Year 7	Year 8	Year 9	Year 10
Total amount that you will have if you rent	213,325.27	237,835.03	263,661.49	290,884.36	319,588.24
Equity in Your Home	239,645.21	274,522.68	311,106.33	349,479.75	389,730.62

Source: Author Calculations.

The second important point to note about this example is that we did not include in the analysis the sale commission that you will have to pay if you sell the house. Normally, the commission is in the range of 3.50% to 5% of the house price, and is paid by the seller. Again, this biased the result of the comparison in favor of the purchase alternative. For example, suppose the sale commission is 4.50% of the condo price while all other variables remain the same as in our example. The effect of the commission on the results is shown in Panel B of Table 11.2. Here, you can see that renting is better than buying for the first three years. With the sale commission, it will take longer for the condo price to go up sufficiently to overcome the upfront costs.

The third important point is that there is a relationship between house prices and rents. Suppose, for example, that you want to buy a house as an investment (i.e., to rent out). The return from such an investment will come from two sources. First, you regularly receive the net rental income (i.e., rent minus expenses on the house such as property taxes, maintenance costs, etc.). Secondly, you expect the house to appreciate in value (i.e., capital gains).

Practice Question *You are considering buying a $300,000 house as an investment. You expect the house price to increase at a rate of 3% p.a. The rent on a comparable house in the same neighborhood is $2,500 per month. The expenses on the house are $4,500 per year in property taxes and $3,000 per year in maintenance costs. What is the rate of return on the investment?*

The total expected return from the investment is the sum of the returns from the two sources:

$$\frac{(2{,}500 \cdot 12) - 4{,}500 - 3{,}000}{300{,}000} + 0.03 = 0.105 \text{ or } 10.50\% \text{ p.a.}$$

Theoretically, the expected total return should be comparable to the return that you expect to get from an investment with the same risk. The two components of return should adjust such that the sum of them is commensurate to the risk of the investment.

In summary, the choices between buying and renting a house have different financial implications. In general, if you plan to stay in your house for a long time, buying is the better choice. However, be careful about the assumptions that you make, especially on the mortgage rate, the expected rate of increase in house price, the investment rate, and the rent payments.

It is important to emphasize that this analysis only compares a buying decision to a decision to rent a comparable place. It does not tell you how much you should spend on a house. Recall from Chapter 5 that mortgage lenders follow a guideline involving your gross-debt-service (GDS) ratio and total-debt-service (TDS) ratio. So you are limited in the amount that you can borrow.

Recall also from Chapter 9 that by owning a house, the risk/return profile of your personal balance sheet will change. This has implications on the kinds of *other* investment that you should take.

11.1.2 Other Aspects of the Decision

For most people, the decision between buying and renting a house does not depend solely on financial considerations. There are other, mostly intangible advantages and disadvantages to either choice. For example, if you rent, you do not have to worry about repairs or maintenance. These are the responsibility of the landlord. On the negative side, renting restricts your freedom to remodel or redecorate the unit. There is also uncertainty about whether you can renew the rent when the existing one expires.

If you own a house, you are secure in the knowledge that you will always have a place to live (if you do not default on your mortgage). A house can also give its owner the pride of ownership because some people enjoy doing the tasks associated with home-owning (e.g., landscaping, repainting, etc.). These are the aspects of home ownership that cannot be easily valued.

In addition, there is an aspect of social capital. **Social capital** is not visible or easy to measure, and, unlike every other form of capital we have discussed so far, does not belong on the personal balance sheet. Social capital is loosely defined as the collection of networks, cooperation, relationship, norms, mutual aid, faith, and various other forms of "glue" that hold a community together. However, what does social capital have to do with housing? There is actually a strong link between home ownership and social capital, which is one of the reasons policymakers in the United States (and, to a lesser extent, in the rest of the world) have encouraged and promoted home ownership.

Please note that we are not veering from our mandate of discussing *normative* personal finance when we mention the role of social capital. The reality is that social capital also serves a smoothing function. How so? If you live in a community or society with very high social capital values, you are much less likely to experience disruptions in your standard of living. Think about the neighborhood or community where you live. If you happen to run out of flour while baking a cake, or need to jump-start your vehicle to get to work one morning, how many neighbors within short walking distance would you feel comfortable borrowing the cup of flour or jumper cables from? All of them? Some of them? None of them? And do you know the names of all your immediate neighbors?

These may sound like unimportant and even off-topic questions, but they can have a profound impact on financial matters. Although social capital does not belong on the personal balance sheet, it is an asset class you can invest in by creating it. Individuals can do this on a community-specific basis. For example, you could arrange a monthly "neighbors' barbecue" for everyone on the block. Specific communities (and religions, and schools) can produce social capital as well. In fact, researchers – mostly sociologists – have developed indices of social capital that they have used to identify regions of the country that score highly versus poorly in this dimension.

At this point, you may be asking what does all of this have to do with housing? Well, according to a recent study by researchers at the Federal Reserve Bank of Chicago and the Office of the Comptroller of the Currency, housing, social capital, and financial well-being are all intertwined. According to the authors of the study, greater home ownership rates increase the social capital of a neighborhood simply because homeowners face larger transaction costs in selling their house and moving away. This reduced mobility incentivizes homeowners to invest in things that increase their property value, which, in turn, also creates more social capital. So social capital is created as a result of home ownership, and property values rise in the process as well. Although you may not think about the investment you are making when you lend that gallon of milk, the logic of investing in social capital is clear.

This relationship between social capital and financial well-being then manifests itself in a number of interesting ways. For example, the authors in the previously mentioned study were able to obtain detailed records of more than 170,000 individual credit card histories over a two-year period, to observe individual payment behavior and bankruptcy filing status for each of these 170,000 individuals. The data set contained enough information so that the individual's age, address, marital status, and home ownership status could be linked to their credit card behavior and in particular could determine whether they filed for bankruptcy protection during the two-year period.

As you might expect, borrowers living in counties and regions with high unemployment and poor economic conditions as well as those individuals who have lower income and wealth status, experienced higher default rates. No surprise there.

However, what is interesting is the following conclusion. We quote from their study: "An individual who continues to live in his state of birth is 9 percent less likely to default on his credit card and 13 percent less likely to file for bankruptcy, while an individual who moves 190 miles from his state of birth is 17 percent more likely to default and 15 percent more likely to declare bankruptcy." This, of course, is consistent with a social-capital story under which the closer you live to your place of birth, the more likely you are to have vested social capital to protect. Along the same lines, it seems that married individuals are 24 percent less likely to default on credit cards and

32 percent less likely to file for bankruptcy. Finally, homeowners – and keep in mind that home ownership provides another proxy for social capital – are 17 percent less likely to default and 25 percent less likely to declare bankruptcy.

In sum, we suspect that people grossly underestimate their home owner-ship expenditures. They overestimate the amount by which the house will appreciate over time. They tend to live where they work (obviously), which means that their housing capital (which is a subset of financial capital) is exposed to the same economic risks as their human capital. And yet, the one thing an investment in housing might achieve is that it creates its own investment in social capital. Perhaps this one factor outweighs the many other negatives and makes home ownership worth pursuing.

11.1.3 Our Recommendation

Where does this leave us in terms of practical housing advice? For one, we think that a large proportion of individuals within the population should not own a house. Instead, they should push the purchase off as long as possible, and in the meantime rent. Anyone that followed this advice in the United States over the last few years, possibly the last few decades, would be much better off today. This is not just us being preachy or dispensing with advice that – with hindsight – proves correct. If you actually go back to one of the first principles we discuss in this book, namely spreading of total resources over the lifecycle, you can arrive at the same conclusion. However, the reason is not as simple as you might think. It is not because housing is a "bad investment" or has performed poorly relative to other asset classes. Instead, it relates to the investment characteristics of your human capital when you are young, and as you age.

A number of recent studies by mathematical economists have developed a control-theory model to derive the optimal or rational approach to housing over the lifecycle. According to these researchers, most "typical" people under the age of forty should not own a house but should rent instead. Again, this is not recommended for the reasons you might think. Here is the argument against home ownership early in life: when you are young the vast majority of your true wealth is locked up in human capital, which is illiquid (i.e., nontradable) and nondiversified. It therefore makes little sense to invest yet another substantial amount of total wealth in yet another illiquid and nondiversifiable item like a house.

Sure, if you could buy a house that has a bedroom in New York City, a bathroom in Los Angeles, a kitchen in Chicago, and perhaps a garage in

Las Vegas, then yes, your home would be diversified. Buying a house as an investment has very strong similarities to someone being convinced that stocks are good investment in the "long run," but they decide to buy only one stock for their portfolio. We do not care how reliable that one stock is or how large the dividends are. That stock portfolio is not diversified. The same goes for housing.

In addition, when you are young your human capital and hence your total wealth is sensitive to the evolution of your wages and income over time. These two factors tend to decline in a recession and bad economic times, just like housing. In other words, there is a good chance that if your wages take a hit, so will your real estate. This should sound familiar from when we discussed the interaction between your future wages and stocks, bonds, and other investments in Chapter 9. For now, it is simply worth pointing out that if your wages are sensitive to economic conditions, it makes little sense to expose a large fraction of your financial capital to the same factors by allocating a significant portion of your assets to a house. In fact, evidence from the U.S.-based Panel Study of Income Dynamics suggests that controlling for levels of wealth, homeowners actually own less stock-based investments, compared to renters, possibly because of this same reason.

Using the lifecycle framework, a strong argument can be made, absent all the emotional factors involved in the decision, that renting is the optimal choice when you are young. However, once you are older (say fifty or sixty) and you have unlocked a large portion of your illiquid and nontradable human capital by converting it into financial capital, then you can afford to "freeze" some financial capital and lock into a home purchase. At that stage, not only do you have more wealth in total, but your balance sheet (and especially your human capital) is likely not as sensitive to the state of the economy as when you were young.

Now, you might justifiably worry here that if you do not buy a house when you are young, you might never be able to afford a house when you are older. We have heard many real estate agents say that it is important to get a foothold into the real estate market or you will never be able to afford a house.

According to the Teranet – National Bank of Canada House Price Index that we alluded to earlier, the compound rate of changes in house prices from 2000 to 2010 is approximately 6.59% p.a. for the whole country and only 5.21% p.a. in the Toronto area. If you calculate the compound rate of return on the TSX Composite Total Return Index over the same period using the data in Table 9.1, you will get 6.64% p.a., which is quite comparable to the changes in house prices. In other words, an investment in the stock market is likely to preserve your ability to buy a house at some point in the future. Note also that the house price index does not adjust for the costs of maintenance, which can often be substantial. If you factor these costs into the estimation, the compound rate of changes in house prices will be even lower.

There is one more dimension that impacts the housing decision; it is the increasing mobility of the labor force. This dimension results in a much higher probability that you might have to relocate for a job or employment opportunities. This is yet another factor that increases the incentive to rent for as long as possible. There is nothing more disruptive to a smooth consumption path than having an illiquid and unsalable house serve as an anchor to a region in an economic distress.

Finally, in case you are truly concerned that you might miss out on the market if you do not buy a house as soon as possible, the authors of one of the articles we cited earlier suggest that you hedge or insure against this risk by investing some money in a mutual fund that is linked to real-estate prices such as a real-estate investment trust (REIT). This way, you can participate in the increased value of housing, without having to mow a single lawn or unclog even one drain.

11.2 Questions and Assignments

1. You are considering buying a $350,000 house. You have saved $70,000 for the down payment and $8,000 for the closing costs. The mortgage rate is 4.50% p.a., monthly compounding. The mortgage is to be amortized over twenty-five years. You expected the house price to grow at the rate of 4% per year. The property tax is 1.50% of the house price at the beginning of the year. The maintenance cost is expected to be $6,500/year (growing by 2% per year). Home insurance premium is $750/year (growing by 2% per year). All of these tax and expenses are payable at the end of each year. Alternatively, you can rent the same house for $1,700/month (inclusive of tenant's insurance premium). The rent will increase by 2% per year. Assume that the rent for the whole year is paid at the end of each year. The after-tax rate on return on cash investment is 4% p.a., annual compounding.

   - Create a spreadsheet to compare the cash flows under the buying and the renting alternatives.
   - How much equity would you have built up if you buy your home and sell it after five years?
   - Which is the better alternative after one year? five years? ten years?

2. Based on question 1, how do your answers change if the average growth rate of the house was 2% per year instead of 4%?

3. You are considering buying a $350,000 house as an investment. You expect the house price to increase at a rate of 4.50% p.a. The rent on a comparable house in the same neighborhood is $2,000 per month. The expenses on the house are $5,000 per year in property taxes and $3,000 per year in maintenance cost. What is the total expected return from the investment?

4. Based on question 3, suppose you want the total expected return to be 10% per year. How much rent do you have to charge?

5. What are some intangible advantages and disadvantages to owning a home?

6. How does investment in housing create its own investment in social capital?

7. Essay: Please comment on this statement: 'You should purchase a home early in life so that you do not miss out on the rising housing prices.'

8. Essay: What is the ratio of annual rent-to-price at which you would decide to rent versus buy? Describe your thought process.

9. Essay: What are the implications of not being able to pay your mortgage? Can you walk away from the house and leave the bank with the house instead? What if the value of the house is less than the amount of the mortgage loan?

10. Essay: Housing prices cannot increase by more than the rate of growth of wages in the long run.

TWELVE

Pensions and Retirement [Canadian Content]

Learning Objectives

In this chapter, you will learn about longevity risk or the risk from not knowing the exact length of life. You will see the impact of this risk on the standard of living and on retirement planning. You then look at financial contracts that can provide lifelong income, and thus can be used to hedge longevity risk. Finally, you learn how the risk is dealt with in the consumption-smoothing framework.

12.1 Longevity Risk

In most of our analyses so far in this book, we assumed that the age at death D is known with certainty. We know exactly how long a person will spend in his or her retirement. This assumption has facilitated many calculations and made concepts easier to understand. Unfortunately, it is also quite unrealistic. In real life, that length of time varies widely. If you peruse, for example, the obituary section of a newspaper on a given day, you will likely see a wide distribution of ages at death. Figure 12.1 shows the distribution of the number of years after age sixty-five that Canadians (both sexes combined) spent prior to their deaths. The data are from Statistics Canada as of 2007 (the latest year available). The average remaining lifetime is 16.86 years. In other word, the average age at death is 81.86 years old. However, as you can see the distribution is quite dispersed, with a standard deviation of 8.43 years.[1] In addition, approximately one in five people

---

[1] Our calculations of the average remaining lifetime and the standard deviation were limited by the fact that Statistics Canada do not provide a breakdown of the ages at death beyond 100 years old (i.e., thirty-five years after age sixty-five). Therefore, in our calculations, we use thirty-five years for the group of people who died after they reach 100 years old. This has an effect of slightly underestimating the average remaining lifetime and the standard deviation.

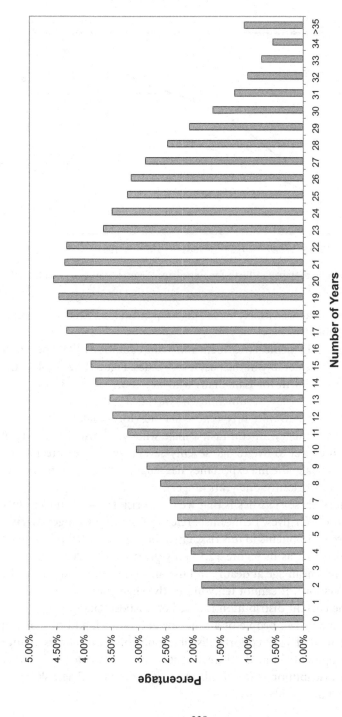

Figure 12.1. Remaining Lifetime of 65-Year-Old Canadians (2007 Data). *Source:* Author Calculations based on 2000 to 2002 mortality rates (Statistics Canada).

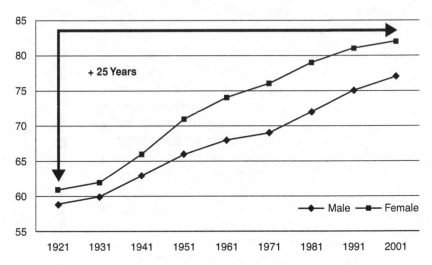

Figure 12.2. Life Expectancy at Birth for Canadians. *Source:* Statistics Canada, Catalogue no. 84-537-XIE.

(i.e., 20%) live to at least ninety years old (or spend at least twenty-five years in their retirement).

With advances in medical treatment and living conditions, life expectancy has increased considerably in the past few decades. Figure 12.2 displays the life expectancy at birth for Canadians who were born at the start of each decade from 1920s to 2000s. Someone who was born at the start of the 1920s could expect to live to only fifty-nine years old (for a male) or sixty-one years old (for a female). In contrast, a male who was born at the start of the 2000s can expect to live to age seventy-seven, which is eighteen years longer. For a female, the life expectancy has lengthened by even more – to age eighty-two (or twenty-one years longer).

The point of these statistics is that we face a risk from the uncertainty in the length of our lives. Economists refer to this risk as **longevity risk**. There are two components to this risk. First, the *current* distribution of the ages at death (such as in Figure 12.1) only gives you an idea of what to expect (i.e., the mean age at death) and the uncertainty around it (i.e., the standard deviation). It cannot tell you exactly when your time will come. Secondly, the current distribution is based on ex-post data of people who have passed away (i.e., people of a previous generation), and so may not be representative of your cohort's distribution, which can always change as new developments in medical treatments come into existence. In other words, your distribution is not fixed; rather it is evolving. The risk lies in not knowing how it will evolve.

Table 12.1. *Amount of money needed for retirement*

Valuation rate (% p.a.)	Length of retirement (years)			
	5	10	20	40
1%	242,672	473,565	902,278	1,641,734
3%	228,985	426,510	743,874	1,155,739
5%	216,474	386,087	623,111	857,954

Source: Author Calulations.

Longevity risk can complicate the retirement planning process, and so should be taken as seriously as other types of risk such as market risk and inflation risk. To get a sense of the effect of longevity risk, consider the following example.

Practice Question *How much money do you need to have at the start of your retirement if you want to consume $50,000 per year (in real term) for the rest of your life?*

This is a present-value-of-an-annuity problem. Prior to this chapter, we always made an assumption about how long the retirement period would be. Here, to see the effect of the uncertainty in not knowing that length, we will do the calculations for four possible lengths: five years, ten years, twenty years, and forty years. The valuation rates are assumed to be 1% p.a., 3% p.a., or 5% p.a. The results are shown in Table 12.1.

As you can see from the table, the amount that you will need for your retirement can vary greatly depending on how long you will live. For example, when the valuation rate is 3% p.a., you need approximately $230,000 if you only live for five years during your retirement. However, if your retirement period lasts for twenty or forty years, you need substantially more than that. The smaller the valuation rate (i.e., the rate of return on your investment), the greater the effect of longer life is on the amount that you will need. Obviously, the uncertainty in the length of life will affect how much you have to save during your working years (which, in turn, determines how much you can consume during the working years).

Another way to look at the effect of this risk is to see how much a fixed amount of nest egg will allow you to consume during your retirement under different assumptions on the length of the retirement period. Consider the next example.

Table 12.2. *Annual consumption during retirement*

Valuation rate (% p.a.)	Length of retirement (years)			
	5	10	20	40
1%	103,020	52,791	27,708	15,228
3%	109,177	58,615	33,608	21,631
5%	115,487	64,752	40,121	29,139

Source: Author Calculations.

Practice Question *Suppose you manage to save $500,000 at the start of your retirement. How much can you afford to spend every year for the rest of your life?*

Let us again look at the results under four possible lengths of retirement period and three valuation rates, as shown in Table 12.2.

As you can see, the longer your life span is, the less you can consume each year given a fixed amount of nest egg. For example, consider the case where the valuation rate is 3% p.a. If you knew that you would only live for ten more years, you could consume almost $59,000 per year. On the other hand, if you thought you could live for forty more years, you would have to reduce your consumption to only about $22,000 per year.

Note also that the lower the valuation rate, the greater the effect of longer life is on your standard of living. When the rate is low, you do not earn much income on the investment of the remaining nest egg, and so you are forced to consume less.

Longevity risk makes retirement planning more difficult. How many years should you be planning for? If you plan for a long retirement period (say, forty years), you will have to save a lot during your working years (which means you will not be able to consume much). You will not be able to consume a lot during your retirement years either. If it turns out that you will not live that long, you would have unnecessarily suffered a low standard of living. On the other hand, if you plan for a retirement period that matches your life expectancy (say, twenty years), you will be able to consume more. However, what if you happen to live longer than expected?

For this reason, you need to be able to deal effectively with longevity risk. In the next section, we discuss two approaches that you can use. The first approach involves retirement plans that provide you with income for the rest of your life, regardless of how long you live. The second approach is based on the consumption-smoothing concept that we introduced in Chapter 4.

12.2 Retirement Plans that Provide Lifelong Income

In Canada, there are primarily three kinds of retirement plans that give you lifelong income. They are (i) the government-sponsored Canada Pension Plan and Old-Age Security Pension; (ii) an employer-sponsored, defined-benefit pension plan; and (iii) a life annuity that you can buy from insurance companies using your own private savings.

12.2.1 Canada Pension Plan (CPP) and Old-Age Security Pension (OAS)

The Canada Pension Plan (CPP) is a public pension plan whose goal is to provide Canadian retirees and their families with basic financial support for retirement (and also in the event of death or disability). The CPP is offered in every province of Canada except Quebec, which has its own Quebec Pension Plan that provides similar benefits.

Income from the CPP is paid monthly to people who contributed to the Canada Pension Plan during their working years. The pension is designed to replace about 25% of the contributor's earnings from employment, up to a maximum amount (for 2010) of $934.17 per month (or $11,210 per year). However, most people do not receive the maximum benefit because the amount of pension income will depend on how much and for how long you have contributed to the plan. For example, in January 2010, the average pension income paid was $502.57 (or $6,030 per year). Typically, people apply for the pension income when they reach sixty-five years old. However, you can choose to start receiving it earlier (from age sixty on). The pension amount will be reduced if you choose to start receiving it early. The reduction rate is 0.50% for each month before age sixty-five. For example, suppose you want to start getting the pension income on your sixty-second birthday (which is thirty-six months before age sixty-five). The amount of your monthly payment will be reduced by $36 \cdot 0.50\% = 18\%$. This will be the amount that you will receive for life.

You can also choose to start receiving the income later than age sixty-five, in which case the CPP increases your pension amount by 0.50% for each month after age sixty-five and before age seventy. The maximum increase is 30%, which occurs if you start receiving your CPP pension at age seventy.

Contributions to the CPP are mandatory for virtually all employees and their employers (including the self-employed). For 2011, the contribution rate is 9.90% of earnings between $3,500 and $48,300. The contribution rate is split equally between the employee and the employer (and so each contributes 4.95% of the earnings). As the maximum contributory earnings is $48,300 − $3,500 = $44,800, the maximum amount paid by the employees and the employer per year is $2,217.60 each (or a total of $4,435.20 per year). People who are self-employed must pay both the employee's and the employer's shares of the contributions.

In addition, the Canadian government provides seniors who are sixty-five years old or older (and have lived in Canada for at least ten years after age eighteen) with **Old Age Security (OAS)** pension. The current maximum amount of this pension is $526.85 per month (or $6,322.20 per year). This maximum is adjusted every three months to account for changes in the cost of living. The actual amount that you receive, however, is calculated based on the number of years of residence in Canada after you turn eighteen years old. The amount will also depend on the amount of income that you have from other sources during your retirement (such as company's pension). The OAS payment will be clawed back once your other income exceeds $67,688 per year, and will be completely eliminated if your other income is more than $109,764 (for 2011).

You can see that both the CPP and the OAS pension will provide a lifelong stream of income, albeit a modest one. The combined maximum from both sources are only about $1,500 a month. Nevertheless, the lifelong nature of their payments helps to reduce the impact of longevity risk on your financial planning.

12.2.2 Defined-Benefit Pension Plan

A defined-benefit (DB) pension plan is one of two traditional types of registered pension plans (RPPs), with the other type being a defined-contribution (DC) plan. RPPs are set up by employers for their employees to provide retirement pension income. Typically, employees make contributions into the plans, and their employers also contribute on behalf of the employees. In some cases, only employers make contributions. RPPs have a tax-deferring benefit because both the employees' and the employers' contributions are not taxed as income in the year they are made. Rather, the funds are taxed when they are withdrawn from the plans (similar to how RRSPs work, as discussed in Chapter 6).

Under a DB plan, the amount of pension income that you will regularly receive is defined (i.e., known) and usually depends on age at retirement, salary level, and years of service. Although the formula for pension amount varies from plan to plan, one commonly used formula in Canada is 2% of the average of the final three to five years of salary, multiplied by number of years of service. For example, suppose you are now sixty-five and have been working for your company for thirty years. The average salary during the past few years is $100,000. If you retire now, you will receive a pension of:

$$2\% \cdot 100{,}000 \cdot 30 = 60{,}000 \text{ per year.}$$

Generally, the number of years of service is capped at thirty-five years, which means that the maximum amount of pension that you get is equal to 70% of your final salary. DB plans are generally designed to replace up to 70% of the income that you make in your working years. The idea behind this is that once you retire, you no longer have to spend work-related expenses such as transportation and clothing. Without these expenses, the replacement rate of 70% should leave you with approximately the same standard of living as before.

The amount that you receive from your DB pension will also be capped by the regulation under the *Income Tax Act.* Remember that money invested inside a DB pension plan (or any RPP) is shielded from tax until withdrawn. As a result, the government limits the amount that can be tax-deferred by imposing the maximum pension income that can be paid out of a DB plan. For 2011, that amount is equal to $2,552.22 multiplied by the number of years of service.

Practice Question *You have been working for your company for exactly thirty-five years. You belong to a DB plan whose annual pension income is 2% of the average salary during the past three years, multiplied by the number of years of service (up to thirty-five years). Suppose that that average is $150,000. What is the amount of annual pension income that you will receive?*

According to the plan's rule, the amount of pension income can be calculated as follows:

$$2\% \cdot 150{,}000 \cdot 35 = 105{,}000 \text{ per year,}$$

which is exactly 70% of your average salary. However, this number exceeds the maximum imposed by the *Income Tax Act.* That maximum is:

$$2{,}552.22 \cdot 35 = 89{,}327.70 \text{ per year.}$$

As a result, your annual pension income will be capped at $89,327.70. This translates to only 59.55% of your average income.

Pension income from DB plans continue for life. In fact, many DB plans also continue the payment to your spouse in the event that you pass away (this is known as a survivorship benefit). The amount of pension income never declined. Rather, some plans offer pension payments that are indexed to inflation in order to adjust for increases in the cost of living.

Because of the lifelong nature of their payments, DB plans provide protection against the decline in the standard of living due to longevity risk. In other words, employers bear the longevity risk of their employees. Employers are in a better position to bear this risk because a DB plan forms a pool of employees where the risk can be shared. Nevertheless, longevity risk may never be completely diversified away. For example, a medical advance can increase the life expectancy of the whole group of employees, which means that, on average, the employer is going to have to make pension payments for a longer period.

Employers also have to make sure that they have enough money to pay to the retirees when the time comes. In this regard, let us look at how employers manage DB plans. A DB plan can be either funded or unfunded. In a funded plan, contributions from the employer and the employees are invested. Because the returns on the investment is random and the length of the benefit periods is uncertain, the employer can never be sure that they will have enough to meet their future obligations. Therefore, the plan's assets and liabilities need to be reviewed regularly by an actuary (normally every three years), and the amounts of contributions be adjusted accordingly. Depending on the contractual agreement, the employees may or may not be asked to change their contributions. If not, then the employer will end up bearing both the investment risk and the longevity risk.

In an unfunded DB plan, no assets are set aside to prepare for benefit payments. Rather, the benefits are paid by the employer as required. This method is referred to as the pay-as-you-go (PAYGO) scheme, and is common among governments around the world. Governments pay pension income to retirees by using the contributions of current employees and taxes. You can think of the PAYGO scheme as an intergenerational transfer of pension. The current employees must then hope that when their retirement comes, there are enough contributions from the next generation of employees to support their benefits, and so on.

The PAYGO scheme is obviously sensitive to the ratio between the number of current employees and the number of retirees. For the scheme to work properly, employers (i.e., governments) need many more workers in the labor force than retirees receiving payments. Unfortunately, the fertility rates in many countries are quite low. This, together with the fact that retirees are living longer, has caused unfunded plans in some countries to become unsustainable. This has forced some governments to alter the terms of the pension benefits.

In summary, DB pension plans benefit employees because longevity risk and investment risk are typically assumed by the employers.[2] This allows employees to better smooth their consumption throughout their lives. However, from the employers' point of view, the plans can be costly, complicated, and risky to manage. This is why the majority of employers (except governments) no longer offer them. Rather, defined-contribution (DC) plans are offered instead. In a DC plan, the amount of your contribution is defined (e.g., a fixed percentage of salary or a fixed dollar amount), but the amount of benefits is not. As you contribute into the plan, your employer will typically match (fully or partially) the contribution. You then have to decide how to invest the funds. Typically, you can select from a variety of stock, bond, and money-market mutual funds. When you reach retirement, the amount of money that you have in your pension account will of course depend on the contributions accumulated and the investment income that they earn. This is the amount from which you will consume during your retirement years.

Consequently, there is no guarantee that you will have enough money to maintain your standard of living for the rest of your life. In other words, in a DC plan, employees bear both the investment risk and the longevity risk. This is why some experts regard DC plans as simply tax-deferring savings plans rather than pension plans. The market's steep decline during 2008 and 2009 simply reinforced the investment risk that members of DC plans face.

Figure 12.3 compares the proportions of Canadian employees enrolled in DB and DC plans in the year 1980 to the proportions in the year 2008. As you can see, the percentage of people who belong to DB plans has declined from 94% to 77%, while the percentage of people who have DC plans has jumped from 5% to 16%.

Figure 12.4 displays the breakdown between the two plans in the public and the private sectors as of 2008. In the public sector, 82 out of every 100 employees have a registered pension plan. Out of these eighty-two people, seventy-seven of them (or 94%) have DB plans (and five of them have DC

---

[2] This argument is predicated on an assumption that employers do not have a complete flexibility in changing the amounts that employees are required to contribute during their working years. Otherwise, employers would always be able to make changes to reflect changing market conditions and life expectancy, in which case employees would end up bearing the market and longevity risks. In general, this assumption is consistent with what goes on in practice.

Pensions and Retirement [Canadian Content]

	1980	2008
Total Members:	4,475,429	5,908,633
Percent DC:	5%	16%
Percent DB:	94%	77%
Percent Other:	1%	7%

Figure 12.3. Members of a Registered Pension Plan (RPP) in Canada. *Source:* Statistics Canada Table 280-0008.

plans). In contrast, in the private sector, only 28 out of every 100 employees have a registered pension plan. Out of these twenty-eight, only seventeen of them (or 61%) have DB plans.

As mentioned earlier, the migration from DB plans to DC plans was caused by the fact that DB plans are costly and risky for employers to manage. The migration was also caused by the fact that many employees over the last few decades saw little value in a benefit that tied them to one company. Many younger workers believed that the chance they would stay at the same company for twenty or thirty years was remote. Therefore, they wanted a pension plan that they could take with them if they decided to move. Because it is very difficult to transfer a DB plan from one employer to another (unlike a DC plan, there is no individual account for each DB plan member), these young workers asked their employers to switch to savings-type arrangements, especially during the equity bull run of the 1990s when an annual return of 20% from the stock market was expected by all.

12.2.3 Life Annuity

The third kind of contract that provides you with lifelong income is a life annuity. A life annuity is a financial contract whereby the issuer (typically an insurance company) promises to make a series of payments to the buyer (or the annuitant) in exchange for either a lump-sum, up-front payment from the buyer or a series of payments that the buyer will make before the payout phase of the annuity.

	Members of RPP	Members of DB
Public Sector	82%	77%
Private Sector	28%	17%

Figure 12.4. Pension Plans in Public and Private Sectors. *Source:* Statistics Canada Table 2002-0008.

In its simplest form, the payments from the annuity are constant and last until the annuitant dies. There are, however, a few variations of life annuities. For example, the annuity payments can be variable and linked to the performance of an equity mutual fund. The annuity may also have a guarantee period where the payments will be made for at least a certain number of years. If the annuitant dies during the guarantee period, the payments will go to his or her beneficiary. On the other hand, if the annuitant continues to live past the period, the payments will continue until he or she dies. Finally, an annuity can be conditioned on more than one life. A couple can buy a joint-life annuity where the payments will continue (in whole or in part) until both individuals die.

Because the annuity's payments last for life, its pricing will depend on mortality probabilities. In Chapter 8, you have already seen one pricing example. Basically, the price of a single-life annuity with no guarantee period is equal to the sum of the discounted values of the expected payoffs (where the expectations are calculated based on the probabilities of survival). For example, consider a life annuity that will pay $1 per year (at the end of each year) for the rest of your life. If you buy this annuity today, you get the first payment of $1 in one year from now. If the valuation rate is v% p.a., the price of this annuity today is:

$$a_x := \frac{_1 p_x}{1+v} + \frac{_2 p_x}{(1+v)^2} + \cdots + \frac{_n p_x}{(1+v)^n} = \sum_{j=1}^{n} \frac{_j p_x}{(1+v)^j} \qquad (12.1)$$

where, if you recall, $_j p_x$ is the probability that an x-year-old person will survive for at least j more years, and n is the maximum age in the mortality table. Each of the terms on the right-hand side of equation (12.1) is the discounted value of the expected payoff (which is $1 multiplied by the probability that you will be around to collect it).

Practice Question *Suppose that the valuation rate is 3% p.a. What is the actuarially fair price of a life annuity that pays $1 per year at the end of each year with no guarantee period for a sixty-five-year-old male?*

We will use the mortality probabilities in Table 8.1 to calculate the probabilities of survival to different ages. The calculation is presented in Table 12.3. The price of this annuity is $12.2249. This is the amount that you have to pay now in exchange for $1 per year for the rest of your life. Note that in the calculation, we assume that no one will live past the age of 110. We assume that people die as soon as they reach their 110th birthday. The impact of this assumption on the annuity price is very minimal (because of the distance to the payoff and the discounting).

Table 12.3. *Actuarially fair price of a single-life annuity with no guarantee period for a 65-year-old Canadian*

Age (x)	j	Probability that an x-year-old male will die within one year (iq_x)	Probability that a 65-year-old male will survive at least j more years (jp_{65})	Expected payoff	PV of expected payoff
65	1	0.01593	0.984070	$0.984070	$0.955408
66	2	0.01752	0.966829	$0.966829	$0.911329
67	3	0.01930	0.948169	$0.948169	$0.867709
68	4	0.02124	0.928030	$0.928030	$0.824543
69	5	0.02329	0.906416	$0.906416	$0.781883
70	6	0.02555	0.883257	$0.883257	$0.739714
71	7	0.02810	0.858438	$0.858438	$0.697989
72	8	0.03104	0.831792	$0.831792	$0.656624
73	9	0.03429	0.803270	$0.803270	$0.615639
74	10	0.03779	0.772914	$0.772914	$0.575121
75	11	0.04165	0.740722	$0.740722	$0.535114
76	12	0.04599	0.706657	$0.706657	$0.495635
77	13	0.05091	0.670681	$0.670681	$0.456701
78	14	0.05631	0.632915	$0.632915	$0.418431
79	15	0.06210	0.593611	$0.593611	$0.381016
80	16	0.06846	0.552972	$0.552972	$0.344594
81	17	0.07555	0.511195	$0.511195	$0.309281
82	18	0.08353	0.468495	$0.468495	$0.275191
83	19	0.09214	0.425328	$0.425328	$0.242558
84	20	0.10129	0.382246	$0.382246	$0.211641
85	21	0.11135	0.339683	$0.339683	$0.182596
86	22	0.12268	0.298011	$0.298011	$0.155530
87	23	0.13566	0.257583	$0.257583	$0.130515
88	24	0.15005	0.218932	$0.218932	$0.107700
89	25	0.16558	0.182682	$0.182682	$0.087250
90	26	0.18264	0.149317	$0.149317	$0.069237
91	27	0.20160	0.119214	$0.119214	$0.053669
92	28	0.22283	0.092650	$0.092650	$0.040495
93	29	0.22086	0.072187	$0.072187	$0.030632
94	30	0.23867	0.054958	$0.054958	$0.022642
95	31	0.25754	0.040804	$0.040804	$0.016321
96	32	0.27751	0.029481	$0.029481	$0.011448
97	33	0.29858	0.020678	$0.020678	$0.007796
98	34	0.32077	0.014045	$0.014045	$0.005141
99	35	0.34406	0.009213	$0.009213	$0.003274
100	36	0.36846	0.005818	$0.005818	$0.002008
101	37	0.39396	0.003526	$0.003526	$0.001181
102	38	0.42053	0.002043	$0.002043	$0.000665
103	39	0.44815	0.001128	$0.001128	$0.000356
104	40	0.47678	0.000590	$0.000590	$0.000181
105	41	0.50637	0.000291	$0.000291	$0.000087
106	42	0.53687	0.000135	$0.000135	$0.000039
107	43	0.56822	0.000058	$0.000058	$0.000016
108	44	0.60036	0.000023	$0.000023	$0.000006
109	45	0.63320	0.000009	$0.000009	$0.000002
Annuity Price					**$12.224910**

Source: Author Calculations based on Statistics Canada mortality table.

The price that we have calculated is an actuarially fair price for the annuity. In practice, insurance companies will also add expenses and profits to the price.

Using the same calculation logic, you can figure out the prices of life annuities for people of different ages and under different valuation rates. We present the results for males and females of ages sixty, sixty-five, seventy, and seventy-five in Table 12.4.

As you can see, annuities are more expensive for females than for males of the same age. This is because females live longer than males do (i.e., their probability of survival to any age is greater than that of their male counterpart). Also, the higher the interest rate, the lower is the annuity price. This is because when interest rates are high, insurance companies can invest the annuity principal (i.e., the amount that you pay up front to buy the annuity) at those high rates. The higher the returns, the lower they need to charge for the annuity.

In practice, annuity prices are quoted in terms of income per a certain amount of annuity principal (e.g., $100). For example, an annuity quote of 7% means that if you buy a $100 dollars worth of a life annuity, you get $7 per year for the rest of your life. You can of course invert this relationship and find out how much you will have to pay up front in exchange for a certain dollar amount of annual income. For example, if you want to receive $10,000 per year, a quote of 7% means that you will have to pay $10,000/0.07 = $142,857 up front.

With this in mind, you can invert the annuity prices in Table 12.4 into annuity quotes. The results are shown in Table 12.5.

Note that the quotes are higher for males than for females at the same age. Males will get more annuity income per year than females do. This is again due to the fact that females have a longer life expectancy. More importantly, note that the rates of annuity income are all higher than the valuation rates (i.e., interest rates). When you buy an annuity, you should get more income than if you invest the same amount of money in an interest-earning account. This is because the annuity income will stop when you die, and your estate will not get the annuity principal back. In other words, when you buy an annuity, you are getting into a pool of people who are sharing their longevity risks. If you happen to live long, you will benefit from the constant stream of income (which, as mentioned, is higher than the interest rate). The insurance company is able to provide you with the high income because it no longer has to make payments to people in the pool who die before you do.

Table 12.4. *Actuarially fair prices of single-life annuities with no guarantee period*

Valuation rate (%)	Male				Female			
	60-years-old	65-years-old	70-year-old	75-year-old	60-years-old	65-years-old	70-year-old	75-year-old
3.00%	$14.3542	$12.2249	$10.0834	$7.9965	$16.3474	$14.2444	$12.0381	$9.7756
5.00%	$11.7742	$10.2854	$8.6997	$7.0686	$13.1131	$11.7272	$10.1762	$8.4835
7.00%	$9.8807	$8.8089	$7.6075	$6.3103	$10.8108	$9.8663	$8.7466	$7.4537

Source: Author Calculations Based on Analytic Mortality Model.

Table 12.5. *Actuarially fair annuity rates for single-life annuities with no guarantee period*

Valuation rate (%)	Male				Female			
	60-years-old	65-years-old	70-year-old	75-year-old	60-years-old	65-years-old	70-year-old	75-year-old
3.00%	6.9666%	8.1800%	9.9173%	12.5055%	6.1172%	7.0203%	8.3070%	10.2295%
5.00%	8.4931%	9.7225%	11.4947%	14.1472%	7.6259%	8.5272%	9.8268%	11.7876%
7.00%	10.1207%	11.3522%	13.1449%	15.8472%	9.2500%	10.1355%	11.4330%	13.4161%

Source: Author Calculations Based on Analytic Mortality Model.

Finally, note that in equation (12.1), the same valuation rate v is used to discount all expected payoffs, regardless of the timing of them. In practice, insurance companies typically use the prevailing term structure of interest rates to price annuities. (A term structure of interest rates is a relationship between interest rates and terms of transactions.)

To summarize this section, you have seen three kinds of financial contracts that give you lifelong income. They all can be used to reduce longevity risk and thus can help you to achieve a smooth pattern of consumption throughout your life. People who do not belong to a DB pension plan should consider creating their own lifelong pension plan by purchasing a life annuity.

12.3 Optimal Retirement Spending Rate in the Presence of Longevity Risk

Another way to deal with longevity risk in the consumption-smoothing framework is to structure your consumption with the risk in mind. Recall that in Chapter 4 you learned how to derive the optimal consumption pattern under the assumption that the length of life is known. You can expand that idea to account for longevity risk. For the purpose of this discussion, let us ignore financial market risk by assuming that all investments are allocated to risk-free, inflation-protected bonds such as real-return bonds issued by the Bank of Canada, or Treasury Inflation-Protected Securities (TIPS) issued by the U.S. Federal Reserve.[3] This simplifying assumption is made in order to focus our attention on the role of "longevity risk aversion" on optimal consumption and spending rates during a retirement period of a random length.

Loosely speaking, by longevity risk aversion, we mean to imply that different people might have differing attitudes toward the "fear" of living longer than anticipated and possibly depleting their financial resources. Some might respond to this risk by spending less early on in their retirement, while others might be willing to take their chances and enjoy a higher standard of living while they are most likely to be alive.

---

[3] Real-return bonds and TIPS are the inflation-indexed bonds whose principal is regularly adjusted to reflect changes in the consumer price index. Its coupon rate is constant. However, the interest amount will change because the (constant) rate is multiplied by the inflation-adjusted principal. Therefore, the holders are protected against inflation. For example, suppose the bond has a face value of $1,000 and a coupon rate of 3% p.a., payable every six months. If the inflation rate over the past six months is 1%, then the principal will be adjusted to $1,010, and the interest payment will be $15.15.

The impact of *financial* risk aversion on optimal asset allocation has been the subject of much research and is by now well understood. Investors who are more worried and concerned about losing money (i.e., risk-averse) invest more conservatively and sacrifice the potential upside, which in effect leads to a reduced lifetime standard of living. In contrast, the impact of longevity risk aversion on retirement spending behavior has not received as much attention. Nor are most financial practitioners even familiar with this concept.

Our pedagogical objective is to contrast the optimal retirement spending policy as derived through utility maximization (i.e., consumption smoothing) with popular recommendations offered by the investment media and financial planners. Moreover, our main point of contention is that counseling retirees to set initial spending from investable wealth at a constant inflation-adjusted rate – for example, the widely popularized 4% rule – is consistent with lifecycle consumption smoothing only under a very limited set of implausible preference parameters. There simply is no universally optimal or safe retirement spending rate. Rather, the optimal forward-looking behavior in the face of personal longevity risk is to consume in proportion to survival probabilities – adjusted (upwards) for pension income and (downwards) for longevity risk aversion – as opposed to blindly withdrawing constant income for life. We will shortly explain this in detail.

12.3.1 Retirement Spending Rates

Within the community of retirement income planners, an often-referenced study is the work by Bill Bengen (a U.S.-based financial planner) in which he used historical (Ibbotson Associates) equity and bond returns to search for the highest allowable spending rate that would sustain a portfolio for thirty years of retirement. Using a 50/50 equity/bond mix, Bengen settled on a withdrawal rate between 4% and 5%. In fact, this is known as the Bengen rule or the 4% rule in the retirement income planning community, and has caught on like a wildfire. For those unfamiliar with this rule, it simply says that for every $100 in the starting retirement nest egg, one should withdraw $4 adjusted for inflation each year – forever, or at least until the portfolio runs dry or life runs out, whichever comes first. Yet this "start by spending x%" strategy has no basis in economic theory and should immediately stand at odds with the "smoothing" we have been advocating in earlier chapters. Our goal here is to illustrate the solution to the lifecycle problem and demonstrate how longevity risk aversion affects retirement spending rates.

12.3.2 Numerical Example

The model that we use is fully described in Chapter 13 (and so the readers can select their own parameter values and derive optimal spending rates under any assumptions). Here, we only mention the logic of the method. Remember that the optimal pattern of consumption that you obtained in Chapter 4 is optimal in the sense that it provides you with the highest total happiness (or utility) over your lifetime (of a known length). In the presence of longevity risk, you will solve the same optimality problem. You maximize the expected total utility from consumption throughout your life, except that now you weigh your future utility by the probability that you will be around to enjoy future consumption.

Recall that in this section, we assume that the only randomness is in the length of life. Our approach forces us to specify a real (inflation-adjusted) investment return. We assume that the real rate of return is 2.50% p.a., which is reasonable for inflation-adjusted values.

As far as longevity risk is concerned, we assumed the retiree's remaining lifetime obeys a (unisex) biological law of mortality under which the hazard rate increases exponentially over time. This is known as the Gompertz assumption in the actuarial literature, and we calibrated this model to common pension (RP2000) tables. The mortality law is described fully in Chapter 13.

What this means is that in most of our numerical examples, we assume an 86.6% probability that a sixty-five-year-old will survive to the age of seventy-five, a 57.3% probability of reaching eighty-five, a 36.9% probability of reaching ninety, a 17.6% probability of reaching age ninety-five, and a 5% probability of reaching 100. Note again that we do not plan using a life expectancy or an ad hoc thirty-year retirement. Rather, we account for the entire term structure of mortality.

Because the main objective of this section is to focus our attention on the impact of risk aversion on the optimal portfolio withdrawal rates (PWR), we display results for a range of values of risk-aversion parameters. We show results for a retiree with a very low γ and a relatively high γ coefficient of relative risk aversion. These concepts were explained in Chapter 7.

To better understand mortality-risk aversion, we offer the following analogy to classical asset allocation models. An investor with a CRRA value of $\gamma = 4$ would invest 40% of his or her assets in an equity portfolio and 60% in a bond portfolio, assuming the equity risk premium is 5% and volatility is 18%. Someone with a lower risk-aversion coefficient (say, $\gamma = 1$) will be less averse to equity investment and will invest more than 40% of his or her

Table 12.6. *Optimal retirement consumption ($y = 4$)*

Age	Real return = 1.5%	Real return = 2.5%	Real return = 3.5%
65	$3.941	$4.605	$5.318
70	$3.888	$4.544	$5.247
75	$3.802	$4.442	$5.130
80	$3.429	$4.007	$4.007

wealth in the equity portfolio. In contrast, a more risk-averse person (say, $y = 8$) will invest less than 40% of his or her wealth in equity.

Finally, to complete the parameter values required for our model, we assume the subjective discount rate ρ, which is a proxy for personal impatience (and which is used to discount future utility), is equal to the risk-free rate (mostly 2.50% in our numerical examples). To compare with the basic lifecycle model without lifetime uncertainty – what we did in Chapter 4 – this implies that the optimal consumption rates would be constant over time in the absence of longevity risk considerations. In the language of Chapter 4, the g_c parameter is zero in real terms.

In the language of economics, when the Subjective Discount Rate (SDR) in a lifecycle model is set equal to the constant and risk-free interest rate, then a rational consumer would spend their total (human plus financial) capital evenly and in equal amounts over time. In other words, in a model with no horizon uncertainty, consumption rates and spending amounts are in fact constant. The question of interest is: *What happens when lifetimes are stochastic?*

We are now ready for some results. Assume a sixty-five-year-old with a (standardized) $100 nest egg with no bequest motive and a risk-aversion coefficient of $y = 4$. At this point, we assume that there is no pension annuity income. Therefore, all consumption must come from the investment portfolio that is earning a deterministic interest rate. Using the model presented in the second half of the book to solve the individual's utility-maximization problem, the optimal consumption rates at various ages and under three different real rates of return are presented in Table 12.6. The numbers shown in the table are the amounts that you should consume at various stages of your life under different interest rates.

Note that some of the optimal consumption rates in Table 12.6 are within the range of numbers quoted by the popular press for optimal portfolio withdrawal rates (i.e., $\approx$ 4%). Thus, at first glance this seems to suggest that simple 4% rules of thumb are consistent with a lifecycle model. Unfortunately, the euphoria is short-lived. It is only under certain combinations of interest rate and age that the numbers (might) coincide. In general, however, the optimal retirement consumption does not remain constant through time. As the retiree ages, they rationally consume less each year – in proportion to their survival probability adjusted for risk aversion. For example, when the real rate of return is 2.50%, the optimal consumption rate drops from $4.605 at age sixty-five, to $4.544 at age seventy, then $4.442 at age seventy-five, then (not displayed in table) $3.591 at age ninety, and $2.177 at age 100, assuming the retiree is still alive.

The optimal pattern requires that you gradually reduce your consumption as you age. The intuition for this result is that because you weigh the utility of future consumption by your probability of survival, later consumption is not valued as highly as early consumption is (because the probability of you being around to consume in the far future is lower than the probability of being around in the near future). In other words, intuitively "smoothers" deal with longevity risk by setting aside a financial reserve and by planning to reduce consumption – if that risk materializes – in proportion to the survival probability, linked to their risk aversion.

12.3.3 Including Pension Annuities

We now employ the same model to examine what happens when the retiree has access to a defined-benefit pension income annuity, which provides a guaranteed lifetime cash flow. We will consider four different cases – (i) no pension; (ii) pension of $1 per year; (iii) pension of $2 per year; and (iv) pension of $5 per year. Note that the income is expressed relative to the standardized nest egg of $100. So, if your nest egg happens to be $1,000,000, the four cases will, respectively, be (i) no pension; (ii) pension of $10,000 per year; (iii) pension of $20,000 per year; and (iv) pension of $50,000 per year.

Table 12.7 displays the optimal portfolio withdrawal rates as a function of the risk-aversion values and preexisting pension income, where we assume that the real rate of interest is 2.50% p.a. By net portfolio withdrawal rates (PWR), we mean the optimal amount withdrawn from the investment portfolio. Thus, for example, when the $\gamma = 4$, which is medium-risk aversion, a retiree who has a nest egg of $100 and a pension of $5 per year will consume $10.551 at age sixty-five. Of this sum, $5 obviously comes from the pension and $5.551 is withdrawn from the portfolio. Thus, the portfolio withdrawal rate (PWR) is 5.551%.

Table 12.7. *Optimal portfolio withdrawal rate at age 65*

Pension income	Risk-aversion coefficient			
	gamma = 1	gamma = 2	gamma = 4	gamma = 8
$0	6.330%	5.301%	4.605%	4.121%
$1	6.798%	5.653%	4.873%	4.324%
$2	7.162%	5.924%	5.078%	4.480%
$5	8.015%	6.553%	5.551%	4.839%

In contrast, if the retiree is only entitled to $1 per year in lifetime pension income, then the optimal total consumption rate is $5.873 at age sixty-five, of which $1 comes from the pension and $4.873 is withdrawn from the portfolio. Hence, the PWR is 4.873%.

So, here for all intents and purposes is the main point of this section in one summary sentence. The optimal PWR depends on longevity risk aversion and the level of preexisting pension income. The larger the amount of the preexisting pension income, the greater the PWR is and thus the greater is the optimal consumption rate.

Basically, the pension acts as a buffer and allows the retiree to consume more from discretionary wealth. Even at high levels of longevity-risk aversion, the risk of living a longer lifespan does not "worry" the retiree as much, because they have pension income to fall back on should that chance (i.e., a long life) materialize. We believe this insight is absent from most of the popular media discussion (and practitioner implementation) of optimal spending rates. If a potential client has substantial pension income from a DB pension, they can afford to withdraw more – percentagewise – compared to their neighbor who is relying entirely on their investment portfolio to finance their retirement income needs.

Table 12.7 confirms a number of other important results. Notice how the optimal portfolio withdrawal rate – for a range of pension income and risk aversion levels – is in fact between 4% and 8%. Remember that these numbers are derived under the assumption that the real interest rate is 2.50%. Adding another 100 basis points to the investment return assumption would add somewhere between 60 to 80 basis points to the initial PWR. Reducing interest rate would have the opposite effects.

Figure 12.5 displays the optimal consumption path from retirement until the maximum length of life as a function of the retiree's level of

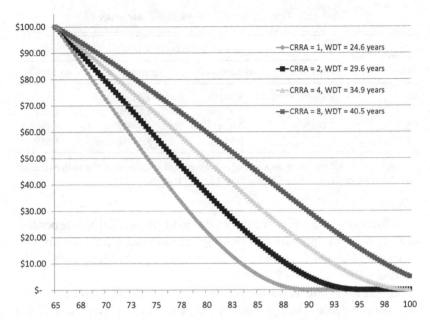

Figure 12.5. Financial Capital: $5 Pension Income and Investment Rate = 2.5%.

longevity-risk aversion (i.e., γ), assuming that the pension income is $5 per year. This figure gives yet another perspective on the rational approach and attitude to longevity risk management. The figure traces out the entire consumption path from retirement at age 65 until age 100.

Notice how the optimal consumption rate declines with age and in relation to the retiree's attitude toward longevity risk as measured by their γ. The figure plots four cases corresponding to differing levels γ. For example, if $\gamma = 2$ (i.e., very low aversion to longevity risk), the individual will start retirement by withdrawing 6.55% from their nest egg plus their pension income of $5. The withdrawals from the portfolio continue until they (rationally) exhaust their wealth at age ninety-five. From what is coined the Wealth Depletion Date (WDT) onwards, all they consume is their pension.

Suppose you have no pension income from your employer. You can create your own lifetime income by using a fixed percentage of the retirement nest egg to purchase a pension annuity (i.e., pensionization). The cost of each lifetime dollar of income from the annuity can be calculated using equation (12.1). We note, however, that the pricing of pension (income) annuities by private-sector insurance companies will usually involve mortality rates that differ from population rates, due to adverse-selection concerns. This could be easily incorporated by using different mortality parameters, but for now

Table 12.8. *Impact of pensionization on retirement consumption rates*

Percent: Initial portfolio and pension	Lower longevity risk aversion $\gamma = 2.0$		Medium longevity risk aversion $\gamma = 4.0$		Higher longevity risk aversion $\gamma = 8.0$	
	Consume at age 65	Consume at age 80	Consume at age 65	Consume at age 80	Consume at age 65	Consume at age 80
0%: W=$100 P=$0.000	$5.3014	$4.5696	$4.6051	$4.2755	$4.1187	$3.9684
20%: W=$80, P=$1.2661	$5.9193	$5.1021	$5.2637	$4.8869	$4.8013	$4.6263
40%: W=$60, P=$2.5321	$6.3760	$5.4958	$5.7963	$5.3815	$5.3858	$5.1893
60%: W=$40, P=$3.7982	$6.7040	$5.7784	$6.2292	$5.7833	$5.8921	$5.6774
80%: W=$20, P=$5.0643	$6.8631	$5.9156	$6.5328	$6.0651	$6.2983	$6.0687
100%: W=$0, P=$6.3303	$6.3303	$6.3303	$6.3303	$6.3303	$6.3303	$6.3303

Source: Author Calculations.

we keep things simple to illustrate the impact of lifetime income on optimal total spending rates.

Table 12.8 displays the total dollar consumption rate at ages sixty-five and eighty for person with a nest egg (as of age sixty-five) of $100 under various assumptions on how much of the nest egg is pensionized – 0%, 20%, 40%, 60%, and 100%. We assume that the annuity is fairly priced and that the real interest rate is 2.50% p.a.

The numbers shown in Table 12.8 are *total* consumption (which includes both the annuity income and the amount that you withdraw from the remaining nest egg). For example, if the (medium risk-averse) retiree allocates $20 (from the $100 available) to purchase a pension annuity that pays $1.261 for life, then optimal consumption will be $1.261 + $3.997 = $5.263 at age sixty-five. Note that the $3.997 withdrawn from the remaining portfolio of $80 is equivalent to an initial portfolio withdrawal rate of 4.997%.

In contrast, the retiree with a high degree of longevity risk aversion $\gamma = 8$ will receive the same $1.261 from the $20 that has been "pensionized" but will only (optimal) spend $3.535 from the portfolio (a withdrawal rate of 4.419%), for a total consumption rate of $4.801 at age sixty-five. In addition, if the entire nest egg is pensionized at sixty-five, leading to $6.3303 of lifetime income, then the consumption rate is constant for life – and independent of risk aversion – as there is no financial capital from which to draw down any income. This is yet another way to illustrate the benefit of converting financial wealth into a pension income flow. The $6.3303 of annual consumption is the largest of all consumption plans. This, by the way, is why most financial economists are strong advocates of "pensionizing" (or at least annuitizing) a portion of one's retirement nest egg.

12.4 Summary

Our focus in this chapter was to illustrate what a lifecycle model actually says about optimal consumption rates. Our intention was to contrast ad hoc recommendations with "advice" that a financial economist would give to a utility-maximizing consumer, and see if there is any overlap and by how much, exactly, it differs. In particular, we shine light on the aversion to longevity risk – the uncertainty of human lifespan – and examine how this affects optimal spending rates.

The main practical insights to remember are as follows:

1. The optimal initial portfolio withdrawal rate (PWR) that the "planning literature" advocates should be an exogenous percentage of one's retirement nest egg, actually depends quite critically on both the consumer's risk aversion – where risk is longevity and not just financial markets – as well as any preexisting pension annuity income. For example, if the portfolio's real investment return is 2.5% per annum, then for individuals who are highly risk-averse the optimal initial PWR can be as low as 3%. For individuals who are less risk-averse, it can be as high as 7%. The same applies to the existence of pension annuity income. The greater the amount of preexisting pensions the larger the initial PWR is, all else being equal. Of course, if one assumes a healthier retiree and/or lower real returns, the optimal initial PWR will be lower.

2. The optimal consumption rate, which is the total amount of money consumed by the retiree in any given year including all pension income, is a declining function of age. In other words, retirees should consume less at older ages. The consumption rate from discretionary wealth is proportional to the survival probability and is a function of risk aversion, even when the subjective rate of time preferences is equal to the interest rate. The rational consumer – planning at age 65 – is willing to sacrifice some income at the age of 100 in exchange for more income at 80.

3. The interaction between (longevity) risk aversion and survival probability is quite important. In particular, the impact of risk aversion is to increase the effective probability of survival. So, imagine two retirees with the same amount of initial retirement wealth and pension income (and the same subjective discount rate) but with

differing levels of risk aversion. The individual with greater risk aversion behaves as if their modal value of life is higher. Specifically, they behave as if it is increased by an amount proportional to $\ln(1/\gamma)$ and they spend less in anticipation of their longer life. Observers will never know if they are longevity-risk averse or just healthier.

4. The optimal trajectory of financial capital (also) declines with age. Moreover, for individuals with preexisting pension income it is rational to spend-down wealth by some advanced age and live exclusively on the pension income. The wealth depletion time (WDT) can be at age ninety – or even age eighty when the pension income is sufficiently large. Greater (longevity) risk aversion, which is associated with lower consumption, induces greater financial capital at all ages. There is nothing wrong or irrational about planning to deplete wealth by some advanced age.

5. The rational reaction to portfolio shocks (i.e., losses) is nonlinear and dependent on when the shock is experienced as well as the amount of preexisting pension income. One does not reduce portfolio withdrawals by the exact amount of a financial shock unless their risk aversion is $\gamma = 1$. For example, if the portfolio suffers an unexpected loss of 30%, the retiree might reduce consumption by only 30% less as a result.

6. Converting some of the initial nest egg into a stream of lifetime income increases consumption at all ages regardless of the cost of the pension annuity. Even when interest rates are low and the cost of $1 of lifetime income is (relatively) high, the net effect is that "pensionization" increases consumption. Note that we are careful to distinguish between real-world pension annuities – in which the buyer hands over an irreversible sum in exchange for a constant real stream – and Tontine annuities, which are at the foundation of most economic models but are completely unavailable in the marketplace.

The "cost" of having a simple analytic expression for spending is that we had to assume a deterministic investment return. Although we used a safe and conservative assumed return for most of the displayed numerical examples, we have for all intents and purposes ignored the last fifty years of portfolio modeling theory. Recall, however, that our attempt was to shed light on the often-quoted rules of thumb and how they relate to longevity risk, as opposed to developing a full-scale dynamic optimization model. That (which is much more mathematical) will be done in Chapters 13 and 14.

12.5 Questions and Assignments

1. You are now thirty years old and have just started working for a company that provides you with a defined-benefit pension plan. The pension income that you get when you retire is equal to 2% of your final-year salary, multiplied by the number of years of service. Your current salary is $40,000 (payable at the end of the year). It is growing at the rate of 1% per year (in real terms). You will retire when you reach sixty-five years old. How much will your pension income be?

2. You have just started working. Your employer offers you a choice between a defined-benefit (DB) pension plan and a defined-contribution (DC) pension plan. Under the terms of the DB plan, your annual pension payment will be equal to 2% of the average of your salary during your final three years, multiplied by the number of years of service. The pension payment will be made once a year (at the end of each year), starting from the year you begin your retirement until you pass away. Under the terms of the DC plan, you and your employer will each contribute $6,000 per year (and hence the total annual contribution is $12,000). The contribution will be invested in a risk-free instrument that earns 5% p.a., annual compounding. (Note that the contribution amounts remain the same year after year.) Your current salary is $50,000, and it increases at the rate of 2% per year. You plan to retire in thirty years, which means that your final-year salary will be $50,000 $\times$ $(1.02)^{30}$. Assume that you will live for thirty years after you retire and that the rate of return will be 5% p.a., annual compounding throughout your life. Disregard income tax in your calculations. What will be your annual pension benefit under each pension plan?

3. Using the mortality table in Chapter 8, how much money does a Canadian male need to have at the start of his retirement (age sixty-five) if he wants to consume $45,000 per year for the rest of his life? Assume that he will not leave anything to his family, and that the valuation rate is 4%.

4. Refer to question 3. Now recalculate your answer for a sixty-five-year-old Canadian female. Please compare these two answers and explain the implications.

5. You have been working for your company for exactly twenty years. You belong to a DB plan whose annual pension income is 2% of the average salary during the past three years, multiplied by the number

of years of service. Suppose that average is $85,000. What percentage of your income will your annual payments be?

6. Suppose that the valuation rate is 2% p.a. What is the actuarially fair price of a life annuity that pays $30,000 per year at the end of each year with no guarantee period for a seventy-year-old female?

7. Based on question 6, what if the annuity has a guarantee period of ten years?

8. Essay: Comment on the 4% withdrawal rule in retirement income planning.

9. Essay: How does longevity risk aversion affect retirement spending rates?

10. Essay: How would a bequest motive (i.e., the desire to leave a legacy for family and loved ones) affect the optimal retirement spending rate?

THIRTEEN

Advanced Material: Part I. Continuous Time and the Calculus of Variations

Learning Objectives

In this chapter we offer a (more) mathematical formulation of the main ideas behind **strategic financial planning** for individuals. The intended audience for this chapter is upper level or graduate students with sufficient calculus training. We start by reviewing some earlier results – which we presented back in Chapters 2 to 5 without much justification – and then move on to obtain some newer ones. Some of the concepts might seem familiar (and perhaps even repetitive), but we urge you to pay special attention to the new context in which they are being presented. As this chapter (and then Chapter 14) progress, the material will get exceedingly mathematical and involve some advanced concepts from differential equations to stochastic processes. Hang in there (or skip to the numerical examples). Our objective is to provide a complete representation of the model for those who want to derive the equations themselves.

13.1 Wages and Salary in Continuous Time

In this section we introduce the notation we will be using in continuous time. Start by assuming that you are x years old, still in school (i.e., not earning any money) and you plan to graduate, start your working life, join the labor force, and earn an **income** at an age denoted by I. From a modeling perspective, it helps to consider the remainder of your lifecycle as consisting of three distinct stages: study, work, and retirement, although we do acknowledge that in practice some people alternate between and merge these stages over their life.

Your inflation-adjusted annual wage (i.e., salary) rate at age x is denoted by w_x, and will be represented by the following equation:

$$w_x := \begin{cases} 0; & 0 \le x \le I \quad \text{Study Period} \\ w_I e^{g(x-I)} & I < x \le R \quad \text{Working Stage} \\ 0; & R < x \le D \text{ Retirement Years.} \end{cases} \quad (13.1)$$

The number w_I is your real (inflation-adjusted) wage rate in your first year in the labor force, while the symbol g denotes the real (inflation-adjusted) rate at which your wages grow until you retire and stop working at the age of $x = R$. Most of our modeling and equations assume that this growth rate g will be constant throughout your working years. On the odd occasion that we need to make it time-dependent (or even random, as we do in Chapter 14), we will denote it by g_t.

Here is the bottom line; your wages drop back to zero between the age of retirement R until the age of death D, which is the reason you have to worry about this (and save for retirement) between age I and age R. In what follows, we assume that R and D are known with certainty (aka exogenous variables), both of which are rather dubious assumptions. Either way, equation (13.1) is the lifecycle model backbone of this book.

Note (again) that we have assumed zero wage income during the retirement years (R, D), which obviously does not include any pensions or retirement income benefits. In practice most people have some form of government pension, like CPP/OAS in Canada, which we will deal with later. However – and this is more than just semantics – we do not consider pension income and entitlements to be part of wages or human capital.

Finally, to bring some life to these symbols, here is one possible set of parameters for this framework. You are $x = 20$ years old and plan to stay in school (or tour Tibet) for another five years until the age of $I = 25$. At that age, you plan to join the labor force (expecting to be) earning $w_{25} = \$50,000$ per year (in inflation-adjusted terms, which means in today's dollars), which then grows by $g = 5\%$ per year until you retire at the age of $R = 55$. This means that you will earn $50,000e^{(0.05)30} = \$224,084.5$ in your final year of work in today's dollars. After that age $(x \ge R)$, you are wageless until you die at $D = 95$. Make sure you understand how all dollars are real (not nominal) values.

13.2 Human Capital Values in Continuous Time

The next step is to value (i.e., discount) the cash flows generated by the human wage process, but using the continuous-time formulation. Following the same summation logic and approach that we took in the earlier parts of this book, the value of your human capital when the wage process obeys equation (13.1) and you are still in school ($x < I$) can be written as:

$$\mathbf{H}_x = \int_x^D w_t e^{-v(t-x)} dt \qquad x \leq I. \tag{13.2}$$

The intuition is as follows. The integral (instead of the summation sign) adds up the instantaneous wage $w_t dt$ earned at age t, and discounts it back $t - x$ years to the present age. The integral is evaluated (added up) from the present age x until the age of death D. However, because the wage process is defined as zero until age I (you are still in school), and zero after retirement R, the integral can be simplified by tightening the upper and lower bounds of integration. Also, instead of the expression w_t, you can substitute the explicit wage value from equation (13.1). This leaves:

$$\mathbf{H}_x = \int_I^R w_I e^{g(t-I)} e^{-v(t-x)} dt \qquad x < I. \tag{13.3}$$

The next step is as follows. Within the integrand, any variable that does not explicitly include t can be pulled out and treated as a constant. This leaves a cleaner expression for human capital:

$$\mathbf{H}_x = \int_I^R w_I e^{gt-gI} e^{-vt+vx} dt \tag{13.4}$$

$$= w_I e^{vx-gI} \int_I^R e^{(g-v)t} dt \qquad x < I.$$

Next, remember that the integral (i.e., anti-derivative) of e^{zt}, for any constant z, is simply $(1/z)e^{zt}$. This is evaluated from the lower bound of integration (age of first job) I, to the upper bound of integration (age of retirement) R. Thus, you can eliminate the integral entirely and arrive at:

$$\mathbf{H}_x = w_I e^{(vx-gI)} \left(\frac{e^{(g-v)R} - e^{(g-v)I}}{g-v} \right) \qquad g \neq v. \tag{13.5}$$

Finally, if you add and subtract an extra term vI, and rewrite $(vx - gI)$ as $-(g - v)I + v(x - I)$ in the first exponent, you can cancel another factor and simplify the second term in the numerator to arrive at:

$$\mathbf{H}_x = w_I e^{v(x-I)} \left(\frac{e^{(g-v)(R-I)} - 1}{g-v} \right) \qquad g \neq v. \tag{13.6}$$

Of course, when $g = v$, the limiting expression is $w_I e^{v(x-I)}(R - I)$.

Note an important thing about equation (13.6). When $x = I$ (i.e., you are just about to start working for the first time) and the projected growth rate of your wages g is exactly equal to the valuation rate v, the value of human capital H_x is equal to $w_I(R - I)$, which is your current wage multiplied by the number of years of work ($R - x$) ahead of you. The intuition for this result is that although your wages are expected to grow over time, the valuation rate v neutralizes the growth in wages. You are left with basic addition.

Here are some numerical applications of equation (13.6) so you can see how it works. You are $x = 20$ years old and plan to start work at the age of $I = 25$, hoping (expecting) to earn $w_{25} = \$40,000$, which is expected to grow at an inflation-adjusted rate $g = 6\%$ per year. Then, assuming an inflation-adjusted valuation rate $v = 5\%$, the value of your human capital (today) is $H_{20} = \$1,532,134$ if you plan to work until age $R = 65$. For future references, we will refer to this case as the **benchmark** case, with which comparisons will be made as we change the values of the parameters.

For example, suppose you decide to delay your first year of work, from $I = 25$ to $I = 26$. In this case, $w_{26} = \$40,000$, and your human capital at age $x = 20$ will decline from $\$1,532,134$ to $\$1,413,424$. In other words, the one-year delay will cost you ($\$1,532,134 - \$1,413,424$) = $\$118,710$ in today's dollars. This might seem extremely steep and counterintuitive, but is mainly due to the high growth rate of wages ($g = 6\%$) compared to the lower valuation rate of ($v = 5\%$). By starting working one year late, you lose not only the first year's wage, but also the opportunity for your wage to grow right away. Here, the high assumed growth rate makes a big difference. In contrast, if you do the same calculation assuming no growth in wages (so that $g = 0$), the cost of the extra year of leisure is a mere $\$30,386$ in today's dollars.

Now, let us come back to the case where you start working at age $I = 25$. What if you are willing to work longer and retire at age $R = 70$? Because the working period is now longer, your human capital will be higher at $H_{20} = \$1,770,408$. The extra five years of wages are worth $\$238,274$ in today's dollars.

Remember that equations (13.2) and (13.6) are meant to be used while you are in school (i.e., when $x < I$), and you are forced to use different periods for wage discounting and wage growth. However, in case you are already working (i.e., $x \geq I$ and so there is no delay until the first wage), the calculus is modified only slightly. In this case, your human capital can be represented as:

$$\mathbf{H}_x = \int_x^T w_x e^{g(t-x)} e^{-v(t-x)} dt \qquad x \geq I. \qquad (13.7)$$

The main difference between equations (13.7) and (13.2) is that you no longer need to keep track of the **initial** wage, w_I, as long as you know the current wage, w_x, and its projected growth rate, g, over time. In this case, after applying the same calculus used to derive equation (13.6), you arrive at:

$$\mathbf{H}_x = w_x \left(\frac{e^{(g-v)(R-x)} - 1}{g - v} \right) \qquad x \geq I, g \neq v \qquad (13.8)$$

with the understanding that when $g = v$, you should use the intuitive $\mathbf{H}_x = w_x(R - x)$. Equation (13.8) is the expression most frequently used in this chapter and the next, and is easy on the eyes and on the memory.

Here it is again. Human capital value is the product of your current wage, w_x, and a multiplication factor that depends only on the difference between the wage's growth rate, g, and the valuation rate, v. Hence, if you are already working (i.e., $x \geq I$), you do not have to make separate assumptions about the values of g and v. All you need is the difference or spread between the two variables. Another nice thing about modeling the problem this way is that it allows us to bypass having to predict (or guess) future inflation rates. If g is a nominal number (growth + inflation) and v is a nominal number (valuation + inflation), then $g - v$ eliminates inflation and becomes a real (inflation-adjusted) quantity.

13.3 A Different Route: Same Destination

Occasionally, when $x \geq I$, you might actually want to represent $\mathbf{H}_x$ in terms of the original initial wage, w_I, instead of the current wage, $w_x = w_I e^{g(x-I)}$. In this case, equation (13.7) and (13.8) can be written as:

$$\mathbf{H}_x = w_I e^{g(x-I)} \left(\frac{e^{(g-v)(R-x)} - 1}{g - v} \right) \qquad x \geq I, g \neq v. \qquad (13.9)$$

The wage multiplication factor in parentheses collapses to $(R - x)$ when $(g = v)$. Note that if (for whatever reason) you decide to use equation (13.9) instead of equation (13.8), you have to specify both g and v. The choice of equation will depend on context and purpose. Do not worry about it now.

To help you understand – one last time, before the calculus gets harder – how all this integration works in practice, here are some numerical examples where you can follow the derivation step-by-step. Think of it as a calculus refresher as well. The next few paragraphs will derive the value of your human capital by brute force, instead of using the (easier) formulas. We use the same example as before where we assume that you are now twenty years old and will join the labor force at the age of $I = 25$, and your initial annual wage is $w_{25} = \$40,000$, which grows at a real $g = 5\%$ per year until retirement at age $R = 65$. As before, the (real) valuation rate is $v = 5\%$ p.a. According to the definition of human capital in equation (13.3), the value is:

$$H_{20} = \int_{25}^{65} 40,000 e^{(0.06)(t-25)} e^{-(0.05)(t-20)} dt \qquad (13.10)$$

$$= 40,000 e^{-(0.06)25} e^{(0.05)20} \int_{25}^{65} e^{(0.01)t} dt$$

$$= 24,261.23 \int_{25}^{65} e^{(0.01)t} dt = \$1,532,134,$$

which is exactly what you obtained before by plugging the six values of x, I, R, g, v, w_I directly into the second part of equation (13.6).

Here is another brute force numerical example. Assume you discount all cash flows at (a much lower) $v = 2\%$ instead of (the relatively low) $v = 6\%$. The corresponding integral value of human capital becomes:

$$H_{20} = \int_{25}^{65} 40,000 e^{(0.06)(t-25)} e^{-(0.02)(t-20)} dt \qquad (13.11)$$

$$= \$3,576,852.$$

Your human capital increases from \$1.532 million to \$3.577 million, which is more than double, when you use $v = 2\%$ instead of at 6%.

To conclude, and to give readers the opportunity to test their own numbers, the following provides a range of values for H_{20} per \$1 of starting annual wage ($w_{20} = 1$), under different combinations of the wage growth rate g and the valuation rate v. Assume, as before, that you will start working at age twenty-five and retire at sixty-five. In the next paragraph, we will use $H_x(v, g, R)$ as long-form notation for the value of human capital, when the current wage $w_x = 1$, the retirement age is R, the wage growth rate is g, and the valuation rate is v, both inflation adjusted.

For example, $H_{20}(1\%, 2\%, 65) = \$46.78$, while $H_{20}(1\%, 8\%, 65) = \$209.88$. Notice how the wage growth rate of 8% versus 2% makes the value of human capital almost four times larger in magnitude. However, when the valuation rate is increased to $v = 5\%$, the relevant values are $H_{20}(5\%, 2\%, 65) = \$18.14$, while $H_{20}(5\%, 8\%, 65) = \$60.23$. Finally, when $v = 7\%$, the values are $H_{20}(7\%, 2\%, 65) = \$12.19$ and $H_{20}(7\%, 8\%, 65) = \$34.66$. Make sure you can replicate these numbers.

13.4 Does Human Capital Grow or Shrink over Time?

Take a careful look at equation (13.9). Notice how the variable x appears twice and in a rather complicated form within the expression for H_x. The derivative (rate of change) of H_x with respect to x, is not necessarily negative. This means that H_x might actually increase with x. Your human capital next year, H_{x+1}, might be worth more than it is today H_x. This may seem puzzling and paradoxical at first. After all, in a world of perfect foresight the sum of $(R - x)$ cash flows should be greater than the sum of $(R - x - 1)$ of those cash flows.

The reason for this (apparent) oddity is that H_x today and H_{x+1} tomorrow are not quite comparable to each other because they represent values and cash flows at different points in time. It is the equivalent of knowing that you might have more money in your bank account tomorrow, compared to today. That does not imply that the discounted (economic) value of your account tomorrow is worth more than it is today. The actual maximum age (in terms of initial wage) depends on the interaction between g and $(R - x)$.

Whether you find this confusing or not, one thing is for certain. If you take the derivative of equation (13.9) with respect to x, set it equal to zero and solve for x, you will see that the function H_x achieves its maximum value precisely at age:

$$x^* = R - \frac{\ln(g/v)}{g - v} \qquad g \neq v. \qquad (13.12)$$

When $g = v$, the value of $x^* = R - 1/v$ (by taking the limit $g \to v$). In the previous example where $g = 6\%$ and $v = 4\%$, the maximum value occurs at age $x^* = 70 - \ln(0.06/0.04)/0.02 = 49.73$. On the other hand, when $g = 0$, the natural logarithm in the numerator in equation (13.12) is negative infinity, which leads to the result that H_x is maximized before you were born. Practically speaking, no growth in wages ($g = 0$) means that the value of your human capital will decline **consistently** as you age. In contrast, positive growth in wages means that the value of your human capital will decline **eventually**. Of course, you can always quit your current job and get another job that pays more and/or whose wages grow at a higher rate (or even retire early). However, that takes you out of the realm of equation (13.1), where it is assumed that g is the same throughout your working years.

Here is the main takeaway. The value of human capital on your personal balance sheet tomorrow – **in tomorrow's dollars** – might be larger than the value of human capital on your personal balance sheet today, **in today's dollars.**

13.5 Implicit Liabilities in Continuous Time

As we argue throughout the book, if you are going to accept and place human capital on your personal balance sheet, you must subtract off the value of implicit liabilities to arrive at a net-human capital value. While we do not want to rehash the earlier discussion in Chapter 3, and for the most part will ignore the messiness of computing liabilities in this chapter, the same calculus technology can be used to arrive at $i\mathbf{L}_x$, the implicit liability.

Consider again the benchmark case. You are now $x = 20$ years old, and you expect to live until you reach $D = 85$. You estimate that you need to spend about \$20,000 per year in today's dollars in order to obtain the minimum standard of living. This cost will increase 2% above the general inflation rate (i.e., in real terms) over time. Assume, as before, that the valuation (discount) rate is $v = 5\%$ p.a. To obtain the current value of these future expenses, we simply take the present value of them. Based on the same logic as the one used in the earlier calculation of human capital, the value of your future expenses is:

$$i\mathbf{L}_{20} = 20{,}000 \left(\frac{e^{(0.02-0.05)(85-20)} - 1}{0.02 - 0.05} \right) = \$571{,}817. \qquad (13.13)$$

Therefore, your holistic balance sheet should show \$571,817 in implicit liabilities (on the right-hand side) in addition to the value of your human capital (on the left-hand side).

13.6 Consumption Smoothing: A Second Look

In this section we derive the optimal consumption function c_t^* by assuming that you want to spread your human and financial capital evenly over your lifecycle. This will provide us with equations for c_t^*, similar to the ones derived in Chapter 4. Later on in this chapter we will do this (much) more formally, by assuming that you want to maximize utility of consumption. The end results are identical **only** when the valuation rates are constants. More on this later.

Let the function $\{c_t; x \le t \le D\}$ denote any one of the infinite number of consumption/expenditure plans that you can implement over the course of your remaining lifecycle (i.e., from your current age, x, to your death at age D). Likewise, the function $\{s_t; x \le t \le R\}$ denotes any one of the infinite number of saving/investment plans you can implement over your working years (i.e., from your current age, x, to your retirement at age R). Notice that consumption plans are structured over the entire period (x, D) while saving plans only make sense over the shorter working period (x, R). After you retire at age R, you live off your previous savings and spend down your financial capital. Remember that c_t and s_t are annual rates that are expressed in dollars. Think, for example, of $100,000 in wages per year, or $10,000 in savings per year, or $90,000 in spending per year, and so on. Finally, the asterisk on the plan $\{c_t^*; x \le t \le D\}$ and $\{s_t^*; x \le t \le R\}$ denotes the unique optimal or most strategic plan from the universe of all available (admissible) plans, $\{c_t; x \le t \le D\}$ and $\{s_t; x \le t \le R\}$.

As we have emphasized throughout the book, c_t^* and s_t^* rates provide strategic guidance as opposed to tactical recommendations. If your fridge unexpectedly breaks today, you have to spend money to fix it. That is not part of our strategic plan and is not something we can predict. Also, although both rates are presented and denoted separately, the relationship between the optimal consumption/expenditure rate at any age t and the optimal savings/investment rate at any age t can be represented by the rather trivial identity:

$$s_t^* = w_t - c_t^*. \tag{13.14}$$

Here w_t, as defined earlier, is your annual wage rate at age t and we have ignored implicit liabilities to keep things as simple as possible in this chapter, because they do not add much to the theory we are about to present. Here we have (truly) ignored required expenses, to keep things simple.

Using the same logic that led to the calculation of human capital, you arrive at the following fundamental identity (again), which is the lifetime budget constraint:

$$\mathbf{W}_x - \int_x^D c_t^* e^{-v(t-x)} \, dt = 0. \tag{13.15}$$

The discounted value of the optimal discretionary consumption plan must be exactly equal to the present value of your current net worth, $\mathbf{W}_x$ (not to be confused with little w_x, which is your wage income).

All of the variables and parameters within equation (13.15) should be recognizable by now. The general function c_t^* denotes the optimal discretionary consumption/expenditure plan at any age $\{t; x \le t \le D\}$, which will be solved for in just a moment. The valuation rate v is used to discount all discretionary consumption cash flows to the present age x, similar to what was done in Chapters 2 and 3, with wages, human capital, and implicit liabilities valuation.[1]

In the language of mathematical optimization, we must locate the optimal lifecycle plan $\{c_t^*; x \leq t \leq D\}$ that yields the highest possible consumption rate at any age provided that consumption changes smoothly by exactly k each year (remember that your k can be positive, negative, or zero) and the lifecycle budget constraint in equation (13.15) is satisfied.

Now let c_x^* be the optimal consumption at the current age x. Because you want consumption to change by k per year, your optimal consumption at any age t where $x \leq t \leq D$, is $c_x^* e^{k(t-x)}$. It then follows that equation (13.15) can be rewritten as:

$$\mathbf{W}_x - c_x^* \int_x^D e^{k(t-x)} e^{-v(t-x)} dt = 0 \qquad (13.16)$$

where two things have now changed. First, the general function $\{c_t^*; x \leq t \leq D\}$ has been replaced by a parametric representation $c_x^* e^{k(t-x)}$, and second, the constant c_x^* (i.e., the optimal consumption at the current age x) has been pulled out of the integral. Other than that, equation (13.16) is identical to equation (13.15).

Just to be clear, the term $c_t^* = c_x^* e^{k(t-x)}$ in the integrand of equation (13.16) did not just come out of the blue. You specified that you wanted (1) a consumption plan over your entire life with no large drops or big jumps, and (2) the amount of your consumption to change by k per year. So, you really have no choice but to accept an exponential representation for your optimal consumption plan $\{c_t^*; x \leq t \leq D\}$. The exponential representation is independent of the value of your financial capital, financial liabilities, human capital, or any other personal quirks (or preferences) that you might have. In other words, whether you know it or not, you actually asked for the integrand in equation (13.16).

Note that by assuming the exponential form for our consumption rate function, we have severely restricted the solution set and choices available. In general, this solution is suboptimal. In the subsequent sections, we will take another look at this problem by using the method of calculus of variations. We will convince you that the exponential function is (not as ad hoc as it might appear, and is) indeed optimal, provided that certain conditions are satisfied.

---

[1] It should by now be clear that our goal is to solve for the optimal **discretionary** consumption. Consequently, we will from this point on omit the term discretionary unless confusion can arise.

We now solve for the exact value of c_x^*, which is the current (today's) consumption rate. This is simply a present-value-of-an-annuity problem, and this is not the first time that we come across a problem like this in this book. By the same logic, we can rewrite equation (13.16) as:

$$\mathbf{W}_x - c_x^* \left(\frac{e^{(k-v)(D-x)} - 1}{k - v} \right) = 0 \qquad (13.17)$$

with the understanding that when $k = v$ the expression collapses to $\mathbf{W}_x - c_x^*(D - x) = 0$.

Here it is in words one last time. Equation (13.17) says that there is a strict relationship between your current economic net worth $\mathbf{W}_x$ and your current optimal consumption rate, c_x^*. It depends only on (1) the number of years until you die ($D - x$), and (2) the difference between your patience parameter and the valuation rate, $(k - v)$.

It then follows that the optimal consumption rate is:

$$c_x^* = \frac{\mathbf{W}_x(k - v)}{e^{(k-v)(D-x)} - 1}, \qquad k \neq v \qquad (13.18)$$

and, when $k = v$, the optimal consumption rate at age x is:

$$c_x^* = \frac{\mathbf{W}_x}{D - x}, \qquad (13.19)$$

which is basic **long division** – evenly spread your economic net worth over the time left in your lifecycle. Conceptually, none of this should be new to you. In Chapters 3 and 4 you saw these formulas in **discrete time**, assuming annual compounding, and in this chapter we are deriving the same results in **continuous time**.

Let us apply the formula and see how (smoothly) the continuous-time expression works in practice. Assume you are currently $x = 35$ years old with $F_{35} = \$100,000$ in financial capital. You earn $w_{35} = \$50,000$ per year, which has been increasing steadily at a real rate of $g = 6\%$ per year. You expect this 6% growth to continue going forward, and would like to retire at the age of $R = 65$, which is in thirty years. The job offers no lifetime pension or retirement income plan. Assume you will live to the age of $D = 95$. Assume also that your minimum, subsistent (i.e., nondiscretionary) level of consumption is $\$20,000$ per year (i.e., $b_{35} = \$20,000$), and growing at 2% above inflation per year. In addition, the valuation rate is $v = 5\%$ per year.

The values of your human capital $H_{35} = \$1,749,294$ and your implicit liabilities $iL_{35} = \$556,467$. Your current economic net worth is $\mathbf{W}_{35} = \$1,292,827$. This is your budget constraint on which you will base your discretionary consumption/expenditure policy $\{c_t^*; 35 \le t \le 95\}$. Now suppose that you want your standard of living to increase by $k = 4\%$ per year. According to equation (13.18), your optimal plan is to start out consuming at a rate of exactly:

$$c_{35}^* = \frac{(0.04 - 0.05)1{,}292{,}827}{e^{(0.04-0.05)(60)} - 1} = \$28{,}654. \qquad (13.20)$$

From this example, $k = 4\%$ and the optimal current discretionary consumption rate is $c_{35}^* = \$28{,}654$. What happens if $k = 5.5\%$? Plugging $k = 5.5\%$ into equation (13.18), your optimal current discretionary consumption becomes $c_{35}^* = \$18{,}476$, which is about 36% lower. You will be consuming (much) less today, and saving (much) more. On the positive side, your consumption rate will be increasing by $k = 5.5\%$ each year (as opposed to $k = 4\%$), which means that it will grow at a faster rate over time. Next year (at age thirty-six), it will be $\$18{,}476e^{(0.055)} = \$19{,}521$, and by age sixty-five it will grow to $\$18{,}476e^{(0.055)30} = \$96{,}206$, which is slightly more than what it would be under the $k = 4\%$ case.

What if you have negative relative patience $(k < 0)$? You are impatient and so you want to consume more now. This means that your optimal consumption will decline each year. For example, suppose $k = -2\%$. Using equation (13.18), you will get that $c_{35}^* = \$91{,}876$, which is far more than you now earn. Your current and near-term consumption will be financed by dipping into financial capital and eventually borrowing money to satisfy your appetite. Of course, the budget constraint will still have to be satisfied. By the time you retire at the age of sixty-five, you will only be consuming $\$91{,}876e^{-(0.02)30} = \$50{,}422$. And, at the age of eighty-five it will shrink to $\$91{,}876e^{-(0.02)50} = \$33{,}799$ per year. These numbers may not look too bad, but assume that you can borrow and lend at the same valuation rate. This will definitely not be the case in practice, and we will address the asymmetry later in this chapter.

Next we look at the effect of wage growth rate g. In general, if you increase the wage growth rate g, and leave every other parameter unchanged, the value of human capital $\mathbf{H}_{35}$ will obviously increase. This, in turn, increases the economic net worth $\mathbf{W}_{35}$, resulting in a looser lifetime budget constraint. It then follows that the optimal current discretionary consumption rate, c_{35}^*, will be higher (remember that it will continue to increase at the same k percent rate per year). The same effect will be observed if you increase the age of retirement R, or increase the current wage w_{35}. They all (uniformly) increase the value of human capital, which then flows into increased consumption at all ages.

The impact of the valuation rate v on the optimal consumption and saving rate is generally more ambiguous. This is because v affects the determination of the optimal consumption rate in two different ways. First, because it is the discount rate used in the calculation of your human capital and implicit liabilities, a higher valuation rate reduces the value of your human capital and your implicit liabilities. The two reductions have opposite effects on your economic net worth. The lower value of human capital causes your economic net worth to be lower, while the lower value of implicit liabilities makes your economic net worth higher. Typically, human capital has a stronger effect and so your economic net worth will be lower when the valuation rate is higher. The reverse is true if the valuation rate is lower. Both your human capital and implicit liabilities will be higher. As before, the effect from human capital is stronger and so your economic net worth will be higher. It then follows that a higher (lower) valuation rate reduces (increases) the optimal consumption rate at all ages.

Secondly, at the same time, a higher valuation rate reduces the present value of your future discretionary consumption. As a result, you can afford to consume more at all ages. In other words, a higher valuation rate allows you to save less because it makes your savings grow faster. Which effect dominates depends on the values of other parameters such as k and g. Generally, however, the second effect will dominate because the time period for consumption (i.e., from age x to death, D) is much longer than the time period for earning wages (i.e., from age x to retirement, R).

For example, if the valuation rate is $v = 7\%$ instead of 5%, the value of human capital is reduced to \$1,295,909. This is almost half a million dollars less than under the $v = 5\%$ case. Now, if you add this to the financial capital $F_{35} = \$100,000$ and then use equation (13.18) to extract the optimal discretionary consumption rate, you will get $c^*_{35} = \$36,510$, which is obviously larger than the \$28,654, which was optimal in the $v = 5\%$ case. This consumption rate is about \$8,000 higher today even though the human capital value and hence your economic net worth are lower. This seemingly counterintuitive result occurs because a higher valuation rate lowers the present value of your consumption, and so you can consume more. Note also that the consumption rate $c^*_{35} = \$36,150$ means that first year's savings are negative (because your nondiscretionary consumption is \$20,000 and your wage in the first year is only \$50,000). You borrow to consume in the first year. You then repay this loan from your wages in later years. Once again, this assumes that v is the rate you pay on borrowing and lending.

Suppose instead that the valuation rate v is reduced from 5% to 3%. The value of human capital is now $H_{35} = \$2{,}432{,}672$, which is obviously much higher, but the optimal discretionary consumption rate is a mere $c_{35}^* = \$19{,}830$. Paradoxically, you might be worth a lot more, but you have to save a lot more as well. In fact, your standard of living – measured by the total amount of consumption over your life – will decline.

Here is the bottom line. In this section we have derived the optimal consumption without a formal optimization procedure. Instead, we computed the value of human capital and assumed that it will be spent over your remaining lifetime (x, D), by increasing at a rate of k per year. This is a very ad hoc way of deriving an optimal consumption rate (especially to an economist), and in the next sections we will arrive at optimal consumption and spending rates – for the third time in this book – by assuming that you want to maximize your utility function of consumption, which is a concept we first addressed in the chapter on risk and insurance.

13.7 Calculus of Variations

To introduce the basic idea for solving the optimal consumption problem more rigorously (i.e., without guessing the functional form of the optimal consumption function), we start with a generic form:

$$J[z_t^*] = \max_{z_t} J[z_t] \quad \text{where } J[z_t] := \int_a^b \phi(t, z_t, \dot{z}_t)\,dt. \quad (13.21)$$

Here the dot denotes derivative with respect to time t, ϕ is a **functional** (a function of functions). The function z_t is free everywhere except at the two end points ($t = a$ and $t = b$). The task we are facing is to choose a particular path z_t^* from a to b so that the integral reaches its maximum value.

This type of problem was first introduced by Johann Bernoulli in 1696 (for physics, not finance!), more than 300 years ago, even though he was not the first to consider such problems. The problem Bernoulli posed was the following: *Given two points A and B in a vertical plane, what is the curve traced out by a point acted on only by gravity, which starts at A and reaches B in the shortest time?* This is the well-known brachistochrone problem, or the curve of fastest descent. The method for solving this type of problem, or the **calculus of variations**, was developed by Euler and Lagrange.

The basic idea of calculus of variations is similar to that used in standard optimization problems you have been exposed to in your first-year calculus course. Recall that when you are searching for the extreme (maximum or minimum) values of a given function, say $y = f(x)$, you look for the candidates x^* by setting the first derivative $f'(x^*) = 0$. The reason behind this is simply that if the extreme of $f(x)$ occurs at x^*, say maximum, you must have $f(x^* + \delta x) \leq f(x^*)$ for all values of δx (usually taken as a small value, both positive and negative). Rearranging the inequality as:

$$\frac{f(x^* + \delta x) - f(x^*)}{\delta x} \begin{cases} \leq 0, & \delta x > 0 \\ \geq 0, & \delta x < 0. \end{cases} \tag{13.22}$$

Taking the limit of $\delta x \to 0$ and assuming the limit exists, we obtain the so-called **first-order condition**: $f'(x^*) = 0$.

To search for the optimal path z_t^* (if it exists), we add a **perturbation** δz_t to it in a similar way. The only difference is that this perturbation is usually not a single number, but instead a function of time t. However, if it helps you to think this way, you could imagine that $\delta z_t = h\eta_t$ where η_t is a given function and h is a number. Now we can carry on as earlier and define

$$\delta J := J[z_t^* + \delta z_t] - J[z_t^*] \tag{13.23}$$

where

$$J[z_t^* + \delta z_t] = \int_a^b \phi(t, z_t^* + \delta z_t, \dot{z}_t^* + \delta \dot{z}_t) dt. \tag{13.24}$$

Using Taylor expansion, we have:

$$\phi(t, z_t^* + \delta z_t, \dot{z}_t^* + \delta \dot{z}_t) = \phi(t, z_t^*, \dot{z}_t^*) + \phi_2(t, z_t^*, \dot{z}_t^*)\delta z_t$$
$$+ \phi_3(t, z_t^*, \dot{z}_t^*)\delta \dot{z}_t + h.o.t. \tag{13.25}$$

Here the subscript 2 and 3 denote partial derivatives to the second and third variables of ϕ. Again, you may find that it is easier to think of this using $\delta z_t = h\eta_t$ because in this case ϕ is simply a function of h and this is just the usual Taylor expansion you have seen in calculus. The term $h.o.t.$ is higher order with respect to δz_t, which means that it goes to zero faster than δz_t (or h as it approaches to zero).

With this in hand, we have obtained the following:

$$J[z_t^* + \delta z_t] - J[z_t^*] = \int_a^b \{\phi_2(t, z_t^*, \dot{z}_t^*)\delta z_t + \phi_3(t, z_t^*, \dot{z}_t^*)\delta \dot{z}_t + h.o.t.\} dt. \tag{13.26}$$

Using integration by parts, we have:

$$J[z_t^* + \delta z_t] - J[z_t^*] = \int_a^b \left\{ \left[\phi_2(t, z_t^*, \dot{z}_t^*) - \frac{d}{dt}\phi_3(t, z_t^*, \dot{z}_t^*) \right] \delta z_t + h.o.t. \right\} dt$$
$$+ \phi_3(t, z_t^*, \dot{z}_t^*)\delta z_t \big|_{z_a}^{z_b}. \tag{13.27}$$

Because z_a and z_b are given, $\delta z_a = \delta z_b = 0$ and the last term disappears. Finally by definition, we have $J[z_t^* + \delta z_t] - J[z_t^*] \leq 0$, and we conclude that

$$\int_a^b \left\{ \left[\phi_2(t, z_t^*, \dot{z}_t^*) - \frac{d}{dt}\phi_3(t, z_t^*, \dot{z}_t^*) \right] \delta z_t + h.o.t. \right\} dt \leq 0 \qquad (13.28)$$

for all δz_t. Therefore, the **necessary condition** for optimality is given by the Euler-Lagrange equation

$$\phi_2(t, z_t^*, \dot{z}_t^*) - \frac{d}{dt}\phi_3(t, z_t^*, \dot{z}_t^*) = 0. \qquad (13.29)$$

Note that the derivative d/dt applies to all the variables that depend on time, not just the first variable of ϕ.

13.8 Smooth Consumption: A Final Look

In this section we put the discussion of smooth consumption on a firm footing by applying calculus of variations for solving the following problem: You are currently at age x and earning a wage that grows with a rate g (as before) and stops at retirement. You will live until the age D (with certainty) and you want to find the best possible consumption rate that will carry you from now until the time of death D. What will that optimal consumption rate look like?

In the utility-maximizing framework, we need to solve the optimal consumption problem:

$$\max_{c_t} E \left[\int_0^{\bar{D}} e^{-\rho t} u(c_t) dt \right] \qquad (13.30)$$

subject to

$$\dot{F}_t = v F_t + w_t - c_t \qquad (13.31)$$

with a given F_0 and $F_{\bar{D}} = 0$. Here ρ (a new variable) is called the subjective discount rate (SDR), which is related to (although not quite equal to) the concept of personal relative patience rates k. You will see how the two are related a bit later.

At this point we should pause and explain the centrality of equation (13.30) to almost everything we have done in this book. Representation of the lifecycle model is the essence of strategic financial planning. It is the mathematical representation on the lifecycle model (LCM) of savings and consumption – originally postulated by Irving Fisher (1930) and refined by Modigliani and Brumberg (1954) – and is at the core of most "modern" dynamic asset allocation models, as well as the foundation of microeconomic consumer behavior. The original mathematical formulation – likely by Ramsey (1928) – assumed a deterministic horizon. However, in a seminal contribution, the LCM was extended by Yaari (1965) to a stochastic lifetime, which eventually led to the models of Merton (1971), Richard (1975), and hundreds of subsequent papers on asset allocation over the human lifecycle.

The conceptual underpinning of the LCM is the intuitive notion of "consumption smoothing" whereby (rational) individuals seek to minimize disruptions to their standard of living over their entire life. They therefore plan for a consumption profile that is continuous, with constant marginal utility at all points, based on the assumption of a concave utility function.

We operate under a constant relative risk aversion (CRRA) formulation for the utility function:

$$u(c_t) = \begin{cases} \frac{c_t^{1-\gamma}-1}{1-\gamma} & \gamma \neq 1 \\ \ln(c_t) & \gamma = 1 \end{cases} \tag{13.32}$$

where the marginal utility of consumption is the derivative of utility with respect to c_t, and defined as $u'(c_t) = c_t^{-\gamma}$. We note that for $\gamma \neq 1$ we will actually use $c_t^{1-\gamma}/(1-\gamma)$ for simplicity as it does not affect the optimal solution. These functions should not be new to you, because we introduced them back in Chapter 7.

This problem can be solved using the calculus of variations. Note that the generic form we have derived in the previous section can be readily applied to this problem by setting $z_t = F_t$, $a = 0$, $b = \bar{D}$, and

$$\phi(t, z_t, \dot{z}_t) = e^{-\rho t}u(w_t + vz_t - \dot{z}_t). \tag{13.33}$$

After some algebraic manipulations, we obtain the following second-order ordinary differential equation (ODE):

$$\ddot{F}_t - (k+v)\dot{F}_t + kvF_t + kw_t - \dot{w}_t = 0 \tag{13.34}$$

for $t \leq \bar{R}$ and

$$\ddot{F}_t - (k+v)\dot{F}_t + kvF_t = 0 \tag{13.35}$$

for $t > \bar{R}$. Here F_0 is given and $F_{\bar{D}} = 0$ and $k = (v - \rho)\gamma^{-1}$. The optimal consumption rate can be obtained by solving

$$\frac{d}{dt}\log c_t^* = k \tag{13.36}$$

as $c_t^* = c_0^* \exp(kt)$. The initial consumption rate c_0^* can be obtained by solving

$$F_0 = -\frac{w_0}{g-v}\left(1 - e^{(g-v)\bar{R}}\right) + \frac{c_0^*}{k-v}\left(1 - e^{(k-v)\bar{D}}\right), \qquad (13.37)$$

which is obtained by integrating the budget equation

$$\dot{F}_t = v F_t + w_0 e^{gt} 1_{\{t < \bar{R}\}} - c_0^* e^{kt} \qquad (13.38)$$

from $t = 0$ to $t = \bar{D}$. Here we have assumed that you have already started earning wage and $\bar{R} = R - x$ is time to retirement.

In sum, we have shown that the (rather ad hoc) smooth consumption policy discussed in most of this book maximizes your discounted lifetime utility and is **optimal** provided that the following conditions hold: (i) borrowing rate is the same as the lending rate and both are constant; (ii) no pension after retirement; (iii) no mortality risk. Next, we relax some of these conditions and consider complications such as the difference between lending and borrowing rates, and the possibility of wealth depletion with the availability of pension income after retirement. Before presenting our lifecycle model, we first discuss some issues related to mortality risk (life and death) in continuous time.

13.9 Life and Death in Continuous Time

In this subsection we introduce the basic concepts needed for modeling – then pricing and optimizing – over uncertain lifetimes in continuous time. Intuitively, we start with the random variable denoted by $\mathbf{T}_x$ and indexed by age x, which represents the **remaining lifetime** for an individual currently aged x. The random variable $\mathbf{T}_x$ has a probability density function (PDF) denoted and defined by $f_x(t)$.

We denote the conditional probability of dying before (or at) the age of $x + t$ with the function $F_x(t)$, which is the cumulative density function (CDF) of $\mathbf{T}_x$. This probability must equal to one when added to $({}_t p_x)$, which is the conditional probability of surviving t more years. Remember that:

$$_t p_x := 1 - F_x(t) = \Pr[\mathbf{T}_x > t]$$

and that:

$$F_x(t) := 1 - {}_t p_x = \Pr[\mathbf{T}_x \leq t]. \qquad (13.39)$$

Because the random variable $\mathbf{T}_x$ is continuous, the CDF is denoted and defined by:

$$F_x(t) = \int_0^t f_x(s)\,ds. \tag{13.40}$$

This probability can be represented in another way, which will be useful in defining the **instantaneous force of mortality**. As long as $(_t p_x)$ is constant or decreasing with respect to t, then we are entitled to represent this function using the following:

$$_t p_x = e^{-\int_x^{x+t} \lambda_s\,ds} \tag{13.41}$$

where the curve $\lambda_s \geq 0$, for all $s \geq 0$. Think of λ_s as the instantaneous rate of death at age s. When $t = 0$, then $(_t p_x) \to 1$, and when $t \to \infty$, we must have that $(_t p_x) \to 0$ so that $\int_x^{x+\infty} \lambda_s\,ds \to \infty$. The probability of surviving to infinity must go to zero because we do not allow for anyone to live forever. It might seem somewhat artificial to worry about these things, but the point is that if we are working in continuous time, we have to make sure the functions are making sense, even under the most extreme situations.

Note that by a simple change of variables $u = s - x$, we can rewrite equation (13.41) as:

$$_t p_x = e^{-\int_0^t \lambda_{x+u}\,du}. \tag{13.42}$$

Integrating the curve λ_s from a lower bound of x to an upper bound $x + t$ is mathematically equivalent to integrating the curve starting at λ_{x+s} from a lower bound of 0 to an upper bound of t. The change will, however, allow us to arrive at some important relationships.

If we take the derivative of both sides of equation (13.42), we arrive at:

$$\frac{\partial}{\partial t}(_t p_x) = -(_t p_x)\lambda_{x+t}.$$

Therefore, the derivative of the cumulative distribution function $F_x(t)$ or $1 - (_t p_x)$, is the probability density function $f_x(t)$, which is equivalent to:

$$f_x(t) = (1 - F_x(t))\lambda_{x+t}. \tag{13.43}$$

Using equation (13.43), we can represent the IFM as:

$$\lambda_{x+t} = \frac{f_x(t)}{1 - F_x(t)} \qquad t \geq 0. \tag{13.44}$$

Note that $F_x(t) \to 1$ as $t \to \infty$ (everyone dies eventually) and therefore $\lambda_t \to \infty$ as $t \to \infty$, unless $f_x(t)$ in the numerator approaches to zero faster.

Thus, the function $F_x(t)$ and its derivative $f_x(t)$ will determine the shape and behavior of λ_{x+t}. Note also that the relationship implied by equation (13.44) leads to:

$$F_x(t) = 1 - \frac{f_x(t)}{\lambda_{x+t}}, \tag{13.45}$$

which then implies:

$$f_x(t) = {}_t p_x \, \lambda_{x+t}. \tag{13.46}$$

Collectively, these equations allow us to move from $F_x(t)$ to $f_x(t)$ to λ_{x+t} and back again.

In summary, these relationships allow us to create mortality laws in two different ways: (i) we can start with a CDF $F_x(t) = 1 - ({}_t p_x)$ and then take the derivative to create the PDF $f_x(t)$ and then use equation (13.44) to get the IFM λ_x; Or alternatively, (ii) we can start with the IFM and build the CDF $F_x(t) = 1 - ({}_t p_x)$ using equation (13.41) and then take derivatives to arrive at the PDF $f_x(t)$.

We can now define the concept of moments and then move onto life expectancy and standard deviation of the remaining lifetime. If T_x is a continuous variable, the first moment of its distribution, or its expected value, is defined as:

$$E[T_x] = \int_0^\infty t f_x(t) dt. \tag{13.47}$$

Note that this is equivalent to:

$$E[T_x] = \int_0^\infty ({}_t p_x) dt. \tag{13.48}$$

The second moment or **the square mean** for the continuous r.v. is:

$$E[T_x^2] = \int_0^\infty t^2 f_x(t) d. \tag{13.49}$$

Taking the root of the difference between the second moment and the first moment squared results in the standard deviation of the random variable:

$$D[T_x] = \sqrt{E[T_x^2] - E^2[T_x]}. \tag{13.50}$$

Exponential Law of Mortality. Assume that the IFM curve satisfies $\lambda_{x+t} = \lambda$, which a constant across all ages and times. In this case, we can build the

$F_x(t)$ and $f_x(t)$ functions using equation (13.41). Note that we have:

$$_tp_x = e^{-\int_x^{x+t} \lambda_s\, ds} = e^{-\lambda t}. \tag{13.51}$$

The integral in the exponent collapses to (i.e., can be solved to produce) a linear function λt. This is the case because, since the function λ_x is a horizontal line, the area under the curve is simply the base $((x + t) - x)$ times the height λ. In this case the current age x does not really affect the probability of survival because all that matters is the magnitude of the IFM, λ. In other words, $(_tp_x)$ is identical to $(_tp_y)$ for any x and y, as long as the underlying λ is the same. At every age, the instantaneous probability of death is the same. This leads to:

$$F_x(t) = 1 - e^{-\lambda t} \tag{13.52}$$

$$f_x(t) = \lambda e^{-\lambda t}. \tag{13.53}$$

Recall that the expected remaining lifetime (ERL), in the case of an exponential model, is:

$$E[\mathbf{T}_x] = \int_0^\infty t\lambda e^{-\lambda t}\, dt = \frac{1}{\lambda}. \tag{13.54}$$

For example, when $\lambda = 0.10$, the ERL is $E[\mathbf{T}_x] = 10$, and when $\lambda = 0.05$, the ERL is $E[\mathbf{T}_x] = 20$. In contrast, the median remaining lifetime (MRL) is obtained by integrating the PDF curve from time zero to the median remaining lifetime and solving for $M[\mathbf{T}_x]$:

$$\frac{1}{2} = e^{-\lambda M[\mathbf{T}_x]} \iff M[\mathbf{T}_x] = \frac{\ln 2}{\lambda} < \frac{1}{\lambda}. \tag{13.55}$$

For example, when $\lambda = 0.05$ the MRL is $M[\mathbf{T}_x] = \ln 2/0.05 = 13.862$ years, in contrast to the ERL of $1/0.05 = 20$ years.

Gompertz-Makeham Law. Like in the case of the exponential law of mortality, the Gompertz-Makeham (GM) law of mortality is constructed using the IFM curve λ_x. In the GM case, the definition is:

$$\lambda_x = \lambda + \frac{1}{b} e^{(x-m)/b}, \quad t \geq 0 \tag{13.56}$$

where m is the selected median life span and b is the dispersion coefficient. According to equation (13.56), the instantaneous force of mortality is a constant λ plus a time-dependent exponential curve. The constant λ aims to capture the component of the death rate that is attributable to accidents, while the exponentially increasing portion reflects natural death causes. This curve increases with age and goes to infinity as $t \to \infty$.

When the individual is exactly $x = m$ years old, the GM's IFM curve is $\lambda_m = \lambda + 1/b$, but when the individual is younger ($x < m$), the IFM curve is $\lambda_x < \lambda + 1/b$, and when the individual is older ($x > m$), the GM IFM curve is $\lambda_x > \lambda + 1/b$. Thus, $x = m$ is a special age point on the IFM curve.

The convention is to label equation (13.56) the Gompertz-Makeham law when $\lambda > 0$ and Gompertz alone, when $\lambda = 0$. In the Gompertz case, typical numbers for the parameters are $m = 82.3$ and $b = 11.4$, under which $\lambda_{65} = 0.01923$ and $\lambda_{95} = 0.26724$. Note that from this point on, we assume that $\lambda = 0$, whenever we work with the GM law. Although this is certainly convenient from a mathematical perspective, this assumption is realistic as well, because λ tends to have a very small value in practice.

By the construction specified in equation (13.41), the conditional probability of survival under the GM IFM curve is equal to:

$$_t p_x = e^{-\int_x^{x+t}\left(\lambda + \frac{1}{b}e^{(s-m)/b}\right)ds} = e^{-\lambda t + b(\lambda_x - \lambda)(1 - e^{t/b})}$$

and $F_x(t) = 1 - {_t p_x}$. Notice how the probability of survival declines – in time – at a rate faster than λ. The additional terms in the exponent are less than zero, and thus accelerate the decline. For example, when $\lambda = 0$, $m = 82.3$ and $b = 11.4$, equation (13.56) results in $F_{65}(20) = 0.6493$ and $F_{65}(10) = 0.2649$ as well as $F_{75}(30) = 0.9988$. By taking derivatives of $F_x(t)$ with respect to t, we recover the probability density function (PDF) of the remaining lifetime random variable $f_x(t) = F'_x(t)$.

We can also use equation (13.46) to obtain:

$$f_x(t) = \left(\lambda + \frac{1}{b}e^{(x+t-m)/b}\right)e^{-\lambda t + b(\lambda_x - \lambda)(1 - e^{t/b})}, \qquad (13.57)$$

which is the $(_t p_x)$ of the Gompertz-Makeham law multiplied by the IFM curve λ_{x+t}.

The **expected remaining lifetime** (ERL) under the Gompertz-Makeham law of mortality is:

$$E[\mathbf{T}_x] = \int_0^\infty e^{-\lambda t + b(\lambda_x - \lambda)(1 - e^{t/b})}dt = \frac{b\Gamma(-\lambda b,\, b(\lambda_x - \lambda))}{e^{(m-x)\lambda + b(\lambda - \lambda_x)}} \qquad (13.58)$$

where the notation:

$$\Gamma(a, c) = \int_c^\infty e^{-t}t^{a-1}dt \qquad (13.59)$$

is the incomplete Gamma function and can be easily evaluated for the parameters a and c in a variety of commercial software packages.

Pension Annuity. Assume that an insurance company commits to pay someone $1 per year for the rest of the person's life. Assuming an effective valuation rate of v per annum, when payments are made in continuous time, the (stochastic) value of this quantity is:

$$\mathbf{a}_x = \int_0^{\mathbf{T}_x} e^{-vt} dt = \int_0^\infty e^{-vt} 1_{\{\mathbf{T}_x \geq t\}} dt \qquad (13.60)$$

where $\mathbf{T}_x$ is the remaining lifetime random variable and the indicator function $1_{\{\mathbf{T}_x \geq t\}}$ takes on the value of one when $\mathbf{T}_x \geq t$ and zero when $\mathbf{T}_x < t$. Note that $\mathbf{a}_x$ is a random variable.

Now imagine that the insurance company sells hundreds and thousands of these pension annuity contracts to different people – all of whom are age x, for example. Some of these people will live a very long time and the insurance company will have to pay quite a lot over the course of their life. Other customers will not live as long and the payments will be much less. On average, though, the insurance company will be paying out an amount that can be computed by taking expectations of equation (13.60). In fact, the more policies they sell, the smaller the variance around this number.

The expected value of this random variable is often labeled the immediate annuity factor.

$$\bar{a}_x = E\left[\int_0^{\mathbf{T}_x} e^{-vt} dt \right] = \int_0^\infty e^{-vt} E[1_{\{\mathbf{T}_x > t\}}] dt = \int_0^\infty e^{-vt} \, {}_t p_x \, dt$$
$$= \int_0^\infty e^{-\left(vt + \int_0^t \lambda_{x+s} ds\right)} dt \qquad (13.61)$$

where the word *immediate* comes from the fact that payments start immediately upon paying the premium $\bar{a}_x$.

Annuities: Exponential Lifetime. When $\mathbf{T}_x$ is exponentially distributed, which implies that ${}_t p_x = e^{-\lambda t}$, the annuity factor from equation (13.61) collapses to:

$$\bar{a}_x = \int_0^\infty e^{-(v+\lambda)t} dt = \frac{1}{v+\lambda}. \qquad (13.62)$$

For example, when $v = 5\%$ and $\lambda = 5\%$, the annuity factor is $\$1/(0.05 + 0.05) = \$10.0$ per dollar of lifetime income. If $v = 4\%$ and $\lambda = 6\%$, the annuity factor is (still) \$10 and the same is true when $\lambda = 4\%$ and $r = 6\%$. Note how it is only the sum of v and λ that matters, and not the individual components. The interest rate v and the instantaneous force of mortality (IFM) λ have the exact same impact on the annuity factor. They both discount the future to the present.

Annuities: GM Mortality. Recall that under the GM law of mortality, the IFM obeys the relationship:

$$\lambda_x = \lambda + \frac{1}{b} e^{\left(\frac{x-m}{b}\right)}. \tag{13.63}$$

The survival probability was shown to be:

$$_t p_x = \exp\left[-\lambda t + b(\lambda_x - \lambda)(1 - e^{t/b})\right]. \tag{13.64}$$

Consequently, the annuity factor under GM assumption can be expressed as:

$$\bar{a}_x = \exp\left[b(\lambda_x - \lambda)\right] \int_0^\infty \exp\left[-(\lambda + v)t - b(\lambda_x - \lambda)e^{t/b}\right] dt. \tag{13.65}$$

We now substitute the change-of-variable $s = \exp(t/b)$, and $ds = dt \exp(t/b)/b$, so that $ds/s = dt/b$, and $s^b = \exp(t)$, which leaves us with:

$$\bar{a}_x = b \exp\left[b(\lambda_x - \lambda)\right] \int_1^\infty s^{-(\lambda+v)b-1} \exp\left[-b(\lambda_x - \lambda)s\right] ds.$$

We change the variable again, let $w = b(\lambda_x - \lambda)s$, so that $dw = b(\lambda_x - \lambda)ds$, and therefore:

$$\bar{a}_x = \frac{b(b\lambda_x - \lambda)^{(\lambda+v)b+1}}{b(\lambda_x - \lambda)} \exp\left[b(\lambda_x - \lambda)\right] \int_{b(\lambda_x-\lambda)}^\infty w^{-(\lambda+v)b-1} \exp(-w) dw$$

$$= b(b\lambda_x - b\lambda)^{(\lambda+v)b} \exp\left[b(\lambda_x - \lambda)\right] \Gamma\left[-(\lambda + v)b, b(\lambda_x - \lambda)\right]. \tag{13.66}$$

This leads to the main expression:

$$\bar{a}_x = \frac{b\,\Gamma\left[-(\lambda+v)b, \exp\left(\frac{x-m}{b}\right)\right]}{\exp\left[(m-x)(\lambda+v) - \exp\left(\frac{x-m}{b}\right)\right]} \tag{13.67}$$

where the last part is obtained by recognizing that $(b\lambda_x - b\lambda)^{(\lambda+v)b}$ can be simplified to $\exp\left[(x-m)(\lambda+v)\right]$, using the original definition of the IFM $\lambda(x)$ in equation (13.63).

Here are a number of numerical examples to help with some intuition for the formulas. Assume that $\lambda = 0$, $m = 86.34$, and $b = 9.5$ for the GM law, in all of the following situations. Under a valuation rate of $v = 4\%$, the annuity factor for ages $x = 65, 75$, and 85 are $\bar{a}_{65} = 12.454$, $\bar{a}_{75} = 8.718$, and $\bar{a}_{85} = 5.234$, respectively. The intuition should be clear. The older the annuitant at the age of annuitization – which is when they purchase a pension annuity – the lower is the cost (and hence value) of each dollar of lifetime income. These numbers can obviously be scaled up. A pension annuity that pays $650 per month – which is $7,800 per year – has a value of $(12.454)(7,800) = \$97,141$ at age sixty-five. This number is not far from the $100,000 premium (price, cost) listed in Table 6.1, which entitled a sixty-five-year-old male annuitant to $655 for life. The reason the two premiums are not *exactly* equal is likely due to different interest rates, mortality estimates, and commissions embedded within the quoted annuity price. We return to this issue later.

If we increase the GM λ value from $\lambda = 0$ to $\lambda = 0.01$ – while maintaining the same m, b, and $v = 4\%$ value – the annuity factors are reduced to $\bar{a}_{65} = 11.394$, $\bar{a}_{75} = 8.181$, and $\bar{a}_{85} = 5.026$, respectively. The same qualitative results follow when we increase the interest rate v from 4% to 6%, while maintaining $\lambda = 0$, $m = 86.34$, and $b = 9.5$. In this case, $\bar{a}_{65} = 10.474$, $\bar{a}_{75} = 7.696$, and $\bar{a}_{85} = 4.832$, respectively. This is identical to the impact of higher interest rates on the value of a (mortality free) fixed-income bond.

Instead of using a GM value of $m = 86.34$, we increase the value to $m = 90$ and retain the dispersion parameter $b = 9.5$. For the three ages considered above, the annuity factors increase to $\bar{a}_{65} = 13.753$, $\bar{a}_{75} = 10.094$, and $\bar{a}_{85} = 6.434$, respectively. The higher values are obviously due to the longer lifespan. Under these parameters, the value of a pension annuity that pays $650 per month is $(13.753)(7,800) = \$107,273$ at age sixty-five.

When $\lambda = 0$, the annuity factor in equation (13.67) can be simplified to:

$$\bar{a}_x = \frac{b\Gamma\left(-vb, b\lambda_x\right)}{e^{((m-x)v - b\lambda_x)}}. \tag{13.68}$$

This is the pure Gompertz (no Makeham) case. In fact, if we let $v = 0$ as well, the equation for the annuity factor collapses to an even simpler:

$$\bar{a}_x = E[\mathbf{T}_x] = \frac{b\Gamma\left(0, b\lambda_x\right)}{e^{-b\lambda_x}}, \tag{13.69}$$

which is the expected remaining lifetime under the Gompertz law of mortality. For example, under the same $m = 86.34$ and $b = 9.5$, when we compute the annuity factor under a zero interest rate, we get $\bar{a}_{45} = 36.445$ years at age forty-five, $\bar{a}_{55} = 27.189$ at age fifty-five, and $\bar{a}_{65} = 18.714$ at age sixty-five.

Finally, the main reason for this section is to present the most general (analytic) expression for the value of a life-contingent annuity under a Gompertz-Makeham law of mortality. The general annuity factor is written and defined as:

$$\bar{a}_x(v,\ T_1,\ T_2,\ \lambda,\ m,\ b) := \int_{T_1}^{T_2} e^{-vt}(_t p_x)dt = \int_{T_1}^{T_2} e^{-\int_0^s (v+\lambda_{x+t})dt}ds.$$

(13.70)

If you replace $(_t p_x)$ or λ_{x+t} with the relevant Gompertz-Makeham version, and after quite a bit of calculus, one arrives at the expression:

$$\bar{a}_x(v,\ T_1,\ T_2,\ \lambda,\ m,\ b) = \frac{b}{\eta}\left\{\Gamma\left[-(\lambda+v)b,\ e^{\left(\frac{x-m+T_1}{b}\right)}\right]\right.$$
$$\left. - \Gamma\left[-(\lambda+v)b,\ e^{\left(\frac{x-m+T_2}{b}\right)}\right]\right\}$$

(13.71)

where the (new) letter η in defined as:

$$\eta = \exp\left[(m-x)(\lambda+v) - \exp\left(\frac{x-m}{b}\right)\right].$$ (13.72)

13.10 The Problem of Retirement Income

In this section we speed up gears and provide a full characterization and the solution of the **retirement income** problem. Our plan is to derive the optimal consumption and savings policy once you no longer have any human capital left, and must live off your financial capital and pension income. This is a relatively easier (and cleaner) problem to solve. Then, in the subsequent section we go back in time and solve for the optimal consumption during the working years. The main idea is the same, but we build in stages.

The classical lifecycle model (LCM) with a random date of death and assuming no bequest motive, first formulated by Menachem Yaari (1965), can be written as follows:

$$\max_{c_t} E\left[\int_0^{\bar{D}} e^{-\rho t}u(c_t)1_{\{t\leq T_x\}}dt\right].$$ (13.73)

As we explained earlier, $\mathbf{T}_x \leq \bar{D}$ is the remaining lifetime satisfying $\Pr[\mathbf{T}_x > t] = (_t p_x)$. In other words, $\bar{D}$ is the time of death, and not the age of death, which was earlier denoted by D. So, if you are currently x years old, and will die – at the latest – by the age of D, then $\bar{D} = D - x$.

Moving on, because the mortality rate is deterministic, one can obviously assume independence between the optimal consumption c_t^* and the lifetime indicator variable $1_{\{t \le T_x\}}$, so that (by something called Fubini's theorem) we can rewrite the value function as:

$$\max_{c_t} \int_0^{\bar{D}} e^{-\rho t} u(c_t) E[1_{\{t \le T_x\}}] dt = \max_{c_t} \int_0^{\bar{D}} e^{-\rho t} u(c_t)(_t p_x) dt.$$

This is a problem within the previously mentioned calculus of variations subject to some constraints on the function c_t. The wealth (budget) constraint can be written as:

$$\dot{F}_t = v(t, F_t) F_t + \pi_0 - c_t \tag{13.74}$$

with boundary conditions $F_0 \ge 0$ and $F_{\bar{D}} = 0$. The parameter π_0 denotes a constant income rate that one can think of as a pension annuity; c_t is the consumption rate and the control variable in our problem. Recall that at this stage there are no wages, because $x > R$ (retirement).

The valuation rate $v_t = v(t, F)$ is a general interest rate function, which from this point onward is defined by:

$$v_t = \begin{cases} v + \xi \lambda_{x+t} & F_t \ge 0, \\ \hat{v} + \lambda_{x+t}, & F_t < 0, \end{cases} \tag{13.75}$$

which effectively imposes a no borrowing constraint when $\hat{v} = \infty$. Equation (13.75) obviously contains some new variables and requires some additional explanation and intuition. First, the reason you see λ_{x+t}, the mortality rate, blended together with the interest rate v, is that in our model we allow for the ability to invest in actuarial notes that are instantaneous life annuities. Basically, you pool your money with other people of the exact same age x, and the survivors gain the interest of the deceased. This might seem completely unrealistic in practice, but is close enough to a conventional life annuity to help serve our purposes. On the other side of the v_t branch, we allow people to borrow money as long as they are charged an interest rate that pays for life insurance as well. Imagine you borrow $100,000 for one day, and have to pay $v/365$ in interest. In addition you must buy life insurance with a face value of $100,000, to pay the lender in case you die. This will cost $100,000(\lambda_{x+t}/365)$, which is the $100,000 times the probability of dying (roughly) in the next day. Finally, the $\xi \lambda_{x+t}$ captures the anti-selection costs we discussed in earlier chapters.

13.10.1 The Euler-Lagrange Equation

We cast the problem in the standard form

$$\max_{c_t} \int_0^{\bar{D}} \phi(t, F_t, \dot{F}_t)dt, \tag{13.76}$$

where $\phi(t, F_t, \dot{F}_t) = e^{-\rho t} u(v_t F_t - \dot{F}_t + \pi_0)\,_t p_x$. The Euler-Lagrange equation is given by (after some algebraic manipulations)

$$\frac{d}{dt}(v_t F_t - \dot{F}_t) = k_t(\pi_0 + v_t F_t - \dot{F}_t) \tag{13.77}$$

with given F_0 and $F_{\bar{D}} = 0$, where $k_t = (v_t - \rho - \lambda_{x+t})\gamma^{-1}$.

When $v(t, F_t) = v$ during the entire interval $(0, \bar{D})$, then the optimal financial capital trajectory F_t must satisfy the following linear second-order, nonhomogenous differential equation over the values for which $F_t \neq 0$.

$$\ddot{F}_t - \left(\frac{v - \rho - \lambda_{x+t}}{\gamma} + v\right)\dot{F}_{x+t} + v\left(\frac{v - \rho - \lambda_{x+t}}{\gamma}\right)F_t$$

$$= -\left(\frac{v - \rho - \lambda_{x+t}}{\gamma}\right)\pi_0. \tag{13.78}$$

When the pension income rate $\pi_0 = 0$, the differential equation collapses to the homogenous case. With the trajectory F_t in hand, the optimal consumption function, which is our ultimate objective, can be recovered from equation (13.74) by subtracting $vF_t - \dot{F}_t + \pi_0$.

13.10.2 Wealth Depletion

When wealth is depleted, $F_t = 0$, there is a question about whether it will be optimal to remain at zero wealth or for F_t to become negative (debt). To find the conditions that will help us determine which scenario is optimal, we go back and apply calculus of variations to the objective functional at $F_t = 0$. Let $J = \int_0^{\bar{D}} \phi(t, F_t, \dot{F}_t)dt$, we have:

$$\delta J = \int_0^{\bar{D}} \left(\phi_{F_t} - \frac{d}{dt}\phi_{\dot{F}_t}\right)\delta F_t dt = \int_0^{\bar{D}} (v_t \zeta_t + \dot{\zeta}_t)\delta F_t dt$$

where we have used $\phi_{F_t} = v_t \zeta_t$ and $\phi_{\dot{F}_t} = -\zeta_t$ and

$$\zeta_t = \exp\left(-\int_0^t (\rho + \lambda_{x+s})ds\right)u'(c_t) = \exp\left(-\int_0^t (\rho + \lambda_{x+s})ds\right)c_t^{-\gamma}. \tag{13.79}$$

Because v_t, defined by equation (13.75), is not smooth at $F_t = 0$, the variation δF_t is one-sided when $F_t = 0$. When J reaches its maximum, we must have $\delta J \leq 0$ for both $\delta F_t > 0$ and $\delta F_t < 0$. In other words, the following conditions must hold:

$$\dot{\zeta}_t + v_t \zeta_t \begin{cases} \geq 0, & \delta F_t < 0 \\ \leq 0, & \delta F_t > 0 \end{cases}. \tag{13.80}$$

Using the fact that $\zeta_t > 0$, we obtain

$$\frac{d}{dt}\log \zeta_t + v_t \begin{cases} \geq 0, & \delta F_t < 0 \\ \leq 0, & \delta F_t > 0 \end{cases}. \tag{13.81}$$

On the other hand, from Equation (13.79), we have

$$\log \zeta_t = -\int_0^t (\rho + \lambda_{x+s})ds - \gamma \log c_t,$$

which leads to

$$\frac{d}{dt}\log \zeta_t = -(\rho + \lambda_{x+t}) - \gamma \frac{d}{dt}\log c_t. \tag{13.82}$$

Combining Equations (13.81) and (13.82), we obtain

$$v_t - (\rho + \lambda_{x+t}) - \gamma \frac{d}{dt}\log c_t \begin{cases} \geq 0, & \delta F_t < 0 \\ \leq 0, & \delta F_t > 0 \end{cases}, \tag{13.83}$$

which can be rearranged as

$$\frac{d}{dt}\log c_t \begin{cases} \leq k_t, & \delta F_t < 0 \\ \geq k_t, & \delta F_t > 0 \end{cases}. \tag{13.84}$$

If it is optimal for $F_t = 0$ over the finite time interval, $c_t = \pi_0$, we must have

$$\frac{v - \rho + (\xi - 1)\lambda_{x+t}}{\gamma} \leq 0 \leq \frac{\hat{v} - \rho}{\gamma}. \tag{13.85}$$

In other words, these are the conditions that must hold when the financial wealth is depleted. When $\xi < 1$, because λ_{x+t} is increasing in time, the first inequality eventually becomes valid over time. The validity of the second inequality depends on how large the borrowing rate $\hat{v}$ is relative to the discount rate ρ. Furthermore, once the wealth is depleted, it stays depleted, again because λ_{x+t} is an increasing function of time. When $\xi = 1$, wealth depletion is optimal only if $v \leq \rho \leq \hat{v}$.

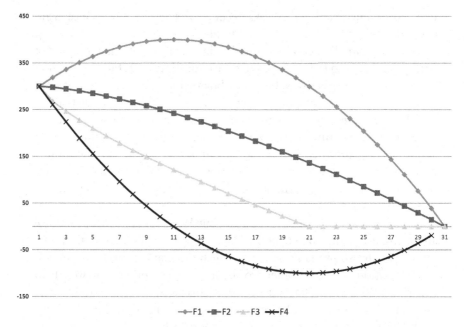

Figure 13.1. Four Possible Trajectories.

13.10.3 Classifying the Different Retirement Trajectories

As far as the economics of the problem is concerned, there are four qualitatively different wealth trajectories F_t that can emerge from our optimization model, based on the assumptions listed in the previous section. These trajectories are crudely displayed in Figure 13.1 and obviously have not been drawn to any scale.

Under regime **I** and **II** the wealth trajectory F_t begins at $F_0 > 0$ and might increase initially (**I**) or decline over the entire range (**II**), but in both cases the trajectory hits zero (only) at the last possible time of death $t = \bar{D}$. Wealth F_t is never depleted and the retiree always has some investment assets at (early) death. Note that our drawing for regime **II** does imply that the optimal wealth trajectory is either concave or convex. More on this later.

In contrast to the first two regimes, in regime **III** the wealth trajectory declines (rapidly) and hits zero prior to the last possible time of death $\bar{D}$, at a so-called **wealth depletion time** (WDT), which we denote by τ. This implies a consumption rate that is higher compared to regimes **I** and **II**. Once wealth is depleted, the trajectory stays at $F_t = 0$ during the remaining time period $(\tau, \bar{D})$, which is only relevant if the retiree is still alive. Note that regime **III** does not allow for a positive derivative $\dot{F}_t$, which means that investment wealth will always decline (or stay constant). Once again concavity or convexity should not be implied.

Finally, regime **IV** denotes a situation in which wealth may or may not be depleted prior to the last possible time of death $t = \bar{D}$, but the function F_t then takes on negative values (i.e., borrowing at a rate of v_t). It then reaches a minimum value, which denotes the maximum loan outstanding and then increases from there to hit zero (again) at $\tau_2 \leq \bar{D}$, which we call the **loan depletion time** (LDT). Recall that in our model the retiree can die at any point in time between $(0, \bar{D})$, which in this regime **IV** might imply death with negative wealth $F_t < 0$. However, recall that the life insurance policy that costs $\lambda_{x+t} F_x$ (annualized) will cover the outstanding loan by construction.

Note that regime **IV** has only one possible WDT and one LDT. Thus, we are essentially ruling out a hypothetical regime **V** – which is not displayed, but can be drawn in many ways – in which there are multiple wealth and loan depletion times. In other words, it is never optimal for wealth to become positive once it has touched zero. Borrowers will never accumulate investment wealth again. We emphasize that this is no longer true if we include the working years as shown in section 13.11.

With the four different trajectories having been described, we now move on to discuss the eight economic cases of relevance in which these trajectories might be observed.

Description	Parameters	$\pi_0 = 0$ (**No Pension**)	$\pi_0 > 0$ (**Pension**)
Relatively Patient:	$0 \leq \rho < v$	Case 1A = [I, II]	Case 1B = [I, II, III]
Neutral Patience:	$\rho = v < \hat{v}$	Case 2A = [II]	Case 2B = [II, III]
Relatively Impatient:	$v < \rho < \hat{v}$	Case 3A = [II]	Case 3B = [II, III]
Extremely Impatient:	$v < \hat{v} \leq \rho$	Case 4A = [II]	Case 4B = [IV]

Here is a brief description of the significance of the eight cases and how they relate to the four possible wealth trajectories. The discussion here is couched in terms of consumption rates, which according to equation (13.74) is the derivative of the optimal wealth trajectory minus the interest and pension income.

Cases 1A and 1B represent a situation in which the optimal consumption rate would increase over time in the absence of longevity risk. This should be quite obvious because the subjective discount rate ρ is lower than the prevailing interest rate v and therefore waiting to consume increases utility. During retirement itself, whether or not the consumption rate increases or declines in the presence of longevity risk depends on a complex interaction among age x, the hazard rate λ_{x+t}, and the pension income π_0. Therefore, qualitatively these preferences and endowments can result in either scenario **I**, **II**, or **III**. Patient retirees do not borrow and scenario **IV** is ruled out regardless of the value of γ and/or how low $v(t, F_t)$ is, as long as it is greater than ρ.

Cases 2A and 2B would theoretically lead to a constant (flat) consumption profile over time were it not for longevity risk. The presence of lifetime uncertainty augments one's impatience and results in a declining consumption profile over time. The only possible trajectories that can emerge are **II** or **III**. Once again, borrowing is shunned.

Cases 3A and 3B will actually result in a more rapidly declining consumption (spending) rate and higher initial consumption rate compared to Cases 2A and 2B. Qualitatively, Case 3A is quite similar to Case 2A and Case 3B is similar to Case 2B. The only possible trajectories are **II** and **III**.

Finally, Cases 4A and 4B are obviously a peculiar (although fully rational) situation in which the retiree's extreme impatience results in a very rapid and steep decline of the consumption rate, and the possibility of borrowing, if he or she is still alive at the wealth depletion time (WDT), have low risk-aversion, and have something (i.e., a pension) to borrow against. In fact, to preview one of our important results, regardless of whether we are in Cases 1A, 2A, 3A, or 4A, the absence of pension income ($\pi_0 = 0$) implies that $F_t > 0$ for all $t < \bar{D}$. No pension implies that trajectories **III** and **IV** are out.

With a better understanding of the possible trajectories and cases behind us, we present the solutions for two special cases. We consider the simpler case of constant mortality rate, followed by a more realistic Gompertz-Makeham mortality model.

13.10.4 Explicit Solution: Exponential Remaining Lifetime

When $\lambda_{x+t} = \lambda$ and $v(t, F_t) = v$ for all t, the coefficients in equation (13.78) are time invariant and the so-called method of undetermined coefficients can be used to find a set of two system basis vectors. More specifically, the ODE is:

$$\ddot{F}_t + (k - v)\,\dot{F}_t - vkF_t = k\pi_0, \tag{13.86}$$

where $k = (\lambda + \rho - v)/\gamma$, which can be either positive, negative, or zero. You will note that this is precisely the personal patience parameter that was the foundation of consumption smoothing in Chapter 7 when $\lambda = 0$.

The general solution, after some manipulation, is:

$$F_t = K_1 e^{-kt} + K_2 e^{vt} - \frac{\pi_0}{v}, \tag{13.87}$$

which then implies that the optimal consumption function is:

$$c_t^* = v F_t - \dot{F}_t + \pi_0$$
$$= (v + k) K_1 e^{-kt}. \tag{13.88}$$

The next step is to solve for the two free constants K_1 and K_2. We do this by invoking the two boundary conditions, namely that initial financial capital at retirement is known to be $F_0 = M > 0$ and that by the time of death $t = \bar{D}$, the financial capital $F_{\bar{D}} = 0$. Note that the boundary condition assumption that $F_{\bar{D}} = 0$ does not preclude the existence of another τ in between 0 and $\bar{D}$ at which $F_\tau = 0$ as well. This should be clear from the earlier discussion.

Either way, these two conditions are enough to obtain explicit values for the constants: K_1, K_2. Specifically:

$$F_0 = K_1 + K_2 - \frac{\pi_0}{v} = M \tag{13.89}$$

$$F_{\bar{D}} = K_1 e^{-k\bar{D}} + K_2 e^{v\bar{D}} - \frac{\pi_0}{v} = 0. \tag{13.90}$$

This would be a good place to note that if the individual (retiree) would like to leave a bequest (financial legacy), the second equation would be set equal to this desired bequest value instead of zero.

Either way, this leads to:

$$K_1 = (M + \pi_0/v)\left(1 + \frac{e^{-k\bar{D}}}{e^{v\bar{D}} - e^{-k\bar{D}}}\right) - \left(\frac{\pi_0/v}{e^{v\bar{D}} - e^{-k\bar{D}}}\right) \tag{13.91}$$

$$K_2 = \frac{\pi_0/v - (M + \pi_0/v)e^{-k\bar{D}}}{e^{v\bar{D}} - e^{-k\bar{D}}}, \tag{13.92}$$

and so we obtain an explicit expression for financial capital F_t from $t = 0$ until $t = \bar{D}$.

For example, assume the relevant preference parameters are $\rho = 5\%$, $\gamma = 4$, the hazard rate is $\lambda = 8\%$ (which is equivalent to a life expectancy of 12.5 years), the valuation rate is $v = 4\%$, the pension income $\pi_0 = \$1$, the initial retirement account $F_0 = M = 10$, and the (last possible) time of death is $\bar{D} = 50$ years. The value of $k = 0.0225$ and the solution coefficients in equation (13.87) are $K_1 = 33.069594$ and $K_2 = 1.9304055$, respectively, which are obviously both positive. The relevant financial capital equation (trajectory of wealth) is:

$$F_t = (33.069594)e^{-(0.0225)t} + (1.9304055)e^{(0.04)t} - 25. \qquad (13.93)$$

The function is **convex** over the entire domain $(0,50)$ and actually hits zero once before $t = 50$. The interior root is at $\tau = 21.313$, at which point the retiree starts to borrow against their pension π_0, and slowly pays this back until death. The optimal (rational) consumption rate becomes:

$$c_t^* = (0.04 + 0.0225)(33.069594)e^{-(0.025)t} \qquad (13.94)$$
$$= (2.0668496)e^{-(0.025)t}.$$

At time zero (retirement) the optimal withdrawal rate from wealth is $(2.0668 - 1)/10 = 0.106,68$, which is almost 1% of the nest egg.

In contrast, when the subjective discount rate is reduced to $\rho = 3\%$ (instead of 5%) and the hazard rate is reduced to $\lambda = 0.5\%$ (instead of 8%), while all other parameters remain the same, the corresponding coefficients are $K_1 = 36.938048$ and $K_2 = -1.9380483$ and the financial capital equation (trajectory) is now:

$$F_t = (36.938048)e^{(0.00125)t} - (1.9380483)e^{(0.04)t} - 25, \qquad (13.95)$$

which is concave over the entire domain and does not hit zero before $t = 50$.

13.10.5 Explicit Solution: Gompertz Mortality

Recall when the (deterministic) mortality rate function obeys the (pure) Gompertz law of mortality the survival probability can also be written as follows:

$$({}_t p_x) = \exp\left\{b\lambda_0(1 - e^{t/b})\right\}, \qquad (13.96)$$

which is a simple rewriting with $\lambda_0 = \exp((x - m)/b)/b$, where time is re-scaled so that x denotes the age at time 0. From the budget constraint equation (13.74) the consumption function and its derivative can be written as:

$$c_t = vF_t - \dot{F}_t + \pi_0 \qquad (13.97)$$
$$\dot{c}_t = v\dot{F}_t - \ddot{F}_t. \qquad (13.98)$$

So, equation (13.78) can be rearranged and rewritten as

$$\ddot{F}_t - v\dot{F}_t + k_t(vF_t - \dot{F}_t) = -k_t\pi_0, \tag{13.99}$$

which – after plugging equations (13.97) and (13.98) into (13.99) – leads to

$$k_t c_t - \dot{c}_t = 0, \tag{13.100}$$

which governs the optimal consumption function. The (optimal) solution to this ordinary differential equation (ODE), denoted by c_t^*, can be obtained and written as:

$$c_t^* = c_0^* e^{\int_0^t k_s \, ds} = c_0^* e^{\int_0^t \left(\frac{v - \rho - \lambda_{x+s}}{\gamma}\right) ds} = c_0^* e^{\left(\frac{v-\rho}{\gamma}\right)t} e^{-\frac{1}{\gamma}\int_0^t \lambda_{x+s} \, ds} \tag{13.101}$$

$$= c_0^* e^{\left(\frac{v-\rho}{\gamma}\right)t} ({}_t p_x)^{1/\gamma},$$

where c_0^* is the optimal initial consumption rate, to be determined, which is the one free constant resulting from equation (13.100). Note that when the interest rate v is equal to the subjective discount rate ρ, and the exponent is zero, the optimal consumption rate at any age $x + t$ is the probability of survival to that age times the initial consumption c_0^*. However, when $\gamma > 1$, which implies higher levels of risk aversion, the optimal consumption rate will decline at a slower rate as the retiree ages.

Longevity risk aversion induces people to behave as if they were going to live longer than determined by the actuarial mortality rates.

Mathematically one can see that $({}_t p_x)^{1/(\gamma+\varepsilon)}$ is greater than $({}_t p_x)^{1/\gamma}$ for any $\varepsilon > 0$ because ${}_t p_x < 1$ for all t. Finally, note that in the Gompertz mortality model evaluating $({}_t p_x)^{1/\gamma}$ for a given (x, m, b) triplet is equivalent to evaluating $({}_t p_x)$ under the same x, b values, but assuming that $\hat{m} = m + b \ln \gamma$. This then implies that one can tilt/define a new deterministic mortality rate $\hat{\lambda} = \gamma\lambda$ and derive the optimal consumption as if the individual has logarithmic utility.

Moving on to a solution for F_t, which is the optimal trajectory of wealth, we now substitute the optimal consumption solution (13.101) into equation (13.97) to arrive at yet another first-order ODE, but this time for F_t:

$$\dot{F}_t - vF_t - \pi_0 + c_0^* e^{\left(\frac{v-\rho}{\gamma}\right)t}({}_t p_x)^{1/\gamma} = 0. \tag{13.102}$$

Writing down the canonical solution to this ODE leads to:

$$F_t = \left(\pi_0 \int_0^t e^{-vs} \, ds - c_0^* \int_0^t e^{\left(\frac{v-\rho}{\gamma}\right)s}({}_s p_x)^{1/\gamma} e^{-vs} \, ds + F_0\right) e^{vt} \tag{13.103}$$

where F_0 denotes the free initial condition from the ODE for F_t in equation (13.102). Recall that we still have not pinned down c_0^*, the initial consumption. We do so (eventually) by using the terminal condition $F_{\bar{D}} = 0$, which is zero wealth at death.

Combining equation (13.103) with the definition of $a_x(v, T_1, T_2, \lambda, m, b)$ for the Gompertz model, presented in equation (13.71), leads to the following analytic expression for the optimal trajectory of wealth:

$$F_t = \left(F_0 + \frac{\pi}{v}\right) e^{vt} - \bar{a}_x(v - k, 0, \tau, \lambda, \hat{m}, b) c_0^* e^{vt} - \frac{\pi_0}{v} \qquad (13.104)$$

where recall that $\hat{m} = m + b \ln \gamma$. Then, using the boundary condition $F_\tau = 0$, where τ is a wealth depletion time (WDT), we obtain an explicit expression for the initial consumption

$$c_0^* = \frac{(F_0 + \pi_0/v) e^{v\tau} - \pi_0/v}{\bar{a}_x(v - k, 0, \tau, \lambda, \hat{m}, b) e^{v\tau}}. \qquad (13.105)$$

We can write down an equation for WDT τ as

$$\left(F_0 + \frac{\pi_0}{v}\right) e^{v\tau} - \frac{\pi_0}{v} = \pi_0 \bar{a}_x(v - k, 0, \tau, \lambda, \hat{m}, b) e^{(v-k)\tau}. \qquad (13.106)$$

This is obtained by substituting expression for c_0^* into equation (13.101) and then set equal to $c_\tau^* = \pi_0$, which is the point in time at which consumption converges to the pension income (only). This concept – that you spend your wealth down to zero – was explained in Chapter 12.

Assume an 86.6% probability that a 65-year-old will survive to the age of 75, a 57.3% probability of reaching 85, a 36.9% probability of reaching 90, a 17.6% probability of reaching age 95, and a 5% probability of reaching 100. These are the values generated by the GM law with $\lambda = 0$, $m = 89.335$, and $b = 9.5$ and the subjective discount rate (ρ) is equal to a risk-free rate $v = 2.5\%$ This implies that the optimal consumption rates would be constant over time in the absence of longevity uncertainty.

Assume a sixty-five-year-old with $F_0 = \$100$. Initially we allow for no pension annuity income $(\pi_0 = 0)$ and therefore all consumption must be sourced to the investment portfolio, which is earning a deterministic interest rate $v = 2.5\%$. The financial capital F_t must be depleted at the very end of the lifecycle, which is time $\bar{D} = (120 - 65) = 55$ and there are no bequest motives. So, according to equation (13.105), the optimal consumption rate at retirement age sixty-five is $\$4.605$ when the risk aversion parameter is $\gamma = 4$ and the optimal consumption rate is (higher) $\$4.121$ when the risk aversion parameter is set to (higher) $\gamma = 8$.

As the retiree ages ($t > 0$) he or she rationally consumes less each year – in proportion to the survival probability adjusted for γ. For example, in our baseline $\gamma = 4$ level of risk aversion, the optimal consumption rate drops from $4.605 at age 65, to $4.544 at age 70 (which is $t = 5$), then $4.442 at age 75 (which is $t = 10$), then $3.591 at age 90 (which is $t = 25$), and $2.177 at age 100 (which is $t = 35$), assuming the retiree is still alive. A lower interest rate (v) leads to a reduced optimal consumption/spending rate. All of this can be sourced to equation (13.101).

A fully rational consumer will actually spend less as they progress through retirement. The lifecycle optimizer spends more at earlier ages and reduces spending with age, even if his or her subjective discount rate $\rho = v$ is equal to the interest rate in the economy.

13.11 Back to the Working Years

As a final case study, we expand the lifecycle model to include wages during the working years, and hence the value of human capital. The basic framework is the same. We want to find c_t such that the following

$$\max_{c_t} \int_0^{\bar{D}} e^{-\rho t} u(c_t)(_t p_x) dt \qquad (13.107)$$

is achieved, with the wealth (budget) constraint modified to

$$\dot{F}_t = v(t, F_t) F_t + w_t + b_t - c_t \qquad (13.108)$$

and $F_0 = F_{\bar{D}} = 0$. The wage function is $w_t = w_0 \exp(\rho t)$ for $0 \le t \le \bar{R}$ and zero for $t > \bar{R}$, while the pension income b_t is zero for $t \le \bar{R}$ and constant π_0 for $t > \bar{R}$. Note that we have assumed that initially there is no existing financial wealth. The cases with a positive and negative (debt) initial financial wealth are left as a project for the students.

The valuation rate $v = v(t, F_t)$ is defined as

$$v(t, F_t) = \begin{cases} v + \xi \lambda_{x+t} & F_t \ge 0, \\ \hat{v} + \lambda_{x+t}, & F_t < 0. \end{cases} \qquad (13.109)$$

To simplify the problem we assume that $\xi = 1$, which means that the life-insurance component on the borrowing rate λ_{x+t} and the mortality-credits term ($\xi \lambda_{x+t}$) are identical.

The optimal consumption c_t^* are a combination of three possibilities: either c_t^* equals the wage w_t, or pension income π_0, or by solving the Euler-Lagrange equation

$$\dot{\zeta}_t = -v(t, F_t)\zeta_t, \quad c_t^* = e^{-\frac{\rho}{\gamma}t}\zeta_t^{-\frac{1}{\gamma}} \tag{13.110}$$

$$\dot{F}_t = v(t, F_t)F_t + w_t + b_t - c_t^* \tag{13.111}$$

with $F_0 = F_{\bar{D}} = 0$. In the appendix, we have established the conditions for the consumption rate and next we shall provide the solutions for several relevant cases with numerical examples, based on three measures of the patience during the working year: (i) relatively patient: $k \leq \hat{k} < g$; (ii) relatively impatient: $k \leq g \leq \hat{k}$; and (iii) impatient: $g \leq k < \hat{k}$.

The main objective of going through these examples is to show that by including working years, the picture of retirement planning becomes more complex so that some of the conclusions arrived at in the previous section need to be revised. We have shown in the previous section that in the later stages of retirement, it is no longer optimal to get into debt once wealth has been depleted. This is in contrast to the accumulation phase in which debt is optimal and quite common in the early stage of the lifecycle.

13.11.1 Patient Individual $k \leq \hat{k} < g$

When $\bar{R} = \bar{D}$, we have shown that $F_t < 0$ for $0 < t < \bar{R}$. When $\bar{R} < \bar{D}$ and $\pi_0 = 0$, we must have $F_t > 0$ for $\bar{R} \leq t < \bar{D}$. Therefore, for $\pi_0 < \exp(g\bar{R})$, the optimal solution is $F_t < 0$ for $0 < t < \tau$ and $F_t > 0$ for $\tau < t < \bar{D}$ for some τ. There are two possible cases: $\tau < \bar{R}$ and $\tau \geq \bar{R}$, which will be considered separately. To simplify the discussion, we have scaled the wage so that initially the wage is unity ($w_0 = 1$).

Case 1. $\tau < \bar{R}$ We obtain the solution as follows. First we have $c_t^* = c_0^* \exp(\hat{k}t)$ and

$$e^{-\hat{v}t}F_t = -\frac{e^{-(\hat{v}-g)t} - 1}{\hat{v} - g} + c_0^*\frac{e^{-(\hat{v}-\hat{k})t} - 1}{\hat{v} - \hat{k}} \tag{13.112}$$

for $0 < t < \tau$. Next we have $c_t^* = \hat{c}_0^* \exp(kt)$ and

$$e^{-vt}F_t = -\frac{e^{-(v-g)t} - e^{-(v-g)\tau}}{v - g} + \hat{c}_0^*\frac{e^{-(v-k)t} - e^{-(v-k)\tau}}{v - k} \tag{13.113}$$

for $\tau < t < \bar{R}$, and

$$e^{-vt}F_t = -\pi_0 \frac{e^{-vt} - e^{-v\bar{D}}}{v} + \hat{c}_0^* \frac{e^{-(v-k)t} - e^{-(v-k)\bar{D}}}{v - k} \qquad (13.114)$$

for $\bar{R} < t < \bar{D}$. The value of τ is the root of the following function

$$f(\tau) = \hat{c}_0^* \frac{e^{-(v-k)\tau} - e^{-(v-k)\bar{D}}}{v - k} + \frac{e^{-(v-g)\bar{R}} - e^{-(v-g)\tau}}{v - g} - \pi_0 \frac{e^{-v\bar{R}} - e^{-v\bar{D}}}{v} \qquad (13.115)$$

where

$$\hat{c}_0^* = c_0^* e^{(\hat{k}-k)\tau}, \qquad c_0^* = \frac{\hat{v} - \hat{k}}{\hat{v} - g} \frac{e^{-(\hat{v}-g)\tau} - 1}{e^{-(\hat{v}-\hat{k})\tau} - 1}. \qquad (13.116)$$

Numerical Example. In Figure 13.2, we have plotted the solution for the case $k = 1\%$, $\hat{k} = 2.5\%$, and $g = 3.5\%$, which corresponds to the case with $v = 6\%$ and $\hat{v} = 10.5\%$ with $\rho = 3\%$, $\gamma = 3$. The other parameter values are $\bar{R} = 35$ and $\bar{D} = 60$ years and $\pi_0 = 0.25$ (25% of the starting wage). In this case it is optimal to borrow for up to $\tau = 14.85$ years. Note also that when we get into retirement phase, we are in a different regime because $g = 0$ and $0 < k < \hat{k}$. This is corresponding to the case that it is optimal to keep $F_t > 0$ until $t = \bar{D}$, as shown by Figure 13.2.

Case 2. $\bar{R} < \tau$. We obtain the solution as follows. First we have $c_t^* = c_0^* \exp(\hat{k}t)$ and

$$e^{-\hat{v}t}F_t = -\frac{e^{-(\hat{v}-g)t} - 1}{\hat{v} - g} + c_0^* \frac{e^{-(\hat{v}-\hat{k})t} - 1}{\hat{v} - \hat{k}} \qquad (13.117)$$

for $0 < t < \bar{R}$, and

$$e^{-\hat{v}t}F_t = -\pi_0 \frac{e^{-\hat{v}t} - e^{-\hat{v}\tau}}{\hat{v}} + c_0^* \frac{e^{-(\hat{v}-\hat{k})t} - e^{-(\hat{v}-\hat{k})\tau}}{\hat{v} - \hat{k}} \qquad (13.118)$$

for $\bar{R} < t < \tau$. Next we have $c_t^* = \hat{c}^* \exp(kt)$ and

$$e^{-rt}F_t = -\pi_0 \frac{e^{-vt} - e^{-v\bar{D}}}{v} + \hat{c}^* \frac{e^{-(v-k)t} - e^{-(v-k)\bar{D}}}{v - k} \qquad (13.119)$$

for $\tau < t < \bar{D}$. The value of τ is the root of the following function

$$f(\tau) = \hat{c}_0^* \frac{e^{-(v-k)\tau} - e^{-(v-k)\bar{D}}}{v - k} - \pi_0 \frac{e^{-v\tau} - e^{-v\bar{D}}}{v} \qquad (13.120)$$

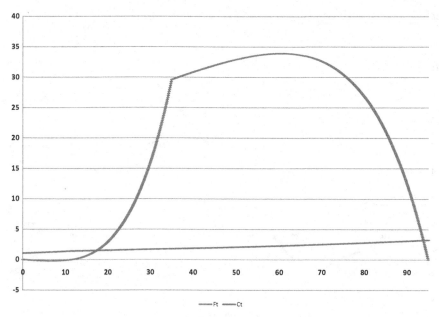

Figure 13.2. Welath vs. Consumption (Case A).

where

$$c_0^* = \frac{\hat{v} - \hat{k}}{e^{-(\hat{v}-\hat{k})\tau} - 1} \left(\frac{e^{-(\hat{v}-g)\tau} - 1}{\hat{v} - g} - \pi_0 \frac{e^{-\hat{v}\bar{R}} - e^{-\hat{v}\tau}}{\hat{v}} \right), \quad \hat{c}^* = c_0^* e^{(\hat{k}-\hat{v})\tau}.$$

(13.121)

Numerical Example. In Figure 13.3, we have plotted the solution for $\pi_0 = 3.25$, while fixing other parameters as in Figure 13.2. In this case, $\tau = 39.43$ years. We note that in this case it is optimal to borrow even into the retirement. Note again that once into the retirement phase, we are in a different regime because $g - 0$ and $0 < k < \hat{k}$. This is corresponding to the case that it is optimal to keep $F_t > 0$ until $t = \bar{D}$. However, because it is optimal to stay in debt while still earning wage, F_t is already negative when we enter the retirement phase. Thus, it takes a certain amount of time to get out of the debt, as shown in Figure 13.3.

13.11.2 Relatively Impatient Individual $k \le g \le \hat{k}$

When $\bar{R} = \bar{D}$, this is the case that one simply consumes the income and maintains $F_t = 0$. When $\bar{R} < \bar{D}$ and $\pi_0 = 0$, we must have $F_t > 0$ for $t \ge \bar{R}$. Thus, for $\pi_0 < \exp(g\bar{R})$, intuitively there exists $0 \le \tau \le \bar{D}$ such

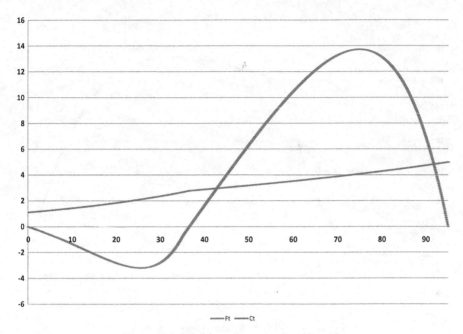

Figure 13.3. Wealth vs. Consumption (Case B).

that $F_t = 0$ for $t < \tau$ and $F_t > 0$ for $t > \tau$. Again, there are two scenarios: $\tau < \bar{R}$ and $\tau > \bar{R}$, which we consider separately.

Case 1. $\tau < \bar{R}$. We obtain the solution as follows. First we have $c_t^* = \exp(gt)$ and $F_t = 0$ for $0 < t < \tau$. Next we have $c_t^* = \hat{c}^* \exp(kt)$ and

$$e^{-vt} F_t = -\frac{e^{-(v-g)t} - e^{-(v-g)\tau}}{v - g} + \hat{c}^* \frac{e^{-(v-k)t} - e^{-(v-k)\tau}}{v - k} \qquad (13.122)$$

for $\tau < t < \bar{R}$, and

$$e^{-vt} F_t = -\pi_0 \frac{e^{-vt} - e^{-v\bar{D}}}{v} + \hat{c}^* \frac{e^{-(v-k)t} - e^{-(v-k)\bar{D}}}{v - k} \qquad (13.123)$$

for $\bar{R} < t < \bar{D}$.

The value of τ is the root of the following function

$$f(\tau) = \hat{c}^* \frac{e^{-(v-k)\tau} - e^{-(v-k)\bar{D}}}{v - k} + \frac{e^{-(v-g)\bar{R}} - e^{-(v-g)\tau}}{v - g} - \pi_0 \frac{e^{-v\bar{R}} - e^{-v\bar{D}}}{v} \qquad (13.124)$$

where

$$\hat{c}^* = e^{(g-k)\tau}. \qquad (13.125)$$

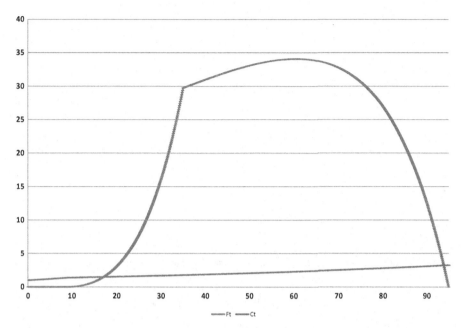

Figure 13.4. Wealth vs. Consumption (Case C).

Numerical Example. In Figure 13.4, we have plotted the solution for $\pi_0 = 0.25$, and increase $\hat{v}$ to 15% ($\hat{k} = 4\%$) while fixing other parameters as in Figure 13.2. In this case, $\tau = 11.65$ years. Because it is never optimal to get into debt in both working and retirement phases, F_t remains nonnegative over the entire lifecycle. In Figure 13.5, we have plotted the solution by setting $\pi_0 = 3.25$. In this case, $\tau = 30.19$, indicating that increasing the value of π_0 increases τ.

Case 2. $\bar{R} < \tau$. This can only occur when $\pi_0 > \exp(g\bar{R})$, i.e., the pension income is greater than the final wage just before retirement. This is an unlikely case. However, for completeness, we obtain the solution for this case as follows. First we have $c_t^* = \exp(gt)$ (simply consumes wage income) for $0 < t < \tau$. Next we have $c_t^* = \hat{c}^* \exp(kt)$ and

$$e^{-vt} F_t = -\pi_0 \frac{e^{-vt} - e^{-v\bar{D}}}{v} + \hat{c}^* \frac{e^{-(v-k)t} - e^{-(v-k)\bar{D}}}{v-k} \quad (13.126)$$

for $\tau < t < \bar{D}$.

The value of τ is the root of the following function

$$f(\tau) = \hat{c}^* \frac{e^{-(v-k)\tau} - e^{-(v-k)\bar{D}}}{v-k} - \pi_0 \frac{e^{-v\tau} - e^{-v\bar{D}}}{v} \quad (13.127)$$

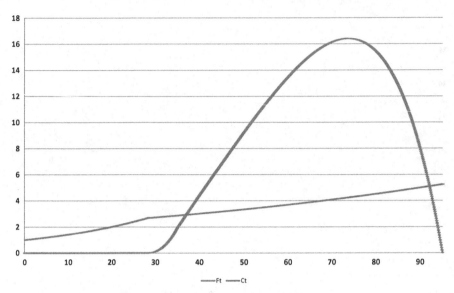

Figure 13.5. Wealth vs. Consumption (Case D).

where

$$\hat{c}^* = e^{(g-k)\tau} \tag{13.128}$$

from continuity of consumption at $t = \tau$.

13.11.3 Impatient Individual $g < k \leq \hat{k}$

In this case, the optimal solution yields $F_t > 0$, that is, no debt. This is because pension income is less than the regular wage income, and in the appendix we have already shown that $F_t > 0$ when $\bar{R} = \bar{D}$. The solution is $c_t^* = c_0^* \exp(kt)$ and

$$e^{-vt} F_t = -\pi_0 \frac{e^{-vt} - e^{-v\bar{D}}}{v} + c_0^* \frac{e^{-(v-k)t} - e^{-(v-k)\bar{D}}}{v - k} \tag{13.129}$$

for $\bar{R} \leq t \leq \bar{D}$, and

$$e^{-vt} F_t = -\frac{e^{-(v-g)t} - 1}{v - g} + c_0^* \frac{e^{-(v-k)t} - 1}{v - k} \tag{13.130}$$

for $0 \leq t \leq \bar{R}$, with

$$c_0^* = \frac{v - k}{e^{-(v-k)\bar{D}} - 1} \left(\frac{e^{-(v-g)\bar{R}} - 1}{v - g} - \pi_0 \frac{e^{-v\bar{R}} - e^{-v\bar{D}}}{v} \right). \tag{13.131}$$

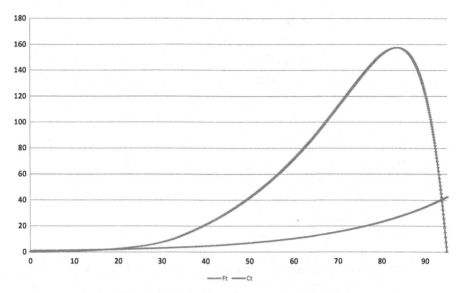

Figure 13.6. Wealth vs. Consumption (Case E).

Numerical Example. In Figure 13.6, we plotted the case with $k = 4\%$ ($v = 15\%$) while fixing other parameters as in Figure 13.5. Clearly, F_t is positive over the entire lifecycle.

The most important difference between the previous examples and the current one is the ability to hedge mortality risk. The situation considered here is idealized in the sense that tontines (mortality credits) and insurance are freely available at no additional cost. Therefore, the same mortality rate is added to the discount rate as well as the interest rate and the net effect is zero. As a result, the law of smooth consumption prevails (in working and retirement years, respectively). The numerical examples are limited only to positive rate of growth for the consumption. Obviously, other choices are possible and it will be left as exercises for the students to investigate the cases with negative growth rates as well as a nonzero starting wealth.

13.12 Conclusion

This chapter has provided a whirlwind (and incomplete) tour of the lifecycle model applied to continuous time. Our underlying objective was to present the lifecycle model (LCM) on a more solid (mathematical) foundation so that we could justify the optimal consumption and saving relationships and formulas we presented in earlier chapters.

13.13 Questions and Assignments

1. Using the formula for the optimal consumption rate under Gompertz mortality, and no pension income, please derive an expression for the age at which your optimal consumption rate is half (50%) of the initial rate at retirement.

2. How does the main formula for the optimal retirement consumption rate change, in the presence of pension income, when the pension increases annually at a cost-of-living (COLA) rate denoted by z%?

3. Please discuss and explain the relationship between the subjective discount rate (SDR), which was denoted by the Greek letter *rho* in this chapter, and the personal patience rate, which we denoted by k, used in earlier chapters.

4. What mortality curve assumption – from retirement until death – would result in the exact same consumption regardless of the level of longevity risk aversion? In other words, for what mortality assumption is risk aversion irrelevant?

5. The first problem of this type (calculus of variations) that mathematicians solved was that of the brachistochrone, or the curve of fastest descent, which Johann Bernoulli proposed in 1696. The problem was posed as follows: *Given two points A and B in a vertical plane, what is the curve traced out by a point acted on only by gravity, which starts at A and reaches B in the shortest time?* Several well-known mathematicians, including Issac Newton, provided solutions. Using the method of calculus of variations, show that the solution is a cycloid $x = \ell(t - \sin t)$ and $y = \ell(1 - \cos t)$ where ℓ is a constant and t is a parameter.

6. In section 13.7, we derived the Euler-Lagrange equation using calculus of variation for the following problem:

$$\max_{c_t} \int_0^{\bar{D}} e^{-\rho t} u(c_t) dt \qquad (13.132)$$

subject to

$$\dot{F}_t = v F_t + w_t - c_t \qquad (13.133)$$

with a given F_0 and $F_{\bar{D}} = 0$.

In the optimal control literature, the problem is often reformulated as

$$\max_{c_t} \int_0^{\bar{D}} (H - \zeta_t \dot{F}_t) dt$$

by introducing a Hamiltonian $H = \phi(t, c_t) + \zeta_t f(t, c_t, F_t)$ where

$$\phi(t, c_t) = e^{-\rho t} u(c_t), \quad f(t, c_t, F_t) = v F_t + w_t - c_t$$

and ζ_t is a Lagrange multiplier.

Using calculus of variation, derive the following optimality conditions:

$$\frac{\partial H}{\partial c_t} = 0, \quad \frac{\partial H}{\partial \zeta_t} = \dot{F}_t, \quad \frac{\partial H}{\partial F_t} = -\dot{\zeta}_t$$

and show that these conditions are equivalent to the results obtained in section 13.7.

7. In section 13.10.5, we have obtained the explicit solution (13.104) for the retirement income problem under Gompertz mortality rate from $t = 0$ until wealth depletion time τ. Show that the solution is consistent with the principle of dynamic optimization; that is, it is also the optimal solution from $t = s$ until wealth depletion time. **Hint:** You need to show that the optimal solution on time interval $[s, \tau]$ is identical to that given by (13.104) on the same time interval.

8. Use the method in section 13.11 to find the solution for two cases: (i). $k = -1.5\%$ and $\hat{k} = -1.5\%$; and (ii). $k = -1.5\%$ and $\hat{k} = 4\%$; with $\pi_0 = 0.25$, $\rho = 3\%$, $g = 3.5\%$, $\gamma = 3$, $\bar{R} = 35$, and $\bar{D} = 60$.

9. [Advanced Project] Solve the following lifecycle optimization problem:

$$\max_c \int_0^{\bar{D}} e^{-\rho t} u(c_t)(_t p_x) dt$$

subject to the wealth (budget) constraint

$$\dot{F}_t = v(t, F_t) F_t + w_t + b_t - c_t$$

with a given initial $F_0 > 0$ and $F_{\bar{D}} = 0$. The wage function is $w_t = w_0 \exp(\rho t)$ for $t \le \bar{R}$ and zero for $t > \bar{R}$, while the pension income b_t is zero for $t \le \bar{R}$ and constant π_0 for $t > \bar{R}$.

The valuation rate $v = v(t, F)$ is given by

$$v(t, F) = \begin{cases} v & F_t \ge 0 \\ \infty, & F_t < 0. \end{cases}$$

Notice that by setting the borrowing rate to be infinite we effectively imposed the no borrowing constraint. We have also removed the mortality-credits term $(\xi \lambda_{x+t})$ from the interest function, because we assume that continuous tontines are not available.

10. [Advanced Project] In this chapter we used calculus of variations as the main tool for solving our lifecycle model. In this project we look at an alternative approach, based on the **principle of optimality** under the framework of dynamic optimization (programming).

Principle of Optimality. Here we establish the main theorem by considering the following generic problem

$$\max_{c_t} \int_a^b \phi(t, c_t)dt + \psi(z_b)$$

$$\text{subject to } \dot{z}_t = f(t, c_t, z_t), \quad z_a = z$$

for given functions ϕ, f, and ψ.

Define a value function $V(t, z_t)$ as

$$V(t, z_t) = \max_{c_t} \int_t^b \phi(s, c_s)ds + \psi(z_b)$$

and we have the following results.

Theorem. *Let c_t^* be the **optimal control**, and z_t^* be the resulting state of the control problem. For $a < \hat{t} < b$, the restricted functions $\hat{c}_t^* = c_t^*$ and $\hat{z}_t^* = z_t^*$ on $[\hat{t}, b]$ form an optimal pair for the restricted problem*

$$\max_{c_t} \int_{\hat{t}}^b \phi(t, c_t)dt + \psi(z_b),$$

$$\text{subject to } \dot{z}_t = f(t, c_t, z_t), \quad z(\hat{t}) = z_{\hat{t}}^*.$$

Furthermore, if c_t^* is the unique optimal control for the original problem, then $\hat{c}_t^*$ is the unique optimal control on the subinterval.

Direct (Numerical) Method for a Lifecycle Model. We consider a lifecycle model where $\phi = e^{-\rho t}u(c_t)\,{}_t p_x$ and $h(t, c_t, F_t) = vF_t + w_t - c_t$ with $a = 0$ and $b = \bar{D}$ and the no borrowing constraint $F_t \geq 0$. We devise a numerical method using the principle of optimality. (Note that this method is more general and works for a generic utility function as well.) First set up a grid in time as t_n for $n = 1, \ldots, N$ with step size Δt to cover the domain $0 < t < \bar{D}$, and the dynamic optimization for the form of

$$V(t_n, F_{t_n}) = \max_{c_t} \left\{ \int_{t_n}^{t_{n+1}} e^{-\rho t}u(c_t)\,{}_t p_x\, dt + V(t_{n+1}, F_{t_{n+1}}) \right\}.$$

Then we set up a grid in F as F_j for $j = 1, \ldots, J$, with grid size ΔF to cover the domain F_{min} and F_{max}. We denote the approximation to $V(t_n, F_j)$ by V_j^n, and approximate the integral as

$$\max_{1 \leq k \leq J} \left\{ \frac{V_j^{n+1} - V_k^n}{\Delta t} + e^{-\rho t_n} u(c_{j,k}^n) \, {}_{t_n} P_x \right\} = 0$$

or

$$V_k^n = V_j^{n+1} + \Delta t e^{-\rho t_n} \, {}_{t_n} P_x \max_k \left\{ u(c_{j,k}^n) \right\}$$

where

$$c_{j,k}^n = v_k^n F_k^n + w_k^n - \frac{F_j - F_k}{(j-k)\Delta t}$$

for $j, k = 1, \ldots, J$ and $n = N - 1, \ldots, 1$. At the terminal time $t_N = \bar{D}$, we apply the condition $V_j^N = 0$ for $j = 1, \ldots, J$.

13.14 Appendix

Here we consider a generic problem that provides the basis for obtaining the results in section 13.11. Suppose that we have a fixed time period $a < t < b$ with $F_a = F_b = 0$. The question is that under the optimal consumption, should F_t change signs or stay positive, or negative in this time interval? It is easy to see that we can assume that F_t does not change sign. If not, we can always break the time interval into smaller ones and consider the case where F_t is either positive or negative. The question now becomes whether F_t is positive or negative, given the parameter values $\rho, g, v, \hat{v}, \gamma$. Without losing generality, we can assume that $a = 0$ and $b = \tau$. Finally, we use $k = (v - \rho)\gamma^{-1}$ and $\hat{k} = (\hat{v} - \rho)\gamma^{-1}$.

On any time interval that F_t does not change signs, the solution can be obtained using the Euler-Lagrange equation. In the following, we will write the solution using v and k with the understanding that if $F_t < 0$, they are replaced by $\hat{v}$ and $\hat{k}$.

$$e^{-vt} F_t = -w_0 \cdot \frac{e^{-(v-g)t} - e^{-(v-g)\tau}}{v - g} + c_0^* \cdot \frac{e^{-(v-k)t} - e^{-(v-k)\tau}}{v - k} \qquad (13.134)$$

where

$$c_0^* = w_0 \cdot \frac{1 - e^{-(v-g)\tau}}{v - g} \cdot \frac{v - k}{1 - e^{-(v-k)\tau}} \qquad (13.135)$$

and

$$c_t^* = c_0^* e^{kt}. \tag{13.136}$$

There are three possible scenarios: (i) patient $k \leq \hat{k} < g$; (ii) relatively impatient $k \leq g \leq \hat{k}$; (iii) impatient $g < k \leq \hat{k}$; and we now show that the F_t is positive, negative, and identically zero.

We consider the second scenario first, that is, relatively impatient $k \leq g \leq \hat{k}$. One can show that neither $F_t > 0$ nor $F_t < 0$ are consistent with the solutions (13.134)–(13.136) and the condition $k \leq g \leq \hat{k}$. Therefore, the only possible case is $F_t = 0$. In other words, it is optimal to consume the entire amount of the wage (or pension $g = 0$) income

$$c_0^* = w_0 \tag{13.137}$$

and

$$c_t^* = c_0^* e^{gt}. \tag{13.138}$$

We can use the similar argument and show that the solution given is consistent; that is, $F_t > 0$ is consistent to the choice v when $g < k \leq \hat{k}$, and $F_t < 0$ is consistent to the choice $\hat{v}$ when $k \leq \hat{k} < g$. Therefore it is optimal to borrow and get into debt. In this case, it is optimal to initially consume more than income, and decrease consumption over time to the level below income at the later part of the time period, given by

$$c_t^* = c_0^* e^{\hat{k}t} \tag{13.139}$$

and

$$c_0^* = w_0 \cdot \frac{1 - e^{-(\hat{v}-g)\tau}}{\hat{v} - g} \cdot \frac{\hat{v} - \hat{k}}{1 - e^{-(\hat{v}-\hat{k})\tau}}. \tag{13.140}$$

When $g < k \leq \hat{k}$, on the other hand, it is optimal to save and never get into debt, and consume less than income initially and increase the consumption level over time, eventually consuming more than income at the second part of the time period

$$c_t^* = c_0^* e^{kt} \tag{13.141}$$

and

$$c_0^* = w_0 \cdot \frac{1 - e^{-(v-g)\tau}}{v - g} \cdot \frac{v - k}{1 - e^{-(v-k)\tau}}. \tag{13.142}$$

FOURTEEN

Advanced Material: Part II. Stochastic Optimal Control and the HJB Equation

Learning Objectives

Until now, we have assumed that there is no uncertainty other than the length of your lifetime. In real life, however, this is not the case. In this chapter we extend the results in the previous chapter by including uncertainties in both investment return and wage income. We start by presenting the standard materials on dynamic optimal asset allocation and consumption under the continuous time framework, originally developed by Robert Merton in a series of papers (1969, 1971) that led to him being awarded the Nobel Prize Memorial in Economics. We then conclude the chapter with a brief presentation of an advanced stochastic lifecycle model.

14.1 Dynamic Asset Allocation and Optimal Consumption

Let us for the time being forget about the lifecycle model (issues related to mortality risk and retirement) and instead consider a classical problem in finance. Suppose that you have inherited or accumulated a certain amount of money M_t at time t. You have a choice between keeping your money in a safe bank account (cash) or investing it in the stock market, which promises a greater return on average. Of course the stock market is volatile and you may lose some or all of your investment (if you are one of the many who bought tech stocks before the great tech bubble burst, for example). So if you are risk averse and belong to those people who will lose sleep worrying about the possibility of losing your investment, clearly you face a dilemma: money in the savings account is safe but the return is low while the stock market might give you a greater return but you face the possibility of losing your investment.

As in every situation you encounter in life, you compromise. You want to invest a portion of your financial wealth in the **risky assets** (stock market)

315

and put the rest in a safer place, a **risk-free** savings account or cash. However, you immediately face another problem, which is how much you want to invest in the risky asset. In other words, is there an **optimal** amount you should invest in the risky asset? If you talk to a financial advisor or consult newspaper columnists, you most likely find that there is no single answer to this question. Typically, after asking about your **risk tolerance**, a financial advisor could recommend a mutual fund with a mixture of assets consisting of a certain percentage of stocks and cash.

The main tools we will be using is stochastic optimal control in continuous time. Instead of providing a detailed treatment of this topic, which is beyond the scope of our book, we will give an informal and intuitive presentation. Our focus is on the financial interpretation of the solution. However, in order to give the readers the main idea of where these solutions come from, we need to go over some basic concepts of stochastic calculus and the dynamic optimization principle.

14.2 Asset Price Model

There is a long history and an ongoing debate on how to model the asset price changes. A popular model for the asset price (and also the simplest) is given by the following equation

$$\frac{S_{n+1} - S_n}{S_n} = \mu_m \Delta t + \sigma_m \Delta B_n, \tag{14.1}$$

where $\Delta S_n = S_{n+1} - S_n$ is the change of the price over time interval $\Delta t = t_{n+1} - t_n$. The upward trend is described by the first term $\mu_m \Delta t$ where μ_m is called the **drift**. The fluctuation is described by the second term $\sigma_m \Delta B_n$ where ΔB_n is assumed to be a normally distributed random variable with variance Δt; that is, $\Delta B_n \sim N(0, \Delta t)$ and σ_m characterizes the amount of fluctuation in the price and is called the **volatility**.

Now instead of using daily opening price, we can use hourly price, or even the price at every minute. If we can take that process to an infinitely small time interval, denoted by dt, we have arrived at our continuous-time asset price model:

$$\frac{dS_t}{S_t} = \mu_m dt + \sigma_m dB_t. \tag{14.2}$$

Here dS_t is the price change over dt and $\mu_m dt$ and $dB_t \sim N(0, dt)$ can be viewed as the limit if $\mu_m \Delta t$ and $\sigma_m \Delta B_n$. This is a **stochastic differential equation** (SDE). Notice that we did not use the rate of change dS_t/dt here because the limit $\sigma_m \Delta B_n / \Delta t$ does not exist. An equivalent formula for the asset price model can be expressed as

$$S_t = S_0 e^{\left(\mu_m - \frac{\sigma_m^2}{2}\right)t + \sigma_m B_t} \tag{14.3}$$

where $B_t \sim N(0, t)$ is a Brownian motion.

This, of course, implies that $\ln(S_t / S_0)$ is normally distributed with a mean value of $(\mu_m - 0.5\sigma_m^2)t$ and a standard deviation of $\sigma_m \sqrt{t}$. Stated differently, the geometric mean return aka growth rate of the risky asset is $\mu_m - 0.5\sigma_m^2$ per annum. Typical values of the parameters μ_m fall in the range of (5%,15%) and typical values of σ_m fall in the range of (5%,50%). The risk-free rate r, which is also the rate at which the family can borrow money, is on the order of magnitude of (1%,5%), which must be lower than μ_m for economic equilibrium purposes.

14.3 A Self-Financed Portfolio

Suppose that you have certain amount of capital (funds) and would like to invest in a mixture of risky and risk-free assets. The simplest self-financed (no additional injection of funds) portfolio consists of one risky asset (stock with price S_t) and one risk-free asset (cash F_t), which grows at the risk-free rate r; that is,

$$dF_t = r F_t dt. \tag{14.4}$$

Assuming that the portion of the total financial wealth M_t invested in the risky asset is α_t, the change in the value of the portfolio is given by the budget constraint

$$\begin{aligned} dM_t &= \alpha_t M_t \frac{dS_t}{S_t} + (1 - \alpha_t) M_t \frac{dF_t}{F_t} \\ &= [(\mu_m - r)\alpha_t + r] M_t dt + \alpha_t \sigma_m M_t dB_t. \end{aligned} \tag{14.5}$$

The variable α_t denotes the fractional allocation of your marketable wealth M_t to the risky asset at time t. Thus, if $\alpha_t = 0$ you allocate all marketable wealth – but no more – to risk-free cash and if $\alpha_t = 1$ you allocate all marketable wealth – but no more – to risky stocks. The model also allows for $\alpha_t > 1$, which would imply leverage. Thus, for example, $\alpha_t = 2$ implies that 200% of wealth is invested in the risky stock. This is financed by borrowing 100% of wealth at some (constant) rate of interest denoted by r. Recall that α_t is under your direct control and is one of the key choice variables in our model.

If you compare equation (14.5) for your portfolio with equation (14.2) for the underlying stock, you can see that the two are similar. The function of α_t will either increase the volatility (risk) if it is greater than one or reduce the volatility (risk) of your portfolio. An optimal dynamic portfolio allocation strategy is the choice of α_t, which maximizes some measure of return or other objectives. Because S_t fluctuates over time (due to its random component), this strategy may involve rebalancing (buying or selling the risky assets) your portfolio constantly. In reality, due to **transaction costs**, it is not practical to rebalance continuously. However, to simplify the discussion, we ignore this important technical issue and assume that you can buy and sell without paying any fees.

14.4 The Asset-Allocation Problem

The model problem Merton (which will be called the Merton problem throughout this chapter) considered is finding the value of α_t so that the **expected utility** of the financial wealth is maximized at the end of an investment period T. Mathematically, this can be stated as

$$\max_{\alpha_t} E[u(M_T)|M_0 = m] \qquad (14.6)$$

subject to the budget constraint

$$dM_t = [(\mu_m - r)\alpha_t + r]M_t dt + \alpha_t \sigma_m M_t dB_t. \qquad (14.7)$$

In words, we look for the optimal allocation, denoted by α_t^* among all possible choices α_t to maximize the **conditional expectation** of the utility of terminal wealth over a given time period. This is a **stochastic optimal control** problem where proportion invested in the risky asset α_t is the control function.

To solve this problem, we recast the problem by introducing a value function

$$J(t, m) = \max_{\alpha_t} E[u(M_T)|M_t = m]. \qquad (14.8)$$

Using the basic principle of the dynamic optimization and stochastic calculus (outlined in the technical appendix), we arrived at the following Hamilton-Jacobi-Bellman (HJB) equation

$$\frac{\partial J}{\partial t} + \max_{\alpha_t} \left\{ [\alpha_t(\mu_m - r) + r]m\frac{\partial J}{\partial m} + \frac{1}{2}(\alpha_t \sigma_m m)^2\frac{\partial^2 J}{\partial m^2} \right\} = 0 \qquad (14.9)$$

with terminal condition $J(T, m) = u(m)$.

This is most likely the first time you have ever seen an equation of this form that consists of partial derivatives as well as an optimization procedure embedded in the equation. Next we briefly describe the approach that is used throughout the rest of this chapter for solving the HJB equation. For readers who are interested in the details of the derivation of the HJB and procedure outlined for solving the HJB, we refer to the book by Bjork (2004, chapter 19) where a relatively gentle introduction to the subject can be found.

First, we note that just as in the previous chapter on calculus of variations, where we have derived the Euler-Lagrange equation for an optimal path (section 13.7), a **necessary condition** for the optimal control function α_t^* can be derived by taking the derivative of the two terms involving α_t in (14.9) with respect α_t and set it to be zero (known as the **first-order condition**),

$$[(\mu_m - r) + r]m\frac{\partial J}{\partial m} + \alpha_t^*(\sigma_m m)^2\frac{\partial^2 J}{\partial m^2} = 0,$$

which leads to the following equation

$$\alpha_t^* = -\frac{(\mu_m - r)J_m}{mJ_{mm}}. \tag{14.10}$$

The HJB equation can be rewritten as

$$\frac{\partial J}{\partial t} + [\alpha_t^*(\mu_m - r) + r]m\frac{\partial J}{\partial m} + \frac{1}{2}(\alpha_t^*\sigma_m m)^2\frac{\partial^2 J}{\partial m^2} = 0 \tag{14.11}$$

with terminal condition $J(T, m) = u(m)$. This equation now only involves partial derivatives (known as a partial differential equation, or PDE for short) but is still quite complicated. In general it is not guaranteed that we can find closed-form analytic solutions for any PDEs, and solving them often relies on good intuition (and luck).

When the utility is of the CRRA form, $u(m) = m_x^{1-\gamma}(1-\gamma)^{-1}$, we can write the value function into a separable form as $J(t, m) = u(m)h(t)$. You may wonder how someone could ever come up with this particular form and the answer is experience (and sometimes good intuition). A simple observation of Equation (14.8) tells us that the value function $J(t, m)$ is scalable in m; that is, $J(t, am) = a^{1-\gamma}J(t, m)$ for any variable a. Thus, choosing $a = m^{-1}$ gives $J(t, m) = m^{1-\gamma}J(t,1) = u(m)h(t)$. With this in our hand, what we need to do now is to show that this assumption is consistent, and then find the unknown function $h(t)$, which can be done by carrying out the following calculations. We start by obtaining the expressions for the partial derivatives J_t, J_m, and J_{mm} as follows:

$$\frac{\partial J}{\partial t} = u(m)\dot{h}(t) \qquad \frac{\partial J}{\partial m} = m^{-\gamma}h(t) \qquad \frac{\partial^2 J}{\partial m^2} = -\gamma m^{-\gamma-1}h(t).$$

Using these expressions, the optimal fraction for the risky asset is given by

$$\alpha_t^* = \frac{\mu_m - r}{\gamma \sigma_m^2}. \tag{14.12}$$

Substituting equation (14.12) into the PDE (14.11), we obtain the following ODE for h as

$$\dot{h} + (1 - \gamma)\left[r + \frac{(\mu_m - r)^2}{2\gamma\sigma_m^2}\right]h = 0 \tag{14.13}$$

with terminal condition $h(T) = 0$, which comes from the fact that $J(T, m) = u(m)h(T) = 0$. Now we need to determine whether the assumption $J(t, m) = u(m)h(t)$ is consistent. Because the equation and the terminal condition for h does not include the variable m, we are assured that h is not a function of m, therefore consistent with our assumption.

You may be surprised to find that the optimal asset allocation is a constant! We note, however, that this does not mean that you are holding a constant number of stocks. Because the asset price changes with time, this formula actually says that you need to constantly rebalance your portfolio to maintain a constant proportion of the total value in the risky assets. When the stocks are up more than expected, the value of the risky assets goes up more than that of the risk-free ones; you need to sell some stocks to bring down the value of risky assets so that its fraction in your portfolio remains unchanged. When the stocks are down, on the other hand, you need to buy more stocks to bring up the value of the risky assets in your portfolio so that the fraction again remains unchanged.

We note that the proportion allocated to risky assets is completely determined by four parameters, namely μ_m, r, σ_m, and γ, and time plays no role even though the value of your portfolio does vary in time with respect to the final time T. The formula (14.12) states that it is optimal to increase the amount in the risky assets if it offers greater expected return (larger $\mu_m - r$), or if it is less risky (smaller volatility σ_m), and if you the investor are willing to take more risk (smaller γ). Furthermore, the value of α_t^* can be greater than 100%, which means that the investor might borrow to invest in the risky asset. For example, if we set some of the parameter values as $r = 3\%$, $\mu = 10\%$, and $\sigma_m = 20\%$ while varying the risk-aversion parameter as $\gamma = 1, 3$, and 6, that is, from risk indifference to relatively risk averse, the optimal allocation to the risky assets is reduced from $\alpha_t^* = 175\%$, to 58% and 29%, respectively.

14.5 The Asset-Allocation-Consumption Problem

So far we have solved the pure asset allocation problem. Another standard problem (Merton problem with consumption) is to add consumption. Instead of maximizing expected utility of terminal wealth, we want to maximize the expected utility of consumption over a certain period of time. The question is how to find the optimal consumption rate c_t^* as well as the asset allocation strategy α_t^* to achieve that objective.

Mathematically, we need to solve the following problem:

$$\max_{\{\alpha_t, c_t\}} E\left[\int_0^T e^{-\rho t} u(c_t) dt \mid M_0 = m\right] \tag{14.14}$$

subject to the budget constraint

$$dM_t = [(\mu_m - r)\alpha_t + r]M_t dt + \alpha_t \sigma_m M_t dZ_t - c_t dt. \tag{14.15}$$

Notice that the difference between this problem and the previous one is the objective function. Previously the objective is to maximize the expected utility of the final wealth. Here the objective is to maximize the utility of expected accumulated consumption.

Similar to the investment problem, we define the value function by

$$J(t, m) = \max_{\{\alpha_t, c_t\}} E\left[\int_t^T e^{-\rho s} u(c_s) ds \mid M_t = m\right]. \tag{14.16}$$

Using similar procedure, the corresponding HJB equation can be obtained as

$$\frac{\partial J}{\partial t} + \max_{\{\alpha_t, c_t\}}\left\{[\alpha_t(\mu_m - r)m + rm - c_t]\frac{\partial J}{\partial m} + \frac{1}{2}(\alpha_t \sigma_m m)^2 \frac{\partial^2 J}{\partial m^2} + e^{-\rho t} u(c_t)\right\}$$
$$= 0 \tag{14.17}$$

with terminal condition $J(T, m) = 0$, which is different from the previous section.

Again, we derive the necessary conditions for the optimal control functions by applying the first-order conditions as before, and rewrite the HJB equation as a nonlinear PDE

$$\frac{\partial J}{\partial t} + [\alpha_t^*(\mu_m - r)m + rm - c_t^*]\frac{\partial J}{\partial m} + \frac{1}{2}(\alpha_t^* \sigma_m m)^2 \frac{\partial^2 J}{\partial m^2} + e^{-\rho t} u(c_t^*)$$
$$= 0 \tag{14.18}$$

where α_t^* and c_t^* (under CRRA utility) are

$$\alpha_t^* = -\frac{(\mu_m - r)J_m}{mJ_{mm}} \tag{14.19}$$

$$c_t^* = e^{-\frac{\rho}{\gamma}t}J_m^{-\frac{1}{\gamma}}. \tag{14.20}$$

For more details, see Merton (1990).

Under CRRA utility, $u(c_t) = c_t^{1-\gamma}(1-\gamma)^{-1}$, we assume again $J(t,m) = u(m)h(t)$ and following the same procedure as in the previous section. The optimal consumption rate and fraction to the risky asset are given by

$$\alpha_t^* = \frac{\mu_m - r}{\gamma\sigma_m^2} \tag{14.21}$$

$$c_t^* = m e^{-\frac{\rho}{\gamma}t}h^{-\frac{1}{\gamma}} \tag{14.22}$$

where $h(t)$ satisfies the following ODE

$$h + (1-\gamma)\left[r + \frac{(\mu_m - r)^2}{2\gamma\sigma_m^2}\right]h + \gamma e^{-\frac{\rho}{\gamma}t}h^{1-\frac{1}{\gamma}} = 0 \tag{14.23}$$

with $h(T) = 0$. This equation can be solved (left as an exercise) and the optimal consumption rate is given by

$$c_t^* = m(k - r + \eta)\left\{e^{(k-r+\eta)(T-t)} - 1\right\}^{-1} \tag{14.24}$$

where $k = (\rho - r)\gamma^{-1}$ and

$$\eta = \frac{(1-\gamma)(\mu_m - r)^2}{2\gamma^2\sigma_m^2}.$$

A careful reader may wonder how the Merton solution is related to the smooth consumption solution in Chapter 13 for the deterministic case. To see this, we consider the scenario when $\mu_m = r$. In this case, $\alpha_t^* = 0$, and all the return is deterministic and the solution becomes

$$c_t^* = m(k - r)\left[e^{(k-r)(T-t)} - 1\right]^{-1}. \tag{14.25}$$

Note that m is the wealth at time t, which means that $m = M_t$, and

$$dM_t = rM_t dt - c_t^* dt.$$

On the other hand, using the results from Chapter 13, we have (replacing v by r and F_t by M_t, and $c_t^* = c_0^* e^{kt}$)

$$M_t = \frac{c_0^* e^{kt}}{k - r}\left[e^{(k-r)(T-t)} - 1\right]. \tag{14.26}$$

These two equations are identical.

14.6 The Asset-Allocation-Consumption Problem with Deterministic Wage Income

Before we examine the full lifecycle model, it is useful to investigate the effect of a (deterministic) wage income on the optimal asset allocation and consumption strategies. Mathematically, we need to solve

$$\max_{\{\alpha_t, c_t\}} E\left[\int_0^T e^{-\rho t} u(c_t) dt\right] \qquad (14.27)$$

subject to the condition $M_0 = m$ and the budget constraint

$$dM_t = [(\mu_m - r)\alpha_t + r]M_t dt + \alpha_t \sigma_m M_t dB_t - c_t dt + w_t dt. \qquad (14.28)$$

Here we assume that the wage grows at a rate g as before; that is, $w_t = w_0 \exp(gt)$. The difference is that the investment return is stochastic.

By now you should be familiar with the procedure we are going to follow. First we define the value function

$$J(t, m) = \max_{\{\alpha_t, c_t\}} E\left[\int_t^T e^{-\rho s} u(c_s) ds \mid M_t = m\right]. \qquad (14.29)$$

Next we write down the corresponding HJB equation

$$\begin{aligned}
\frac{\partial J}{\partial t} + \max_{\{\alpha_t, c_t\}} &\left\{ [\alpha_t(\mu_m - r)m + rm + w_t - c_t] \frac{\partial J}{\partial m} \right. \\
&\left. + \frac{1}{2}(\alpha_t \sigma_m m)^2 \frac{\partial J}{\partial m^2} + e^{-\rho t} u(c_t) \right\} = 0
\end{aligned} \qquad (14.30)$$

with terminal condition $J(T, m) = 0$.

The only difference between this problem and the ones in the previous sections is that we then seek a closed-form solution by setting $J(t, m) = u(\hat{m})h(t)$ with $\hat{m} = m + w_0(g - r)^{-1}\{\exp[(g - r)t] - 1\}$. The optimal consumption rate and proportion of risky asset can be obtained as (by applying the first-order conditions)

$$\alpha_t^* = \frac{(\mu_m - r)}{\gamma \sigma_m^2} \frac{\hat{m}}{m} \qquad (14.31)$$

$$c_t^* = \hat{m}(k - r + \eta)\left\{e^{(k-r+\eta)(T-t)} - 1\right\}^{-1} \qquad (14.32)$$

where $\hat{m} = m + w_t(g - r)^{-1}\{\exp[(g - r)(T - t)] - 1\}$. The derivation of the closed-form solution will be left as an exercise problem.

Recall from Chapter 13 that the value of human capital during the time period $[t, T]$ for the wage growing at a rate g can be computed as

$$\int_0^{T-t} w_t e^{g(s-t)} e^{-r(s-t)} ds = \frac{w_t}{g - r}\left[e^{(g-r)(T-t)} - 1\right],$$

which is the amount included in $\hat{m}$ in addition to financial wealth m. This is consistent with the earlier discussion that human capital is an integral part of our total wealth. In addition, it is interesting to note that the future wage is discounted using the risk-free rate even though a risky asset with a potentially higher return is available for investment. The decision on asset allocation and consumption is now based on the total wealth ($\hat{M}_t = M_t + w_0(g - r)^{-1}\{\exp[(g - r)t] - 1\}$), not just the financial wealth M_t. In particular, the consumption rate is proportional to the total wealth $\hat{M}_t$ including human capital, instead of financial wealth M_t. Furthermore, the amount of wealth invested in the risky asset is adjusted by a factor $\hat{M}_t/M_t$, toward the risky asset. In other words, we can now take more risk knowing that there is a steady stream of wage income. For example, when the human capital is 100% of the financial wealth, the optimal fraction in risky asset is now doubled compared to the case without human capital. Note here we have used capital letters to emphasize that both the financial and total wealth are stochastic due to uncertainty in the return of the risky asset.

In the next section, we explore the effect of human capital further with several important extensions. First of all, we will introduce uncertainty in wage income. Secondly, we include mortality risk and insurance and solve the optimal asset allocation and consumption problem inside a lifecycle model framework. Finally, we use a more general utility function to reflect the reality of consumption floors faced by many households.

14.7 An Advanced Stochastic Lifecycle Model

In the previous sections we have ignored several important factors in the lifecycle model discussed in earlier chapters such as retirement and mortality risk. In this section we offer (a very brief) overview of what happens in our advanced lifecycle model, when the financial wealth M_t and the wage rate W_t are stochastic and possibly correlated with each other. Also, we will consider a family – as opposed to an individual – that relies on a breadwinner, which introduces the need for life insurance. In particular, our learning objective is to derive the **optimal** asset allocation denoted by α_t^* (as before), as well as the **optimal** amount of insurance and annuities as a function of one's human capital. This section ties together three sources of risk that people face over their lives: (i) investment returns, (ii) wage income, and (iii) how long they live.

In an effort to keep the mathematical content at a minimum level, we will gloss over the basic model and move to the presentation of the closed-form solutions for several special cases including the ones when the wage and the risky asset is perfectly correlated and anti-correlated. Our plan is to focus on the general framework, numerical results, and provide ample intuition. If you are interested in the derivations of the solutions, you can consult a detailed description in Huang and Milevsky (2008).

14.7.1 Model Specifications

As before, and following Huang and Milevsky (2008), the variable t denotes the current time, but in this section we work with three dates of interest. The first date is the time horizon $\bar{H}$ of the family, which is assumed exogenous and deterministic on the order of 50 to 100 years. The second date is the time of retirement $\bar{R} < \bar{H}$, which is when the wage/income process (job) terminates and the breadwinner enters his or her retirement years. The third date of interest is the death of the breadwinner, and the end of the wage/income process, which takes place at a random stopping time denoted by $\tau = \mathbf{T}_x$, which is the remaining lifetime random variable. The wage/income process W_t therefore jumps to zero at the earlier of $\bar{R}$ and τ. The time horizon of the family can actually extend beyond the (maximum) remaining lifetime of the breadwinner, which we denoted by $\bar{D}$ earlier.

We assume the family purchases short-term insurance on the life of the breadwinner that is renegotiated and guaranteed renewable on an ongoing basis at a predetermined schedule, which is driven by an **instantaneous force of mortality (IFM) curve** denoted by λ_{x+t}, where x is the age of the primary breadwinner at inception of the model. We then let I_t denote the insurance premium (in dollars) payable per unit time; a variable that is under the direct control of the family. (The symbol I_t is not to be confused with I used in previous chapters, which was the age you enter the labor force and start working.)

One can think of I_t as a budget for insurance that will then induce a certain face value or death benefit I_t/λ_{x+t}. For example, if the IFM curve at age $x = 35$ is $\lambda_{35} = 0.001$, and the family spends $I_t = 50$ dollars on life insurance, this entitles the family to a death benefit of $50/0.001 = \$50,000$ if the insured dies at the age of thirty-five.

The family is also allowed to purchase annuity tontines on behalf of the breadwinner. To make the problem simple, we assume that the annuity can be treated as a negative insurance: instead of paying the premium, the family receives an annuity payment, also indicated by I_t. Upon the death of the breadwinner at time t, the family has to pay back the face value of the annuity policy in a lump sum I_t/λ_{x+t}. We note that in reality, the face value is usually paid up front, instead of at the time of death, but in this section we will assume for simplicity.

We let M_t denote the market value of the family's assets that include the value of all (risky) stocks and (risk-free) cash on a mark-to-market basis. We assume that M_0 denotes the initial marketable wealth (think financial capital) at time $t = 0$. Heuristically, the breadwinner works and converts labor and time into wages and income. A portion of this income is consumed and the remainder is saved in a diversified portfolio consisting of risky stocks and safe cash, to finance consumption after retirement or death.

As before, we let c_t denote the instantaneousness consumption rate of the family (in real terms) per unit time. In general, our model is specified in real (after inflation) terms and all parameters and choice variables will reflect this. Note that the consumption rate is our third and final choice (aka control) variable and c_t is chosen to maximize the family's *utility* of consumption.

Even though a more realistic state dependent instantaneous utility function can be used, we adopted a so-called HARA utility function in this section. The precise functional form is

$$u(c) = \begin{cases} u_l(c) \equiv \frac{1}{1-\gamma}(c - c_l)^{1-\gamma} & t < \tau \\ u_d(c) \equiv \frac{1}{1-\gamma}(c - c_d)^{1-\gamma} & t \geq \tau \end{cases} \tag{14.33}$$

for $\gamma > 0$, which (as before) is the coefficient of relative risk aversion. c_l and c_d are the consumption floors for the family, before and after the death of the breadwinner. Here τ is used to denote the random time of death.

As before, we let W_t denote the real (after-inflation) wage/income rate of the family's breadwinner per unit time. This stochastic process is expected to increase in real terms over time and might be correlated with the investment performance of the "risky asset." We assume the wage process satisfies the following geometric Brownian motion (GBM), but with specification:

$$dW_t = \begin{cases} gW_t dt + \sigma_w W_t dB_t^w & t < \min[\tau, \bar{R}] \\ 0 & t \geq \min[\tau, \bar{R}] \end{cases} \tag{14.34}$$

where g denotes the drift rate of wages, and σ_w denotes the diffusion coefficient of the process, and B_t^w denotes the Brownian motion driving the wages process W_t. Similar to the risky asset, we assume that the real wage at any future time $t + s$ is lognormally distributed with parameters (g, σ_w). Note that the Brownian motion B_t driving the risky asset is instantaneously correlated with the B_t^w driving the wage process via the relationship $d\langle B_t, B_t^w \rangle = \theta \sigma_m \sigma_w dt$. Later we talk about this correlation variable θ, which is the primary focus of our numerical case study and results.

As mentioned earlier, the instantaneous force of mortality (or hazard rate) is denoted by λ_{x+t}, where x is the initial age. As we explained earlier, the quantity $\lambda_{x+t}dt$ can be thought of as the rate of death within a small time interval dt at time t.

It is important to stress that in our model the family unit knows exactly how much they will have to pay for insurance – regardless of how much and when they want to purchase it – from the current time t, to the time of retirement $\bar{R}$. Thus, in addition to precluding whole-life and other more complicated forms of insurance, we do not allow for stochastic mortality rates or anti-selection effects that might complicate the insurance purchase problem. Thus, once again, if the family purchases (invests) I_t dollars in life insurance at time t, they will be entitled to a death benefit of I_t/λ_{x+t} if the breadwinner dies at time t. For now, we ignore loading and commissions that can easily be handled by working with a loaded mortality rate.

Based on the construction of the wage/income process W_t and the evolution of the risky asset price S_t, the family budget constraint for the marketable wealth process M_t will satisfy the following stochastic differential equation:

$$dM_t = W_t dt - c_t dt - I_t dt + \alpha_t M_t(\mu_m dt + \sigma_m dB_t) + (1 - \alpha_t)r M_t dt$$
$$= \left[(\mu_m - r)M_t \alpha_t + r M_t + W_t - c_t - I_t\right] dt + \sigma_m \alpha_t M_t dB_t \quad (14.35)$$

for $t \leq \min[\tau, \bar{R}]$, and

$$dM_t = -c_t dt + \alpha_t M_t(\mu_m dt + \sigma_m dB_t) + (1 - \alpha_t)M_t r dt \quad (14.36)$$
$$= \left[(\mu_m - r)M_t \alpha_t + r M_t - c_t\right] dt + \sigma_m \alpha_t M_t dB_t$$

for $t > \min[\tau, \bar{R}]$. To simplify the problem, we have ignored retirement income either in the form of a jump in the wealth at retirement or in the form of pension income after retirement. Notice that for the post-death period we simply have the Merton problem (with consumption). For the pre-death period, however, we have several new features included in our model, namely stochastic wage and insurance/annuity.

The intuition for the various pieces in equations (14.35) and (14.36) are as follows. First, we add wage income – when there is some – via $W_t dt$. Then, we subtract consumption $c_t dt$ and insurance premiums $I_t dt$. Finally, we add instantaneous investment returns from the allocation to the risky asset, $\alpha_t M_t dS_t/S_t$ as well as allocations to the risk-free asset $(1-\alpha_t)M_t r\,dt$. Finally, we have substituted dS_t/S_t from equation (14.2) to eliminate any reference to S_t from here on.

The final part should be familiar by now. When the breadwinner is still alive, the family unit or household objective function is defined by:

$$J(t, m, w) = \max_{\{\alpha_s, I_s, c_s\}} \left\{ E_t \left[\int_t^{\bar{H}} e^{-\rho s} u_l(c_s) ds \,|\, M_t = m, W_t = w \right] \right\}$$

(14.37)

where ρ is the subjective discount rate and $u(c_s)$ denotes the utility function, in the form of $u_l(c_s)$ or $u_d(c_s)$ depending on whether the breadwinner is alive or not. In words, the family is searching for an asset allocation strategy α_s, an insurance buying strategy I_s, and consumption strategy c_s that maximizes the discounted value of utility of consumption between time t (now) and the terminal horizon of the family unit.

Similarly, when the breadwinner has died, the household objective function is defined by

$$\Phi(t, m) = \max_{\{\alpha_s, c_s\}} \left\{ E_t \left[\int_t^{\bar{H}} e^{-\rho s} u_d(c_s) ds \,|\, M_t = m \right] \right\}$$

(14.38)

because there is no wage income and it is optimal not to purchase insurance.

14.7.2 HJB Equation for the Lifecycle Model

The HJB equation for the portfolio choice and human capital problem can be derived as follows (Huang and Milevsky, 2008):

$$
\begin{aligned}
\lambda_{x+t} J ={} & \frac{\partial J}{\partial t} + \max_{c_t} \left(e^{-\rho t} u_l(c_t) - c_t \frac{\partial J}{\partial m} \right) \\
& + \max_{I_t} \left(\Phi\left(t, m + I_t \lambda_{x+t}^{-1}\right) \lambda_{x+t} - I_t \frac{\partial J}{\partial m} \right) \\
& + \max_{\alpha_t} \left[\alpha_t(\mu_m - r) m \frac{\partial J}{\partial m} + \frac{1}{2}\alpha_t^2 \sigma_m^2 m^2 J \frac{\partial^2 J}{\partial m^2} \right. \\
& \left. \qquad + \alpha_t \theta \sigma_w \sigma_m w m J \frac{\partial^2 J}{\partial m \partial w} \right] \\
& + rm \frac{\partial J}{\partial m} + w \frac{\partial J}{\partial m} + \mu_w w \frac{\partial J}{\partial w} + \frac{1}{2}\sigma_w^2 w^2 \frac{\partial^2 J}{\partial w^2}
\end{aligned}
$$

(14.39)

for $t \leq \bar{R}$ and

$$\lambda_{x+t} J = \frac{\partial J}{\partial t} + \max_{c_t} \left(e^{-\rho t} u_l(c_t) - c_t \frac{\partial J}{\partial m} \right)$$
$$+ \max_{I_t} \left(\Phi \left(t, m + I_t \lambda_{x+t}^{-1}, t \right) \lambda_{x+t} - I_t \frac{\partial J}{\partial m} \right)$$
$$+ \max_{\alpha_t} \left[\alpha_t (\mu_m - r) m \frac{\partial J}{\partial m} + \frac{1}{2} \alpha_t^2 \sigma_m^2 m^2 \frac{\partial^2 J}{\partial m^2} \right] + r m \frac{\partial J}{\partial m}$$

$$(14.40)$$

for $t > \bar{R}$. And Φ satisfies the following HJB (without wage and insurance)

$$0 = \frac{\partial \Phi}{\partial t} + \max_{c_t} \left(e^{-\rho t} u_d(c_t) - c_t \frac{\partial \Phi}{\partial m} \right)$$
$$+ \max_{\alpha_t} \left[\alpha_t (\mu_m - r) m \frac{\partial \Phi}{\partial m} + \frac{1}{2} \alpha_t^2 \sigma_m^2 m^2 \frac{\partial^2 \Phi}{\partial m^2} \right] + r m \frac{\partial \Phi}{\partial m}. \quad (14.41)$$

Because there is zero-bequest, the terminal conditions are

$$J(\bar{H}, m, w) = \Phi(\bar{H}, m) = 0. \quad (14.42)$$

14.7.3 Closed-Form Solution

For the lifecycle model, closed-form solution can only be obtained for three special cases: post-death period of the breadwinner, pre-death period when the wage and risky asset are perfectly correlated or anti-correlated. Next we shall provide these solutions and some insights.

Post-Death Period
After the death of the breadwinner, the solution is given by Φ, which can be obtained (following Merton, 1969) and explained earlier by writing it in the form

$$\Phi(t, m) = \frac{h(m - g_d)^{1-\gamma}}{1 - \gamma}$$

where h and g_d are given as

$$h(t) = e^{-\rho t} \left[\frac{e^{\eta_h(\bar{H}-t)} - 1}{\eta_h} \right]^{\gamma} \quad (14.43)$$

$$g_d(t) = \frac{c_d}{r} \left[1 - e^{-r(\bar{H}-t)} \right] \quad (14.44)$$

with

$$\eta_h = -\frac{\rho}{\gamma} + \frac{1-\gamma}{\gamma}\left[r + \frac{(\mu_m - r)^2}{2\gamma\sigma_m^2}\right].$$

The optimal controls are given as

$$c_t^* = c_d + e^{-\frac{\rho}{\gamma}t}h^{-\frac{1}{\gamma}}(m - g_d) \qquad (14.45)$$

$$\alpha_t^* = \frac{\mu_m - r}{\gamma\sigma_m^2}\left(1 - \frac{g_d}{m}\right). \qquad (14.46)$$

In words, we work our way backwards from $\bar{H}$ (the point at which the breadwinner has died and hence the family is (only then) faced with a conventional portfolio choice problem) to $\tilde{H}$. These types of problems in which the mortality risk has obviously been eliminated, are the optimal asset allocation-consumption problems discussed at the beginning of this chapter with the exception that the CRRA utility is replaced by an HARA function.

In addition to their intermediate role in the optimal solution, here is how to think of the g_d variable/quantity from a financial economic perspective. Basically, the optimal policy – both in terms of the demand for insurance and the allocation to the risky asset – is driven by the need to satisfy the minimal consumption level c_d, which is required by the family once the breadwinner is deceased. The effect of consumption floor is represented by the function g_d, which is essentially the funds set aside (discounted by the risk-free rate) to cover the consumption floor c_d. Indeed, if the time horizon $\bar{H} = \infty$, and the family is concerned with perpetual consumption, then $g_d = c_d/r$, which is the discounted value of perpetual consumption, or the market value of a console bond at the rate of r. Once the family has this level of wealth, it can secure or lock in the floor by investing g_d in the risk-free asset.

The allocation and consumption strategies are in the same form as in the CRRA case, except that they are now based on the wealth available, that is, financial wealth M_t minus g_d, instead of M_t. As a result, the allocation to risky asset is reduced by a factor $(M_t - g_d)/M_t$.

Pre-Death Post-Retirement Period
We seek the solution in the form

$$J = \frac{h(m - g_l)^{1-\gamma}}{1-\gamma}$$

where $g_l = \delta g + g_d$ and

$$\delta g = (c_l - c_d)e^{-\int_t^{\bar{H}}(r+\lambda_{x+s})ds}\int_t^{\bar{H}} e^{\int_z^{\bar{H}}(r+\lambda_{x+s})ds}dz. \quad (14.47)$$

The optimal controls are now

$$c_t^* = c_l + e^{-\frac{\rho}{\gamma}t}h^{-\frac{1}{\gamma}}(m - g_l) \quad (14.48)$$
$$\lambda_{x+t}^{-1}I_t^* = -\delta g \quad (14.49)$$
$$\alpha_t^* = \frac{\mu_m - r}{\gamma\sigma_m^2}\left(1 - \frac{g_l}{m}\right). \quad (14.50)$$

Similar to g_d, the quantity g_l can be viewed or treated as a type of present of discounted value of this required level of consumption over the horizon of the family before the death of the breadwinner.

The amount of the financial wealth over g_l plays a similar role in the asset allocation and consumption strategies, after taking the consumption floor c_l into consideration. As in the case earlier, the allocation to risky asset is reduced by a factor $(M_t - g_l)/M_t$. An additional quantity is the amount of insurance the family should purchase, which is given by $I_t^*\lambda_{x+t}^{-1} = -\delta g$. Here $\delta g = g_l - g_d$ is the amount needed to cover the difference in consumption floors for the pre- and post-death periods of the breadwinner. Because c_l is in general greater than c_d, the value of δg is positive. Thus the optimal amount of insurance is in fact a negative amount, which suggests that the family should buy annuity (sell insurance) instead of buying insurance in this case.

Pre-Death Pre-Retirement Period
We look for the solution in the form of:

$$J(t, m, w) = \frac{h(m + \pi w - g_l)^{1-\gamma}}{1 - \gamma}$$

where h and g_l are given earlier, and

$$\pi = \begin{cases} e^{\int_t^{\bar{R}}\eta_\pi(s)ds}\int_t^{\bar{R}} e^{-\int_s^{\bar{R}}\eta_\pi(t)dt}ds & t \le \bar{R} \\ 0 & t > \bar{R} \end{cases} \quad (14.51)$$

were $\eta_\pi(t) = \mu_w - r - \lambda_{x+t} - \beta(\mu_m - r)$ and $\beta = \theta \sigma_m / \sigma_w$. The optimal controls are now

$$c_t^* = c_l + e^{-\frac{\rho}{\gamma} t} h^{-\frac{1}{\gamma}} (m + \pi w - g_l) \qquad (14.52)$$

$$\lambda_{x+t}^{-1} I_t^* = \pi w - g_l + g_d \qquad (14.53)$$

$$\alpha_t^* = \frac{\mu_m - r}{\gamma \sigma_m^2} \left(1 + \frac{\pi w}{m} - \frac{g_l}{m} \right) - \beta \frac{\pi w}{m}. \qquad (14.54)$$

Compared to the solutions for the post-death and post-retirement cases, the only new feature of the solution for the pre-death and pre-retirement case is the addition of human capital. It is interesting to also compare the optimal strategies for asset allocation and consumption for the Merton's problem with deterministic wage income discussed in the previous section. The evaluation of the human capital, represented by π, is now based on the quantity $\eta_\pi = \mu_w - r - \lambda_{x+t} - \beta(\mu_m - r)$, instead of $g - r$ when the wage is deterministic. Note g is the growth factor for the wage.

There are several very interesting observations that can be made here. Obviously the growth rate for the wage is now μ_m instead of g. The risk-free rate is now adjusted by the hazard rate λ_{x+t} due to mortality risk. However, a more important fact is that the evaluation rate is also adjusted by $\beta(\mu_m - r)$. This means that the true value of the human capital is also affected by the risky asset and its correlation with the wage. If the wage is perfectly correlated with the risky asset (financial market), then the wage income should be discounted by an additional factor of $\mu_m - r$. In this case, the evaluation rate for human capital is given by $\eta_\pi = \mu_w - \mu_m - \lambda_{x+t}$, that is, the growth rate in wage discounted by the drift of the risky asset and mortality rate. On the other hand, if the wage income is anti-correlated with the financial market, an extra premium $\mu_m - r$ should be included to evaluate the wage income. The evaluation rate for human capital is given by $\eta_\pi = \hat{\mu}_w - r - \lambda_{x+t}$ with $\hat{\mu}_w = \mu_w + \mu_m - r$, that is, the apparent growth rate in wage $\hat{\mu}_w$ discounted by the risk-free rate and mortality.

Discussion: Life Insurance or Pension Annuity?

Even though the closed-form solutions obtained are for special cases, it is instructive to examine this solution more closely in an attempt to extract some economic insights. In particular, based on our closed-form solution, the optimal demand (either positive or negative) for mortality-contingent claims is given by:

$$\lambda_{x+t}^{-1} I_t^* = \pi w - \delta g. \qquad (14.55)$$

Note that this expression has two components. The first term is the protection against human capital. The second term is purely driven by the extra HARA constant in the utility function and determines how to maintain the minimal level of consumption the family desires, both before and after death. This is the difference between CRRA and HARA utility.

There exists a critical wage level $w_c = \pi^{-1}\delta g$. When $W_t \geq w_c$, life insurance is desirable and demanded, but when the wage level is lower than w_c, the pension annuity is preferred. This does not occur under CRRA utility as there is no difference in consumption levels. In other words, the specification of a minimal consumption floor forces people to start buying annuities prior to the retirement date.

It is interesting to observe that the wealth level itself does not appear explicitly in the insurance/annuity demand or cost. Instead, it is determined by the instantaneous wage as well as the difference between g_d and g_l, which are the amounts of wealth set aside to guarantee the consumption needs specified by the floors c_d and c_l.

We now examine several special cases to show how these consumption floors affect the value of δg.

Uniform consumption floors: $c_l = c_d$. When $c_d = c_l$, we have $\delta g = 0$, or $g_l \equiv g_d$. In this case the optimal insurance payment is simply:

$$\lambda_{x+t}^{-1} I_t^* = \pi w, \tag{14.56}$$

which is the same as the CRRA. Thus, the level of consumption floor has no impact on the optimal amount of insurance. No annuity is necessary. In this case, the wealth level also has no effect.

Different consumption floors: $c_l > c_d$. When the consumption floors are different, $\delta g > 0$, therefore the level of optimal insurance is lower (annuity is higher). The actual amount is also affected by the mortality rate and two typical examples are next.

(i) **Constant λ_{x+t}.** When $\lambda_{x+t} = \lambda$. In this case we have:

$$\delta g = \frac{c_l - c_d}{r + \lambda} \left(1 - e^{-(r+\lambda)(\bar{H}-t)} \right) \tag{14.57}$$

(ii) **Gompertz mortality.** A more realistic mortality rate is the Gompertz rate:

$$\lambda_{x+t} = \lambda_0 + \frac{1}{b} e^{\frac{x+t-m}{b}} \tag{14.58}$$

Table 14.1(a) and (b). *Asset allocation and insurance as a function of theta*

	$\theta = 1$	$\theta = -1$	$\theta = 1$	$\theta = -1$	$\theta = 1$	$\theta = -1$
			(a)			
γ	1	1	3	3	6	6
α_t^*	10	19	2.4	7.8	0.52	5.0
$I_t^*/\lambda_{(x+t)}$	\$1,109	\$1,740	\$1,109	\$1,740	\$1,109	\$1,740
			(b)			
γ	1	1	3	3	6	6
α_t^*	2.7	8.8	0.13	4.0	-0.50	2.8
$I_t^*/\lambda_{(x+t)}$	\$829	\$1,216	\$829	\$1,216	\$829	\$1,216

Parameter values: $M_0 = \$200$, $W_0 = \$50$, $x = 45$, $\rho = 3\%$, $\mu_m = 10\%$, $\sigma_m = 20\%$, $\mu_w = 4\%$, $\sigma_w = 5\%$, retire at 65, death at 120. HARA ($c_d = \$20$, $c_l = \$25$).

In this case the solution for δg can be worked out as

$$\delta g = (c_d - c_l)be^{-(r+\lambda_0)(x+t-m)+e^{\frac{x+t-m}{b}}}$$
$$\times \left[\Gamma\left(-(r+\lambda_0)b, e^{\frac{y+\bar{R}-m}{b}}\right) - \Gamma\left(-(r+\lambda_0)b, e^{\frac{x+t-m}{b}}\right) \right].$$

Here the incomplete gamma function is defined as

$$\Gamma(a, b) = \int_b^\infty t^{1-a}e^{-t}dt.$$

Tables 14.1–14.3 provide summary results for the lifecycle model we have just presented for $\theta = \pm 1$. The solution for the more general case $-1 < \theta < 1$ can be obtained using the numerical method, which will be left as a possible student project.

Table 14.2(a) and (b). *Asset allocation and insurance for CRRA vs. HARA*

	$\theta = 1$	$\theta = -1$	$\theta = 1$	$\theta = -1$	$\theta = 1$	$\theta = -1$
			(a)			
γ	1	1	3	3	6	6
α_t^*	1967	4519	437	1883	55	1224
$I_t^*/\lambda_{(x+t)}$	\$1,310	\$1,740	\$1,310	\$1,740	\$1,310	\$1,740
			(b)			
γ	1	1	3	3	6	6
α_t^*	722	3274	22	1468	-153	1016
$I_t^*/\lambda_{(x+t)}$	\$1,213	\$2,162	\$1,213	\$2,162	\$1,213	\$2,162

Parameter values: $M_0 = \$1$, $W_0 = \$50$, $x = 35$, $\rho = 3\%$, $\mu_m = 10\%$, $\sigma_m = 20\%$, $\mu_w = 4\%$, $\sigma_w = 5\%$, retire at 65, death at 120. HARA ($c_d = \$20$, $c_l = \$25$).

Table 14.3(a) and (b). *Asset allocation and insurance for CRRA vs. HARA*

	$\theta = 1$	$\theta = -1$	$\theta = 1$	$\theta = -1$	$\theta = 1$	$\theta = -1$
			(a)			
γ	1	1	3	3	6	6
α_t^*	3.5	4.5	0.97	1.7	0.34	1.0
$I_t^*/\lambda_{(x+t)}$	$469	$559	$469	$559	$469	$559
			(b)			
γ	1	1	3	3	6	6
α_t^*	0.82	1.9	0.079	0.85	−0.11	0.60
$I_t^*/\lambda_{(x+t)}$	$427	$517	$427	$517	$427	$517

Parameter values: $M_0 = \$400$, $W_0 = \$50$, $x = 55$, $\rho = 3\%$, $\mu_m = 10\%$, $\sigma_m = 20\%$, $\mu_w = 4\%$, $\sigma_w = 5\%$, retire at 65, death at 120. HARA ($c_d = \$20$, $c_l = \$25$).

The main qualitative insights from our model are as follows. First, the optimal amount of life insurance and allocation to stocks depends on the correlation between wage shocks and the investment return on stocks. As we mentioned in the earlier part, by varying only the correlation between wage shocks and market shocks we are essentially comparing the demand for insurance and asset allocation for two individuals who have identical discounted value of wages (because the wage process parameters are the same). The economic value of their human capital is obviously different, as evidenced by the fact that the amount of life insurance is lower when the correlation is greater than zero. In other words, the lower amount of life insurance is a proxy for a reduced economic value of human capital. Indeed, if the economic value of human capital was the same, the amount of insurance would be the same as well.

For example, a forty-five-year-old who earns $50,000 per annum and who already has $200,000 in accumulated savings will optimally purchase between $829,000 and $1,216,000 of life insurance depending on the correlation between wages (i.e., human capital) and markets (financial capital). If this individual is working in a job/career whose wages profile is countercyclical to the financial market ($\theta = -1$), then the optimal amount of insurance is $1,216,000. On the other hand, if the wage profile is perfectly correlated with financial markets, the optimal amount of life insurance is a lower $829,000. The economic intuition for the impact of wage-market correlations on the optimal demand for insurance is that when human capital is highly correlated with financial capital, the **utility-adjusted value** (i.e., economic value) of human capital is much lower and hence the family requires less life insurance. Also, when the wage process is highly correlated with the returns from the risky asset, the allocation to financial risky asset is reduced to counteract the existing (and implicit) allocation to risky assets within the wage process. A number of other researchers – including the classic paper by Zvi Bodie, Robert Merton, and Robert Samuelson (1992) – confirm this. Notice, however, that the optimal face value life insurance, I_t^*/λ_{x+t}, does not vary with the risk aversion of the family in the case that the wage and investment returns are perfect (anti-) correlated. For example, when both consumption floors are zero, and assuming perfect wage to market correlation ($\theta = 1$), the optimal face value is approximately $1,109,000, which is more than twenty-two times the breadwinner's annual wage. This number is somewhat higher than the often-heard rule of thumb that people should have five–eight times their annual income in life insurance. Notice, however, that the amount of insurance goes down as consumption floors are increased, to $829,000. When we examine the numbers for a different scenario of a fifty-five-year-old retiree with $50,000 wage income and a financial wealth of $400,000, the optimal amounts of insurance are now $469,000 (CRRA) and $427,000 (HARA) for $\theta = 1$, which are about eight–nine times of the wage income. This is due to the reduction in human capital at a more advanced age.

Some might find it puzzling that our utility-based model does not predict even higher levels of life insurance for families that are more risk averse. On a theoretical level, it is important to remember that we did utilize fair actuarial pricing. In practice though, this invariance is fairly consistent with practitioner intuition when it comes to life insurance. Namely, a family should be protected with a minimal level of insurance regardless of how risk tolerant the family (or breadwinner) considers itself. Of course, risk tolerance and risk aversion have a very strong impact on the demand for the risky asset α_t^*, as one would expect. Families that are more risk tolerant will allocate more financial and marketable wealth to risky equities, in highly leveraged amounts, as evidenced by our numerical values of $\alpha_t^* \gg 1$.

Finally, we note that the results discussed here are based on the special cases where wage income and risky asset is either perfectly correlated or anti-correlated. For the more general case when the correlation is not perfect, we need to rely on numerical methods to find solutions. We have listed it as a possible class project for mathematically advanced students. In Table 14.4, we provide a snapshot of the results for a family when the breadwinner is relatively close to retirement (age fifty-five) with intermediate risk tolerance ($\gamma = 3$), when the correlation parameter θ varies between -1 and 1. As you can see, the qualitative picture remains unchanged. You tend to allocate more wealth into the risky asset and buy more insurance when the wage is

Table 14.4(a) and (b). *Asset allocation and insurance for CRRA vs. HARA*

	$\theta = -1$	$\theta = -0.5$	$\theta = 0$	$\theta = 0.5$	$\theta = 1$
			(a)		
α_t^*	1.75	1.51	1.31	1.14	0.977
$I_t^*/\lambda_{(x+t)}$	\$559	\$530	\$506	\$485	\$469
			(b)		
α_t^*	0.851	0.578	0.292	0.220	0.0815
$I_t^*/\lambda_{(x+t)}$	\$517	\$478	\$447	\$435	\$427

Parameter values: $\gamma = 3$, $M_0 = \$400$, $W_0 = \$50$, $x = 55$, $\rho = 3\%$, $\mu_m = 10\%$, $\sigma_m = 20\%$, $\mu_w = 4\%$, $\sigma_w = 5\%$, retire at 65, death at 120. HARA ($c_d = \$20$, $c_l = \$25$).

negatively correlated with the risky asset and less when the correlation is positive, whether there is a consumption floor or not.

14.8 Questions and Assignments

1. Verify the optimality conditions (14.19) and (14.20) and the solution c_t^* (14.24) in section 14.6.
2. Drive the closed form solutions (14.31) and (14.32) in section 14.6.
3. Find the solution of the asset allocation problem under HARA utility $u(m) = (m - \bar{m})^{1-\gamma}/(1 - \gamma)$ by maximizing terminal wealth, that is,

$$\max_{\alpha_t} E\left[u(M_T)| M_0 = m\right]$$

subject to the budget constraint

$$dM_t = [\alpha_t(\mu_m - r) + r]M_t dt + \alpha_t \sigma_m M_t dB_t.$$

Compare it with the solution using CRRA utility.

4. Find the solution of the optimal consumption problem under HARA utility $u(c) = (c - \bar{c}_t)^{1-\gamma}/(1 - \gamma)$ where $\bar{c}_t = \bar{c}_0 e^{\nu t}$ for a constant v,

$$\max_{\{\alpha_t, c_t\}} E\left[\int_0^T e^{-\rho t} u(c_t)dt| M_0 = m\right]$$

subject to the budget constraint

$$dM_t = [\alpha_t(\mu_m - r) + r]M_t dt + \alpha_t \sigma_m M_t dB_t - c_t dt.$$

5. Verify the closed-form solutions of the lifecycle model in section 14.7.
6. Using the parameter values related to Table 14.3, plot the critical wage $w_c = \pi^{-1}\delta g$ vs. time to retirement.

7. Derive the closed-form solution in the lifecycle model with pension income π_0 after retirement.
8. The optimal asset allocation and choice between risky and risk-free assets in a model with human capital included, depends critically on the covariance (or correlation) between shocks to the wage process and stock returns. This number obviously depends on your particular job and career prospects. Please discuss how you would go about doing calibration for this coefficient and what type of data you would need in order to get a statistically significant estimate.
9. (Project) In recent years, the so-called target date funds (TDFs) are becoming popular. These are mutual funds with a target date for the investors (usually retirement date) and typically start with a high risky to risk-free assets mix and slowly winding down to a lower ratio. The problem facing the investors is how to evaluate various available TDFs so that the **best** funds can be chosen. The objective of this project is to use a simplified version of the lifecycle model here to evaluate a given TDF by removing insurance and consumption in the accumulative stage (before retirement).
10. (Advanced Project) In the lifecycle model, closed-form solution cannot be obtained when the wage and risky asset is not perfectly correlated ($\theta = 1$) or anti-correlated ($\theta = -1$). When this is not the case, numerical methods have to be used to obtain the solution of the HJB equation. In this project, you will apply the method outlined in the technical appendix to find the numerical solution for:

   a. $\theta = \pm 1$ and compare it with the closed-form solutions; and
   b. $-1 < \theta < 1$ and verify the results in Table 14.4.

14.9 Technical Appendix

14.9.1 Elementary Stochastic Calculus in Finance

Here we list a few important results in stochastic calculus and intuitive interpretations. For a more detailed treatment, see Roberts (2009).

Brownian Motion
B_t is a Brownian motion (or a random walk, or a Weiner process) if it satisfies the following conditions:

- B_t is continuous;
- $B_0 = 0$;

- $B_{t+s} - B_s \sim N(0, t)$ for any $t, s \geq 0$;
- $B_{t+s} - B_s$ is independent of any details of the process earlier than s.

The key word here is **independent**. For example, one can define a stochastic process $Y_t = \sqrt{t}Z$ with $Z \sim N(0,1)$. This is **not** a Brownian motion because $Y_{t+s} - Y_s = (\sqrt{t+s} - \sqrt{s})Z$ is not independent of $Y_s = \sqrt{s}Z$. The other important fact about the Brownian motion is that it is time homogeneous, or **stationary**. In other words, if B_s is a Brownian motion, then $B_{s+t} - B_s$ is also a Brownian motion and can be written as B_t. The correct way to view B_{t+s} is that it is the sum of two independent quantities B_s and B_t. Let $s = t_1$ and $t_2 = s + t$ and $\Delta t = s = t_2 - t_1$; we can write $B_{t_2} = B_{t_1} + \Delta B_{t_1}$ where $\Delta B_{t_1} = B_s = B_{\Delta t}$. Of course we do not have to stop here. You can imagine that B_t is the accumulative sum of all the independent quantities $\Delta B_{t_i} = B_{\Delta t_i}$.

When the time intervals Δt_i are infinitesimally small, usually denoted by dt, we write $d B_t = B_{dt}$, which are the infinitesimal Brownian motion. This is an important step forward because when you have a finite step size Δt (we have dropped the subscript here to simplify notation), you need to keep the higher order terms with respect to Δt. For example, the j-th moment of ΔB_t can be computed as

$$E[(\Delta B_t)^j] = \frac{(2\Delta t)^{\frac{j}{2}} \Gamma\left(\frac{j+1}{2}\right)}{\Gamma\left(\frac{1}{2}\right)} \tag{14.59}$$

for an even j. (The j-th moment is zero when j is odd.) However, for $d B_t$, the j-th moment is nonzero only when $j = 2$, which is $E[(d B_t)^2] = dt$ because the higher order terms vanish. Therefore, $(d B_t)^2 = dt$ with probability one.

Ito's Calculus
Let B_t be a Brownian motion and $f(t, b)$ be a smooth function and $Y_t = f(t, B_t)$; then we have Ito's formula:

$$dY_t = \left(\frac{\partial f}{\partial t} + \frac{1}{2}\frac{\partial^2 f}{\partial b^2}\right)(t, B_t)dt + \frac{\partial f}{\partial b}(t, B_t)d B_t. \tag{14.60}$$

Here we have used b to denote the values (real numbers) that B_t can take. Compared to the deterministic case, there are two main differences: (1) there is the second-order term $\frac{\partial^2 f}{\partial b^2}$; and (2) there is the Brownian motion term $\frac{\partial f}{\partial b}(t, B_t)d B_t$.

At first glance, the Brownian motion part may be natural but the second-derivative term seems strange. To see how Ito's formula is actually a very natural result, we look at a similar situation with finite time step size Δt **formally** as opposed to **rigorous**,

$$
f(t + \Delta t, B_t + \Delta B_t) = f(t, B_t) + \frac{\partial f}{\partial t} \Delta t + \frac{\partial f}{\partial b} \Delta B_t
$$
$$
+ \frac{1}{2} \frac{\partial^2 f}{\partial t^2} (\Delta t)^2 + \frac{\partial f^2}{\partial t \partial b} \Delta t \Delta B_t + \frac{1}{2} \frac{\partial^2 f}{\partial b^2} (\Delta B_t)^2
$$
$$
+ h.o.t. \tag{14.61}
$$

We note that the mean and variance of the second-order term $\Delta t \Delta B_t$ is zero and $(\Delta t)^2$, which vanish as Δt becomes infinitesimally small. In fact, all the higher-order moments vanish as Δt becomes infinitesimally small, or when Δt is replaced by dt and ΔB_t replaced by dB_t. Thus, the term $dt\,dB_t = 0$ with probability one. Similarly, you can imagine similar things happen to other higher-order term denoted by $h.o.t$ except the term $(\Delta B_t)^2$, which has a mean Δt. However, even for this term, the higher-order moments are higher-order of Δt, which means that when Δt and ΔB_t are replaced by dt and dB_t, all the higher-order moments vanish and the mean is dt, or $(dB_t)^2 = dt$ with probability one.

Now we can take the leap and write

$$
dY_t := f(t + dt, B_t + dB_t) - f(t, B_t) = \frac{\partial f}{\partial t} dt + \frac{\partial f}{\partial b} dB_t + \frac{1}{2} \frac{\partial^2 f}{\partial b^2} dt
$$
$$
\tag{14.62}
$$

and combine the two dt terms, we obtain Ito's formula as stated earlier.

Using a similar approach, we can now write down Ito's formula in a more general form, known as Ito's lemma. Let $dZ_t = \mu dt + \sigma dB_t$ and $Y_t = f(t, Z_t)$ where $f(t, z)$ is a smooth function, we have the following formula:

$$
dY_t = \left(\frac{\partial f}{\partial t} dt + \mu \frac{\partial f}{\partial z} + \frac{\sigma^2}{2} \frac{\partial^2 f}{\partial z^2} \right) dt + \mu \frac{\partial f}{\partial z} dB_t. \tag{14.63}
$$

Here μ and σ can be functions of time t as well as Z_t in general.

This is the formula we will use in the rest of this technical appendix. Although the actual details may vary, the basic idea remains the same. You expand the function $f(t + dt, Z_t + dZ_t)$ into a Taylor series, keeping the first-order terms, and the only higher-order term that remains is the one involving $(dB_t)^2$. Before we move on, we note that the differential form of

Ito's formula can be viewed as a short-hand notation of the integral term

$$f(b, Z_b) - f(a, Z_a) = \int_a^b \left(\frac{\partial f}{\partial t} dt + \mu \frac{\partial f}{\partial z} + \frac{\sigma^2}{2} \frac{\partial^2 f}{\partial z^2} \right) dt + \int_a^b \mu \frac{\partial f}{\partial z} dB_t$$

(14.64)

where the hand-waving arguments and intuitions we have provided here (and in the rest of the technical appendix) can be made precise. We will use either formula whenever it is more convenient for the discussion.

14.9.2 Stochastic Dynamic Optimization

Here we present the basic idea of stochastic dynamic optimization. Suppose that we have at our disposal a **control** that is a function of time, denoted by c_t. The action of the control will change the state, Z_t, which is given by the following SDE:

$$dZ_t = \mu(t, c_t, Z_t)dt + \sigma(t, c_t, Z_t)dB_t$$

(14.65)

where μ and σ are given functions with desirable properties. Note that we have assumed that the control as well as state functions are scalars for simplicity purposes. Our objective is to find c_t to maximize the conditional expected value in the form of

$$E \left[\int_a^b \phi(t, c_t, Z_t)dt + \phi(Z_T) | Z_0 = z \right].$$

(14.66)

Let

$$J(t, z) = \max_{c_s} E \left[\int_t^b \phi(s, c_s, Z_s)ds + \phi(Z_T) | Z_t = z \right].$$

(14.67)

Bellman's principle of optimality says that

$$J(t, z) = \max_{c_s} E \left[\int_t^{\hat{t}} \psi(s, c_s, Z_s)ds + J(\hat{t}, Z_{\hat{t}}) | Z_t = z \right]$$

(14.68)

for any $a \le t < \hat{t} \le b$.

Applying Ito's lemma,

$$J(\hat{t}, Z_{\hat{t}}) = J(t, Z_t) + \int_t^{\hat{t}} \mathcal{L}J(s, c_s, Z_s)ds + \int_t^{\hat{t}} \sigma \frac{\partial J}{\partial z} dB_s$$

(14.69)

where

$$\mathcal{L}J(t, c_t, Z_t) = \frac{\partial J}{\partial t} + \mu \frac{\partial J}{\partial z} + \frac{1}{2} \sigma^2 \frac{\partial^2 J}{\partial z^2}.$$

(14.70)

Substitute it into Bellman's principle, we have

$$J(t, z) = \max_{c_s} E\left[J(t, Z_t) + \int_t^{\hat{t}} [\psi(s, c_s, Z_s) + \mathcal{L}J(s, c_s, Z_s)]ds \right.$$

$$\left. + \int_t^{\hat{t}} \sigma \frac{\partial J}{\partial z} dB_s | Z_t = z \right]. \tag{14.71}$$

Because $E[J(t, Z_t)|Z_t = z)] = J(t, z)$ and

$$E\left[\int_t^{\hat{t}} \sigma \frac{\partial J}{\partial z} dB_s | Z_t = z \right] = 0,$$

we obtain the following equation:

$$0 = \max_{c_s} E\left[\int_t^{\hat{t}} [\psi(s, c_s, Z_s) + \mathcal{L}J(s, c_s, Z_s)]ds | Z_t = z \right]. \tag{14.72}$$

Using the fact that this equation is valid for all $\hat{t} > t$, we conclude that the integrand must be zero at $s = t$, and we obtain the Hamilton-Jacobi-Bellman (HJB) equation

$$\max_{c_t} \psi(t, c_t, z) + \mathcal{L}J(t, c_t, z) = 0. \tag{14.73}$$

From the definition, we have the terminal condition by setting $t = b$, $J(b, z) = \psi(z)$.

For derivations of HJB using stochastic optimal control approach for optimal asset allocation and consumption problems, we refer the readers to Bjork (2004) and the paper by Huang and Milevsky (2008) and references therein.

14.9.3 Finite Difference Method for Solving the HJB Equation

The closed-form solution obtained in this chapter is useful because it provides useful insights as well as a calibration benchmark for special cases. For more general cases, closed-form solutions are no longer available and we must use numerical means to find approximate solutions. Obviously one can apply a numerical method to the two-dimensional HJB equation directly, and this has been done by others. However, if one can locate a similarity variable and reduce the dimension of the equation, numerical solutions can be obtained more efficiently. A helpful technique is to take the ratio between the wage w and the wealth m as the main variable and then apply the similarity-reduction technique. Here we use a more general similarity variable:

$$y = \frac{w}{\hat{m}} \qquad (14.74)$$

where $\hat{m} = m + \pi w - g_l(t)$ is the adjusted wealth including the human capital portion (πw). We then seek solution in the form of:

$$J(t, m, w) = \frac{\hat{m}^{1-\gamma} F(t, y)}{1 - \gamma}. \qquad (14.75)$$

Note that $\hat{m}$ is always positive. Thus, the approach used here is valid for all financially relevant scenarios, including the case of $m < g_l$ or even $m < 0$. After algebraic manipulations, we obtain a simplified one-dimensional equation for F:

$$F_t + c_0 F + c_1 y F_y + c_2 y^2 F_{yy} = 0 \qquad (14.76)$$

where the subscripts t and y denote the partial derivatives with respect to that variable. The terminal condition is given at retirement $\bar{R}$,

$$F(y, \bar{R}) = h(\bar{R}).$$

This is a second-order nonlinear partial differential equation because the coefficients are functions of the F_y and F_{yy} as well as y and t, as shown next.

$$c_0 = -\lambda_{x+t} + (1 - \gamma)(\mu_m - r)\beta\pi y + \gamma(\hat{c} + \lambda_{x+t}\hat{I})$$
$$+ (1 - \gamma)(\lambda_{x+t} + r) + (1 - \gamma)\hat{\alpha}(\mu_m - r) \qquad (14.77)$$
$$- \frac{\gamma(1 - \gamma)}{2} \left[(\sigma_w \pi y + \rho\hat{\alpha}\sigma_m)^2 + (1 - \rho^2)(\hat{\alpha}\sigma_m)^2 \right] \qquad (14.78)$$

$$c_1 = -(\mu_m - r)\beta\pi y - \frac{\gamma}{1 - \gamma}(\hat{c} + \lambda_{x+t}\hat{I}) - (\lambda_{x+t} + r) - \hat{\alpha}(\mu_m - r)$$
$$+ \frac{\gamma}{2} \left\{ (\sigma_w \pi y + \rho\hat{\alpha}\sigma_m)^2 + [\sigma_w(\pi y - 1) + \rho\hat{\alpha}\sigma_m]^2 \right.$$
$$+ 2(1 - \rho^2)(\hat{\alpha}\sigma_m)^2 - \sigma_w^2 \} \qquad (14.79)$$
$$+ \mu_w \qquad (14.80)$$

$$c_2 = \frac{1}{2} \left\{ [\sigma_w(\pi y - 1) + \rho\hat{\alpha}\sigma_m]^2 + (1 - \rho^2)(\hat{\alpha}\sigma_m)^2 \right\} \qquad (14.81)$$

and

$$\hat{c} := \frac{c_t^* - c_l}{\hat{m}} = e^{-\frac{\rho}{\gamma}t}G^{-\frac{1}{\gamma}} \tag{14.82}$$

$$\hat{I} := \frac{\lambda_{x+t}^{-1}I_t^* + m - g_d}{\hat{m}} = h^{\frac{1}{\gamma}}G^{-\frac{1}{\gamma}} \tag{14.83}$$

$$\hat{\alpha} := \frac{\alpha_t^* m}{\hat{m}} = \frac{\frac{\mu_m - r}{\sigma_m^2}G + \beta y G_y}{\gamma G + y G_y} - \beta \pi y \tag{14.84}$$

and

$$G = F - \frac{y F_y}{1 - \gamma}, \quad H = \pi G + \frac{F_y}{1 - \gamma}. \tag{14.85}$$

To solve the equation (14.76) numerically, we use a one-step backward Euler method for the time discretization and central and upwind difference formulas to approximate F_{yy} and F_y, respectively. Our method is semi-implicit because controls (14.82)–(14.84) are computed using the solution at the previous time step:

$$\frac{F_j^{n+1} - F_j^n}{\Delta t} + c_0 F_j^n + \frac{c_1 + |c_1|}{2} y_j \frac{F_{j+1}^n - F_j^n}{\Delta y} + \frac{c_1 - |c_1|}{2} y_j \frac{F_j^n - F_{j-1}^n}{\Delta y}$$
$$+ c_2 y_j^2 \frac{F_{j+1}^n + F_{j-1}^n - 2F_j^n}{(\Delta y)^2} = 0 \tag{14.86}$$

where F_j^n is an approximation to $F(t_n, y_j)$ on the grid points (t_n, y_j). The semi-infinite domain $0 < y < \infty$ is truncated into a finite one $0 \leq y \leq y_{max}$. The main challenge is to find numerical boundary conditions at the computational boundaries $y = 0$ and $y = y_{max}$. One possibility is to apply the asymptotic relation $F_y = 0$. The discrete system for F is then solved using a so-called tridiagonal solver.

FIFTEEN

Concluding Thoughts and Next Steps

The last two chapters might have been a bit more than what you were expecting (or bargaining for) from a book on personal financial planning. Indeed, when we mention the terms *Ito's lemma, control theory,* or *diffusion processes* to graduate students and university colleagues – when asked about the tools of our research trade – they immediately assume that we work in the esoteric field of option pricing or derivative hedging. For most of the 1980s and 1990s that would have been the only conclusion to draw, but not anymore.

Indeed, most people are surprised to learn that one can actually use these mathematical concepts to analyze and provide guidance on *practical questions* such as how much and which type of life insurance you should purchase, the best age at which to start drawing a retirement pension annuity, or the optimal home mortgage loan for their family. Indeed, the models of quantitative finance that spawned a revolution in the 1970s and 1980s, which then filtered through to corporate finance and strategy in the 1980s and 1990s, have arrived at your personal doorstep in the last decade or two. The objective is crystal clear: to use the concept of "consumption smoothing" – in all its mathematical glory – to help individuals make better personal wealth and risk management decisions. We call it strategic financial planning (SFP) over the lifecycle. In the last decade financial luminaries such as Harry Markowitz, William Sharpe, and Robert Merton have penned articles, given presentations, and encouraged research on this same topic.

Our main objective in this book was to give the reader a taste of these developments and how to "think" about personal finance from a more financial and economic perspective. Let us bring this book to a conclusion by summarizing and reviewing some of the main ideas as well as offering some suggestions about interesting and current problems that might appeal to graduate students who perhaps are looking for research topics in the future.

Let us take one final random walk over the human lifecycle.

15.1 Portfolio Selection with Human Capital

Although classical Markowitz theory and the ubiquitous efficient frontier predates much of modern financial economics, the application of this concept to human capital and broader wealth management has only started recently. Recall from Chapter 3 that to appreciate the value of human capital and its role in portfolio selection, you must imagine an individual investor as a small, privately held, and poorly diversified corporation called You, Inc.

In contrast to Financial Accounting Standard Board (FASB) or Generally Accepted Accounting Principles (GAAP) standards applied to publicly traded companies, we place an asset called human capital on the left-hand side of the personal balance sheet. Human capital is the measure of the present value of future wages, income, and salary that will be earned over the human lifecycle. Sure, you cannot really touch, feel, or see human capital. However, like an oil reserve deep under the ocean, it will eventually be extracted, and so it is definitely worth something today. That was one of the main points in this book. More importantly, it has its own risk and return characteristics and can be modeled as a random variable that is correlated with a variety of economic factors. In fact, you can think of your human capital as a continuous-time stochastic process that is subject to unpredictable jumps and discontinuities. This process pays a lumpy stream of dividends and eventually converges to zero – if you are still alive. Your objective is to maximize these dividends in some risk-adjusted manner. Remember that you can control your human-capital process by investing in education, making prudent career choices, and eating healthy. We provided a flavor of this advanced way of thinking in Chapter 14.

With this preliminary framework in mind, recall that the Markowitz paradigm dictates that total capital – both human and financial – should be properly diversified and *consumed evenly over the course of the lifecycle.* Thus, in the early stages of the lifecycle, financial capital and investments should be used to hedge and diversify human capital. Think of investable assets as a defense against adverse salaries and wages as opposed to an isolated pot of money that has to be allocated.

To understand the implications of modeling human capital as a random variable, let us revisit the example we gave earlier in the book. For tenured university professors such as ourselves, human capital – and the subsequent defined benefit pensions we are entitled to – has the risk and return properties of a fixed-income bond fund paying monthly coupons. In a sense, we are an inflation-adjusted real return bond. Therefore, we have very little need for fixed-income bonds, money market funds, and other guaranteed products in our discretionary financial (retirement savings) portfolio. In fact, much of our personal savings are quite heavily invested in individual equities and broad-based investment funds. The opposite advice would be relevant for the MBA and other graduate students we teach, who intend to work in the financial services sector when they graduate.

Thus, one of the fertile areas of research in this field – which we touched upon in Chapters 9 and 10 – evolves around how to construct a financial portfolio and where to invest your personal savings so that your total portfolio is properly diversified. This line of research examines the wage profile of various career occupations and then models their covariation with general financial markets to arrive at tailor-made investment solutions based on unique idiosyncratic factors. This goes far beyond tailoring personalized investment portfolios for dentists, lawyers, and doctors. The ideas can be used to examine and think about a number of other issues.

15.2 Asset Location vs. Asset Allocation

Although income tax regulations are country specific – and we focused primarily on Canada for the numerical examples in this book – most all jurisdictions around the world offer individual tax shelters and concessions for long-term savings in which capital gains, dividends, and even interest income is tax-deferred. These products might also be associated with personal pension plans or be part of standalone life insurance and saving policies. Regardless of the exact substance or form, these strategies often leave individual investors with a difficult decision regarding which assets should be subjected to which tax treatment. This is known as the *asset location* problem as opposed to *asset allocation* problem, which has spawned yet another interesting avenue of research within strategic financial planning. From a mathematical point of view, these multi-period optimization problems are highly path-dependent due to the peculiar tax asymmetries, and they quickly escalate in dimensionality. For example, in general the gains on a stock are usually taxed more favorably compared to gains on a bond. However, if they are placed within tax shelters and held for short periods of time the situation might be reversed, especially when considering that loss cannot be deducted or used to reduce income tax liabilities.

Indeed, personal income taxes can severely distort optimal trading, hedging, and investment strategies to a point far beyond the perfect and frictionless markets envisioned by the purists.

15.3 Home Mortgage Financing

Beyond investment and portfolio issues, most individuals purchase a personal residence at some point in their lives, yet very few have the liquid wealth to pay for this transaction in cash. Mortgage financing is usually the way in which this leveraged positioned is accomplished, and we described this process in Chapters 5 and 11. Just like publicly traded companies face a myriad of choices between fixed- and floating-rate obligations in their capital structure, so too individuals must decide on the composition and characteristics of their debt. Depending on the jurisdiction and country, consumers must decide whether to go "long" or "short" term, or whether to "close" or leave "open" their home mortgages. In some cases, individuals must further decide whether to borrow in real (after-inflation) or nominal terms or whether to link their payments to a given index. In all of these personal deliberations, a robust and dynamic model for the evolution of the term-structure of interest rate is required. In most of this book, the interest (or valuation) rate was constant and known throughout life. That was only the start. Moreover, these models must do more than explain the evolution of the curve over short periods of time, akin to what an option trader might need. They must also provide realistic long-term forecasts and risk metrics taking into account the option to default, prepay, and move. The presence of complex penalties and prepayment charges further fuels the demand for rigorous and sound advice. This too is a fertile area of research.

15.4 Life and Health Insurance

Personal risk management is an exercise in protecting human as well as financial capital. We covered this in Chapters 7 and 8. Recall that both forms of capital should diversify each other. So too property insurance should be viewed as a hedge against the loss of financial capital, and life insurance should be treated as a hedge against the unsupportable loss – to the surviving family – of human capital. Thus, all forms of life, health, and disability insurance should not be acquired as an investment; rather they are purchased for their hedging properties. If something happens to human capital, the insurance will pay off. However, if nothing (bad) happens to human capital, the insurance will perform poorly. Insurance is an asset class with a negative expected rate of return (on a pre-tax basis, at least), but nevertheless forms part of the optimal portfolio because of the negative correlation matrix. The concept might sound simple but the broad menu of insurance choices available – such as term life, whole life, and universal life, to name a few – generates yet another difficult portfolio selection problem. In many cases, insurance products provide guaranteed renewability and contain implicit options on mortality tables. Adverse selection, which is at the heart of insurance pricing, becomes an optimal strategy in its own right. In this book we obviously just touched the surface.

15.5 Employee Compensation and Proper Incentives

A more mathematical approach to strategic financial planning can also lend insights into the optimal design of employment compensation contracts. The trend toward company stock-linked compensation and incentive stock options creates a need for normative advice on optimal exercise strategies in the presence of highly illiquid and concentrated portfolios. Furthermore, if granting more options to a greater number of employees only serves to increase their risk profile, the incentive effects might be counterproductive. A sound mathematical model of the trade-off between the various risk factors is required for a careful analysis. Indeed, the recent accounting debate surrounding the cost of an incentive stock option must be prefaced on a solid understanding of how individuals value these illiquid instruments. If individuals seek a smooth consumption plan over their lives, how do companies create optimal contracts that compensate employees for sharing their human capital?

15.6 Choice of Defined Benefit vs. Defined Contribution Pensions

For many years, the venerable defined benefit (DB) pension plan was the mainstay of retirement pension provision. An individual worked for the same company during his or her entire life, and earned a pension annuity based on career average earnings and/or the number of years of credited service. As we explained in Chapter 12, in DB plans the "risk" was borne by the employer who had to provide and support the guarantee. However, over the last ten to fifteen years, there has been a sharp and noticeable shift toward defined contribution (DC) pension provisions around the world. Under these plans, the employee is entitled to fixed periodic contribution and has full control over its allocation, but the risk is squarely in the hands of the employee as well. Although it is debatable what is best for individuals at which point in their life, the transition process from DB to DC often involves a number of choices that lend themselves to mathematical modeling. For example, what is the value of the option to choose which plan to belong to? Or what is the optimal mix between DB and DC plans from a portfolio perspective? Yet another question to ponder in the growing world of mathematics of personal finance.

15.7 Starting a Retirement Pension Annuity

The decision of when to retire can lead to some fascinating and complicated optimal stopping problems. On the one hand, we have the illiquidity and irreversibility of a pension annuity that would lead people to delay annuitization. On the other hand, we are faced with lifetime uncertainty and the desire to hedge against longevity risk. A number of recent models have been developed to help consumers understand and appreciate these trade-offs. Once again, we must turn to a holistic risk and wealth management framework to provide proper guidance. The models we presented in Chapter 14 can easily be modified to address these and similar questions.

15.8 Estate Planning and Tax Arbitrage

Many countries impose estate and wealth taxes on individuals upon their demise. The United States is a good example of such a system. While death and taxes are truly unavoidable, the ability to minimize the impact of the former on the latter is a rich and fertile endeavor for many lawyers and accountants specializing in estate transfers. Interestingly, a number of provisions within the tax code allow for mortality and tax arbitrage by allowing portions of the estate to escape taxation. The precise construction and implementation of these strategies often comes down to satisfying certain internal rate of return criteria or probabilistic thresholds that, once again, fall naturally within the domain of the tools we presented in Chapters 13 and 14. (Can a course called Ito Calculus for Attorneys be far behind?)

15.9 The Real Options in Your Life

From a broader perspective, many of the previously mentioned optimization problems involve an element of timing and irreversibility, both of which bring to mind the classical call and put option analogy. You might recall from the field of option pricing that American options differ from their

European counterpart in that one can choose when to exercise the option. Taking this concept further, we can frame many decisions – financial as well as non-financial ones – that people face over their life as option-pricing problems. Viewed from this perspective, the optimal career, time to purchase a house, and even age at which to get married, have children, and get divorced all become an exercise in American option pricing, or at the very least a dynamic programming problem. Time constraints prevent an in-depth elaboration, but one can imagine the numerous additional applications.

Indeed, one of the defining features of control-theoretic personal finance (for lack of a better term) is that, in contrast to the recent work in behavioral financial economics that sheds light on the psychological biases that lead to consistent human mistakes, our book advocates a normative prescriptive approach by trying to help people make better *strategic personal financial decisions*.

What follows in our bibliography is a list of some classical as well as more recent articles and books – some elementary and some advanced – covering many of the areas discussed herein.

Bibliography

Babbel, David F. and Eisaku Ohtsuka (1989), Aspects of Optimal Multiperiod Life Insurance, *Journal of Risk and Insurance*, Vol. 56, 460–481.

Bayraktar, E. and V. R. Young (2007), Correspondence between Lifetime Minimum Wealth and Utility of Consumption, *Finance and Stochastics*, Vol. 11(2), 213–236.

Becker, G. (1993), *Human Capital: A Theoretical and Empirical Analysis with Special Reference to Education* (3rd edition), The University of Chicago Press.

Benartzi, S. and R. H. Thaler (2001), Naive Diversification Strategies in Defined Contribution Savings Plans, *American Economic Review*, Vol. 91, 79–98.

Benartzi, S. and R. H. Thaler (2002), How Much Is Investor Autonomy Worth?, *The Journal of Finance*, Vol. 57(4), 1593–1616.

Bjork, T. (2004), *Arbitrage Theory in Continuous Time*, Oxford University Press, New York.

Bodie, Z. (1990), Pensions as Retirement Income Insurance, *Journal of Economic Literature*, Vol. 28, 28–49.

Bodie, Z., Merton, R. C., and Samuelson, W. (1992), Labor Supply Flexibility and Portfolio Choice in a Life Cycle Model, *Journal of Economic Dynamics and Control*, Vol. 16, 427–449.

Butler, M. (2001), Neoclassical life-cycle consumption: A textbook example, *Economic Theory*, Vol. 17, 209–221.

Cairns, A. J. G., Blake, D., and Dowd, K. (2006), Stochastic lifestyling: Optimal dynamic asset allocation for defined contribution pension plans, *Journal of Economic Dynamics and Control*, Vol. 30, 843–877.

Campbell, J. and Viciera, L. (2002), *Strategic Asset Allocation: Portfolio Choice for Long-Term Investors*, Oxford University Press, New York.

Campbell, J. Y., J. F. Cocco, F. J. Gomez, and P. J. Maenhout (2001), Investing Retirement Wealth, in A Life-Cycle Model, in *Risk Aspects of Investment-Based Social Security Reform*, 439–482, National Bureau of Economic Research.

Charupat, N. and Milevsky, M. A. (2001), Mortality swaps and tax arbitrage in the Canadian annuity and insurance market, *The Journal of Risk and Insurance*, Vol. 68(2), 124–147.

Cocco, J., F. Gomes, and P. Maenhout (2005), Portfolio choice over the life-cycle, *Review of Financial Studies*, Vol. 18, 491–533.

Constantinides, G. (1979), A Note on the Suboptimality of Dollar-Cost Averaging as an Investment Policy, *Journal of Financial and Quantitative Analysis*, Vol. 14(2), 443–450.

Daly, M. J. (1981), The role of registered retirement savings plans in a life-cycle model, *Canadian Journal of Economics*, Vol. 14(3), 409–421.

Dammon, R. M., C. S. Spatt, and H. H. Zhang (2001), Optimal Consumption and Investment with Capital Gains Taxes, *Review of Financial Studies*, Vol. 14(3), 583–616.

Davies, J. B. (1981), Uncertain lifetime, consumption, and dissaving in retirement, *Journal of Political Economy*, Vol. 89, 561–577.

Deaton, A. (1991), Saving and liquidity constraints, *Econometrica*, Vol. 59(5), 1221–1124.

Dybvig, P. H. (1995), Dusenberry's Racheting of Consumption: Optimal Dynamic Consumption and Investment Given Intolerance for any Decline in Standard of Living, *The Review of Economic Studies*, Vol. 62(2), 287–313.

Fischer, S. (1973), A life cycle model of life insurance purchases, *International Economic Review*, Vol. 14(1), 132–152.

Fisher, I. (1930), *The Theory of Interest: As Determined by Impatience to Spend Income and Opportunity to Invest It*, Macmillan, New York.

Friedman, A. (1957), *A Theory of the Consumption Function*, National Bureau of Economic Research, New York and Princeton University Press.

Friedman, A. and W. Shen (2002), A variational inequality approach to financial valuation of retirement benefits based on salary, *Finance and Stochastics*, Vol. 6(3), 273–302.

Gallmeyer, M. F., R. Kaniel, and S. Tompaidis (2006), Tax management strategies with multiple risky assets, *Journal of Financial Economics*, Vol. 80, 243–291.

Garlapp, L. and G. Skoulakis (2010), Solving Consumption and Portfolio Choice Problems: The State Variable Decomposition Method, *Review of Financial Studies*, Vol. 23(9), 3346–3400.

Goetzmann, W. N. (1993), The Single Family Home in the Investment Portfolio, *Journal of Real Estate Finance and Economics*, Vol. 6, 201–222.

Gomes, F., A. Michaelides, and V. Polkovnichenko (2009), Optimal savings with taxable and tax deferred accounts, *Review of Economic Dynamics*, Vol. 12, 718–735.

Hakansson, N. H. (1969), Optimal investment and consumption strategies under risk, an uncertain lifetime, and insurance, *International Economic Review*, Vol. 10, 443–466.

Horan, S. M. (2006), Withdrawal location with progressive tax rates, *Financial Analysts Journal*, Vol. 62(6), 77–87.

Horneff, W. J., Maurer, R. H., and Stamos, M. Z. (2008), Lifecycle asset allocation with annuity markets, *Journal of Economic Dynamics and Control*, Vol. 32, 3590–3612.

Huang, H. and Milevsky, M. A. (2008), Portfolio Choice and Mortality-Contingent Claims: The General HARA Case, *Journal of Banking and Finance*, Vol. 32, 2444–2452.

Ibbotson, R. G., Milevsky, M. A., Chen, P., and Zhu, Z. (2007), *Lifetime Financial Advice: Human Capital, Asset Allocation, and Insurance*, The Research Foundation of the CFA Institute, Charlottesville, Virginia.

Kau, J. B., with D. Keenan, W. Muller, and J. Epperson (1990), The Analysis and Valuation of Adjustable Rate Mortgages, *Management Science*, Vol. 36(12), 1417–1431.

Koo, H. K. (1998), Consumption and Portfolio Selection with Labor Income: A Continuous Time Approach, *Mathematical Finance*, Vol. 8(1), 49–65.

Kotlikoff, L. J. and A. Spivak (1981), The Family as an Incomplete Annuities Market, *The Journal of Political Economy*, Vol. 89(2), 372–391.

Kotlikoff, L. (March 2008), Economics' Approach to Financial Planning, Boston University working paper and *Journal of Financial Planning*, Vol. 21, 5–10.

Lachance, M. (2012). Optimal onset and exhaustion of retirement savings in a life-cycle model, *Journal of Pension Economics and Finance*, Vol. 11(1), 21–52.

Leung, S. F. (1994), Uncertain Lifetime, the Theory of the Consumer and the Life Cycle Hypothesis, *Econometrica*, Vol. 62(5), 1233–1239.

Leung, S. F. (2007), The existence, uniqueness, and optimality of the terminal wealth depletion time in life-cycle models of saving under certain lifetime and borrowing constraint, *Journal of Economic Theory*, Vol. 134, 470–493.

Markowitz, H. M. (1991), Individual versus Institutional Investing, *Financial Services Review*, Vol. 1(1), 9–22.

Martin-Jimenez, S. and A. R. Sanchez Martin (2007), An evaluation of the life cycle effects of minimum pensions on retirement behavior, *Journal of Applied Econometrics*, Vol. 22, 923–950.

Merton, R. C. (1969), Lifetime portfolio selection under uncertainty: The continuous time case, *Review of Economic Studies*, Vol. 51, 247–257.

Merton, R. C. (1971), Optimum consumption and portfolio rules in a continuous time model, *Journal of Economic Theory*, Vol. 3, 373–413.

Merton, R. C. (1990), *Continuous-Time Finance*, Blackwell Publishing, Oxford, UK.

Milevsky, M. A. (2006), *The Calculus of Retirement Income: Financial Models for Life Insurance and Pension Annuities*, Cambridge University Press, UK.

Milevsky, M. A. and H. Huang (2011), Spending Retirement on Planet Vulcan: The Impact of Longevity Risk Aversion on Optimal Withdrawal Rates, *Financial Analysts Journal*, Vol. 67(2), 45–58.

Milevsky, M. A. and V. R. Young (2007), Annuitization and asset allocation, *Journal of Economic Dynamics and Control*, Vol. 31, 3138–3177.

Modigliani, F. (1986), Life cycle, individual thrift, and the wealth of nations, *The American Economic Review*, Vol. 76(3), 297–313.

Modigliani, F. and R. Brumberg (1954), Utility analysis and the consumption function: An interpretation of cross-section data, in *Post Keynesian Economics*, 338–436, New Brunswick, Rutgers University Press.

Olshansky, S. J. and B. A. Carnes (1997), Ever since Gompertz, *Demography*, Vol. 34(1), 1–15.

Olshansky, S. J., B. A. Carnes, and C. Cassel (1990), In search of Methuselah: Estimating the upper limits to human longevity, *Science*, Vol. 250, 634–640.

Poterba, J. (2001), Estate and Gift Taxes and Incentives for Inter Vivos Giving in the U.S., *Journal of Public Economics*, Vol. 79, 237–264.

Pratt, J. W. (1964), Risk aversion in the small and in the large, *Econometrica*, Vol. 32, 122–136.

Ramsey, F. P. (1928), A mathematical theory of saving, *The Economic Journal*, Vol. 38(152), 543–559.

Reichenstein, W. (2001), Asset allocation and asset location decisions revisited, *Journal of Wealth Management*, Vol. 4(1), 16–26.

Richard, S. (1975), Optimal consumption, portfolio and life insurance rules for an uncertain lived individual in a continuous time model, *The Journal of Financial Economics*, Vol. 2, 187–203.

Roberts, A. J. (2009), *Elementary Calculus of Financial Mathematics*, SIAM, Philadelphia.

Samuelson, P. A. (1969), Lifetime portfolio selection by dynamic stochastic programming, *Review of Economics and Statistics*, Vol. 51, 239–246.

Sheshinski, E. (2008), *The Economic Theory of Annuities*, Princeton University Press, New Jersey.

Smith, M. L. (1982), The Life Insurance Policy as an Options Package, *Journal of Risk and Insurance*, Vol. 49, 583–601.

Stanton, R. (2000), From cradle to grave: How to loot a 401(k) plan, *Journal of Financial Economics*, Vol. 56, 485–516.

Stock, J. H. and D. A. Wise (1990), Pensions, the option value of work, and retirement, *Econometrica*, Vol. 58(5), 1151–1180.

Sundaresan, S. and F. Zapatero (1997), Valuation, optimal asset allocation, and retirement incentives of pension plans, *Review of Financial Studies*, Vol. 10(3), 631–660.

Yaari, M. E. (1965), Uncertain lifetime, life insurance, and the theory of the consumer, *Review of Economic Studies*, Vol. 32, 137–150.

Yagi, T. and Y. Nishigaki (1993), The inefficiency of private constant annuities, *The Journal of Risk and Insurance*, Vol. 60 (September, 3), 385–412.

Index

asset classes (*cont.*)
  commodities. *See* commodities
  correlations among, 194, 194t, 221
  diversification and, 194–197
  equities. *See* equities
  historical returns, 191–194

balance sheets, personal, 28-33, 29t, 30t, 38t
balanced funds, 198
bankruptcy, 229, 233
Bellman principle, 312, 341
benchmark case, 269, 273
Bengen, B., 255
bequests, 298
Bernoulli distribution, 209
Bernoulli utility, 263
binomial distributions, 210
blended payments, 81
Bodie, Z., 336
bonds
  assets and, 30n1
  balance sheet and, 28, 29t, 30
  balanced funds and, 198
  default risk, 187
  discount rate and, 37
  fixed income and, 187
  human capital and, 196
  interest income and, 115
  interest-rate risk and, 188
  junk bonds, 198
  mutual funds and, 187
  portfolio and, 202
  real-return bonds, 254, 347
  risks and, 187, 188
  RRSPs and, 132
  safety and, 115
  self-directed plans and, 128
  taxes and, 115
  terms of, 187, 192
  TFSAs and, 132
  TIPS and, 254
borrowing. *See* debt
brachistochrone problem, 279, 310
Brownian motion
  asset price model and, 317
  geometric (GBM), 326
  models for, 339–341
Brumberg, R., 2
budget constraint, 58

CAGR. *See* compound annual growth rate
calculus of variations, 266–314
  brachistochrone problem and, 279, 310

Brownian motion and. *See* Brownian
  motion
Euler-Lagrange equation and, 281, 293,
  303, 310, 313
first-order condition, 280–281
perturbations and, 280
Canada Mortgage and Housing
  Corporation (CMHC), 84
Canada Pension Plan (CPP), 104
  death benefits and, 160–161
  OAS and, 243–244
  RRSPs and, 126
Canada Revenue Agency (CRA), 116
Canadian Bank Act, 79
capital gains/losses, 119–120
  Canada and, 104, 119
  index funds and, 192
  RRSPs and, 129
  taxes on, 119–120, 126, 189
  See also specific types
cash equivalents, 186–187
cash-value life insurance, 161, 179
central limit theorem, 212–214
CMHC. *See* Canada Mortgage and Housing
  Corporation
commodities, 186–191
compound annual growth rate (CAGR),
  193
constant-growth annuities, 14
  annuity due and, 18–21
  delayed (DGOAs), 16, 53
constant relative risk aversion (CRRA), 282,
  330, 334t
consumption, 263, 291
  age and, 60t, 62, 63t, 64t, 69t, 71t
  asset-allocation and, 315–316, 321–324
  assumptions for, 49–50
  consumption floor, 330, 333
  discretionary, 51–55, 57, 61, 74, 275n1,
  277
  exponential representation, 275
  implicit liabilities and, 184, 273
  initial, 301
  interest rates and, 302
  investment and, 183–186
  life insurance and, 336
  lifetime budget constraint and, 274
  longevity risk and, 254–261, 297
  Merton problem and, 321, 327
  net worth and, 276
  nondiscretionary, 59
  optimal, 275, 281, 298, 315–316. *See also*
  consumption smoothing

364 Index